CHOW HAYES

GUNMAN

CHOW HAYES

GUNMAN

DAVID HICKIE

A division of HarperCollins*Publishers*

DEDICATION

To my comrade, ally and confidante
Jennifer Caspersonn
who reminded me there's always time to laugh.

AN ANGUS & ROBERTSON BOOK

First published in Australia in 1990 by
Collins/Angus & Robertson Publishers Australia

Collins/Angus & Robertson Publishers Australia
A division of HarperCollins Publishers (Australia) Pty Ltd
Unit 4, Eden Park, 31 Waterloo Road, North Ryde
William Collins Publishers Ltd
31 View Road, Glenfield, Auckland 10, New Zealand
Angus & Robertson (UK)
16 Golden Square, London WIR 4BN, United Kingdom

National Library of Australia
Cataloguing-in-Publication data:

Hickie, David, 1953–
Chow Hayes: Australia's most notorious gangster.
ISBN 0 207 16012 0.
1. Hayes, Chow. 2. Gangs — Australia.
I. Title.
364.1092

Typeset in 10.5 Baskerville by Best-set Typesetter Ltd.
Printed in Australia by Australian Print Group

5 4 3 2 1
95 94 93 92 91 90

ACKNOWLEDGEMENTS

Chow Hayes telephoned me in April 1985, following publication of *The Prince and the Premier*. We met soon after and he agreed to allow me to tape-record his life story. Nearly three years of weekly recording sessions in the lounge room of his Lidcombe flat followed. Hayes placed no conditions on his participation. I, however, laid down one: that if, at any time, I felt he was straying from the complete truth, I'd end our project immediately. Subsequently I found my real problem was in deciding how, legally, to use all the no-holds-barred "on the record" information he provided about life at the top of Australia's criminal world over four decades.

Special thanks to Jill Wayment for all her enthusiasm and encouragement over nearly four years — from her initial reading, back in 1987, of the hundreds of pages of unedited transcripts of tape-recordings between myself and Hayes, right through to her professional judgement and advice in editing the final manuscript.

Finally, thanks to Jenny Caspersonn, Belinda Roberts, Emma Dane and Karen Caspersonn for help with the massive Index.

DAVID HICKIE
August 1990

CONTENTS

1 Chow Hayes — Gunman

At a touch after 11.30 pm on 29 May 1951 Sydney's two most notorious gunmen, Chow Hayes and Joey Hollebone, slipped quietly inside the front door of the Ziegfeld Club in King Street.

The Ziegfeld was renowned for its late-night revelry. Always among the throng that frequented it were the mobsters and standover merchants, the pimps and prostitutes, the spivs and touts and crooks and conmen who brazenly paraded as high-profile "celebrities" of Sydney nightlife throughout the 1940s and early 1950s.

This evening was to be the climax of legendary gunman Chow Hayes's criminal career. These were the final moments in a chain of sensational events which would explode into the cold-blooded massacre, before 80 witnesses, of a well-known boxer, Bobby Lee.

From the street-level foyer, Hayes and Hollebone peered downstairs into the smoke-filled room, slowly searching the beer-swilling crowd of boisterous dancers for their victim. Hayes spotted Lee within a minute. As the band played and the customers cavorted with abandon, the two hoods strode purposefully down the wide staircase.

Soon the three men faced each other across a small table. Almost 40 years later, Hayes still recalls every detail: "Lee said: 'You wouldn't do it in here, with the lights shining and all the people around.' So with that I pulled out the .45 from my belt and held it just above the table. . . And I said: 'I'll fucking give it to you here, don't worry about that!'

"But he said: 'No you won't. There are too many witnesses.' Then I said: 'Are you going to come outside. . .?' But he replied: 'You get fucked!' So then I just said: 'Well, here's yours!' And I fired and hit him twice in the chest.

"He fell over and out the back of the chair. Then I stood up and walked around the table, because he'd fallen out of sight. When I arrived above his slumped body I pumped another slug into his side and two more into his back. I fired three more times

— and by this point the band had stopped playing and people were running everywhere, screaming at the tops of their voices." Hayes and Hollebone walked out of the club.

During the ensuing police investigation and eventual courtroom drama, the sensational details of life in the Sydney underworld would be displayed publicly as never before.

One magazine later summed up the incident: "Shots rang through a Sydney nightclub. A man slumped to the floor, dying. And the underworld fought to save a ruthless murderer from justice...In the course of an Inquest and three trials the evidence was unswervingly of underworld hatred and suspicion, of smouldering rage and finally sordid murder." Hayes was described as "a feared and hated figure in the underworld...a 'standover man' who used threats, intimidation and violence for extortion from fellow crooks", and "a potential menace to any man who might get in the way of his ruthless gun or his savage ambitions".

• • •

By the time he shot Lee in 1951, Chow Hayes had become the most notorious gunman Sydney had ever known. He had stolen, intimidated and murdered brutally and callously. And he had successfully manipulated the legal and prison systems to his own ends.

Above all, the career of Chow Hayes epitomises life in the Sydney criminal *milieu* during the twentieth century. For in Sydney, amid what passes for the smart set, politicians and captains of commerce, sporting and entertainment personalities, glitterati and professional poseurs mix freely with sly-groggers, illegal bookmakers, mobsters and tramps, and the smiling butterflies of the Sunday social pages.

Typically, during his life Chow Hayes partied with criminal friends at the Moore Park private home of up-and-coming politician Bill McKell, who was later to become Premier of New South Wales. Hayes was also employed by, and received huge cash payments from, Sydney's most flamboyant medico, Dr Reginald Stuart-Jones. At the same time he provided the muscle for legendary illegal casino czars Perce Galea and Dick Reilly, and, over four decades, for the boss of Thommo's two-up school, Joe Taylor.

Now, in 1990, Chow Hayes remains the last living link with the infamous "celebrities" of the Sydney underworld of the Roaring Twenties, Thirties and Forties.

More than 50 of Hayes's criminal associates were murdered between 1920 and 1980. "And there wasn't a 'lifer' who went through jail between 1928 and 1977 whom I didn't know," Hayes still boasts.

2 The Railway Gang

John "Chow" Hayes came from traditional, working-class, rural Australian stock. His grandfather, Patrick Hayes, had been an amateur jockey around the New South Wales provincial and bush racetracks. He married a country lass named Rose and they raised seven children — four boys and three girls.

Chow's father, Robert John Hayes, born in 1891, was the third of those children. At that point the family already prided itself on the fact its ancestors had been in Australia several generations. Robert Hayes duly married Elizabeth Mary Hill and they, in turn, had two children: a boy, John, whom the family referred to as "Jackie" from an early age, but whom his street mates later tagged "Chow"; and a younger girl.

John Frederick Hayes was born in Baradine, near Coonabarabran in western New South Wales, on 5 September 1911.

At the outbreak of World War I in 1914, when young Jackie was 3 and his father still only 23, the family moved to Sydney so his dad, who had been ringbarking in the Baradine area, could join up. On 22 January 1915, aged 24, he left with the Light Horse for overseas duty in various theatres throughout Europe and Egypt.

The rest of his family moved into a terrace house — 55 Shepherd Street, Chippendale — off what was then the western arm of Sydney's major transport thoroughfare, George Street. (It later became known as The Broadway.) The household comprised young Jackie and his grandfather Patrick, who took a job on the Sydney City Council, and three females: Jackie's mother, Elizabeth; his grandmother, Rose; and his Aunty Josephine, who was nicknamed "Ninny". Six and a half months after his father's departure, young Jackie's sister was born. "She didn't meet Dad until he came back from the War," Hayes recalls. "My mother was carrying her when he left."

Jackie avoided formal education until he was seven years old. Then he started at the parish primary school beside the nearby

St Benedict's Catholic Church, on the corner of Abercrombie Street and George Street, about 800 metres from Sydney's bustling Central Railway Station.

In 1921 the infamous "Black Plague" swept through Sydney's working-class terrace suburbs. Deadly and highly contagious, bubonic plague had originally reached Australia in 1900. Fleas from rats in the holds of ships docked in Sydney Harbour then transferred the disease to humans. During the early years of the century, over 1200 cases were officially treated and many wharves were closed; large areas of harbourside Sydney were whitewashed and disinfected, and scores of old and insanitary houses were demolished in the historic Rocks area. A bounty of a penny per head (later reduced to a halfpenny) was paid for plague rats. Thereafter, sporadic outbreaks continued until the plague again flared up on a large scale in 1921.

Grandfather Patrick Hayes was one of the victims. Jackie was 10 years old, but recalls the events vividly: "Grandad had to wear a white mask because the plague was so contagious. And I remember everyone had to pull on those masks. All the men and women and kids in Sydney wore them. The plague struck down scores of people. You had to wear the mask everywhere, inside and outside, and you even used to sleep in it. You'd change them about three times a day. The Government supplied them, and if you wanted more you could go and get them."

Meanwhile, Jackie's father had been badly injured in the War. Suffering severe shell shock, he lay hospitalised in various English and European medical centres from 1918 to 1920, when he was well enough to be transported home to Australia by ship. After he returned, he worked spasmodically on the Sydney City Council. But more often than not he was in and out of hospital — and eventually died from his battle injuries in 1924.

Meanwhile the family remained in Shepherd Street, until Jackie's mother remarried about 18 months after his father's death.

• • •

Young Jackie Hayes grew up as part of a traditional, working-class Catholic family. Father Malone was the parish priest at St Benedict's and Jackie's grandmother took his sister to church every Sunday. Aunty Ninny politely declined invitations to join them — and Jackie was more or less left to go his own way.

During the week Jackie attended school at St Benedict's.

Jackie hated the whole idea from the outset. He had no favourite subjects, and found classes boring. "Without a father," he recalls, "I had no discipline at all."

By the age of 11 he was selling afternoon newspapers after school at Railway Square, outside Central Railway Station. And before long he was often skipping school altogether and heading straight for Railway Square.

Sydney's two afternoon papers in the early 1920s were the *Evening News* and the *Sun*. A large group of tough young inner-city lads, aged between 11 and 15, worked for the newspaper companies through representatives who directed operations around Railway Square. The best-known "reps" during those years were Jim Black from the *Evening News* and "Fatty Joe" from the *Sun*. They held court at Railway Square where the trucks deposited their papers for distribution among the paperboys.

Young Jackie Hayes quickly became mates with a group of like-natured scallywags including Billy Verney and his brother Tommy Verney (they were tagged "Little Rot" and "Big Rot"), Eddie Stewart, Fred Buckley, Dougie Broomfield and Albert "The Fly" Meggs. They, with others, formed a group known as the Railway Mob.

They sold newspapers to busy railway passengers for one penny each; purchased at a cost price of eightpence per dozen from the company reps, that left the paperboys with fourpence-a-dozen profit. In an average afternoon a lad would sell about four dozen copies of each paper, and pocket about three shillings profit, which, as Hayes is fond of recalling, was "a lot of money then".

One day a heated argument developed between Hayes and Meggs over a batch of papers. It climaxed in a fist fight in the lane behind the nearby Grand and Railway Hotels, next to what later became Her Majesty's Theatre. "It was one of the very few fights I won legitimately," Hayes recalls. "And when 'The Fly' finally climbed up off the pavement he yelled at me: 'You Chow bastard!' He was referring to the fact that my eyes had a narrow slant to them. And that's how I earned the nickname 'Chow'."

Jackie sold papers on and off until he was 15 — and it meant he always had money in his pocket. But the precocious youngster, unsupervised and spending much of his time running wild around the streets, was picking up bad habits. "I must have been a bastard when I was a kid," he sums up bluntly.

Sydney's Central Railway Station

Central Station viewed across Belmore Park in 1922. As a teenager, Chow Hayes and a dozen other paperboys and truants spent most of their time committing petty crimes in its vicinity as part of the Railway Gang.

At the Railway in those days two jewellery stores, Saunders and Orchards, stood on opposite sides of the corner where Quay Street runs into the main thoroughfare, George Street. "When I was wagging school," Hayes recalls, "I'd go to Saunders about once a year to pacify my grandmother and Aunty Ninny. You could buy a little statue of a cricketer for only 1s 6d, and for an extra ninepence they'd engrave your name on it. So I'd arrange for it to say I'd won the best batting trophy at cricket. Then I'd take that home and I'd be the best in the world around there for a few days.

"Another time I'll never forget, we knocked off a box of chocolates. There used to be a confectionary shop next to the Railway Hotel and one day a truck pulled up right in front of a group of four of us. So we pinched a dozen huge boxes from the back. And, gee, I felt sick later!

"Anyway I took one box home and said to my grandmother: 'Look what I won at the school raffle!' But my grandmother said they were too good for her and never opened them. Instead, she went down to St Benedict's to see Brother O'Connell. Her intention was to take the chocolates back and let the school authorities re-raffle them.

"That's when all hell broke loose, because O'Connell told her he thought I had been attending some other school. See, quite a few months earlier I'd arranged for a mate to write a note informing Brother O'Connell that, from now on, I would be going to another school. So O'Connell told my grandmother I hadn't been at school for three or four months — and, boy, did I cop a long lecture when she arrived back home. And, of course, then she also knew I'd pinched the chocolates — even though I insisted they'd literally fallen off the back of a truck."

Then, when Hayes was only 11 years old, he was sent to Guildford Truant School. The school authorities had notified the local inspector that Hayes was missing classes day after day. Initially, the inspector visited his home and issued his grandmother with a summons requiring young Jackie to appear in Albion Street Children's Court in Surry Hills. There, the magistrate delivered the standard lecture about returning to school. But Hayes would return for only a day or two before again taking off for the high life down at the Railway.

His poor grandmother and aunty thought he was back at school, especially as he'd pretend to head off for classes by shrewdly leaving the house each morning with his sister. But while she made it to St Benedict's he headed for the Railway. And so Hayes and his grandmother duly trooped down to the Children's Court three or four times over the following months before the magistrate, in despair, packed him off to the notorious Guildford Truant School for his first stint of enforced detention.

Guildford was for boys only, up to the age of 14. There Hayes found himself part of a population of about 120 social misfits, all aged between 10 and 14. Anyone who was there on his fourteenth birthday was discharged, because then he could leave school legally. Hayes recalls his stint at Guildford: "One of the chaps in charge at one point was named Delano. He was the boss and he was a bastard...

"The boys in those days were a lot tougher than they are today. They were streetwise.

"When I was first sent there, they didn't send you for a set period. It was up to the people in charge to decide when they thought you might have learned your lesson.

"We slept in big dormitories — they had about eight, with 15 boys in each — which were numbered 1, 2, 3... up to 8. We were woken at 6 am and had a wash — but didn't shower until later in the afternoon, after school. Breakfast consisted of porridge and toast, with the occasional sausage as a special treat.

"We wore uniforms, and at 7.30 am we fell into muster, just like in the army. Then they gave each gang — each dormitory — an assignment for the day. It might be roadwork or pushing wheelbarrows full of broken bricks or chopping down trees. Since it was mostly all bush around Guildford in those days, the jobs involved virtually clearing the suburb.

"We walked in gangs to and from the work site. We worked on the roads from 8 am until midday, with no breaks. And they were pretty tough on anyone slacking...it was back-breaking work, especially when you weren't used to it.

"At midday, we knocked off and trooped back to the school by about 12.10 pm. Then we had another wash and ate lunch. It wasn't a hot meal. It'd be a sandwich of some sort, usually without any meat on it, just jam or treacle or something. Then at 1 pm school started. Lessons went until 4 pm. There were four classrooms and we rotated between them for the various subjects, which went for about 45 minutes each. Then at 4 pm you'd knock off and have your shower for the day.

"At 4.45 pm we had dinner, which was the best meal of the day, a hot meal. Then at 5.30 pm each 'company' as they called them, went into its dormitory. There were no radios or anything like that, only a library down at the end of the dormitory. At 8 pm sharp the lights went out and that was it. A supervisor sat up all night in each dormitory — one from about 4 pm until 11 pm, and then they'd change shifts and another would sit from 11 pm until 6 am.

"Between 5 pm and 8 pm, if you didn't like reading books, you just sat around talking with nothing else to do. There were no toys there. Exercise such as cricket or footy was restricted to Sunday afternoon. The school and roadwork took place six days a week, including Saturdays.

"Sunday was the only rest day. Sunday morning they'd dress us in our 'home clothes' (our civvies) and they'd march us right into the heart of Guildford to the Catholic church for mass. Afterwards they'd march us back again.

"Then about 90 minutes after we arrived back we'd have lunch. In the afternoon, families came out to visit their boys. My grandmother and Aunty Ninny came to see me about every three weeks, and we'd sit on the grass and have a bit of a picnic and just talk. They were allowed to stay from around 2 pm until 3.30 pm, and I really looked forward to their visits.

"Meanwhile boys whose relations weren't visiting on any particular Sunday were allowed to play cricket or football or some other sport. We'd take our civvies off as soon as we returned from church and change back into our uniforms. Cricket was my favourite sport; I was a bit of a batsman, but I wasn't much good. Cricket was by far the most popular sport among the boys — it was very big generally in society in those days. . .

"You had to earn points for everything at the Truant School — points for schoolwork, points for roadwork, and so on. They added them up each weekend and they'd calculate a grand total at the end of each month. If you had 90–100 you were doing very well. (I was usually about 80. There were a lot who did worse than me, but also a lot did better too.) That's how they determined when they'd release you from Guildford. It was like an early release scheme. It was their way of monitoring how you were going. I don't think anyone was there longer than about nine months. I stayed four and a half months the first time.

"Anyway, when I was sent home from Guildford after that initial stint, I returned to the terrace house our family was renting in Regent Street. I went back to school for about three weeks, but then I started skipping it again. However it was 14 or 15 months before the authorities caught up with me again with another summons. When the inspector came that time, I'd fled over to Forest Lodge to another aunty of mine named Emily. My grandmother told the inspector she didn't know where I was, but actually she'd taken me over there herself.

"Aunty Emily and her husband had two daughters of their own and were renting a terrace in Forest Lodge. Emily was one of my father's sisters. I lived with them, in hiding, for about three weeks. But Aunty Emily was far too strict for my liking, and I quickly decided I couldn't stand the place. So I returned to Regent Street — and the authorities eventually collared me, when I was 13½, down at the Railway.

"At the time, I was out roaming the streets all day every day, though I'd avoided being nabbed officially for any other trouble. But the day they collared me the police came and grabbed me while I was selling papers (they knew me by sight, because I only lived two doors away from the police station in Regent Street). They'd ignored me for a while, until they were forced to do something about my permanent absence from school. So they took me back to Albion Street to the magistrate again. He remanded me for a week or a fortnight, and then sent me back to Guildford.

"I never returned to school after that. I spent six months at Guildford — which was a breeding ground for criminals — until they let me go the day before I turned 14, because they couldn't keep you there any longer than that. Then I went back to Regent Street again. My sister and Aunty Ninny and my grandmother were still living there, and I was spoiled absolutely rotten by them all." The day he was released was a very special one for the budding young criminal. His aunt and grandmother took him into the city and bought him his first suit with long trousers.

Since he was no longer obliged to attend school, Hayes's grandmother urged him to take a job down the road at the Dairy Farmers depot in Harris Street, Ultimo. In those days dairy deliveries were made by horse and cart, and she knew one of the drivers. Each driver employed a young teenage boy as an offsider on his cart. "So she lined me up for a job as an offsider," Hayes recalls, "but I didn't even start. The pay was five bob a week — big deal! I was earning at least that much each day at the Railway. Anyway the Monday after I returned from Guildford, it must have been 3 am, and my grandmother came to my room and said: 'Jackie, your boss is here and he's waiting for you.' Well, I just rolled over and said I was sick — and that was the beginning and end of the job with Dairy Farmers!"

So Hayes went back to selling afternoon newspapers at the Railway. Most days he would not rise from his bed until midday. And in the evenings, after he'd finished selling papers at about 7 pm, he would head down to the city centre with the other paperboys to the *Evening News* and *Sun* buildings in Elizabeth and Market Streets. The lads, still too young to venture into hotels, played cards in the dock and toilet areas of the newspaper premises. Sometimes they would also play cards over the subway which ran into Elizabeth Street, at Railway Square. All the paperboys would stick together and play cards and steal a few newspapers. The card games went until 1 am or 2 am, sometimes even 4 am. Other nights the boys would head over to George Street to the picture theatres, which issued "pass-outs" around 8 pm. "Now if you didn't have a pass-out," Hayes recalls, "the bloke on the door would let about a dozen of us in for a shilling. So it'd cost us a penny each, when everyone else was paying about fourpence. And we'd work our way up from Broadway to the Town Hall. They were all silent films in those days, with a bloke down the front playing the piano and so on."

Officially, during that era, a lad had to obtain a special, diamond-shaped badge (which he wore on his arm) to be allowed to sell newspapers. And he had to be 14 years old before he could apply for a badge — the rationale was that this would stop younger boys wagging school. But it proved little deterrent to Jackie Hayes: "I arranged my first badge when I was only 12. You went down to the Children's Court and paid 2s 6d for them. I collected mine by just saying I was 14 and they didn't check up. You'd go up there with any adult — for example, George "Bombardier" Williams, a local crook, took me up there once — and you'd simply supply a dud name and a dud address. Another reason for getting a badge was that newsagencies would only give you papers to sell if you had a badge."

• • •

Some 18 months after Hayes's father died in 1924, his mother re-married. Thereafter Jackie, now 14, and his sister were raised by his grandmother and Aunt Ninny. "When mother re-married she moved to the Waverley area," Hayes recalls. "From that point, she only contacted us at birthdays and Christmas. I thought she'd gone on a holiday — she didn't actually explain to me that she was leaving for good. I didn't know much about the man she'd left with, only that his name was O'Brien. I only saw him twice in my life."

What was left of the family group lived in a terrace house at 17 Regent Street. "The rent was very cheap in those days," Hayes remembers. "My grandmother was on the pension and Aunty Ninny was working as a waitress. Then Ninny leased the café right opposite our house in Regent Street and eventually she bought it outright. So Ninny was actually making most of the income upon which the family lived.

"In Regent Street, you had Taverna's café, with four storeys and 80–100 rooms. Frank Taverna owned the leading racehorse Valamita, which raced against the champions of that era like Limerick and Pantheon. [In the 1926–27 season, Valamita finished third in both the Cumberland Stakes and AJC Plate behind those two immortals of the Australian turf.] Taverna used to feed Valamita on lettuce leaves and cabbages, and Jackie Toohey used to ride it. Taverna would even bring Valamita into the city pulling a sulky — can you imagine any of the other champion racehorses being used to pull sulkies? Then he'd pose for photos with the horse outside the café. Alongside Taverna's was No 2 Police Station — that later became one of my main homes-away-from-home! On the other side of the police station, Gould Street ran into Regent Street, and then there was a sort of little garage and then came our house."

During those days young Jackie Hayes spent much of his time with the Railway Gang roaming the streets around the old fruit markets (which later housed Paddy's Market during the 1970s and 1980s) in inner Sydney's Haymarket district. They were about 18 tough young teenagers in the Railway Gang's "Little Mob" and another dozen older youths in the "Big Mob". "Members of the little gang were all around my age," Hayes recalls. "We used to think the members of the big gang were old men, but actually they were only 18 and 19 and 20."

The gangs spent a good deal of their time shoplifting and thieving. But their most important activity was fighting other inner-Sydney gangs to prove who were the toughest. The major gangs, known colloquially as "mobs" or "pushes", included the Surry Hills Mob, the Loo Mob (from Woolloomooloo), the Newtown Mob, the Glebe Mob, the Redfern Mob and the Rocks Mob. "Whenever they ran into each other," Hayes explains, "it was a matter of daring one another until a bit of a scrap broke out.

"The Surry Hills Mob was really the Ann Street Mob, and its territory ran from the Railway up to Darlinghurst and back through Riley Street and Surry Hills. They were a really tough bunch. But not as tough as the lads in the Rocks Mob — they were willing!

"Now the Glebe Mob hung out at the Australian Youth Hotel in Bay Street, Glebe. We called it McGrath's Hotel, after the owner, Mick McGrath, who had it for years and years. Mark Shelton, the SP bookie, ran his operation from the Australian Youth Hotel and lived just around the corner from that pub...

"Even the local police were scared of the Newtown Mob — they used to throw stones at the coppers and so on. The Newtown Mob hung around Newtown railway station, just down the road from the police building in Australia Street. When Joe Taylor [who later became one of Sydney's illegal casino kings] was managing The Hub theatre there, he told me that if there was any trouble the lads from the Newtown Mob were much more help than the police. Joe would immediately send someone to grab a few of the Mob to come over to the theatre and turf out the troublemakers. The Newtown Mob toughs would arrive in half the time it took the police — and they'd do the job instantly."

Members of the Newtown Mob's arch rivals, the Redfern Mob, roamed the narrow inner-suburban lanes which ran off Cleveland Street — the natural boundary between Surry Hills and Redfern. Redfern Mob boys congregated every afternoon outside the Norfolk Hotel (on the corner of Walker Street) and across the road on the steps of the Empire picture theatre at 303 Cleveland Street.

Hayes's gang, the notorious Railway Mob, patrolled a large home territory which extended from Grace Bros on Broadway, down past Central Railway and the Haymarket, and up George Street to the Sydney Town Hall. The territory began in earnest where Broadway was intersected by Harris Street on the Ultimo side and Regent Street (with the police station) on the Redfern side.

A pedestrian walking through Railway Mob territory (along the left hand side of Broadway) toward central Sydney, came first to Robertson's dance hall, where many youngsters of the era learned to waltz and foxtrot. It was upstairs, on the first floor. Underneath it stood an old picture show, The Kings, and almost next door was the famous Glaciarium with its huge indoor ice-skating rink.

Then came the vaudeville-style variety theatre, Clay's, where Roy "Mo McCackie" Rene appeared with his partner, "Stiffy". Directly across the road was the Mayfair dance hall. Still heading toward central Sydney came the Savoy dance hall (downstairs below street-level) where Chow Hayes's mate, Dick Reilly (later to become an infamous gangster during the 1950s and 60s), held an early job as the bouncer. Then, almost next to one another, stood the two pubs which became most popular with Hayes and his teenage cohorts, the Railway Hotel and the Grand Hotel.

Next, on the corner of George Street and Quay Street was Saunders jewellery shop (today part of the Central Plaza Hotel site), and on the opposite side was Orchards jewellery shop. Just around the corner from Saunders, about 50 metres down on the left-hand side in Quay Street, on the corner of Bijou Lane, the

Empire Theatre picture show (now Her Majesty's) was refurbished by the big-punting turf tipster Rufe Naylor early in the Depression.

Continuing along George Street, past Orchards' corner, were the Lyric theatre, the Great Southern Hotel (with the Crystal Palace Hotel opposite) and, downstairs, the Eden billiard room. The Eden, where Hayes and his mates spent much of their time, was run by A. W. "Nick" Winter, who had represented Australia and won an Olympic gold medal in the hop, step and jump (now triple jump) at the 1924 Paris Olympics. Winter's partner was Charlie Purdy, a New Zealand boxer who at one point held an Australian championship. (Some years later, after he split from Winter at the Eden, Purdy opened another billiard room at Stanmore just down from the Petersham Inn Hotel. It quickly became a popular hangout for Sydney's criminals.)

Nearer central Sydney, one came to the Haymarket picture show. Queenie Paul and Mike Connors later took it over and turned it into a variety show, with Roy Rene as their star attraction. The Haymarket charged 1s 6d for front stalls, 1s for back stalls and sixpence upstairs in "the gods". A little further on stood the Haymarket Post Office. Nearby, Campbell Street marked the northern border of the Railway Gang's unofficial territory.

In the middle of this unofficial territory (where George Street now becomes The Broadway) large crowds would gather in front of Central Railway waiting for public transport, even at 2 am in the morning. From this terminus, the trams ran out to Leichhardt, Glebe and Annandale. And rattling in from the eastern suburbs came the constant stream of trams from Coogee, Bronte, Bondi and Oxford Street; these would then turn around a loop near Sam Barnes's old factory and circle back past the Railway before heading east again to the beaches. The large area which, in the 1980s, has become the main George Street bus stop beside the Railway, used to be a men's toilet block and a fruit stand. The Big Railway Mob would congregate on top of it. Nearby, in the passage beside the old post office building, the Little Mob congregated. Andy Boyle's paper stand was at the entrance to the passageway, and beside him stood the fruit stall where Hayes and his confreres left their weapons and anything they had stolen but did not wish to carry around. The nearby back areas, where the trams turned around, were also part of the Railway Gang's territory. "But," Hayes remembers, "if you ventured out of your area — like over into Surry Hills or Glebe or Annandale — you were liable to cop a kicking from members of one of the other gangs."

Hayes quickly became known around the Railway as a delinquent who spent most of his time involved in hooliganism, shoplifting and petty crime. "I was allowed to run around all night from the time I was about 12 years of age," Hayes explains, "and it was very uncommon, I know that myself. In those days most household doors were open all night, and you didn't have to bolt them or anything like that. But the reason I did what I pleased was that there were no older men in my life. My father had been at the War and my grandfather had died, and there was no older male who could stand over the top of me. By this time my grandmother was 70 years old, and her daughter Ninny was nearly 50. I was virtually doing what I liked. There were about 15 or 20 of us running wild. We were roaming the streets all night, down at the Railway and the newspaper offices and in the subway. There was no-one to stand up to me and make me do the right thing. And of course my grandmother and my Aunty Ninny spoilt me and I couldn't ever do a thing wrong in their view. I was the apple of their eyes — and if I was ever pinched for anything, even though I was one of the ringleaders, as far as they were concerned I was always just one of the group led into trouble by others."

The more time young Jackie spent around the Railway Mob, the more he became involved in shoplifting. One of their favourite spots was the toy department at Grace Bros. "In those days," Hayes recalls, "the second Grace Bros building at Broadway (the one now on the eastern corner of Bay Street, nearest the Railway) hadn't been built. So Grace Bros then consisted of the older building on the Sydney University, or western, side of Bay Street. And behind the older building ran a narrow roadway officially named Grose Street.

"When I was about 12 or 13 a group of us used to go up to the toy department on the second floor and we'd take cricket bats, footballs, tennis balls, dolls, scooters, bikes, rocking horses, little prams — anything at all, it didn't matter how big it was! The stuff would be worth a fortune today. Three of us would go in, and another half a dozen would wait down below in the back lane. We'd kid at playing around there, especially at Christmas time. And when the shop assistants weren't looking we'd throw the toys out the window for our mates to catch below. What they couldn't catch broke on the pavement, and they'd simply push the bits and pieces into the gutter and leave them there. We used to sell the stuff to the kids who were going to school — for example we'd sell a football, which might cost four shillings, for one shilling or ninepence. Later, when I was 18 and 19, we worked the ground floor, shoplifting socks, ties and so on."

One favourite caper of Hayes and his paperboy mates involved a short piece of roadway, officially listed as Lee Street, which ran beside the Railway. "We used to play a trick which involved meeting someone on the corner of George Street and Pitt Street," Hayes recalls. "Now most people would say they run parallel and, therefore, you couldn't meet someone on the corner of George and Pitt Streets. But they actually run into each other at what used to be the old Marcus Clark building on the corner opposite the Railway.

"We'd spot a fellow we thought might have 10 bob and we'd start arguing the point and we'd make sure the mug could hear us. Then one would turn to him and say: 'Am I right or am I wrong?' And the mug would agree there was no corner of Pitt and George Streets. So then the bloke who reckoned there was would chip in: 'Well, I'll bet you five bob too.' Then he'd reveal how, if you continued along Pitt Street past the subway tunnel, you came to Lee Street, where Pitt and George met. It was only about 100 yards [90 metres] long, and ran from the Railway up to Regent Street and the police station."

Just past Regent Street Police Station was the old mortuary, where the trains could roll in. "We used to sell flowers there," Hayes explains. "They only buried people on a Sunday in those days. Even if you died on Monday or Tuesday you wouldn't be buried until the following Sunday.

"And they never took the coffins to the church. If you died in hospital, the undertaker would come and put you in a coffin and then take you back home, always to the front room. And your family hung white sheets up around the walls, and stood two candles at the top of the coffin and two at the bottom. Then a few days later the undertaker would come back and seal down the casket. But the coffin would remain there until Sunday, and then he'd come and pick it up.

"On Sundays there used to be five or six trains which would leave from the platform at the Railway mortuary. There'd be a dozen carriages per train, with two at the back for the coffins. These trainloads of people would all be travelling out to Rookwood Cemetery. But they weren't all going to mourn relatives and friends who'd died that week; there'd also be many returning to visit other old graves. The trains would continue right up to Rookwood, and then the mourners would step off and carry the coffins down the road.

"So we used to sell flowers, for threepence a bunch, to the passengers as they arrived at the mortuary platform. We'd keep a penny per bunch, and the owner of the flowers received twopence. But we'd still make a profit of seven or eight bob each, because you could sell hundreds of bunches. There were at least two or three thousand people travelling up to Rookwood every Sunday to the graves."

• • •

In those days there were several well-known characters around Railway Square. One was a loner named Butler (nicknamed "Fatty Arbuckle" after the American comedian), who lived in Abercrombie Street, Chippendale. "He'd walk past the Railway," Hayes recalls, "and if there were two or three of us sitting around, he'd shout us to the pictures. He'd buy us ice-cream and chocolate and so on, as long as we read the subtitles to him. They were all silent movies and he couldn't read or write. So we'd whisper to him what the subtitles said — and there were always people in the seats alongside and behind telling us to keep quiet. Later, when the talkies came in, I had to laugh, because then Butler gave us all the arse — he didn't need us any more!"

Another well-known character was a woman the boys nicknamed "Jimmy Pike", after the leading jockey of the era, because she wore a little peaked hat similar to a jockey's racing cap. Her real name was Ruth Morrison and she lived at the top of Glebe Point. "In those days all the women wore their dresses down around their ankles," Hayes explains, "but she didn't, she wore hers up to her knees. She'd walk around the streets, mostly in white, and everybody would stare at her. She'd always walk from Glebe all the way down to Circular Quay. She'd lost her son in World War I and she used to walk down to the Quay to watch the boats come in. And even if it was a Manly ferry, she'd ask the first people coming off if there were any soldiers on board. And when she was told 'No', she'd walk all the way back to Glebe again. She did that every single day, year after year."

The boys tagged another neighbourhood eccentric "Rainy Day" because he always carried an umbrella. Even in the middle of summer he would wear several jumpers, an overcoat, a rain hat and galoshes, and carry his umbrella. "One day Leslie 'Spud' Murphy and I were looking into the window at Mick Simmons sports store in George Street," Hayes recalls. "We used to go shoplifting in there during lunchtime, because they had only three employees and two took lunch at the same time, between 12 noon and 1 pm. We'd just wait until a customer walked in and then, while the remaining assistant was busy attending to him, we'd stroll in and pinch mostly golf balls (they were worth about ninepence each and we'd sell them for threepence). We'd grab two boxes at a time.

"Anyway this day we were looking in the window and 'Rainy Day' came over. He was standing beside me and Murphy was on my other side. So Murphy said: 'Why don't you do your washing, "Rainy Day"?' And with that 'Rainy Day', who thought it was me, turned around with his umbrella and belted me right across the forehead and yelled: 'I do my washing, you rotten little bastard!' He gave me a real nice pay-out."

Another notorious character was the religious crank the lads called "Father". "He arrived down at the Railway every Sunday night around 9 o'clock," Hayes explains. "He'd announce to all and sundry that he was Jesus Christ, the Son of God. He used to sing it out at the top of his voice, right in the middle of George Street. And if you joined his congregation you'd receive sixpence each, so we'd all line up to grab our 'zac'. He'd hold the trams up and start a traffic jam and we thought it was a great laugh. We'd encourage him to stand right in the middle of the tram lines. The tram drivers all knew him, and some would just jump out and move him, but others would sit there ringing their bell. And we'd keep geeing him up, telling him to continue with his sermon and ignore the trams and so on. We'd be telling him that we believed he was indeed the Son of God because he could hold up trams and motor cars and the whole lot."

(In those days threepence was a "trey"; sixpence was a "zac"; a shilling was a "deener" or a "bob"; two shillings was a "swy"; five shillings was a "caser"; 10 shillings was a "saner"; one pound was a "quid"; £25 was a "pony"; £50 was "half a spot"; £100 was a "spot"; £500 was a "monkey"; and £1,000 was a "grand".)

A favourite time of the year was Easter, which brought the Royal Easter Show to town. "You'd collect sample bags out at the Sydney Showground and you could take away as many as you wanted to carry," Hayes recalls. "They were all free, with little bottles of tomato sauce, and pieces of round cheese and paste and all that. Well, you could grab hundreds and hundreds and take them home and they'd last about a fortnight for the whole family."

Also with Easter came free hot cross buns on Good Friday at the Hippodrome in Campbell Street. "That was before the Hippodrome was ever known as the Capitol Theatre," Hayes explains. "The people who owned the Hippodrome used to bring the circus there over Easter, and kids would come from everywhere for the buns. They gave you a dozen hot cross buns and a bottle of ginger beer — and you could back up for more again and again. It was one of the few times each year when a truce prevailed between the mobs, because we all wanted to jump in for the buns. They'd also let you see a bit of the circus — but not the whole thing, because it wasn't open on Good Friday. But you could see the animals."

3 Gosford Boys' Home — "A Breeding Ground for Crims"

Throughout the early 1920s, young Jackie Hayes's life was one of petty crime. But he was growing up fast, and by the age of 13 was becoming closely acquainted with more serious crimes.

He had a cousin named Thomas Esmond "Ezzie" Bollard who, with his mate Stan Vincent, belonged to the Redfern Mob. Bollard was four years older than Hayes. When Bollard was 17 (and Hayes 13) he and Vincent spotted a lone member of the rival Surry Hills Mob in Exhibition Park with a girl.

A couple of months earlier, Vincent had been involved in a confrontation with this youth and had come off second best, copping a decent kicking during the ensuing brawl. So Bollard and Vincent, upon sighting the rival, immediately wrenched a couple of palings from a nearby fence. Unfortunately one piece of timber had a rusty nail protruding from the end, though Bollard later told Hayes that neither he nor Vincent realised this at the time.

Bollard and Vincent gave the Surry Hills lad a bashing with the palings — and later proudly boasted that they'd also landed several hefty whacks upon his "sheila" before she ran away. But the rusty nail pierced the youth's skull, penetrating his brain. He was unconscious for over a year, and eventually died from the injury.

The two youths were charged with attempted murder. But they were lucky. After six months they made a deal with the authorities to plead guilty to a common assault (at that point, no-one imagined the victim might actually die). So the Crown accepted the guilty pleas to assault charges, and Bollard and Vincent were each sentenced to two years in jail. Eventually the

Surry Hills lad died and, if Bollard and Vincent had not agreed to plead guilty to the lesser charge, but had instead sought continuing remands, they would eventually have faced a murder charge and received death sentences.

After his two years in Long Bay Jail, Bollard was the first person to tell Jackie Hayes about life inside prison. "Bollard was living with his mother in Cleveland Street," Hayes recalls. "My mother and Bollard's mother were sisters. So my grandmother, with whom I was living, was Ezzie's grandmother too. He came down to our place when he was released and told me what a bastard of a place jail was — and that he'd never go back. It was the same old thing every crim says when he first gets out — but, of course, he went back in again time after time. And, of course, he warned me never to end up out there. And I said there was no way I intended to end up anywhere near a jail."

• • •

Hayes was growing up in other ways, too. In late 1925, aged 14, he was seduced for the first time.

He recalls vividly: "We used to call them a 'prick relation' — that meant some distant relative who introduced you to sex. She was my grandmother's cousin's daughter and she came from Yass. I don't know to this day what happened, but they said she left her husband. She was about 24 and, as women go, she was one of the ugliest bastards I've ever seen; she was so bloody ugly I thought she was more like 50!

"At the time I used to stay out nearly all night. But I'd pulled a hamstring muscle in my leg when I was jumping off a tram. There were only two bedrooms at Regent Street. My grandmother and Aunt Ninny used to sleep together in one double bed in the front room, and in the back there was only my bedroom (at that stage, my sister was boarding at St Mary's Convent at Wollongong).

"Now Aunty Esmay was her name. She was only there for about four months — though afterwards I wished she'd stayed longer! Anyway there was nowhere to put her up. The only thing they could do was buy a second-hand single bed and dump it in my room. So about a fortnight later I pulled the hamstring in my leg and the doctor came and looked at it. He said to keep the leg very warm and prescribed some silly ointment. It had to be applied twice each day, once in the morning and once at night.

"For the first couple of nights — when I was ready to go to sleep—my grandmother came to my bedroom and I lay on the bed and she rubbed in the ointment. I could hardly walk on the bloody thing. Then Aunty Esmay butted in and said: 'I'll do it for him tonight, Ma, and then it'll be real warm when he pulls up the sheets.'

"Now about 8.30 that night I wanted to go to sleep. So she sat up and half undressed and grabbed the ointment and came over and started to rub my leg. And the way she was rubbing. . . She was going a bit higher and a bit higher all the time, and every so often she stopped to ask things like: 'Do you know how babies are made?' Well, I knew alright, but at that time I'd never interfered with a girl. And she kept asking questions like had I interfered with a girl before, and I said 'No.' Then she asked did I know how to do it, and I said I had a rough idea, that you lay on top of them. Well, eventually she took hold of my 'old fella' and I developed an erection, and so then she said: 'I'll show you.' She unbuttoned my pyjamas and then took off her own clothes and jumped into my bed and showed me. When it was finished she asked whether I liked it, and I said 'Yes.' She insisted that I mustn't tell Ma (my grandmother) or Ninny. Well I had no intention of telling them. So for the next three or four evenings she stayed in my bed all night. After that, as soon as the others went to bed (and they used to retire early at about 8 pm or 8.30 pm because there was hardly any wireless in those days) she'd be into my bed.

"Anyway the leg recovered after a few weeks, but I still used to come home early. Even the Little Mob didn't know why I wanted to go home early, by 10 pm or so. I had her for about four months.

"Then one day they suddenly told me that she was gone. I came home about 10 pm and my grandmother and Ninny were in bed. I went up to my room but she wasn't there. I thought she might have gone to the pictures or something. So I went to my grandmother's front room and knocked on the door and asked: 'Aunty Esmay's not home. Has she gone out?' And they told me 'No', she'd left that afternoon, that her husband had come and taken her back. So I lost Aunty Esmay, and I pulled my clothes straight back on and I went out again, back down to the Railway."

• • •

Life at the Railway and around the adjacent fruit markets was full of mischief and adventure. Transport was mostly horses, drays, pushbikes and hansom cabs, with horse troughs about every 100 metres along the main thoroughfares (George Street, Pitt Street, Elizabeth Street and Castlereagh Street) in central Sydney.

One of the paperboys' favourite stunts involved the old Chinese vegetable gardeners from the then orchard-covered southern suburbs of Botany and Mascot. "They'd jump onto their carts about 1 am," Hayes recalls, "and doze off to sleep during the trip into town. The old horses knew where to go and would always take the same route all the way to Paddy's Market. About once a month we'd see a cart with a sleeping driver going past the Railway at 2.30 am or 3 am. So we'd slip quietly over and grab the horse by the bridle and turn it around. Then instead of going on to the markets, the horse would head for home. Sometimes the old Chinaman would be almost back at Botany Bay before he woke up.

"Anyway, they complained to the police at Regent Street Station, and the coppers would come down, especially one known as 'The Mad Digger'. His real name was Toohey and he'd come back from World War I. He was fair dinkum mad, and he'd fight you, no worries. If he was confronted with a big mob, he'd say: 'Alright, any one of you, we'll go around into the lane. And don't worry, if you beat me that'll be alright. But if I beat you, then I'll pinch you.' He'd always take his coat off before one of these fights. Well, Toohey came down to see us about the old Chinamen, and he warned us: 'Now look, you bastards. You keep this up and I'll give it to the lot of you.' Then he gave us a good kick up the bum to go on with and sent us on our way."

Another racket Hayes and his mates fancied during those years involved stealing the horse-and-carts belonging to second-hand dealers and other merchants loading fruit and vegetables around the Haymarket area. "We'd wait until the cart was about three-quarters full," Hayes recalls. "Then, while the owner was in the markets, three or four of us would jump on and drive it away — to Balmain, Ultimo, Redfern or Glebe, where we could sell the stuff to fruit shops and the like for about a quid or 30 bob for the lot. Then we'd leave the cart in the street and take the horse up into the University Park [now part of Sydney University] and let it loose. There must have been 15 or 20 horses grazing there at one point!"

Another favourite caper involved the Sargents refreshment rooms and cake shops then popular around Sydney. "We used to gather over in Exhibition Park instead of going to school," Hayes

THE MARKETS

The No. 1 Vegetable Market (which provided accommodation for about 310 carts with horses, and a similar number of stalls) was the first major development in the rebuilding of the Haymarket complex between 1909 and 1914. This view is from the corner of Hay and Thomas Streets. Chow Hayes and the Railway Gang spent much of their time around the markets, and Hayes later lived in Thomas Street.

remembers, "and we'd pick out the cleanest one among us. And if he didn't have a good pair of shoes, someone who had a polished pair would lend them to him. Similarly if he didn't have a clean shirt or something, one of us would give him that. And he'd put a pencil behind his ear and carry a little notebook and he'd go into Sargents, and we'd all follow him over and look in the doorway.

"We did this caper at Sargents shops all over Sydney, though this particular one was a few doors up from Grace Bros on Broadway. He'd make out that he was an office boy, and he'd order half a dozen pies, six sandwiches and six of something else, cream puffs and the lot. And while the girl was collecting it all, she'd stack them up on the counter in front of him. When he thought he had enough, he'd pick out something about four or five yards [3.5–4.5 metres] away — where she had to go and stretch to reach it — and meantime we'd just walk in and scoop up what was already on the counter in the little parcels and walk out again. And when she came back he'd say the boys took all the parcels, and she'd run out after us but we'd be gone by then."

Another favourite eating spot was Grace Bros, which was the first department store to include a cafeteria. "You would go in and take a tray and pick out whatever you wanted to eat," Hayes recalled. "Then at the bottom they'd add it up and give you a ticket. But you didn't pay there. Instead you sat down at a table and ate your meal, and then you paid as you went out the other door.

"So one day Charlie 'Kicker' Kelly, Eddie McMillan, Leslie 'Spud' Murphy and I were in there. While we were having our lunch, Kelly decided he was thirsty and went back for a glass of milk. And when he went and picked it up, the girl gave him another ticket for one penny. So then we thought, what a good idea — and we went back for three more glasses of milk and collected three more tickets for one penny each. When we went out, instead of handing in our tickets for the full lunch for about 2s 6d, we just gave over the tickets for one penny each. And the girl we had to pay as we went out had no idea what we'd eaten back inside. That rort went on for months and months, and we told a lot of people about it. The old folk used to come in from everywhere to do it — Newtown, Annandale and Surry Hills — and they'd bring all the kids with them. One women used to take about eight or nine kids and they'd only pay a penny each for a glass of milk."

In those days the Rush refreshment room at the Railway was open 24 hours a day. "It was open every day, Christmas and all," Hayes recalls. "We used to go in there and walk down an aisle and snatch a couple of sandwiches and put them in our pockets, and a couple of cakes or something and then we'd reach the end and buy a penny cup of tea. So we'd only pay the one penny for the tea, and then we'd go and sit at the table and eat all the rest of it.

"I saw Jack Haines the boxer there one night. [Haines won the Australian middle-weight championship in November 1929.] We'd just come from the Stadium, but I didn't know Haines from a bar of soap. We were sitting at a table talking about the fight, and I was saying what a good boxer Haines was. And this fellow stuck his head in from next to us and said: 'Haines wouldn't beat time.' But it was really Haines himself geeing me up."

At one point a small confectionary shop opened next to the

Lyric picture show in George Street, almost opposite the Crystal Palace Hotel. One day the owner walked up to Central Railway station and asked Hayes and the other paperboys whether they were interested in a Sunday job selling chocolates, peanuts and sweets down in the Domain park and over at Taronga Zoo. "He said he'd supply a tray just like they used to have in the theatres," Hayes recalls. "Well, we jumped at the chance, and turned up on the Sunday morning about 9 o'clock. He gave us each a tray filled with chocolates and peanuts and so on — and, of course, we already knew what we were going to do, which was sell as much as we could and then take off with the money at the end of the day.

"So we did that the first time, and then we sent word out about the caper and some of the other mobs had a go at it. I went down to the Domain myself, but I only sold about a quarter of the goods, and just took the rest home. There was about £5 worth of merchandise on the tray, which was a lot in those days. Of course, after about six months he went broke...

"Afternoons down at the Domain during those years were among the funniest times of my life," Hayes says. "There'd be 20 speakers on soapboxes, and a quarter of Sydney used to congregate down there on Sundays and listen to the speeches about religion and politics and so on. Even the 'squareheads' [law-abiding citizens] would laugh at them and sing out and jeer and heckle. And a couple of the speakers — when they had the money — would slip us 10 bob to go and interrupt the others and heckle them and pull their boxes from under them and throw rotten fruit."

Also in that era, politicians still stood on local street corners and addressed their constituents. "There was no television then," Hayes laughs. "On one corner might be the Conservatives and, at the same time, down on the next corner might be a Labor speaker. Of course, everyone around my area was Labor. All my people had been Labor. Few citizens thought for themselves, they just went with the majority. Anyway, the politicians would spruik on the corners and, gee, we used to have a lot of fun, heckling them and calling them bastards and all that. When the politicians gathered to speak, they'd attract hundreds of people and it became an open go for the 'dips', the pickpockets. But luckily they couldn't pickpocket too much, because most people had almost nothing to lose."

Another big event was Bonfire Night, then on New Year's Eve.

"Residents in every street around Glebe and Ultimo would compete to see who could build the biggest bonfire," Hayes recalls. "They'd be stacked up in the middle of the road and all the residents would throw on top their carboard boxes and wood and papers and anything else that would burn. People would store rubbish all year round for it, hoarding things in their backyards and sheds. And during the night the fire brigade worked overtime racing from one bonfire to another. The next day the scene was awful, with all the streets in a terrible state with the piles that were left. I remember one night in Row Street we set one off and the coppers arrived and wanted water to put it out and one smartie gave them half a bucket of kerosene! It nearly took them up in flames too, and one copper was seriously burnt."

One of the local policemen on the beat around Central Railway was a chap named O'Neill. "Now there was a popular song about that time titled 'Sweet Peggy O'Neill'," Hayes explains. "And this young lass, aged about 19, would arrive at the Railway around 5.30 pm each evening and talk to O'Neill for 10 minutes. Then he'd put her onto her tram out to Leichhardt or somewhere. And one night we heard him say to her: 'Goodnight, Peggy.'

"Soon after, 'Duke' Molloy (who was part of the Big Gang up at the top end of the Railway) came down to our end. But I didn't know he fancied himself as a ventriloquist and used to have them all laughing up with the Big Mob. Molloy walked down and stood near me and two or three of my mates. And when O'Neill helped Peggy onto the tram, Molloy started to sing the song 'Sweet Peggy O'Neill'. Well, Molloy was the best ventriloquist you've ever heard. The copper turned straight around and you'd have sworn blind that the voice had come out of my mouth. So O'Neill ran over to me and yelled: 'You dirty rotten bastard! If I ever hear you say that again I'll take you round the back (that was behind Saunders' jewellery shop) and kick the shit out of you.' But at the time I didn't know what he was talking about, because it was the first time I'd ever heard a ventriloquist. Then O'Neill started to walk away and the voice came out again: 'You and who else?' So he ran back and threatened me again and, gee, he was red in the face.

"This continued, on and off, for about two months. Molloy would shoot the voice to a squarehead and O'Neill would turn around and he'd think it was the squarehead who said something. So he'd run over and front the bloke and declare: 'What's up with you, you dirty rotten lair!' Eventually one night he knocked a bloke down over it, and the fellow went up to Regent Street Police Station and reported him. After that they shifted O'Neill to another district."

After the crowds came out of the various dance halls near the Railway (the Savoy and the Mayfair and the Glaciarium) on Friday and Saturday nights, large groups of youngsters would congregate in the street and around the tram stops, many still dancing about "doing the Charleston" and so on. The young boys were tagged "lairs" and the girls were known as "sheilas".

"Now one of our big jokes," Hayes explains, "was to pin condoms onto the boys' coats while they were dancing. They called the condoms 'french letters' in those days. We used to persuade a sheila to go and dance with some bloke. And we'd fill a french letter up with water, put a pin in it and encourage her to pin it on his coat while she was dancing with him. Then we'd laugh at all the blokes, mostly squareheads, heading home with these things pinned to the backs of their coats. But after about six or seven weeks the coppers came down and told us we had to cut it out."

• • •

Sydney in the late 1920s, despite the antics of young Hayes and his teenage mates, was still an extremely conservative and ordered society. Even the larrikins knew when to observe social customs. "For example, when a hearse was passing along a street," Hayes recalls, "everyone would stop until it went by. And all the womenfolk — the wives, sisters, mothers and close female relations — used to dress in black for up to 12 months. Everyone wore hats then, both men and women. And the man would tie a black crepe armband — sometimes it was a bit of silk — around his left arm, as a mark of respect for the dead.

"But then I remember all that — the women in black and the men wearing armbands for 12 months — going out of fashion. First they broke it down to only about three months. Then later they'd take the band off their arm after about a week and put it around their hat. But everyone would still line the street until the funeral had passed. It just shows how the world has changed — these days if a funeral goes past, people don't even stop to raise their hats!"

• • •

From the time he was about 14 years old Hayes, not content with his fourpence-a-dozen profit margin, had also begun stealing additional newspapers and selling them. "A paper by the name of *Beckett's Budget* came out; it was like *Truth* later on, with all the divorce court proceedings and so on in great detail. It was the hottest paper I'd ever read," Hayes remembers. "We used to steal papers from the trams which delivered them around town. We'd push two bundles of *Beckett's Budget*s off the tram for each boy. So if there were six of us, we'd push 12 bundles and carry one in each hand.

"*Beckett's Budget* only came out on Fridays. Now one particular Friday when I was about 16½, Billy Earle and I pushed four bundles off the moving tram in Botany Road, near Henderson Road. But we were seen by a policeman on a pushbike, and he started to chase us on foot. I was a better runner than Billy, so I stayed just behind him as we ran off. I was a pretty fair runner, so I kept looking over my shoulder and the policeman wasn't catching us. But one time as I looked over my shoulder I clipped Billy's heels in front of me. I stumbled and fell and the policeman nabbed me.

"He took me down to Redfern Police Station and I knew I was in big trouble. He recorded my name and address, and to make sure I was telling the truth — at this stage I was still in the charge room — they contacted Regent Street Police Station. There were hardly any phones in those days, so someone from Regent Street went and contacted my grandmother and she came up to Redfern Station. After some talk they allowed me to go as long as I appeared in Albion Street Children's Court the following Monday.

"So I went to court on the Monday and obtained a remand. I didn't have a lawyer. The remand was for a fortnight or three weeks and then the magistrate more or less branded me a no-hoper and sent me to a home for uncontrollable youths at Gosford. You went there from age 14 or 15 through to about 18. I travelled there by train about a fortnight later. In the meantime I stayed in the children's shelter at Albion Street until there was a group of about eight of us ready to be taken up there. My grandmother and Aunty Ninny and everyone were most upset, but they'd virtually despaired of me by then. On the other hand, I still couldn't do anything wrong in their eyes — it was always the other party's fault, not mine."

Hayes was 16½ when he was sent off to Gosford, and returned home on his seventeenth birthday. "Gosford was a real bastard of a place," he recalls, "a breeding ground for crims. I met blokes like Guido Calletti and 'Scotchy' McCormack — blokes who were murdered later in life. All the kids up there later became heavy criminals and many ended up being killed in underworld activities. I'd say that, of the boys at Gosford, I finished up seeing 99 per cent of them again at Long Bay Jail later on." Indeed, during one court case the eminent barrister Jack Thom declared that his experience showed that "criminals served their apprenticeship to crime in the Gosford Boys Home." In another case a barrister named Wishart described his 17-year-old client as a "graduate of Gosford" while telling Judge Clancy that the corrective system that applied to the lad had failed, as he had been in and out of jail continuously since he was 10, with his sentences already totalling six years.

The daily routine at Gosford involved hard physical work: chopping down trees and clearing paths for roads for the Forestry Commission. The young inmates rose at 6 am sharp, worked from 8 am through till 12.30 pm, took a half-hour break for lunch and then resumed work until 4.30 each afternoon. The labour gangs walked out from the camp to their respective work sites, a hike usually taking between 10 minutes and half an hour. "That was really hard work, five days a week," Hayes recalls. "Then on the weekends we could play sport. The centre didn't have walls, like a prison, to keep you in. But there wasn't anywhere to run off to, because it was mostly bush around there at that time.

"All I basically did there was learn more bad habits for later on. There were fights every day. I wasn't a particularly big bloke, but I always knew how to look after myself. I was only about 10½ stone [67 kilograms] and 5 ft 9 in [175 centimetres], but I'd been brought up in a tough school and I never backed off— you could never lose face. I was quiet, rather than a gregarious youngster, but I finished up a leader rather than a follower. I mixed easily with everyone."

4 The Shoplifting Caper

Hayes was duly released from Gosford on his seventeenth birthday and came back to Sydney, but not to Regent Street. While he'd been away the family had moved out of Regent Street and back to Chippendale, to another terrace house, at 5 Rose Street, which ran off Shepherd Street. The family never owned any of these houses, they were always rented.

Young Jackie decided there wasn't much future going back to selling papers. So he moved into fulltime shoplifting. "I never sought a legitimate job," he recalls, "but just went back to hanging around with the old gang, the Railway Gang. I moved up then from the 'Little Mob' to the 'Big Mob'. We carried knives, razors, guns — though I didn't carry a gun myself at that stage; I carried a razor. The notorious Sydney razor gangs started around that time. However, I never needed to use my razor on anyone. I mainly just pulled it out to frighten people, though if I'd had to use it I certainly would have done! I remember Leslie 'Spud' Murphy used his to slash one bloke across the forehead and he needed a lot of stitches. . . We left all our weapons (razors, iron bars, socks with stones in them) at the fruit barrow at the Railway. This was from when I was 16–17 years old right through until I was 28–29. . .

"But back when I was 17 we spent most of our time shoplifting in Gowings, Farmers, Anthony Horderns, Mark Foys and Lowes. We'd pinch everything and anything upon which we could lay our hands. Then we'd sell the spoils to people like Kate Leigh or Tilly Devine. That's when I met those famous characters and started making a name for myself. We'd pinch stuff every day.

"I was caught many times before I eventually went to jail for shoplifting. The first few occasions they caught me I walked away with fines. I appeared mostly in Central Court and copped a fine each time — maybe a £5 fine, which was still a lost of money in those days. And, for example, you weren't fined £5 or 10 days — you received £5 or a *month* in jail! But every time, I paid the fine because through my stealing I had quite a bit of money."

However, Hayes and his mates became so well known as a shoplifting team that most of the bigger department stores eventually stuck up the youths' photos in their offices. "After that, there was only one way of beating the big stores," Hayes explains. "Blokes arrested for shoplifting on a Tuesday, Wednesday, Thursday, Friday or Saturday would all be remanded to the following Monday. And the shop detectives used to go down to the court to look at the boys who'd been caught. Well, there were five or six of us in our gang, and one would go down to the court and see which shop detectives were down there. Then we'd head for the store which we knew had its shop detective in court that morning. Our bloke would stay at the court watching where the detective went, while we went to his store."

One of Hayes's most lucrative activities involved horse saddles stolen from Anthony Horderns. "I was with 'Spud' Murphy," he says. "We used to wear overcoats (or a dustcoat in summer) when we were pinching things. We went to Anthony Horderns and Murphy went behind the showcase and came out with these two saddles, which were only about 1½ lb or 2 lb [700 or 900 grams] in weight. He simply walked out with them both under his coat — I was merely accompanying him — but he didn't have anywhere to sell them.

"Later, during the afternoon, we were up at the Railway near the fruit stand where we used to stash all our stolen goods. A chap named Andy Boyle had a paper stand next to it — his father and mother and brother, Jackie, worked the stand with him. I started talking to Andy and I said how silly it was that 'Spud' had knocked off the two saddles. But Boyle said he'd like to see them. So I went over and collected them from the fruit stand. Boyle said he might be able to offload them for us. He asked how much we'd want for them and I said whatever he could get.

"Boyle knew an old-time jockey, Laurie Sharp, and Boyle went and saw Sharp. I don't know how much Boyle really received for them, but he came back the next day and told me he could only obtain £10 each for them. Well I thought £10 each was millionaire's money so I couldn't grab hold of the £20 quick enough. I never found out how much Boyle actually made on the deal, but I'd have taken 10 bob for them. In fact, I wouldn't have taken the saddles in the first place. Since we were working together, 'Spud' and I split it £10 each.

"Well, we thought we were onto a goldmine. So we all went down to Anthony Horderns and, over a short period, we stole about 30 saddles from the showcase before they stopped stocking them anymore. We were selling them to Laurie Sharp who, in turn, was supplying all the other jockeys. And we were still collecting £10 per saddle through Boyle. Pretty soon every second jockey on the racecourse was using a stolen saddle."

However, the Anthony Horderns antics stopped suddenly when Marie Barr, the store's shop detective, spotted Hayes (then aged 17 years and seven months) and Murphy as they were walking out of the shop with about eight shirts each. "She was a funny woman," Hayes recalls, "in fact, more like a man. Horderns was in the big building in George Street, and we used to run out of the shop and jump on a tram while it was going past. We thought we'd lose Barr that way, but she was a really athletic woman and, on this occasion, she jumped aboard the tram after us. So we darted along the footwalk of the tram to try and race away from her, but she followed us along blowing her little whistle. Then we jumped off — but she jumped off and continued chasing us.

"Anyway she knew us by name and she gave all the details to the police, who came and arrested us. Two coppers, who knew me very well by this stage, came down to the Railway and one said to me: 'How long have you been home, Chow?' I replied about five or six months and he said: 'Well, I'll tell you what to do. I don't want to see you go back to Gosford, but you'll be sent back for sure. So when I charge you we'll arrange a remand and then you say you're 18 and you'll only cop a fine and won't have to return to Gosford.'" Hayes duly appeared at Central Court and, as he'd been instructed, said he was 18. He was granted a remand, before eventually being fined £2 or 14 days. He happily paid the fine.

Over the following four years Chow copped a series of fines and, sometimes, three- and six-month jail terms. "I did the short terms at Long Bay," he recalls. "The first time at The Bay was an awful bloody shock! I was just about the youngest bloke out there. I said I'd never do it again, that I'd made up my mind. But I was no sooner back on the streets than I was shoplifting again that very afternoon.

"I kept on shoplifting, and copped fines and 'three-monthers' and 'six-monthers'. I've amassed an awful record. But in those days you could appeal. So if you were pinched on a Monday and you appeared before the Court and copped three months, well it really gave you an 'open go'."

It worked this way: Hayes would appeal against the sentence and be granted bail; then, in the meantime, he'd attempt to procure enough cash to pay the fine instead. So, thereafter, each time he was subsequently arrested he'd keep appealing. Eventually he would have half a dozen appeals pending at any one time. Then he'd go to the Crown Law Department and announce that he wanted to withdraw all his appeals — and the biggest sentence, say six months, would then become his total sentence. "So because they'd be concurrent, all you'd have to serve was six months," he explains, "when you'd accumulated maybe six convictions against you."

Hayes's first convinction had been for indecent language at the age of 15. Two years later he came under regular police notice, when he became known as a standover merchant with, as *Truth* later reported, "Central Railway frankfurt and roll sellers as his frightened victims. 'Give us a swy' was his favourite demand. Those who attempted to refuse were soon persuaded by a nick from a razor blade embedded in a cork. From these small beginnings, however, Hayes developed his criminal status with amazing speed."

From late 1928, when he turned 17, Chow Hayes quickly amassed a lengthy criminal record:

- 10/10/28: "break and enter" and "malicious damage" at Redfern Petty Court.
- 10/12/28 and 18/2/29: "indecent language" (swearing at police) at Central Petty Court.
- 19/2/29: "riotous behaviour", which involved a brawl between two of the gangs.
- 8/4/29: "steal from the person" at Central Petty Court. This was a pickpocket charge. Hayes recalls: "It was at the Grand Hotel in George Street, between Quay Street and Campbell Street. A bloke was boarding a tram, and I jumped in front of him to hold him up and my mate Tommy Verney pinched the money from his back pocket. The bloke yelled out, and two people sitting in the tram grabbed me. But Verney ran away

and was never charged. That was the first time I went to jail. I copped one month hard labour with no option of a fine."

- 1/5/29: "demand money by menaces" and "threatening words" at Central Petty Court. This was an early attempt by young Chow to extract money using standover tactics.
- 18/6/29: "assault" and "evade tram fare" at Central Petty Court. Hayes caught a tram to Glebe. "The fare was only twopence — it was threepence from Circular Quay to Glebe Point, and the first section ended at Railway Square, where I jumped on," Hayes recalls. "In most of the working-class suburbs in those days, the tram conductor wouldn't ask you for your fare. He simply left it to you whether you wanted to pay or not. So I gave him a wink, but he said that he wanted my fare. Then I got my back up and said he wasn't getting it. One thing led to another and I hit him on the eye."
- 25/6/29: "suspected person" at Kogarah Petty Court. "Leslie Murphy, 'Kicker' Kelly and I were up there shoplifting," Hayes recalls. "Murphy went into a men's store and Kelly and I were outside watching. I leant on a car and a copper came along and asked what I was doing — he thought I was looking in the car, but I wasn't. Now 'suspected person' in those days meant they could suspect you of stealing anything at all, or of any involvement in any crime. It was a very hard charge to beat. So the copper took me down to the police station and charged me and I was granted bail. But the charge was later withdrawn because people I knew 'got at' him. Basically my grandmother knew an old sergeant at Regent Street station named Rose and he did the business."
- 22/7/29: "riotous behaviour" at Central Petty Court.
- 2/9/29: "riotous behaviour", "indecent language" and "not paying for drinks" at Central Petty Court; it involved an incident in a hotel and the "indecent language" charge involved swearing at police.
- 19/10/29: "riotous behaviour", "indecent language" and "assaulting police" at Paddington Petty Court. "That was a fight in Oxford Street, where I assaulted a uniformed policeman," Hayes recalls. "It started when he told me to move on and I told him to get fucked. I was by myself and I told him it was a public place and that I was waiting to see a girl. Then he said I was under arrest and we ended up in a brawl."

- 6/11/29: two "stealing" charges at Paddington Petty Court. "I was charged with stealing money and silverware from a house," Hayes recalls. "It was a party — what they used to call a 'crush party' — where someone would be invited and he'd tell all his mates and we'd all go. The people in the house called the police who came and picked me up. But the matter was eventually discharged because I threatened the householders. I met the owner in a hotel in Oxford Street and told him that if I went to jail a lot of trouble would come his way. He was a family man and didn't want any trouble, so he suddenly refused to give evidence, and the matter was discharged."
- 6/11/29: "riotous behaviour" at Central Petty Court.
- 15/11/29: "stealing" (shoplifting) at Central Petty Court.
- 19/11/29: "stealing" and "assault" at Central Petty Court. "That was all to do with assaulting a shopwalker in Lowes, just opposite the Town Hall," Hayes recalls. "He tried to grab me for shoplifting and we had a fight. It was inside the store. I was also charged with stealing stetson hats — they used to have three or four in a box, and you'd take them out and press them down into another box and end up with 10 or 12 in one box. 'Kicker' Kelly was with me that day, but he got away."
- 1/2/30: "malicious damage" at Central Petty Court.
- 17/5/30: "offensive behaviour" at Central Petty Court.
- 2/6/30: "suspected person" at Burwood Petty Court. "Leslie Murphy and I went to a menswear store in Burwood Road, just up from the station," Hayes explains. "We were walking around the shop deciding what to pinch — it was only ties and shirts and stuff in there — but the owner telephoned the police while we were looking around. He thought we seemed suspicious, and a detective and two uniformed coppers came down and nabbed us. They took us into the owner's office and searched us. We had nothing on us, so they charged us with 'suspected person'. I copped three months' hard labour in jail and Murphy received two months.

  "We'd caught the train out there because we weren't known among the shopkeepers around that area, and there were no organised mobs out at Burwood. Not that we were afraid of the other mobs, it was just that if you were in their territories you'd have to be constantly on the lookout; plus they were already organising a lot of shoplifting themselves in their areas. For example, the Newtown Mob were already robbing most of the shops in their district. Other outer suburbs we'd visit included Arncliffe and Leichhardt and Botany, where there were no organised mobs. We also caught trains to Newcastle and Wollongong for the day (it only cost about three bob to go all the way to Newcastle then)."

- 16/6/30: "assault" and "indecent language" at Central Petty Court.
- 3/10/30: "riotous behaviour" at Redfern Petty Court.
- 15/10/30: "riotous behaviour" at Central Petty Court.
- 20/10/30: "indecent language" at Central Court.
- 27/10/30: "indecent language " at Central Petty Court.
- 6/11/30: "stealing" and "assaulting police" at Central Petty Court. "That involved shoplifting 18 shirts from Anthony Horderns," Hayes explains. "There were four of us down at the Railway — Eddie McMillan, 'Kicker' Kelly, 'Spud' Murphy and I — and we were standing around the fruit barrow where we used to leave the stuff which we'd pinched. But the bag with the shirts in it was alongside me when a copper, 'Mad Digger' Toohey (he was the mad bastard who'd come back from the War) arrived to try and pinch us. He tried to take two of us at once, but he couldn't, so he just grabbed me. The others came around and gave him a few clips behind the ear and so on, but he held onto me and charged me. He knew who the others were, but he never charged them later on. Someone had dobbed us in. So I copped a six-month hard-labour jail sentence for the shoplifting, and one month accumulative for the assault plus spitting at Toohey in the charge room at Regent Street police station."
- 6/6/31: "riotous behaviour" and "indecent language" at Central Petty Court.
- 9/6/31: "riotous behaviour" and "indecent language" at Central Petty Court.
- 29/6/31: "indecent language" at Central Petty Court. All these involved incidents with police. "Those type of charges were basically when the coppers just wanted to have a go at you," Hayes claims.
- 14/7/31: "assault and robbery" at Central Petty Court. "I assaulted and robbed a bloke in George Street," Hayes recalls.

"I took his chain watch and some money. But after I attacked him he went to Regent Street police station and gave a description of me. I was well known by then and the police knew who to look for immediately. So they came to my home the next morning and arrested me. But I finished up 'getting at' him. A mate of mine who happened to know him went and paid him off. My mate told the bloke that I could receive three or four years for it. I think he offered him £50 originally, but he eventually only gave him £25; he was supposed to receive the other half after the case, but he never got it."

- 20/7/31: "riotous behaviour" at Central Petty Court.
- 27/7/31: "common assault" and "malicious damage" at Central Petty Court. "The assault was on a stranger at Redfern," Hayes explains. "It was a fight in a pub and the 'malicious damage' was to his clothes. I eventually went to jail for three months' hard labour on the assault."
- 28/7/31: "riotous behaviour" and "malicious damage" in Glebe Petty Court. "That was in a fish shop," Hayes recalls. "I was chatting up a sheila named Tibby, who was working behind the counter, when a young copper came in. He'd only been in Glebe three or four days, and I didn't know him. He didn't have his tunic on — only his shirt and trousers — though I could tell he was a copper. I said something to Tibby and the copper stuck his head in and, the next minute, we were into a brawl. But later she wouldn't come to court to give evidence, so the malicious damage (to the shop) charge was dismissed with no evidence to offer. Fortunately I was sweet with her, and she moved out of her place for a couple of weeks until things died down. So the copper was only able to proceed with the riotous behaviour charge."
- 28/12/31: two charges of "indecent language" at Central Petty Court.
- 6/1/32: "suspected person" at Central Petty Court. "That was outside Mark Foys and I copped three months' hard labour," Hayes says. "I was on my own and I was about to go in shoplifting. Two or three of my mates were already inside. We'd sent one bloke to Central Court to see which shopwalker was down there giving evidence this day and it was the one from Mark Foys. Anyway, I was the member of our gang who stayed outside the store this time to watch when the shop-

walker came back. Then I would walk into the store — and if I did that, I didn't have to speak to the others or anything, because when they saw me inside they knew it signalled that the shopwalker had returned and they'd leave the store quickly. But a group of plain-clothes coppers arrested me this time and I copped three months — you could be sentenced up to six months on a suspected person charge."

- 12/1/32: "steal from person" at Central Petty Court; Hayes was charged after an attempt to rob a taxi driver named John Harte of 14 shillings and twopence at Darlinghurst.
- 18/1/32: "indecent language", "assaulting police" and "stealing" at Central Petty Court. "They were all to do with shoplifting at Anthony Horderns," Hayes recalls. "I was held until the police arrived and I copped six months' hard labour."
- 1/2/32: "assault" and "robbery" at Central Petty Court. "That was an assault on the owner of the Exhibition Hotel," Hayes explains. (The Exhibition Hotel used to stand on the corner of Glebe Point Road and Broadway, just down from Sydney University; Exhibition Park was on the opposite side of the road.) "We were robbing the till in the parlour — the Ladies' Bar they used to call it. The proprietor came in and saw us and grabbed hold of the bloke with me. I tried to help and the owner then grabbed hold of me. I hit him on the chin and he fell down and I ran away. But I was pinched later that day. It was eventually discharged because a lot of my friends knew him and they 'got at him' and he refused to appear in court."
- 11/7/32: "indecent language" at Central Petty Court.
- 18/7/32: "riotous behaviour" at Central Petty Court.
- 26/7/32: "indecent language" at Glebe Petty Court.
- 6/8/32: "street betting" and "assaulting police" at Glebe Petty Court. "There was an SP joint in a house in Glebe Point Road," Hayes recalls. "The coppers arrived and pinched me on the premises, and during the arrests I assaulted a copper. I can't remember if I was there to have a bet or just put the bite on the owner, one of the two. On the trip back to the station I was threatening to bring half of Glebe as witnesses that I never bet there, but was just visiting the house. So eventually they dropped the 'street betting' charge and only went on with the 'assaulting police' charge. I paid a £5 fine on that."

- 23/8/32: "assault occasioning actual bodily harm" at Central Petty Court. "That was in a house in Pine Street, Chippendale," Hayes explains. "I went to an ethnic SP bookie named 'Snowy' Costello to stand over him. He'd been giving me money previously, £5 and £10 at a time. But this time it was more or less my own fault, because he told me he was going bad and didn't have anything for me — though I knew he could rake up £2 or £3. So I assaulted him. He contacted the police in a fit of temper, but then friends of mine 'got at him' afterwards to drop it. So it was discharged."
- 26/8/32: "indecent language" at Central Petty Court. "That relates to when I went back and abused Costello," Hayes explains. "The police also charged me with that one, and they went on with it. I paid a £5 fine, but actually Costello paid it. He gave the money to me in 'Snowy' Flynn's hotel on the eastern corner of Liverpool Street and George Street. Actually he gave me £25: £5 to pay the fine and £20 for me. But he wanted a receipt to show I'd paid the fine. So I sent a prostitute named Lizzy Turner, who was in the pub at the time, up to Central to pay the fine for me."
- 10/10/32: "indecent language", "assault police" and "resist arrest" at Central Petty Court.
- 8/11/32: "robbery" at Sydney Quarter Sessions. "It was actually an armed robbery in Lansdowne Street in Surry Hills," Hayes recalls. "It was SP bookie Hector Hodgman's joint and I was standing over him. I put a gun in his belly. He didn't pay me anything there and then, but told me to come back later. Like a fool I went back and the police were waiting. But I didn't have the gun with me when I went back. So they took me away and charged me. But I was acquitted because we got at him — some friends of mine stood over him and he dropped off."
- 11/10/32: "suspected person" at Central Petty Court. "That was in Lowes — there were four or five of us in there at the time — and the shopwalker saw me and contacted the police," Hayes recalls. "By this time our pictures were up in all their offices and they knew us well; even a lot of people behind the counters began to know us by sight. A couple of plain-clothes police nabbed me and I copped six months' hard labour."
- 13/10/32: "consorting" at Central Petty Court. "I was arrested at the Railway," says Hayes, "and it was for consorting with

everyone about the place. I pleaded guilty, because you had no chance of beating a consorting charge. I received six months' hard labour."

- 26/4/33: "stealing" at Central Petty Court. "That was in a small shop called Collar Kings, in George Street, just down from the fire station," Hayes recalls. "I was grabbed inside the shop by a young relation of the owner and copped another six-month sentence..."
- 9/6/33: "stealing" at Central Petty Court. "I was arrested by the shopwalker inside Murdochs men's store, which was next to Lowes. I was with a group of other blokes, but I was the only one caught. Since I had such a bad shoplifting record I copped 12 months this time."

• • •

Hayes served the last part of his one-year sentence for shoplifting at Bathurst Jail. There he renewed his acquaintance with a leading criminal, Patrick Brady, whom he had first met, on the outside, in the early 1930s.

"When I arrived at Bathurst," Hayes recalls, "Brady was already there serving three years for forgery. He was a very quiet man, and later he never talked about his central role in the famous Shark Arm case. [In 1935 Brady was acquitted of the murder of billiard-hall boss, James Smith, whose body was never found, but whose severed arm with a rope tied around the wrist and featuring a unique tattoo of two boxers in fighting pose, had been regurgitated by a 3.5-metre tiger shark at Coogee Aquarium.] At Bathurst, neither Brady nor I would work, so we were both stuck in Number 4 Yard with a broom...

"Now, three or four days before I was due to be released from Bathurst, Brady called me aside in the yard. He wanted me to deliver a special message to his wife. He insisted it was extremely important, but said I couldn't deliver it verbally. So he asked if I'd take a secret letter to her. He made a tiny letter by sticking cigarette papers together. Then, after he'd written on it, he screwed it up into a small ball and wrapped it in a piece of silver paper. Then my job was to carry it in my mouth, under my tongue; and if I was caught, I was to chew it up and swallow it.

"In those days, when you were released from Bathurst, you needed three shillings for a taxi fare at midnight — you were technically due for release then. Otherwise you had to wait until 10 o'clock the next morning. Now the day before your release, they'd call you at 3.15 pm and take you down to the office, where you'd 'sign off' and collect your personal belongings. Then you were taken to B Wing — it had 64 cells, with four special cells just inside the entrance for imminent discharges. At 3.30 pm you were put into one of those cells. Now initially I had Brady's letter in my pocket; then, on my way back to B Wing, I'd put it under my tongue. Upon arrival at B Wing, I was stripped out of my prison clothes, and walked into the cell naked. Inside the cell they'd laid out my suit, shirt, shoes and so on. Then the prison officers locked the door behind me. But once I'd been put in there, I knew I was sweet.

"The screws came back again at 11.15 pm and made sure I was awake and ready. Then they returned at 11.50 pm and took me to the office. But there was no further search from that point on. At 12.02 pm they took me to the prison gate, where my taxi was waiting to take me to the station for three shillings. These, of course, were still the days of the old steam trains, and it took another six hours to reach Sydney.

"Brady's wife was living in Australia Street, Newtown. When I arrived with the letter, she was expecting me. She offered me a £1 note, but you never accepted that sort of thing. Later she wrote back to Brady with a message in code that she'd received my letter."

• • •

One extremely lucrative caper of Hayes's shoplifting career involved the docket books from major department stores such as David Jones and Farmers. "The big stores would have three or four receipt books on their counters," Hayes explains, "and printed across the front cover was the shop's name. We'd pinch one of these from each of the major stores. Then we'd also buy a little receipt book, a common one, for sixpence at a newsagent.

"Once, for example, we pulled this caper at the Westminster Hotel, where the owner was a bloke named Hector Allsop. He always left the hotel on Monday to do his banking and general business. He'd be away for several hours, and then maybe he'd have lunch somewhere with a couple of business associates or friends. So one of us followed him to see where he went. In the meantime, the others got a small box — the type you'd put jewellery in — and wrapped it up and went to the hotel and asked to speak to his missus or the manager. The boy who fronted put the receipt books in his pocket and a couple of pens in the top pocket of his shirt. Then he told Mrs Allsop that her husband had just bought this jewellery package an hour or so before, at David Jones or Farmers or wherever, but he didn't have enough money on him at that time. So he'd said to bring it down to the hotel. (In those days the prices were all in guineas.) So we'd tell Mrs Allsop or whoever that it was cash on delivery and we had the receipt book to prove we were from David Jones or wherever.

"I was pulling this caper with all the same blokes with whom I was shoplifting: Eddie McMillan and 'Kicker' Kelly and 'Spud' Murphy and so on.

"We conned 375 guineas from Allsop, which was a fortune in those days. We did a number of hotels, including the St Clair Inn at Broadway. We pulled this caper a dozen times, at amounts like 250 guineas and 325 guineas, so it really was a small fortune during that era.

"And we didn't restrict it to hotels. Once we pulled it off at McIlwraiths, which was the big food shop, something like a Flemings supermarket today. McIlwraiths had about five stores in Sydney in those days, but the main shop was just down from City Tattersalls Club in Pitt Street. We conned the manager at McIlwraiths in Pitt Street with the same caper."

• • •

Around this time, young Chow Hayes met Dick Reilly — who was later to become one of Sydney's most notorious underworld and illegal gambling figures — when Reilly was working as a doorman at the Savoy dance hall. "It was just down from the old Glaciarium," Hayes recalls, "and you went downstairs to enter it. In those days among the things we used to shoplift were women's stockings. Now the Savoy always had a special dance during the week — sometimes twice a week — called the Spotlight Dance. You had to be in a certain spot when the music stopped — it might be under a light or up against a particular wall or something — and they turned on the spotlight. And if you were standing in the spot, you won a prize.

"So if I had a girl with me whom I wanted to impress, I'd give Reilly half a dozen pairs of stockings — he would keep three for himself and give the girl the other three as her prize — and then he'd tell me the secret spot in advance. That always made me pretty sweet with the girls."

Another favourite ploy to impress the girls involved the fortune-teller Gipsy Lilly. "Lilly was never pinched because she took care to hang a notice above her door," Hayes remembers. "It said she didn't charge for her services, but you could donate something, like sixpence or a shilling or two shillings, in the box. So when you went in she'd be sure to say she wasn't going to charge you, but if you'd like to make a donation, put it in the box. Of course, if you didn't make a donation then you didn't have any fortunes told.

"One Friday night I was with Leo Murphy (he wasn't related to 'Spud' Murphy) down at the markets, and I saw a sheila named Linda with two or three other girls. I commented to Murphy that I'd like to 'knock her off' and he said why didn't I give it a go. So I walked over and fronted her and started talking. I asked her name and where she lived and how many brothers and sisters she had and so on. I squeezed quite a bit of information out of her, and then I said I'd see her down at the markets again the next Friday evening.

"Then we'd go to see Gipsy Lilly and give her the information and she'd write it down. So I told Lilly about Linda and said I'd bring her up to the shop the following Friday night to have her fortune told.

"So I met Linda on the Friday night and began talking to her again. Then I asked if I could walk home with her. She asked where I came from and I told her some silly place, but was careful not to mention the Railway Mob. She nodded while I talked on — and I didn't know that she was actually going out with a bloke from the Surry Hills Mob. As we were walking I asked if she believed in fortune-tellers. She said 'Yes'. Then I announced there was one just up the road and, while I didn't believe in them myself, this one was supposed to be good. So we went up there, just past the Lyric Theatre, and I gave her a shilling and told her to go in and have her fortune told. But Linda said she didn't like giving only a shilling, she wanted to give two shillings and receive a really good session. So I gave her two shillings. Then she went in — but was only inside about two minutes when she came out again. I asked what Gipsy Lilly had told her. And Linda said Lilly had read her palm and declared that Chow Hayes was a mongrel and to go and get fucked!

"What had happened was that, on the first night I'd talked to her, someone had recognised me and tipped her off that I was Chow Hayes from the Railway Mob. So she'd known all along that I was conning her, and she didn't even put the two bob in Lilly's box. Well, I had to laugh about it all. Anyway, that was the time I came undone — but I'd conned about 10 or 12 other girls before that and they were all sweet when they came out."

In those days Dick Reilly was also a doorman at the Prince of Wales Hotel, opposite the Lyric Theatre. "I used to see him often, but he wasn't big time then," Hayes explained. "I always found him a mighty fellow. He was fair dinkum and straight down the line with you, there was never any shit with him. If he could do you a good turn, then he'd do it. And he was generally a very quiet man. He was a big, solid bloke, and so was his brother, Gerry, who used to do a bit of boxing — only six- and eight-round stuff.

"They were two very good street fighters, though old George 'Bombardier' Williams was the best street fighter of all. One time Williams and Gerry Reilly were about to start a brawl, and then Dick poked his head in so Williams said he'd fight him instead. Anyway Dick and Williams fought under the arches in Eddy Avenue at the Railway for about 45 minutes. In the end old 'Bombardier' got away with Dick and beat him fair and square, no kicking or anything. What made it even more incredible on old George's part was that when he finished with Dick, he turned to Gerry and said: 'Right oh, Gerry, I'll take you now.' Gerry was a lot taller than Dick — Dick was about 6 ft 1 in [185 centimetres], and Gerry was another 3 or 4 inches [8 or 10 centimetres] taller than him. But that fight only lasted another 10 minutes before Williams knocked Gerry out cold."

• • •

Even before he had graduated from the Railway Gang's "Little Mob" up to the "Big Mob", Chow Hayes had gained a reputation for being one of the toughest youngsters on the streets of Sydney. He and his mates in the "Little Mob" prided themselves on the fact that they never backed down to anyone. "With all respect to them," Hayes explains, "I really think that in those days the Little Railway Mob was a lot harder and tougher and vicious than even the Big Mob. The Big Mob carried guns, but I'd say only one of them would actually have used a gun, a bloke named Hadey Futeler. (He later served half a dozen years in jail.) But in the Little Mob, we'd pick up anything — bottles, stones, iron bars, blocks of wood — to use in a fight. Even the police used to say that, at that point, the members of the Little Mob at the Railway were a lot tougher than the big fellows."

One night Hayes was at the Railway and a fellow named Jackie Hardacre, a shoplifter who was more or less a loner, arrived with his girlfriend, Rosie Morris. "She was a real top sort," Hayes recalls. "I was only 16 at the time and she was about 18, and Hardacre came along — I think he was going to see another sheila, but he told me he was going to a party — and asked me to take Rosie to the pictures. He gave me a 'caser' (five bob) to take her to the flicks and then see that she arrived home at Leichhardt safely afterwards. I said alright, and he went up the other end of the Railway to meet her and then brought her back down and introduced me to her. He explained to her that he had to go and see a sick friend or some other yarn, and said: 'Chow will take you to the pictures and then take you home.'

"After about five minutes, when he was gone and we were standing there talking, I asked which theatre she wanted to go to and she said the Haymarket. I said I'd seen the film showing there, even though I hadn't really seen it. So then she said the Empress and I said I'd seen that too (that was a bit out of my territory, to tell the truth; it was up near the Town Hall and the Rocks Mob had the territory there). Then she said I obviously didn't want to go to the pictures, and I admitted I didn't. I said I'd buy her a milkshake instead. So we did that, and she admitted she didn't want to go to the pictures either. Then I suggested we go and sit in the park instead — Belmore Park, which was a bit dangerous too, because it was actually in the Surry Hills Mob's territory. We walked there and, to cut a long story short, after a while we went and rented a room.

"We stayed in the room (at Ma Dooley's place in George Street, just up from where Mick Simmons sporting store is now) for eight days. I think I had about 32 shillings, which was a lot of money in those days, and it was three bob a night for a room. We used to come out and buy more beer and go back in again. She had about £3 in her purse, so we pooled our money. But after the eight days were up we'd run out of cash. And by then I knew the Little Mob would want to know where I was. They knew I'd gone away with her, but they'd want to know why I hadn't been 'working' — 'working' was what we termed shoplifting.

"So I left Rosie near the Railway and went home to Regent Street and told Ninny and the others some lie about staying at a mate's place for eight days. They were just glad to see me and find out that I wasn't in any trouble. I changed my clothes and went straight down to the Railway. It must have been about 4 pm. 'Spud' Murphy, 'Kicker' Kelly and Eddie Miller were there — they'd been out shoplifting and had come back to the Railway. They wanted to know where I'd been all week and what I'd done with Rosie. I said she'd gone home and they reckoned that

Hardacre was threatening to kill me, that he'd been running around madly looking all over Sydney for me. 'Kicker' Kelly asked what I was going to do, and I said there was only one thing to do and that was to front Hardacre and take it from there. They all said they'd back me up in any brawl. But I said 'No', I didn't want anyone with me, that I'd done the wrong thing by Hardacre and I'd just let him sort it out.

"Hardacre didn't arrive at the Railway until about 7.15 pm. The blokes in the Big Mob would drink in the hotel until 6.10 pm (it was 6 pm closing and then you had about 10 minutes to finish your drinks and get out). Then they'd go and have something to eat. So at about 7.15 pm Hardacre came down from the top of the Railway to where he knew the Little Mob congregated. He asked where Rosie was and I said she'd gone home. Then he asked where we'd been, so I told the truth and said we'd rented a room. Well, he called me a dirty rotten bastard and so on, and threatened that he was going to go on with me. He raved how he was going to do this and do that to me. But he only got it half out before 'Kicker' Kelly, who was standing alongside him, king-hit Hardacre. It wasn't pre-arranged.

"The punch broke Hardacre's nose and knocked out a couple of his teeth. And when he went down Eddie Miller and Kelly and I gave him a bit of a kicking — not too much because it was only just after 7 pm and there were still a lot of people around the Railway.

"The Big Mob duly heard the commotion and they ran down and 'Snowy' Molloy, who was in charge of them (he was no relation to 'Duke' Molloy, the Big Mob's ventriloquist), broke it up and said we'd done the wrong thing. But I told him he could go and get fucked, and if they wanted to put on a stink then we'd go around the corner behind Saunders and finish it.

"However, just then Rosie Morris came along, and Hardacre said to her: 'Look what these bastards have done to me!' She replied: 'What do you expect me to do about it?' So then Hardacre threatened: 'I'll give it to you later!' But Rosie replied: 'You won't give it to me later, because I'm not going with you.' So 'Snowy' Molloy asked which bloke she wanted to go with, Chow or Jackie. And she replied 'Chow'. With that Molloy told Hardacre to come with them back up the other end of the Railway and clean himself up in the toilet there. After that Hardacre hated me, but in the meantime I took up with Rosie for a while."

Prior to that time, Hayes and his shoplifting comrades had never ventured into the ladieswear sections of the big department stores. "We stuck to the menswear," Hayes recalled, "but Rosie had done a bit of shoplifting with Hardacre, so I asked whether she wanted to do a bit with me. Rosie had a friend named Thelma Barton, so I said to bring her too. Thereafter, 'Kicker' Kelly and I and Rosie and Thelma started working the ladies' departments and it was a real open go in all of them. It was just so easy in those sort of shops — much easier than in the menswear. There was only one lady detective in the shop and you could watch her down one end while your partners were pinching stuff up the other. And if we pinched some ladies' shoes — they were about 25 or 30 bob a pair in those days — we wouldn't take one pair, we'd grab seven or eight at a time and stuff them in a big gladstone bag and fill it up as soon as we got in there. We'd do the same with women's bags and stockings and those slips they used to wear; you could take dozens of them and they'd never miss them.

"Eventually one day, when I'd turned 17 and Kelly was the same age, we rented a room in Myrtle Street, Chippendale — about number 56. It was a two-room place and the four of us moved in there. Its main function was to serve as a base to store all the stuff we were pinching. But we also stayed there a few nights a week — Kelly with Thelma and Rosie with me.

"One day we went to the ladies' department at Mark Foys, where they had these expensive fur coats worth about £300 (that'd be at least $30,000 today — people were only earning about £2 6s a week then, so £300 was several years' wages for the working man). Anyway, the four of us were sitting in Hyde Park, across the road from Mark Foys, and I asked Rosie: 'Would you be game to put on one of those fur coats and walk out?' She replied 'Yes', so I said we'd go back at lunchtime and try it. I told her what to do — how to remove the labels from the neck and sleeve and put them in the coat pocket and then just walk out. I said 'Kicker' and I would be about five metres behind — and if anyone tried to intercept her we'd take them on.

"So, initially, that was the arrangement. But then Rosie stopped and said she wasn't going in and taking all the risk for Thelma to receive a whack of the profit — we used to split everything four ways. However, Thelma replied we didn't have to worry about her. She said she was surprised at Rosie's complaint, and that if Rosie put one on, she'd put one on too. So then we had to alter our plan: I'd go in with Rosie and look after her if anyone tried to intercept her, and 'Kicker' would look after Thelma. When we went inside, I immediately told Rosie to grab the dearest one and it came to about 300 guineas. Thelma's choice was worth about 250 guineas. And they got away with it and we walked back over into Hyde Park. But then the problem was wearing the expensive coats from the park back to Chippendale — you'd feel as though everyone in Australia was looking at you walking down the street in them. However, we eventually made it home to Chippendale, and then I went off to see a fence named Billy Chambers. He operated in a shop above Nick Winter and Charlie Purdy's Eden billiard hall. The Eden was downstairs, and on top of it were three little shops and Chambers had one of them and Gipsy Lilly had another.

"Billy Chambers was the biggest fence in Sydney. He would buy absolutely anything, from a pin-up to a motor car, a tractor even, and he'd be able to sell it again. And he had been touching us for years. If you took something to him worth £5 he'd only give you £1.

"I went and saw Chambers and he wanted to know how big the coats were and I said they fitted Rosie, whom he knew. Initially, he tried the line that he didn't think he'd be able to unload a fur coat, which I knew was a lie because he could get rid of anything. Then he asked how much we wanted for them and I said 100 guineas each. He replied that he didn't think we'd get 200 guineas, but to bring them down and give him a look at them. I said it was too late to bring them down that evening so we'd return in the morning.

"Then I went back and told the others what happened, and Rosie and I decided to go to the pictures while Thelma and Kelly stayed home. So we went to the pictures and, because it was the middle of winter, Rosie insisted on wearing the bloody fur coat. We went to the State Theatre, and when we came out at interval some people were looking at us, though most didn't even notice. But I kept imagining everyone was looking at us. Then on the way home Rosie told me how warm the coat was and that she thought she'd keep it. I immediately replied pig's arse she would, but she said she'd pay the 100 guineas by giving Kelly and Thelma and I our 25 guineas each and keep it. Then I explained she couldn't keep it because any copper who saw her with a coat like that would know immediately that it was hot. Eventually she agreed that she couldn't keep it. Later we pinched other fur coats from Anthony Horderns and Grace Brothers. And we went back to Mark Foys about eight weeks later — if we returned to any store before that the thefts would become too obvious and they'd realise the coats were missing. So we took our time and grabbed about 10 of them over a period of 12 months.

"Meanwhile, the morning after the first job at Mark Foys I went back to see Chambers. He said he'd seen a fellow and the most he'd give us was 100 guineas for both coats. We had no other way of disposing of them, because you couldn't walk around the hotels trying to flog fur coats. So I said okay and the girls later wore the coats down to Chambers' shop right in the middle of the day. Then Rosie and Thelma headed off into town — Rosie went to buy her mother a present or something — and Kelly and I went up to the Railway Hotel and we met them about two hours later.

"Rosie had gone into Prouds jewellery shop and put down a lay-by on a little pendant for her mother. She could have bought it there and then, but she didn't because the bloke behind the counter was trying to pitch for her. So then she started kidding to him and spun some yarn about how the main reason she went in was to look at engagement rings. She said she was going to marry a fellow and he was rich and so on, and she wanted to see an expensive ring. He pulled out a tray with half a dozen on it, including one worth 750 guineas.

"Rosie came back and told us about it. Now the bloke behind the counter was aged around 30, but he wanted to take her out, even though she'd told him she was engaged. She'd purposely led him on a bit. She told us she thought she could steal that ring, if we went back to Prouds to help her. She planned to tell him that she wanted to look at the engagement ring in the sunlight near the door; then, when she bolted, Kelly and I would stop him chasing out after her.

"We thought about it for two or three days and then, on a Friday, she went back and asked him to show her the 750-guinea ring again. She tried it on her finger, and while she had it on she let him chat her up. Eventually she said: 'I shouldn't do this, but you seem a nice chap. So I'll let you take me out tomorrow night.' So he made an appointment with her for the Saturday evening and took down her name and address and so on — which naturally was a bodgie name with a bodgie address. Then Rosie said she'd like to look at the ring in the sunlight. He said that was alright, and she walked to the door where, outside, Kelly was on one side and I was on the other. So she walked out and he was about three yards [2.75 metres] behind her. Then she stopped — and when she stopped, he stopped, still about three yards behind her. And she glanced around and kidded to be looking at it in the sunlight and then moved to walk away. Of course he went to walk after her, but Kelly and I bustled him back in, saying we wanted to 'buy a cigarette case, mate' which stopped him getting out the door. He kept trying to push past us, but we held him up. So Rosie got away — and we later collected 150 guineas from Chambers for the ring.

"But about four days later Rosie was pinched over it. The police showed the bloke photographs and he identified her. He also said that she'd originally been accompanied by another woman, but he couldn't identify Thelma. The police charged Rosie with stealing a ring worth 750 guineas. However, to cut a long story short, she beat it with an alibi: her mother and two sisters all said she was home at that particular time so she couldn't have been in Prouds shop. And he was a squarehead, and made a couple of mistakes while he was giving his evidence in the witness box. Jim Kincaid was Rosie's barrister — he was the leading criminal barrister at the time.

"But just after that Kelly was pinched for consorting and copped six months in jail. He'd actually been pinched earlier and had been out on bail pending his appeal. When he went 'inside' for six months, I told Rosie that Thelma had to leave Myrtle Street, because we couldn't have her there now that Kelly was in jail. But Rosie was a queer bastard, in that one minute she'd want to be with you and the next she wouldn't. And, to tell the truth, I was becoming a bit sick of her by this time. Anyway, she said that if Thelma was going, then she was going too. I said that suited me and to pack her port and get out. She was the type who starts to take over your life."

• • •

About 10 months later, after Kelly had been back from prison for four months, he and Hayes were in the Eden billiard room after a shoplifting spree from which they had each pocketed roughly £2. "We were sitting in the billiard room and Chambers came to see me," Hayes recalls. "And when he went I commented to Kelly that Chambers had been touching us for years. So I said I thought I might hold him up, and asked whether Kelly wanted to be in it. I said that if he didn't, I could do it on my own anyway, but since he'd been touched too he might want to be in it. Kelly said he'd be only too happy to be in it. I was now 18 and I asked Kelly if he had a gun and he said he did.

"All the police in Sydney knew Chambers was a fence. He must have been 'slinging' to some of them so they would let him continue to operate — and he would also give information about other criminals to them. Anyway it was about 1 pm and I said we'd hold him up in the morning. But then Kelly said 'No', not tomorrow (which would have been a Wednesday) but on Friday because Chambers always pulled his money out of the bank on Friday to buy up stuff over the weekend. So we agreed to hold him up to 10.30 am on the Friday morning.

"We met on the Friday, just around the corner in Quay Street, and we both had a gun. I had a .32 and Kelly had a .22. We walked in and Chambers's first words were: 'What have you boys got for me today?' With that, Kelly closed the door and fastened the latch and I pulled my gun out. I said: 'You bastard. You've been robbing us all our lives, now we're going to rob you!' At first, he thought it was a joke. But I told him it was no joke and I stuck the gun as far as I could into his guts. Then he knew I was serious. So he sat down in his chair, but just then there was a knock at his door. It must have been another thief trying to sell him something — there was always a constant stream of thieves and shoplifters in and out. I whispered to him to tell the knocker that he was busy and to come back in half an hour. So he sung that out loudly and we heard the footsteps going away.

"Then we ordered Chambers to pull his wallet out, which he did, and we made him empty his pockets and put everything on the table. All the while I still had the gun on him. Kelly had his gun out too, but he transferred it into his left hand and went over and picked up all the money and stuffed it inside his shirt. Then I told Chambers: 'Now open the safe.' It was a little safe, and he protested that there was nothing in it. But I insisted that he open it just the same. So he opened it, but he'd been telling the truth and there was nothing in it. Then I said: 'Now look, Bill, you can't go to the police. But if you do I'm going to tell them the names of every thief in Sydney from whom you've been buying stuff and you'll be charged with receiving.' I added that I knew he was sweet with the coppers, but he could please himself, because if he did go to the police, I also had a lot of friends and if we got pinched they'd blow his head off.

"Then he said: 'Well, give me half back.' But I said: 'No, not a penny.' I said that if we were going to take his money, we were taking the lot. Well he never went to the police and we got away with £2800 — that was £1400 each. That was the first time I ever bought a house full of furniture."

(Charles Russell "Kicker" Kelly and Hayes remained close friends until the early 1940s. On one occasion during that period Kelly received a six-month jail sentence for punching a female shop inspector, and on another he was described in court as "the champion shoplifter." "We more or less drifted away from one another — though we never lost complete contact — just before I copped four years' jail in 1941," Hayes recalls. "He went into the breaking and entering caper and began using dynamite to blow up safes. One night he and two other fellows, who came from the Loo, went to a factory in Surry Hills to blow the safe. But he put too much gelignite into the keyhole of the safe — I've never done a safe myself. It went off alright, but it blew his left leg off with it. Of course, when the neighbours heard all the noise they rang the police. Meanwhile Kelly nearly bled to death before the ambulance arrived. After that he had a wooden leg and only lived another eight or nine years. I met him one day and asked why those other two blokes didn't get him away. But he said it'd have been no use.")

• • •

Hayes sums up his shoplifting career thus: "I did a few spells in Long Bay — three months when I was 18½ and six months when I'd just turned 19 and so on. I remember very well that when I was 21 I copped 12 months, and that was the maximum for shoplifting. Among the favourite things we'd pinch were socks, ties, shirts, all types of hats, overcoats and watches. And we were selling a lot of it to Kate Leigh and Tilly Devine, and the Big Mob down at the Loo, and Jim Devine (Tilly's husband) and 'Slack' O'Brien. There were always lots of people to whom you could sell things.

"So from the age of 17½ until I was 21 I spent most of my time shoplifting. And I also copped a few charges for assaulting police, and one thing and another. All this time I was still living with my grandmother, Aunty Ninny and sister in Rose Street, Chippendale.

"But when I copped the 12-month sentence I was sent to Bathurst Jail (they didn't want you at Long Bay for longer sentences). Actually my first sentence outside Long Bay was at Parramatta, where I did three months. One of the blokes I met at Parramatta was Billy Phillips, who eventually spent 41 years straight in jail and died there. Back in the early 1920s he'd killed one of the Arnotts' grand-daughters at the Arnott's biscuit factory out Petersham way...

"Anyway, once I received the maximum of 12 months for shoplifting and was sent to Bathurst, I knew I was going to be given the maximum every time from then on. So that's when I began to give shoplifting away."

5 Frank Green, Nellie Cameron and "Pretty Dulcie" Markham

When Hayes and his mates finally decided it had become "too hot" to continue shoplifting, they began kicking in shop windows at night. "We used house bricks and iron bars," Hayes explains, "and it was like a smash-and-grab. We'd wait till a tram was coming past about 1 am in the morning and then we'd let go and take whatever was in the window. Then we'd jump on the tram as it rattled past. Most of the stuff was jewellery — for example, from Grace Bros where they'd take the good stuff out overnight but leave things such as watches in the window display.

"The only two jewellery shops around the Railway we didn't smash were Saunders and Orchards. We left them alone because they were situated too close to the 'teams' — that is, the Big Mob and the Little Mob. Smashing into them would have immediately brought the coppers after us. And as much as anything, we had to be nightwatchers there because the Glebe Mob or the Loo Mob or the Surry Hills Mob might try and sneak up there and smash something. Anyway, after a while Saunders and Orchards paid us money to keep the other mobs away from them.

"One day the manager from Saunders came across the road to Railway Square and told half a dozen of us that he'd pay us £1 a week to stop breaking his windows. And he told the manager at Orchards, who followed suit. So then we were receiving £2 each week to protect their windows. So we basically smashed into any other shop in our area which had jewellery, except the two shops right at the Railway.

"We'd sneak into another mob's territory and smash windows in their areas too — say the Ann Street Mob's Surry Hills territory. For a while those smash-and-grab raids became the main reason for all the mobs fighting each other. Also in those days it was pretty much the law of the jungle after dark, because there weren't many police cars around. I remember when the

'PD' cars came in — the 'PD' on the front and back stood for 'Police Department'. They were a joke. Their top speed was around 30 miles [50 kilometres] an hour, so they were no trouble to us and you could see them coming 400 yards [370 metres] away.

"In those days there weren't many cars around, day or night. It was mostly still horses and carts and drays and sulkies. I remember when the first taxi cabs started in Sydney. Up to that point it had been all hansom cabs — and you could catch one from the Railway to Circular Quay for three shillings (30 cents today) or from the Railway to Randwick racecourse for three bob. But the hansom cabs only took two people — three at a pinch. At taxi ranks in those days you'd see a row of hansom cabs. The first taxi cabs I remember in Sydney were the 'Yellow Cabs' — they were coloured yellow all over and stood out easily. Then came the 'Check Cabs', which featured black-and-white checks down both sides."

Next, Hayes and his mates moved into what they called the "Swap Game". "It involved a diamond ring worth about £200," Hayes explains. "We'd buy one, and then have an imitation made at somewhere like Saunders — especially at Saunders because they made really good imitations and you'd swear blind it was the same ring. But it cost only about £1 or 25 bob!

"Then you'd put it in a little white bag about four inches long and two inches wide [10 centimetres by five centimetres] and you'd put that in your pocket, and you'd also have the good ring. In other words, we'd buy the good ring at Saunders, and then we'd also buy the imitations at the same place. As a matter of fact we bought three or four every fortnight for over 12 months from Saunders and nobody asked any questions.

"So we'd have the good ring in a little white bag, exactly the same as the imitation. Then we'd go to a publican or down to City Tatts in Pitt Street. For example, if we went to a publican we'd tell him it was hot and that he could take it away and have it valued, and they all did that — except for one mug, a bookie or punter or something in the street outside City Tatts, who just bought it without even bothering to have it valued. Anyway, the publican would find out that the ring was indeed valued at about £200 and we'd asked him for £50, a quarter of the price. But then as soon as he went to give you the £50, you'd suddenly say: 'Oh no no no, I want £100.' And you'd put the ring back in your pocket. Of course, the buyer would insist that we'd said £50, and then we'd kid to go into a little huddle to discuss it between ourselves and eventually we'd agree to give it to him for the original £50. But when you pulled it out again, you'd pull out the other identical bag with the imitation in it.

"'Kicker' Kelly used to do that caper with me. And a mate of mine named Alex 'Lug' Sheedy put us onto several suckers. (I'd first met Alex — who was 'three parts dark' — when he used to sell frankfurts down at the Railway). We kept up the Swap Game for about 12 months — virtually until we ran out of customers, because there were no more publicans or bookmakers. It was no good going to a worker with it."

• • •

The young criminals had a number of other nefarious activities to fall back on, several of them involving the racetrack.

During the late 1920s the notorious pony races at Sydney's now defunct Victoria Park, Rosebery, Kensington and Ascot tracks began around 10 am. The program often featured 16 races on the one day, with an entrance fee of five shillings into the Paddock. The pony tracks were a favourite venue among Hayes and his mates, but they were loath to hand over the admission price.

"Now it was too hot to try before the first race," Hayes recalls, "but after each race they'd give you a 'pass-out'. You'd simply tell the bloke on the gate that you'd lost your money on the previous race and you were going out to get some more. Then we'd sell the 'pass-out' to people arriving for 2s 6d — and if you did it four or five times, well, that was 12s 6d, which was good money in those days.

"See, we knew spots at each track to climb back over or through the fence. We continued the fence rort at the racecourses for about six or seven years. Sometimes we wouldn't even have to jump over the fence, because we'd just put an iron bar in and pull off a few palings. And, of course, once there was a hole some of the paying customers would charge in after us."

Another lurk at the ponies involved the infamous "run-offs" for the main race of the day. The organisers might list four heats of the main event during the afternoon, and then the winners of the heats would race in a run-off after the last race for, say, £50 prizemoney. "Well, the owners would get their heads together," Hayes recalls, "and decide to back the outsider or the second favourite. And while it lasted, they made a lot of money from the bookies from the run-off racket. So the trick for us was to find out which one they were going to back and get on too."

Another racket during those years involved outsmarting the

SP bookies in the pubs. "You couldn't do it too often," Hayes explains, "and you couldn't do it at the SP houses, only at the pubs, because the blokes in the houses used to go to the pubs to get the results. But in those days a telegram boy used to ride around to the hotels and deliver the race results to the SP bookies. If the race was on at 2.15 pm, for example, then about 3 pm the telegram boy would come to the bookmaker and give him the result. And then he wouldn't pay out that day, he'd pay out the next day on the *Sydney Morning Herald*'s official SP prices.

"So what we did with a couple of telegram boys about half a dozen times — no more because there'd be a big blue over it — was to 'neck' him. See he'd only be a kid about 14 or 15 years old. So we'd neck him, and take the telegram, see the result and then give it back to him and hold him for a couple of minutes while one of our mates sneaked up ahead and placed a bet on the winner. Meantime we'd threaten the kid not to say a word. We'd only bet five or six bob — you couldn't put too much on or the bookie would get wise to us."

During that era the newspapers and newsletters, such as the *Arrow* and the *Referee*, all competed vigorously to outdo each other at tipping race winners.

"Now Tommy Verney, who was known as 'Big Rot', developed an idea for a thing called *Top Notch*," Hayes recalls. "It was only written on a bit of writing pad and he listed four horses and tried to pick a winner. He went to a printer and had it printed up, and the first time he had 500 done and they sold like hot cakes — because it was the first time he'd come on the market. He sold them for one shilling each, and we used to keep sixpence per copy for selling them for him.

"It was only a single sheet of paper in an envelope, but Verney had placards made and *Top Notch* was the only tipsheet sold outside the course (the others were sold through the newspapers). On the Friday we'd go into town and sell it in King Street and around all the clubs and so on. And the placards would boast how we tipped three winners last week and, of course, that was all rubbish. But Verney used to pick a winner now and again, and he finished up selling about 4000 or 5000 each week. It went for nearly two years and then it fell off altogether. I was about 17 when I was distributing *Top Notch* and I'd sell about 30 or 40 each week, which meant I made about £1 or a bit more out of it. That was real good money in those days."

One of their more colourful competitors for a fast buck was a man named Vockler. He was a very tall chap who used to wear a long hat, with "Vockler" displayed on top, around the course. "Now his caper," says Hayes, "revolved around the fact that in those days there were huge crowds at the weekend meetings, and they didn't have as many tote windows open as they do today. So, for example, he'd pick the placed horses and if the dividend was 15s 6d for 5s, then he'd stand at the end of the pay-out queue and offer you 15s for your ticket, to save you having to wait. We used to think he was a fool at the time. But later he told me that he made a lot of money out of it — indeed, on days like Epsom, Metropolitan, Doncaster, Sydney Cup and Derby Day, he'd make enough to last him for the rest of the year."

Another racecourse character of the era was old Herbie Golding. He lived in a terrace in Jones Street, Ultimo. "He used to kid to be blind," Hayes recalls, "but he had as many convictions as I did. He would stand outside the tracks with a big placard over his shoulder featuring the words 'Help The Blind'. Of course he could see anyone coming. Sometimes the police would pinch him, and eventually they charged him and he copped a six-month jail sentence. That's when he gave it away — before that he'd only been copping fines."

Another haunt of Hayes and his friends was the famous Sydney Stadium down at Rushcutters Bay. "Some nights blokes like Ambrose Palmer and Jack Haines fought for only £100 and they'd go 20 rounds for that. And on Wednesday nights they'd have a main bout and also a variety show, but the fight wouldn't involve top-liners. So they'd then have singers and dancers in the ring.

"One Wednesday the manager came to a group of us — Eddie McMillan, 'Kicker' Kelly, 'Spud' Murphy, Dougie Broomfield and I. He picked four of us out and told us the layout before we entered the ring. They put a blindfold over our heads and placed each of us in one corner. But they left a little bit of a hole so Eddie McMillan could see. So he was the one who'd knock you down, and they told him not to hit us too hard, just to whack us on the chin to drop us on our arse. But what we didn't know was that there were also four attendants, one in each corner, with a long broom with a glove on the end of it. And as we were going around the ring, they were hitting us too. When they hit you, you'd swing around and swipe a punch back but there was no-one there, because they'd quickly pull the broom back each time. That only went on three or four times, but we collected two bob each for it, and we also got in for free. We saw all the good fighters — but, of course, in those days they fought for peanuts."

One of the boxers of the era was Arthur Messenger, who fought under the name Art Walker. In one celebrated incident in April 1930 he was, according to the *Sydney Morning Herald*, "fired at by a gangster outside a Surry Hills restaurant" but "the bullet was deflected by a button and merely grazed his stomach."

"Walker couldn't really fight," Hayes recalls, "but he was a real crowd-pleaser. There was no way in the world anyone could ever knock him out. They'd put him on the program nearly every week; even when there was a major fight, they'd make sure they included Walker in one of the preliminaries. But he used to take an awful hiding most times.

"Anyway, 'Spud' Murphy and I once had a blue with him at The Hole In The Wall restaurant near the Railway. We knocked him down and gave him a kicking, but he kept getting back up. He followed us all over Sydney that night wanting to fight. And every time he saw us after that he'd still want to fight; no matter how much serve we gave him we still couldn't stop him. Finally a fellow in the Big Mob, named Andy, advised us that he'd drop off if, the next time he fronted us, we just told him: 'No, Artie, you'd win, you're too hot for us.' And it worked too...

"Years later, during World War II, Messenger was at Luna Park when the Yanks were out here. He was a bit punchy and, coming back from Luna Park on the ferry one Friday or Saturday night, he got into an argument with three or four Yankee sailors. Apparently they were pretty drunk and ended up throwing him overboard into the harbour. When they threw him over, they then threw the lifebuoy after him. But Messenger, being such a punchy bloke, swam away from it instead of grabbing hold, and he drowned. They found his body the next day."

• • •

During the late 1920s and early 1930s the notorious gunman Francis Donald "Frank" Green controlled much of the underworld activity — notably prostitution and SP betting — in the Woolloomooloo district. In one celebrated incident, a rival slashed him with a razor and the wound required 60 stitches.

Green featured regularly on the front pages, notably:

- in November 1930, he was attacked outside a Lithgow dance hall and received a fractured skull, but refused to give any information about the matter to police;

- in October 1931, he was wounded in the stomach by a bullet and found lying in the street behind St Vincent's Hospital;
- in August 1932, he was charged with robbing another infamous criminal, "Big Jim" Devine;
- in January 1933, after a consorting conviction, he undertook to leave New South Wales for two years;
- but in May 1933 he was sentenced to six months' jail for consorting and another six months for breaking the bond given in January;
- in August 1936 he was injured in a wild brawl in Brisbane; and
- in both August and November 1937 he was convicted of carrying an unlicensed pistol.

Chow Hayes vividly remembers the first time he met Frank Green: "I'd just been released from Parramatta Jail. I was about 19 and that night I went down to Charles 'Chilly' Smith's house at 219 Palmer Street, Darlinghurst — it was an iron-railing terrace among a row of five or six right opposite the Tradesman's Arms Hotel. Smith had just come out of jail and I had a verbal message for him from a bloke named Jim Tombleton whom I'd met in jail. [The message was along these lines: Smith should not come back out to Parramatta Jail to visit Tombleton, because the coppers would be waiting for him. Apparently he'd abused them on a previous visit and they now knew the name he'd put in the visitors' book was a false one. But they didn't know where to find him unless he came back out to see Tombleton again.]

"Smith was running a small SP operation from his house and Green was more or less looking after him, like his backstop. I arrived at Smith's place about 5 pm but he wasn't there. I didn't know that, in fact, he was over the road in the Tradesman's Arms Hotel. Since I hardly knew anyone down around the Loo, I went back up to Oxford Street and had tea.

"Then I returned about 7 pm and Smith was home. I gave him the message and he asked me to have a drink while I was there. Green was also present, with his girlfriend and one of his offsiders named 'Snowy' Chapman. While we had a few drinks I noticed out of the corner of my eye that Green was staring at me. And I swear to this day that I wasn't pitching for his sheila, but apparently he thought I was.

"Anyway, we drank three or four bottles of beer and then 'Chilly' Smith gave me 10 bob for my trouble. But as I was

FRANK GREEN

During the early 1930s, notorious gunman Frank Green controlled much of the underworld activity — notably prostitution and SP betting — in the Woolloomooloo District. During one confrontation Chow Hayes bashed Green repeatedly with a block of wood, breaking Green's jaw and knocking out eight of his teeth.

leaving Green stopped me in the hallway and said: 'What was the idea of trying to pitch for my sheila?' I said I wasn't and Smith told Green to break it down. But Green wanted to go on with it, and he king-hit me. I went down on the ground and then Chapman jumped in and pulled Green away.

"So I wiped my mouth — it was only cut a bit and I wiped away the blood — and had another couple of beers and then I told 'Chilly' that I was going. But I didn't really go. Instead I walked across the road, near the hotel — it was shut due to the 6 pm closing curfew during that era — and I waited in the dark until about 9.45 pm. I saw Chapman come out and leave. But I wasn't sure if Green had stayed inside or not. So I decided to wait until midnight and see if he came out; if he hadn't emerged by then, I was going to piss off.

"In the meantime I noticed that workmen had been digging up the road nearby and there was a stack of little blocks of wood on the footpath. I grabbed hold of one of them, took off my shirt and made a sort of waddy [club] out of it.

"Green finally emerged about 10.30 pm with the sheila. I followed him down the road and waited until he'd walked 50 or 60 yards [45–55 metres] away from Smith's place. Then I sang out: 'Frank! Just a minute. I want to see you.' Well, by this time he was pretty drunk and replied: 'What do you want?' I said: 'I want to give you this!' And with that I got stuck into him. I broke his jaw and knocked out seven or eight teeth, and I gave him a good booting too. Meanwhile his sheila didn't scream out at all at that stage; the only time she screamed was when I was walking away and was 30 or 40 yards [25–35 metres] down the street. So I don't know whether she was glad that I gave it to him or not. But while I was thumping him she just stood there, up against the fence.

"After that I went home. And, of course, the next day I heard from various people that Green was threatening to do all sorts of things to me. But then apparently 'Chilly' Smith got into his ear and told him something like 'this Hayes fellow is an up-and-comer, so you'll be taking a risk because you know what young kids are like when they don't worry about fear', and so on. Anyway, Green kept threatening that he was going to get me, but he never did and I saw him many, many times over the years."

• • •

Frank Green and his arch-rival Guido Calletti ruled the roost among the racketeers who frequented Woolloomooloo during that era.

Calletti had a long career in crime, beginning with a conviction as an uncontrollable child at the age of nine. Thereafter he faced the courts on 56 occasions in three States.

Among his headline-grabbing exploits were:

- in February 1929, he was charged with intent to murder after Ernest Connelly was shot during a party in Womerah Avenue, Darlinghurst;
- in February 1930, he was sentenced to six months in jail and then in May 1931, he was sentenced to a further two years in jail after conviction for "assault with intent to rob" on a train; and
- in February 1933, he had been out of jail just 19 days when sentenced to another six months for consorting.

In one celebrated incident in November 1934 Calletti instituted a libel action against the *Truth* newspaper. "At the time he'd opened a fruit shop somewhere in Paddington," Hayes recalls. "Anyway, he won the court case — but the damages were only one farthing! Well, we all laughed and laughed, because his reputation was only worth a farthing. So *Truth* sent him a penny stamp to cover it, and Calletti kept it for years and years. He even had a little frame made in which to display it."

During the 1930s Calletti muscled in on the lucrative SP business as a standover man. But it was a particularly risky occupation. Calletti found himself regularly involved in gun battles and street brawls. Nevertheless he developed a cavalier attitude to the daily dangers. At one point the Sydney *Sun* reported: "Having survived gunshot wounds on five occasions, it was Calletti's proud boast that no bullet would ever finish him off."

However, most of the gunmen of the era inevitably met their maker sooner rather than later. And in August 1939 Calletti, aged 34, duly died in St Vincent's Hospital with two .32 bullets in the stomach.

The *Sun* explained: "Behind the underworld slaying lay a long-standing feud between two mobs. Calletti's lot had carved out an area in Palmer Street as its preserve. Not far away, in Brougham Street, their bitter rivals for the spoils of crime and corruption were entrenched."

Calletti had barged into a party in a house in Brougham Street unannounced. Wild scenes followed as bottles of liquor and pieces of furniture were hurled around the room. Revolvers

Guido Calletti

Having survived gunshot wounds on five occasions, Guido Calletti proudly boasted that no bullet would ever finish him off. But at the height of an underworld feud in 1939 Calletti barged into a vice-district party and the house erupted — bottles of liquor and pieces of furniture were hurled around the room, revolvers flashed, and Calletti lay prostrate on the carpet in a pool of blood.

flashed. Partygoers fled. And Calletti, bleeding profusely, was left prostrate on the carpet. A mate called a taxi to rush the gravely wounded Calletti to hospital. The driver surveyed the carnage and refused, and then called the police. Robert Branch (alias Jackson) and George Allen (alias Cave) were later charged with his murder, but both were subsequently acquitted.

Extraordinary scenes took place at the Darlinghurst mortuary where Calletti's body lay enclosed in an ornate silver and maple coffin. An estimated 5000 people filed past. The crowd outside was so dense that police, caught offguard, had to summon reinforcements. The *Sunday Telegraph* declared: "They gave Guido the most spectacular criminal funeral Sydney has ever seen. . . ."

The scene was repeated at the graveside at Rookwood Cemetery. More than 200 wreaths arrived. One in particular stood out. It was in the shape of a four-foot-high [120-centimetre] cross from his estranged wife in Queensland.

• • •

Calletti's wife was Nellie Cameron, a woman almost as well known around Sydney's seedy vice and gambling districts as her husband. The *Sunday Telegraph* described Cameron as "a sexy redhead with a ripe figure and provocative china blue eyes". She had become famous throughout the State for her ability to attract the toughest mobsters of the era like proverbial bees to a honeypot. The *Sunday Telegraph* summed up: "The list of her lovers reads like a Who's Who of the razor-gang era. The vicious gang bosses of the 1920s and 30s — the dope-pushers, razor-slashers and standover men — fought over her like jungle animals. That was how she acquired her title 'The Kiss of Death Girl'. . . Police used to say that Nellie Cameron was responsible for more brawls than any other woman in Sydney's history." At least four notorious gangsters of the period who courted Nellie Cameron — Guido Calletti, Alan Pulley, Norman Bruhn and Ernest Connelly — died from gunshot wounds.

At 14 Nellie Cameron had run away from her North Shore home to work as a prostitute in the notorious red-light districts around Darlinghurst and Kings Cross.

"For years Nellie was in the middle of all-out warfare between rival gangs for control of Sydney's narcotics, sly grog and vice rackets," one newspaper later explained. "She did not emerge unscathed from that violent era and at times was shot, razor-slashed, beaten insensible, robbed and terrorised."

Cameron participated in several celebrated fist-swinging brawls with other she-cats of the slumland streets. For many years Surry Hills and Woolloomooloo residents talked about the day Cameron and another harlot, known as "Black Aggie", slugged it out. The *Sunday Telegraph* reported that, stripped to the waist, the two women fought in a tenement backyard for the streetwalking rights to a couple of lucrative blocks along William Street. "Black Aggie" had at least a 12-kilogram weight advantage, but Nellie's ability to punch like a man more than compensated. After 20 minutes her bruised and bleeding foe cried enough.

Cameron's first underworld lover was the Melbourne hoodlum Norman Bruhn, who made his money standing over cocaine pedlars. One night in June 1927 an unknown assassin pumped five bullets into Bruhn when he called at a house in Charlotte Lane, behind Liverpool Street, to collect a pay-off from a drug runner.

Then Nellie took up with swarthy Ernest Connelly — until he too was gunned down, in 1929, while strolling along Womerah Avenue.

Connelly's place was taken by Alan Pulley, until he was shot in Wentworth Street, Glebe. Chow Hayes remembers that episode vividly. "Pulley was shot by Florrie O'Halloran's husband, Ned O'Halloran, who was another well-known criminal. Florrie and Ned O'Halloran lived in a house at 31 Wentworth Street, just two doors along from the house where my wife, Topsy, grew up.

"Ned O'Halloran was in hiding at the time, because he'd assaulted a policeman. And while he was away, Pulley had been trying to stand over Florrie. Florrie ran an SP book. Anyway, she went and told Ned that Pulley was trying to stand over her, and the first thing he asked was: 'Where are Chow and Benny?' That referred to myself and Benny Gorman, because we were supposed to help out if there was any trouble. We weren't being paid, it was just helping out as friends. Anyway Florrie said she couldn't find us. Meanwhile, after the Wednesday race meeting, she told Pulley to come back on the Saturday afternoon. Pulley was trying to squeeze £50 out of her, which was a lot of money in those days.

"Ned told Florrie that if she couldn't contact Chow and Benny by the Friday, to give him another ring. Well she wasn't able to contact us, so she rang him and he went back to Wentworth

Nellie Cameron

Described by one newspaper as "A sexy redhead with a ripe figure and provocative china-blue eyes", she was famous for her ability to attract the toughest mobsters like bees to a honeypot. The list of her lovers read like a who's who of the razor-gang era — and included several of Chow Hayes's close mates.

Street in the middle of the night, about 1 am, and took a rifle with him. Pulley arrived about 2.30 on the Saturday afternoon with another well-known gunman, "Hoppy" Gardiner. Ned was upstairs with the rifle and he heard them talking to Florrie downstairs. Then he suddenly came down and shot Pulley dead on the spot, and Gardiner ran for his life.

"The police arrived, after she rang them, but by that time she'd prepared her story — that she'd shot Pulley herself for trying to stand over her and that she was acting in self-defence. She also emphasised that she had two young children in the house at the time. Pulley did have a gun with him, so she was able to say he'd threatened her and the kids. And while the police were questioning her, Ned was still upstairs hiding under the bed.

"Anyway, they believed her story (of course the police already knew she was an SP bookie) and she eventually got out of it all at the Coroner's Court. It was some months later before the police found out she didn't do it, but Ned had done it. Just after that Ned, who was very sick with an ulcer, died in Prince Alfred Hospital when the ulcer burst."

After Pulley's sudden departure, both the cold-blooded Frank Green and the squat, gorilla-strong Calletti entered the picture. When they both became interested in Nellie Cameron, one newspaper noted, "the underworld erupted into a violent see-sawing contest between them."

It started with a ferocious fist fight in a Woolloomooloo street before an audience which quickly swelled to over 500. "For an hour the two men slugged, gouged, kicked and wrestled each other," one paper reported, "until their clothes were bloodied tatters and neither was capable of continuing."

However, soon after, Calletti was sentenced to two years in Long Bay for armed assault. Green was left to pursue Nellie — though twice over the ensuing months he staggered into Sydney Hospital after brawls with rival admirers. Once his right hand was nearly severed by a savage knife slash. On the other occasion he copped a bullet in the chest when he arrived home unexpectedly and found someone under his mistress's bed. When police questioned Nellie, she denied any acquaintance with Green's assailant. "I didn't know he was there," she insisted. "He must have been a prowler!"

At one point when Green was sought by police after a shooting, he hid in a bushland cave and Nellie made daily trips with food and liquor. Police eventually followed her on one of her visits and arrested Green.

Later, police sought Nellie for questioning about narcotics being supplied to Sydney's callgirls. They discovered she was convalescing in Newcastle Hospital after undergoing an operation under the name Mrs Russell. Knowing she faced arrest as soon as she was discharged, Nellie suffered a "relapse" and sent word to Frank Green, who drove up to Newcastle. Late that night he climbed the fire escape and entered Nellie's private room, wrapped her in a blanket, carried her back down the fire escape to his waiting car and, within a matter of hours, had her safely concealed in a Darlinghurst hide-out.

Meanwhile, however, Calletti had just been released from jail. The following night, while Green was out, Calletti called on Nellie and convinced her that she could best escape the unwanted attentions of the New South Wales police by eloping with him to Queensland. In Brisbane, soon after, they married.

In 1934, satisfied that their police troubles had blown over, Cameron and Calletti returned to Sydney. Green quickly reappeared and this time, in early 1935, Nellie headed back to Queensland with him. Calletti immediately followed — with a couple of gunmen to back him up. He had vowed he was "going to finish that wife-stealer once and for all."

However, Sydney police alerted their Brisbane colleagues, and detectives were waiting when Calletti and his henchmen arrived. They were taken into custody, and Green and Cameron were also rounded up. That same evening all the Sydney visitors were placed on a southbound train and warned not to set foot in Queensland again.

On the journey a settlement was reached, and Nellie went home with her husband, Calletti. Frank Green left her alone thereafter — and eventually died from a knife thrust in his heart by another woman.

Calletti, meanwhile, copped a six-month sentence under the new Consorting Act. During his prison term police began a crackdown on the Sydney vice trades and, with her income drastically cut, Cameron moved to Queensland yet again. There she found business so lucrative that even after Calletti was released in 1936 she preferred to stay in Cairns.

Calletti was shot to death one night in August 1939. In 1942 Cameron returned to Sydney to cash in on the booming wartime vice rackets which accompanied the arrival of American troops.

After the War, Nellie Cameron's fortunes nosedived. In March 1952 she was found crawling down a passage outside her Darlinghurst flat, blood pouring from a bullet wound in her spine. She was rushed to hospital, where doctors found two other healed bullet wounds and numerous old razor-slash scars which had never been officially reported. Police charged a man with attempted murder, but when she recovered Nellie went into court and said the man in the dock was not guilty. She insisted she'd been shot by a stranger who came at her out of the shadows as she was about to enter her flat. The magistrate was forced to discharge the accused man, and he and Nellie left the court arm-in-arm.

One night in November 1953 Nellie Cameron gassed herself in front of her kitchen stove. She had just been told by her doctor that as a result of the old bullet wounds she had an inoperable cancer.

• • •

Another infamous female of the era was "Pretty Dulcie" Markham. Sydney's *Daily Mirror* summed up her career in crime thus: "Dulcie Markham saw more violence and death than any other woman in Australia's history."

Hayes's friends "Scotchy" McCormack and "The Egg" Talpin were among her early lovers, and Hayes remembers how Dulcie's mother and sister lived in a Newtown terrace at 189 Missenden Road, on the corner of Campbell Street, where Dulcie visited them every few weeks.

Dulcie Markham had been born into a respectable Sydney family in 1913 but, before her sixteenth birthday, ran away to the bright lights of sleazy Kings Cross and its environs. Sydney's *Sun* later waxed lyrical: "She came shimmying onto the underworld scene in 1929, at the age of 16, and promptly created a sensation. Admirers described her as 'tall, slim, well-groomed and shapely as a mannequin'."

During an extraordinary life of violence and bloodshed, however, at least eight of her gentlemen friends died courtesy of the blade or bullet, earning her a series of ominous sobriquets including "The Black Widow", "The Bad Luck Doll" and "The One-Way Ticket".

In May 1931, Hayes's mate, 21-year-old standover man Cecil William Bethel "Scotchy" McCormack, who'd wooed her away from another lad, was walking with Dulcie near the corner of William and Bourke Streets. The jilted boyfriend confronted them and stabbed McCormack through the heart, killing him on the spot.

By that time Chow Hayes, now aged 19½, was well on his own way to a life of violent crime. He already knew, and mixed nocturnally, with many of the city's leading criminals and underworld figures. He remembers "Scotchy" McCormack's death well.

"McCormack was a 'bludger' who was on with 'Pretty Dulcie'," says Hayes. "'Bludging' meant living off the earnings of prostitutes, and he already had a conviction for that. I got to know McCormack well in Parramatta Jail when we were both in the boys' section. He was about 18 months older than me and he was serving a 'sixer' [six months] for consorting.

"As it worked out, we were both to be discharged on the same day in May 1931. Since we knew the date three or four weeks in advance (it was a Wednesday), we arranged to meet at 9.30 pm the following evening, the Thursday, in the Campbell billiard room, which was upstairs in a building opposite the Capitol Theatre (then the Hippodrome) in Campbell Street. I went there at 9.30 pm but McCormack wasn't there. Nobody had seen him, so I left word with a few fellows to say that I'd dropped in and I'd call back the next night. But I picked up the following morning's newspaper and found out he'd been murdered. He was stabbed through the heart. A bloke named Alfred John Dillon had confronted 'Scotchy' and Dulcie as they walked along the street. While 'Scotchy' had been in jail, Dillon had been on with Dulcie, and the blow-up had been over her. Dillon copped a 13-year manslaughter sentence for it. His mother ran what was known as a 'residential' (which was really a brothel) in George Street just down from the Plaza Hotel. You went up a narrow stairway to enter it."

In December 1937 another of Hayes's mates — and Dulcie's admirers — 23-year-old hoodlum Arthur Kingsley "The Egg" Talpin, was shot in a hotel bar in Swanston Street, Melbourne. (In 1933 Talpin had himself been sentenced to three years' jail for shooting with intent to murder; and during 1936 he was fined £100 for carrying an unlicensed pistol and then later charged with assault with intent to rob.)

And when Guido Calletti was fatally shot during the gunfight in the house in Brougham Street, Kings Cross, in August 1939, the newspapers reported that Calletti bled to death with two bullets in his stomach and his head on Dulcie's lap.

In 1940 Dulcie's first husband, mobster Frank Bowen, was shot dead in Kings Cross. In June the same year another boyfriend, John Charles Abrahams, was shot dead outside an illegal gambling joint in Collingwood, Melbourne. In January 1945 her close friend Donald "The Duck" Day was gunned down in a sly-grog den in Crown Street, Surry Hills.

In September 1945 Dulcie was in Melbourne and closely associated with notorious thug Leslie Ernest "Scotland Yard" Walkerden, who provided protection for a Richmond baccarat den. Three enemies lay in wait at 2.30 am when he came out of the game to discover one of his tyres was flat. As he began

"PRETTY DULCIE" MARKHAM

Eight of Dulcie Markham's lovers died from either gunshot or knife wounds — including Chow Hayes's good friends "The Egg" Talpin and "Scotchy" McCormack — leading one Sydney newspaper to sum up her career in crime thus: "Dulcie Markham saw more violence and death than any other woman in Australia's history."

pumping it up, three guns took aim — a .32 bullet ricocheted from a nearby post, a .45 hit a fence and a shotgun charge slammed into Walkerden's side. At the Coroner's Court, Dulcie later explained she had been "keeping company" with Walkerden.

In September 1951, when Dulcie was 38, she and a group of friends were drinking brandy at her St Kilda home when two men burst in, one armed with a pistol and the other with a rifle. One drinker, Gavan Walsh, was killed; his brother Desmond was wounded; and Dulcie had her hip shattered by a bullet. She spent nearly three months in hospital, but did not let that detail slow her down: while immobilised, she married Leonard "Redda" Lewis. Dulcie received her wedding guests lying in bed — there were 60 witnesses, a parson, a three-tier cake and an 18-gallon keg.

The newlyweds settled in Sydney. But on a trip to Melbourne in April 1952 Lewis answered a knock at his mother's Prahran front door at 1.15 one morning and copped three bullets in the stomach. As his wounded victim staggered about in the doorway, the gunman fired three more times.

Dulcie later spent six months in jail on a consorting charge, and in 1959 was convicted for failing to file tax returns. During that case she admitted that she engaged in "nocturnal activities"; that she was "a practising member of the oldest profession"; and that she had, in fact, never lodged a tax return.

At various times this extraordinary woman called herself Tasca de Marca, Tasca Damarene, Tosca de Marquis, Dulcie Taplin, Mary Williams, Dulcie Whittingham and Dulcie Johnson — indeed it was widely said that she changed her name as often as she changed her men. At one point she was badly injured when thrown out of a block of beachside flats. Her police record included convictions for consorting, vagrancy, soliciting, assaulting police, brothel-keeping, drunkenness and driving under the influence.

In 1976, aged 63 and living with her third husband at Bondi, she went to bed and lit a cigarette — 30 minutes later firemen had extinguished the fire but found Dulcie dead from asphyxiation. Next morning the *Daily Mirror* recalled her as "the former prostitute and gun moll once called the Mistress of the Cross".

• • •

During the years when the various youth "pushes" had Sydney informally divided into their own territories, violent clashes were regular affairs. And those delivering the beatings and bashings one week were just as likely to be on the receiving end the next.

Chow Hayes was no exception. He recalls vividly: "I certainly didn't escape those years scot-free. For a start, I copped two fractured skulls. The first was in the Railway Hotel in August 1928 when I was almost 17. Two blokes from the Rocks Push happened to see me going in, so they jumped off the tram and checked to see that I was on my own. I was — so they went and grabbed an iron bar and walked back into the hotel and got stuck into me. I copped a fractured skull and 15 stitches in my head. The next time I woke up I was lying in Sydney Hospital. I was kept there for about three weeks.

"But once I got out, I only had a couple of days at home convalescing before I started running around the streets again. We went looking for those blokes for a while, and I think if we'd looked hard enough we'd have found them. But you couldn't just arrive down at the Rocks because there were too many of their mob down there (even neighbours would jump in and help them in a fight down there) so you had to catch them somewhere else while they were out of their own territory." At the time, the *Sydney Morning Herald* noted merely that Hayes's injuries appeared to be the result of "an underworld feud", and that he had "refused to give police any information" about the attack.

"The second major injury," Hayes remembers, "involved the Surry Hills Mob. They were very vicious. They caught me one day in Elizabeth Street and they kicked the shit out of me. I was about 19 then. I needed 11 stitches in the back of my head and the doctors told my grandmother the fracture was so bad that I'd have died (from the pressure build-up inside my brain) if my skull hadn't been open. They had all these tubes running into it to drain it out. That was the second fracture I'd copped within two years, and I was in hospital about 10 weeks that time.

"Of course, I also had numerous broken arms at different times, and that many black eyes and bruises all over my body that it's impossible to count them all...

"Back in the 'push days', there were never any fights in the daytime, because we were all shoplifters. But any night if you were caught on your own — or only two or three out — they'd kick the living daylights out of you.

"The coppers in those days patrolled in pairs. But if they knew there was a fight on, they'd go the other way. Their attitude was to let the gangs crack each other's skulls.

"However, on Friday nights there were no fights because

Paddy's Market was open until 9 pm. But then, say after 10 pm, the fights could be on again."

• • •

During the Depression years (the late 1920s and early 1930s) a number of memorable cafés and "cheap eat" joints sprang up around the Railway end of the city.

Mason's café in Elizabeth Street, between Foveaux Street and Campbell Street, offered a three-course meal for sixpence. "But you can imagine what it was like," Hayes laughs. "They even had the knives and forks chained to the tables so people couldn't pinch them. And once they'd been used, the waitress would just walk around with two dishcloths — one was wet and one dry — and wipe the cutlery over and they'd be there for the next customer.

"Now in those days, if you wore a suit you always wore a vest with it. The man who ran Mason's was Harry Lawrence and he didn't have a coat on, but he always wore his vest. And if customers wanted pepper or salt on their meals, Lawrence would come around with pepper in one waistcoat pocket and salt in the other and he'd dispense it himself so you couldn't have too much.

"It was the funniest café you ever saw in your life. Sometimes he'd advertise in the window that a special was on: 'Chicken'. Well I reckoned he got those chickens from the dead ones — which had been thrown in the gutter — down at the markets. But Mason's always did a roaring trade.

"About two doors away from Mason's was old Ernie Good's wine bar, another very well-known spot in those days. You could take an empty beer or lemonade bottle in and have it filled up with wine for threepence. A lot of the toughs from Surry Hills and Woolloomooloo used to congregate there." At one point the proprietor, Ernest Ambrose Good, was charged with manslaughter when he shot a young criminal named Lancelot MacGregor Saidler inside "E. A. Good's Wine Saloon" in September 1930. The jury found it to be a justifiable homicide.

"But the best meal of the lot in those days," Hayes recalls, "was at the old Hole In The Wall restaurant in Pitt Street, about 100 yards [90 metres] from the Railway arches. Charlie McDonald ran it for years and years. You got three curried sausages plus peas and potatoes for sixpence — and it was always good food. Or you could have curried steak for eightpence. It was such good value that I've seen them lined up 20 and 30 in the queue to get in."

6 Buying a Gun and Moving into "Standover"

During the early 1930s Parramatta Road, the main traffic artery heading west from central Sydney, was lined daily by desperate men humping their blueys (which consisted of a blanket, pan and billy), trying to hitch a lift into the countryside in search of work. "This was the Depression — and they were hard days," Hayes recalls. "Thousands of unemployed men were heading off to the bush seeking labouring jobs at £1 a week plus their keep. And most were sending that £1 back to their wives and children.

"But luckily I was very streetwise by that stage. I always thought to myself that, no matter what happened, I'd never fall into that lifestyle — though now, of course, I can look back and think I might have been better off if I had. But then it all seemed too much like hard work. Those blokes would go to a farm and work picking apples or peas, or shearing or whatever, and they'd only earn that paltry £1 a week. And anything they'd buy with the money would be almost all tinned stuff, and they'd send that back to their families.

"Of course, a few would go from one town to another and collect the dole under different names. You only received 7s 6d on the dole then, and if you were married you copped an extra five shillings for your wife. But you didn't collect that in cash; in Sydney you had to go down to Circular Quay to the wharf and they'd give you coupons and you'd use them at the stores there beside the wharves. They had a butcher shop and bread shop and so on."

• • •

One of Sydney's better-known gunmen during this era was Norman "Mickey" McDonald, whose favourite caper involved standing over SP bookies and molls. He had a reputation as a particularly vicious hoodlum, but Hayes has never taken much notice of reputations.

One night, Hayes and "Kicker" Kelly were playing snooker in the Eden billiard room. "I was only about 19 at the time and still running around doing a lot of shoplifting," Hayes recalls. "We had some of the new swimming costumes. The old-fashioned full-length ones were being replaced with the new shorts with no top and Jantzen was the brand name. It was all the go and everybody wanted to get their hands on a Jantzen swimming costume.

"'Spud' Murphy, Eddie McMillan, 'Kicker' Kelly and I had been pinching quite a few of them, and we had half a dozen this night in the billiard room. McDonald came over and asked if he could have a pair and I said yes. They cost 12s 6d each, which was pretty expensive for those days. Anyway I gave McDonald a pair and he went outside for a while. Then he came back and asked how many more we had. In the meantime we'd sold another two, so I said three or four, and he asked for a look at them. I showed him — but he just put them under his arm and started to walk out. I asked what he thought he was doing, and he replied: 'You stole them; now I'm stealing them.' So he walked straight out the door with them. Now Kelly and I knew his reputation — he was about 27 or 28 and stood over a lot of people at that point; he had half of Sydney terrified.

"But I said to Kelly that we couldn't let him get away with that. However, we didn't have a gun or a razor or any other weapon with us. We were just talking about getting a gun, when McDonald came back in again. But he didn't have the swimming costumes with him. He started playing a game of snooker and I went over and asked whether he was only joking about the costumes. But he said he didn't joke about things like that. Then I said well he'd better bring them back, and he just laughed at me. So I returned to Kelly and sat down for a minute. Then I thought bugger him, I'll give it to him with a cue. I went over to the rack along the wall and chose the heaviest cue of the lot. Then I told Kelly to grab hold of one too, and we'd go over to the next table and pretend we were waiting for it to become vacant. But when I saw the opportunity I was going to smash McDonald with the cue.

"As luck would have it, we walked toward the table just as McDonald bent over to pot a ball. So I let him have it with all my fucking might right on top of his head. The blow fractured his skull — but none of his mates jumped to his defence, no one at all. He was in the hospital three or four weeks; he needed 30 stitches in the cut, and some sort of infection set in as well. Meanwhile he was sending out threats through his friends about what he was going to do to me when he was eventually discharged.

"When he finally did come out of hospital, they arranged for me to meet him in the Crystal Palace Hotel. I went along and I had another bloke, my uncle Herbert 'Hubie' Hayes, with me and he had a gun. McDonald was sounding off about what he was going to do to me. But I just told him he was all talk and that he'd robbed me after I'd given him a costume for free. Two or three others were there and they said we should forget all about it, rather than start a big blue over it again. But I kept insisting that this bastard wasn't standing over me. Finally he said he didn't want to stand over me, that he didn't want to know me again. Then we shook hands and left it at that...

"And a funny thing, McDonald was supposedly so tough and hard and all that. Well, in September 1936 he and a close mate of his John Joseph 'Jackie' Finnie [an ex-fighter later shot by Hayes] had a stink over money and Finnie shot him as they crossed the railway bridge at St Peters, near the old dogtrack behind Erskineville. (They used to trial the greyhounds there on a Sunday morning from 8 am to 11 am, and then later on they'd pitch a two-up game.) I think Finnie fired four shots, and three bullets went into McDonald.

"They took McDonald to hospital and he was very close to death. For two days it was real touch and go. Finnie went into hiding, but only for that afternoon, because he thought no matter what happened McDonald would never give anyone up, let alone his best mate. So the coppers came to Finnie's place and took him to the hospital — and Finnie didn't mind going because he was certain McDonald would never testify against him. But as soon as they took Finnie into the ward at Prince Alfred, McDonald told the police that Finnie was indeed the man who shot him.

"Finnie was flabbergasted. He was committed for trial for attempted murder, but eventually beat it by saying that McDonald had a gun with which he'd threatened Finnie, and he therefore had acted in self-defence. That was the first time I ever heard of a mob man coming straight out and dobbing in another crim. Just after that McDonald copped three years himself for assault and robbery. Later he had an old tin shed out Newtown way and he'd travel around all the houses and collect the little leftover bits of soap and make his own soap in a big drum. Then he'd sell it for scrubbing floors and the like."

Even before shooting McDonald, Finnie was no stranger to violent crime:

- in May 1931 he had been charged with the murder of bookmaker George Alfred Cooper at Redfern and was acquitted;
- in December 1931 he was sentenced to one year in jail for demanding property with menace at Waterloo;
- in August 1933 he was badly wounded, along with McDonald, in what the *Sydney Morning Herald* described as a "rain of bullets" at Mascot; and
- in February 1935 he began another jail term, the length of which the trial judge increased after referring to Finnie's propensity to "terrorise his victims".

After the McDonald trial, Finnie continued his regular court appearances. They included: a consorting charge in September 1936; a charge of occasioning actual bodily harm to Dick Reilly's brother, Gerald Vincent Reilly, in November 1937; three months in jail for consorting in December 1937; and acquittal on an assault charge in February 1938.

• • •

During the 1930s, Hayes's own reputation for violence was being consolidated.

One afternoon in the early 1930s, Hayes was drinking with his cousin, Ezzie Bollard, in the Lansdowne Hotel when Jim "Pansy" Barron walked in. (The son of an old-time boxer also named Jim, Barron was nicknamed "Pansy" because he used to pinch sunflowers from the front gardens of the local cottages and display one in his lapel every day.) A few weeks earlier, Bollard had made off with Barron's woman at a dance hall. But Bollard had since broken his leg and Barron, spotting the cast, snapped at Bollard: "Pity it wasn't your fucking skull that was broken."

Soon after, Bollard pretended to go out to the toilet, but as he walked back into the bar he belted Barron across the head with his crutch. To Bollard's astonishment, however, Barron merely shook his huge head, turned around and threw a punch which knocked Bollard out.

The barmaid screamed, and ran to help Hayes lift Bollard up off the floor. Then Hayes grabbed hold of the crutch, took an almighty swing and clobbered "Pansy" with all his might. The blow broke Barron's nose and smashed several of his teeth, and he immediately ran out the hotel door and off down City Road. Hayes then loaded Bollard over his shoulder and carried him back to the Hayes household in nearby Shepherd Street.

Thereafter Barron, who lived two blocks away in Ivy Street, always avoided Hayes in the local streets around Chippendale and Darlington.

• • •

Shoplifting and violence were not Hayes's only preoccupations during the thirties: in 1932, when he was 21, he married Gladys Muriel King.

"We'd gone to St Benedict's School together," Hayes explains. "I used to call her 'Topsy'; everyone did. She was 18 months younger than me and lived with her married sister at 27 Wentworth Street, Glebe, off Bay Street. I met her again when I was about 17½ and started to go out with her. We often met on the corner of Wattle Street and George Street (it wasn't called Broadway then) opposite St Benedict's.

One of Hayes's best mates lived opposite Topsy in Wentworth Street. His home backed onto a garage (on the corner of Wentworth Park Road and Bay Street) where police cars were serviced. "He and I and a couple of other mates, who lived nearby, used to climb over the fence and let the tyres down and smash the windows and inflict any other damage we could," Hayes recalls.

Topsy King viewed Hayes's teenage shenanigans in basically the same way as his grandmother and aunty. For a while, she took over from them in trying to point Hayes in the right direction. But her efforts had no effect.

Dennis King, Topsy's father, was a butcher. The King family operated two butcher shops in Parramatta Road, one near the top of Taverner's Hill on the right-hand side leaving the city, and the other at the bottom of the hill on the left-hand side. They owned the shops for several decades, until the early 1950s.

Topsy's mother was named Mary, and Topsy had three sisters and three brothers. The sisters were Elizabeth Simmons (mother of two people who later figured prominently in Hayes's life, Dolly and Danny Simmons); Bonney (a religious woman who died in church from a heart attack); and Kathleen. The brothers were Mickey (who died when he was about 21); Georgie (who walked out of the Lewisham Hotel half-drunk and was knocked down and killed by a car); and Billy (who died from a heart attack while walking along Parramatta Road).

Hayes was "going steady" with Topsy when he was sent to Bathurst Jail for a year at the age of 20. When he returned 10 months later, he had decided to give shoplifting away because he would now receive the maximum sentence with each subsequent conviction. "So I took a step up and bought a gun and started running around standing over people — sly-grog dens and SP joints," he recalls. "The blokes at Bathurst had told me there was a quid in it.

"I bought my first gun from a knockabout named Joe Green, a petty thief. He asked me did I want to buy one and I said 'Yes.' I paid him £5. It was a .22 and I learned how to use it by shooting at trees in Centennial Park in the evenings with a few mates. You didn't need a licence or anything then. You'd just walk into a sporting store like Mick Simmons and buy the ammunition. If you couldn't buy it, you'd thieve it. But I never had to steal it because it was so cheap — about 7s 6d for 100 bullets."

Hayes and Topsy married four months after he returned from Bathurst. "Topsy didn't know I was carrying a gun for the first eight or nine months of our marriage, because I never kept it at home," Hayes admits.

The wedding ceremony took place in the Catholic church at Malabar, about half a mile from Long Bay Jail. Hayes recalls: "We went out to Malabar on the tram, and then afterwards there was a reception back where I was living in Rose Street. It wasn't a big wedding; only our relations attended. My best man was a longtime mate named Ernie Means, who lived in Jones Street at Broadway. Topsy's girlfriend Rita Turner, a real 'squarehead', was the bridesmaid."

Soon after, the young couple moved to 156 Bridge Road at Glebe and for the next 18 months rented two rooms in a boarding house. "The rent was very cheap, about 11s 6d a week," Hayes recalls. "Topsy didn't hassle me because I didn't have a job. It was the Great Depression, and you couldn't get a job. She worked during the day at a laundry in Leichhardt, so she was bringing in a steady wage — though it was only 32s 6d for five days a week. At the start I just told her I was earning my money at the two-up games."

Before long, however, Topsy had her worst fears confirmed when she discovered Chow was carrying a gun during his "night shift". "One day I took the gun home, but didn't hide it carefully enough," says Hayes. "Up to that point I used to leave it at the home of a mate, Freddie Buckley. He was involved in the standover with me. He wasn't married and was living in a room, so it was easy to leave guns at his place. But he'd had an argument with his landlady and she ordered him to leave. So he decided to go to Melbourne and I had to take my gun home with me. I had it there for three or four days under the mattress. But then I got up one day about 4 pm and forgot to take it with me. Later Topsy came home and went to make the bed and there it was. I was in the kitchen and she sang out: 'What's this?' I said I was only minding it for a fellow. So she told me to give it back to him, but I said I couldn't because he'd gone away. After that I put it in the wardrobe, and she felt bloody awful about it."

During this period Hayes spent most of each day at home, before venturing out on the town after sunset. As he sums up, "That's when the sly grog joints were operating...Now by standover, I mean we used to just walk into them and ask for money. More often than not the boss would readily give us cash to leave him alone. If he didn't we'd smash the place up. We'd get £10 a week from most of them."

Hayes's early standover revenue sources included some of the best-known nightspots of Sydney's high-profile 1930s demimonde: Ma Brown's illicit booze joint in Riley Street; Kate Leigh's series of sly-grog dens; and Bub Brown's two-up game in the big yard at the back of two terraces at 15–17 Young Street, Redfern.

"I was earning big money," Hayes explains. "But I was also spending up big — gambling, mostly on the races. I used to go out to the track. My biggest win was £700 at Victoria Park one day.

"After that big win we moved from Glebe to a terrace in Thomas Street, Ultimo. We were still renting, but I bought a house full of furniture for about £400 — and it was really good furniture too."

With no consistent daytime employment, he became a regular at the racetracks. Among his favourite characters of the era was the legendary scoundrel and huckster Rufe Naylor. "Naylor used to go on the radio, on 2KY, and sell his tips," Hayes recalls. "He used to pay for the air-time, but he had a big following, and he'd sell his tips through the daily paper. If you sent him 5s he'd post back his code, and then you could check in the newspaper and find out his code special. Of course 5s was a lot of money in those days.

"And I remember the time, around 1932 or 1933, when he

touted a £5 special that was to go off two months later. While very few people had £5 in those days, a lot of neighbours and mates around the suburbs pooled their money into little syndicates. Well the special turned out to be a pony named Kentucky, which raced at Victoria Park one day. But there were only three starters and Kentucky was 15–1 on or 20–1 on — and even though it won nobody had enough money to back it at those odds. And the other two starters, of course, were 'dead'."

As well as Bub Brown's Redfern operation, other two-up sites paid Hayes weekly tribute, among them Australia's best-known game, Thommo's, just up from Central Railway. Joe Thomas ran it himself at that time (later, Joe Taylor took over and put Hayes on the permanent payroll).

Hayes was pocketing £2 or £3 a week from each of the two-up games. They were basically paying to be able to let potential troublemakers know: "There are some particularly heavy characters on our payroll if we need to call on them." Thommo, for example, employed boxers to stand on nearby corners as "cockatoos", on the door as bouncers and inside the game as ringkeepers. But if they couldn't handle the trouble, then he'd call in Hayes and his colleagues, the gunmen.

"I wouldn't go to Thommo's every night and hang around in the background," Hayes explains. "We'd simply leave word where we could be easily contacted if we were needed. And there were never any problems in those days about getting the word out very quickly if we were required. We'd usually be at a hotel around the Railway.

"Our job was to more or less 'put a frighten' into someone. They usually needed our services about once a month. You'd show the gun and you'd threaten the troublemaker, and you might even threaten his family and tell him that if you couldn't get him then you'd get one of his family. They were mainly just workers complaining about losing their money. The average wage was only about £2 16s then. But if a bloke lost all his money, Thommo would give him 10 bob to take home...

"In those days I fired the gun a couple of times at people, but missed them more or less on purpose. I was only really trying to scare them and would fire in their general direction. The first time I fired at the two-up was in 1932. George 'Bombardier' Williams wanted a fight and he wasn't a bad brawler. I knew him as a tough around the place who was working on the wharves. He was disgruntled about losing his money. He had a

AN ILLEGAL TWO-UP GAME

Chow Hayes collected regular standover payments from all the major two-up games, including Thommo's, which was run by leviathan racetrack punter Joe Taylor in Surry Hills, and Bub Brown's Redfern operation. When the boxers employed as regular bouncers and ring-keepers "couldn't handle the trouble", Hayes and his fellow gunmen would arrive with their revolvers to "put a frighten" into the troublemakers.

reputation as a fighter who carried firearms and razors and that sort of thing.

"I came down to Thommo's and Williams was standing outside arguing the point. So I pulled the gun and as soon as he saw it he took off. I chased him around the archway opposite Sydney Hotel and into Belmore Park, where I fired two shots in his direction without trying to hit him. So I let him go and he sent word back that he wouldn't return to Thommo's if I forgot all about it. Well, I was satisfied with that — and I became good mates with him later on . . .

"The fact that I'd had to fire the gun didn't have any effect on me. I wasn't scared to use it."

Other gamblers from whom Hayes was making money were the SP bookies — well-known identities such as Mark Shelton in Glebe and Paddy Roach in Young Street at Redfern. "We were collecting from half-a-dozen SP chaps operating within a couple of miles of the Railway," Hayes recalls. "Sometimes we'd get £2 a week, but other times we might get nothing because he'd had a losing day. It was similar to the two-up arrangement: they'd pay us to be on hand if they needed us, mostly to hassle someone who hadn't paid his debts. But we rarely had any problems, because we knew where they lived, since they were all locals. In contrast, if you went to the two-up games, the players might come from all over the place — Summer Hill or Bellevue Hill or Strathfield or anywhere at all. But the SP's clients all lived within a few streets of his operation, so everyone knew one another well. It was virtually the same as debt collecting. But most folk would only bet to their limit and then pay their debts. If they were going to take the knock [fail to pay] on anyone, it'd be the corner shop before the SP bookie."

Among the notorious sly-grog joints on Hayes's weekly round were Ma Brown's two houses in Crown Street, Surry Hills. She was paying Hayes about £1 a week for the same sort of service as the two-up games, but she only ever required his services a couple of times a year. "She basically sold beer all night," Hayes explains. "There were also lots of little hotels which used to sell a bit of sly-grog. But there weren't many cars in those days and Ma Brown had most of the clients. Any taxis which were taking customers to a sly-grog joint would mostly drive people to Ma Brown's places. She had the taxis tied up — she'd slip the drivers two bob for their trouble, and two bob was big money for them in those days."

One of the best-known police during that era was Joe Chuck. At one point Ma Brown had a beer house in Riley Street, and Chuck was finding it impossible to catch her "in the act" because she would serve only people she knew well. "So Chuck lined up a young copper named Price and put him in a horse and cart selling ice-cream," Hayes recalls. "And every Sunday about 2 pm he'd make sure that he pulled up outside Ma Brown's, on the opposite side of the street, and he'd sell these penny ice-cream cones to the local kids. It went on for several weeks and she'd always be on the verandah watching him and they'd nod at one another. Eventually one Sunday he had an old 10-shilling note in his pocket and the police took the serial number and had it marked. It was a hot day, and Price walked over to her and said: 'Oh gees, it's warm, missus. Can I get a drink?' And she said: 'Yeah. What do you want? Water or beer?' Well, he replied that he'd only wanted water, but actually he'd rather have beer. So she said she'd sell him a couple of bottles if he was interested. He gave her the marked 10-shilling note and no sooner had the money changed hands than Chuck and his men raced around the corner. She went to shut the door, but then the young copper said: 'It doesn't matter, Mrs Brown, because I'm a policeman too.' "

Chuck was also determined to close down a two-up game that operated on Sunday afternoons on top of the hill in the middle of Moore Park. But cockatoos strategically positioned at each of the four corners of the crowd, kept constant watch down the slopes, making it virtually impossible for the police to catch the gamblers in action. "So Chuck rounded up coppers from the suburban stations at places like Rockdale and Mascot and so on and took them out of uniform and put them into cricket gear and made up two teams," Hayes remembers. "They played on different parts of the park over three or four weeks. Then one of them went up and had a few bets. The next week a few more went up, and so on. Now Chuck wasn't interested in the people playing the game; he wanted the Ross brothers, who were running it. And eventually when his police busted the game, Chuck nabbed them and the ringkeeper and so on."

During that era Hayes also collected cash by simply standing over innocent citizens. "For example," he explains, "someone would tell you they'd had a win at the races or the Game [Thommo's] or somewhere and you'd go and ask for a sling. They'd quickly get the hint that you were a fairly heavy person and they ought to pay you a quid or two to piss off."

• • •

Hayes's nightly routine involved strolling around the hotel bars and underworld haunts of inner Sydney, drinking bottle after bottle of blackmarket beer with his criminal mates and standing over the plethora of illegal gambling and sly-grog dens. And as often as not he would finish up in the arms of female company other than his wife. "It was a fairly regular thing," he admits. "My wife didn't know until years after; she thought I was working at the two-up game. I chased a lot of girls both before and after I was married. For years I was a bloody scallywag...

"You wouldn't believe this, but one time there was a girl who lived in Derwent Street, Glebe, named Anne. She wasn't a bad sort. Three or four of us were pitching for her. And she wasn't a harlot or anything like that, she was a clean-living girl. Finally one day I managed to start talking to her and I asked her to go out with me. Initially she replied: 'No, I wouldn't take the risk going out with you!' However, eventually we made a date for a Saturday afternoon. I was on my best behaviour and took her to the pictures at the Lyric. I walked her home and I became pretty sweet with her over the next two or three weeks. But I could never entice her out in the night time, until one Friday evening when she wanted to go to the markets and she said I could walk her down there. (The markets used to be open there until 9 pm). On the way she asked: 'Jackie, why did you want to take me out?' So I replied: 'To make love to you, of course.' She just laughed, and we walked about another 10 or 15 yards [metres], and then she said: 'If I made love to you it'd be on one condition.' And I said: 'What's that?' And this is the gospel truth, she replied: 'You show me the underworld.' Well, I immediately said: 'Yeah, I'll do that.'

"So after we went to the markets I was planning to take her up to Surry Hills and Campbell Street and the like and show her all the seamy places. But as we were walking along Broadway, she kept looking in the gutter and I couldn't make it out. And we'd walk another 50 or 60 yards [metres] and she'd look in the gutter again. So when we reached the jewellery store at Railway Square I asked: 'What the bloody hell are you stopping and looking in the gutter for?' And she answered: 'I want to know when you're going to take me down!' I said: 'Take you down where?' And she replied: 'To the underworld.'

"She really thought that you went down the drains, underneath the streets to reach the underworld. It took me another bloody hour to convince her that it wasn't true... Anyway I eventually did a bit of business with her for an hour or so in Rest Park, on the corner of Glebe Point Road and Bridge Road, in Glebe...

"In those days I'd often stay out all night and end up with a girl. I very rarely came home before sunrise. Meanwhile Topsy was going off to work during the day and she didn't really have much idea what I'd been up to until years later."

Topsy bore four children between 1932 and 1939: in March 1933 the first son, John Patrick, was born, but lived only two days and died of "something like pneumonia"; on 31 March 1935, Patrick Frederick was born (the Patrick in both names was in memory of Chow's grandfather); in August 1937, Robert Herbert was delivered stillborn; and then on 21 December 1939, Gladys Veronica was born. She was later also tagged "Topsy"; she was a big girl but referred to as "Little Topsy", in contrast to

Hayes's wife, who was a smaller woman but known as "Big Topsy".

Throughout all these years Mrs Hayes would take the children to church at St Benedict's on Sundays. "Sometimes she'd look at me out of the corner of her eye and I could see her thinking: 'I'll never change him'." Hayes recalls. "All the police of the time used to treat her as a fine upstanding woman in spite of my antics. I remember a senior policeman once said to her: 'I don't know how you stay with him, Topsy. He'll finish either in jail or in the gutter with a bullet in him!'

"But my wife never went through my pockets or anything like that. She left my business up to me, even though I'd often have a lot of money — say £10 — in my pocket. I was never short of cash. But we were still renting in Thomas Street and there were no big family plans to save up and buy a house or anything like that.

"So why didn't I ever buy a house in my younger days, especially since I had enough money to buy a dozen houses at various times? You could purchase a good house in those days around Balmain or Glebe or Rozelle or Lilyfield or Ultimo or Redfern or Surry Hills for £700. And when I went to Thomas Street to live, it was a five-room house — and they were large rooms — and a kitchen and the rent was only 13s 6d a week. But in those days it just never entered my head to buy a house, which is what I should have done. My wife never talked about it either. She was quite content to rent. But, of course, if I'd known then what I know now, I'd have bought a dozen houses and been a millionaire . . .

"Similarly, I never put any money into a bank. Instead, I had a wooden dressing table, and I'd take out the bottom drawer and keep my cash in an Arnott's biscuit tin on the floor under that bottom drawer. Sometimes I had £8000 or £9000 cash in it. There were seven houses in our row in Thomas Street, when we lived in Ultimo, and I could have bought the lot."

7 Kate Leigh and "Tilly" Devine

As the Depression dragged on, Hayes, now in his early twenties, became a regular visitor to Sydney's inner-suburban police stations, most frequently on charges of assaulting police and consorting.

The consorting bookings involved all the worst criminals of the era: Guido Calletti and Frankie Green; Clarrie Thomas, a thief who was later declared an habitual criminal before Hayes's buddy, mobster Dick Reilly, eventually shot him dead in November 1937; and Donald "The Duck" Day, who ran two of Sydney's best-known brothels in Elizabeth Street and was eventually gunned down at one of his string of sly-grog shops.

Hayes explains: "At that time most of the big names in the Sydney criminal world hung around together and I was booked for consorting with them all — men like 'Paddles' Anderson, 'Face' McKeon and his brother Lawrie McKeon, Cecil 'Hoppy' Gardiner, Barney Dalton, Alan Pulley, Charlie Bourke, Jackie Clarke, 'Chicka' Reeves, Billy McCarthy and 'Baldy' Mason. And it was the same with the Melbourne fellows. I was booked while I was down there a couple of times. And on three or four occasions when 'Snowy' Cutmore came up from Melbourne, I happened to be in his company and was booked. Soon after Cutmore went back to Melbourne and killed 'Squizzy' Taylor. Most of these men were charged with murder at some stage of their careers — and some, like myself, were charged with murder on several occasions."

In one three-month period in early 1935 Hayes, now 24 years old, appeared in court on half-a-dozen different matters:

- 22/2/35: a "consorting" charge at Central Petty Court. "I was pulled up in the street in Surry Hills and told to get into the car," Hayes recalls. "The police said they wanted to see me down at the station, where they had a present for me. I copped six months' hard labour and appealed."

- 14/3/35: charges of "stealing" and "threatening words" at Glebe Petty Court. "That was at Grace Bros," Hayes explains. "The shopwalker came up and I threatened him with assault. I copped three months' hard labour and appealed again."
- 16/3/35: a "drunkenness" charge at Glebe Petty Court.
- 4/4/35: an "evade taxi fare" charge at Central Petty Court.
- 9/4/35: charges of "stealing from the person", "stealing" and "demanding money by menaces" at Central Petty Court. "They all involved my attempts to pickpocket at the Showground over Easter," Hayes explains. "I put my whole hand in some bloke's pocket, and I was pinched and sentenced to four months' hard labour."
- 15/4/35: hearing of all the appeals Hayes had pending. He withdrew the lot and served the sentences concurrently.

Despite his constant run-ins with the constabulary, Hayes proudly boasts that he never paid the police to leave him alone. "I took the line that if I stole money from different people, why should I pay it to the police?" he says. "However, the police weren't as corrupt back in my younger days. They were much more honest and there weren't really many crooked police. Of course, things changed greatly by the time I reached middle age in the 1950s. But back in the 1930s you could buy anyone for £50 or £100 — nothing like the thousands they talk about today."

• • •

Another difference between the 1930s' and today's law and order systems was that the death penalty was then still on the statute books. And Hayes was twice at Long Bay Jail when prisoners were hanged.

In August 1932 William Cyril Moxley (a well-known criminal who had previously hit the headlines when he refused to speak to police after being shot at Parramatta in October 1930) was executed at Long Bay for the double murder of Burwood youngsters Frank Wilkinson and his girlfriend, Dorothy Denzel. They had been kidnapped from Wilkinson's red Alvis sports car while parked in a lovers' lane near Liverpool. After a massive police search, their bodies were found in shallow graves in the Holdsworthy area. Their hands were bound behind their backs with strips of rug and stocking, they had been shot from behind and their heads had been bashed.

Then in May 1936 Edwin John Hickey, 17, was hanged at Long Bay for having (at the age of 16) bashed to death Conciliation Commissioner Montague Henwood with a water bottle as Henwood sat sleeping in a train. Henwood's body had been found beside the railway line near Linden, in the Blue Mountains west of Sydney.

"They didn't put the victim in the condemned cell the night before, as many people thought," Hayes recalls. "They moved him from the OBS (the observation unit) to the condemned cell at 6 am. I saw the hanging gear. It was a sort of straitjacket which they put over the victim. It had a belt which came around, with one handcuff on each side, so that his hands were held beside him. Underneath was a sort of saddle which had me intrigued — they put that between his legs and around his arse. One warder told me it was important because 'with some of them their guts fall out when they drop'. I didn't know that. Then they also had a bit of rope which they fitted around the ankles, so that the victim could only walk one pace at a time with it on. But they didn't fit that part until they had him in the condemned cell. Back in the OBS they fitted the straitjacket, but then they let the prisoner walk to the condemned cell. Once inside that cell — about 15 minutes before he was to be hanged — they'd attach the leg-rope. Then the priest and the doctor would go in.

"They always hanged people at 8 am. They'd shift everyone over from Long Bay's B Hall and A Hall to the Ranges — 1 Range and 2 Range. And that was the only time they'd give you a couple of cigarettes and three matches each. The cigarettes were to keep you quiet — but everyone kept quiet at these times, they never put on a turn when a hanging was on. The authorities would hang him, and leave him swinging for a couple of hours. Then they'd cut him down and take the body over to a little tomb opposite the hospital and lay it on a slab. Then the undertaker would come [and take it away].

"But they didn't do that with Moxley. He was buried inside the prison grounds at 'The Bay' — he was the only one I knew to whom that happened — because no-one claimed his body. However, a few old-timers told me there were some others buried in the jail grounds too. In contrast, Hickey's family claimed his body and he was buried outside.

"At the time — I was 20 years old — I didn't give a bugger about Moxley, because I never imagined that I'd ever be in the same position. At that point I was only involved in shoplifting. The death penalty was in vogue then because the conservatives were in power — the Labor Party never believed in it."

• • •

Another vivid jail memory from those years involved an old drunk, nicknamed "Peg Leg Joe", who had a wooden leg.

"They put all the drunks and vagrants and winos into what they called the chat yard," Hayes recalls. "That was at Long Bay between the OBS and 1 Wing. They were so dirty that even the screws wouldn't go in and search them. Sometimes these hobos were arrested two or three times each week.

"One day, over at the bathroom, someone suggested hollowing out Joe's wooden leg — and 'Peg Leg' became our postman. Only six or seven of us knew anything about it, and it went on for months and months. He only took letters out: we wouldn't risk him bringing any in. We'd send him out to one home — one day my place and the next time to 'Skinny' Brett's place — with a batch of letters. Then the wife at that address would deliver all the letters from there. She'd give 'Peg Leg' £2 or £3 for his trouble. And he'd take the money, immediately buy himself some grog for a party in Belmore Park and, for several hours, be the happiest man in the world — and end up back in jail again the next day! So, for a while, that's how we used to smuggle our letters out without the prison authorities seeing them."

• • •

Outside jail, two of Chow Hayes's most infamous colleagues in crime were Australia's most celebrated female criminals — Kate Leigh and Tilly Devine. Their rise to notoriety occurred in the twenties and thirties, just as Hayes was making his own mark on the Sydney underworld. He knew both women well over four decades.

People magazine once described Kate Leigh's territory as "the noisome slum which begins across the road from Sydney's Central Railway Station and whose squalid, dirty, narrow streets rise and fall across Surry Hills to Taylor's Square, Darlinghurst. . . The Hills are crammed with ancient hovels and terraces. . . and life is characterised by the personalities of people, the rottenness of crime, the roughness of jungle justice, and the generous impulses of the badly-off towards the worse-off." The writer went on to brand Kate Leigh's domain as "an empire of brothels, gambling joints, verminous flop-houses, sly groggeries and gin mills" inhabited by "prostitutes, pimps, thugs, blackmailers, thieves, bludgers and strong-arm toughs."

And the *Daily Mirror* summarised the career of "fat, blowsy, leathery-faced Kate Leigh" thus: "For more than half a century Kate Leigh was an institution in Sydney as the city's most notorious sly-grog racketeer. As such she coined a fortune in the years between the Wars when hotels and wine bars closed at 6 pm. In the process Kate Leigh built a police record of more than 100 convictions and served 13 terms of imprisonment. She dealt in drugs and stolen goods as well as liquor. . . Her convictions included keeping a house frequented by thieves, stealing, vagrancy, carrying an unlicensed pistol, assault and consorting."

But there was another side to Kate Leigh. Down in Surry Hills people insisted she had a heart of gold. It was a side Chow Hayes knew well. "Every Christmas old Kate would erect makeshift barricades at both ends of the block in Lansdowne Street where she had her main beer house. Then she'd pay two or three drunks to dress up as Santa Claus, and she'd put out big tables stacked with chocolates and cakes and lollies and lemonade for all the local kids. And three or four other tables would be covered with toys — dolls and train sets and so on. Of course, much of it was stolen stuff, from shoplifting. But she turned it on every Christmas for the hundreds of slum children in Surry Hills. Naturally, there was method in her madness. By doing that she encouraged all the customers — all their fathers — to visit her place during the year, because they'd all say 'Kate's alright, she puts on a party every year for the kids.' That went on for years. If you were sweet with Kate, she'd do anything for you and give you anything. But if you crossed her, she'd shoot you."

During the Depression, Kate Leigh was supposed to have saved half of Sydney's down-and-outs from starvation. "I could never knock a man back for a feed or a drink or a few bob," she once explained to the newspapers.

Born Kathleen Behan in 1880, she was one of 13 children in the family of a small-time Dubbo horse-trainer. She ran away to Sydney as a teenager and worked as a factory girl and waitress before marrying at 18. Her husband, Jack Leigh, was a 30-year-old carpenter and within two years the marriage had broken up.

Chow Hayes remembers Kate and her perennial rival, Tilly Devine, working as prostitutes: "They used to have terrible fights, and Kate always came out on top. When I was a teenager,

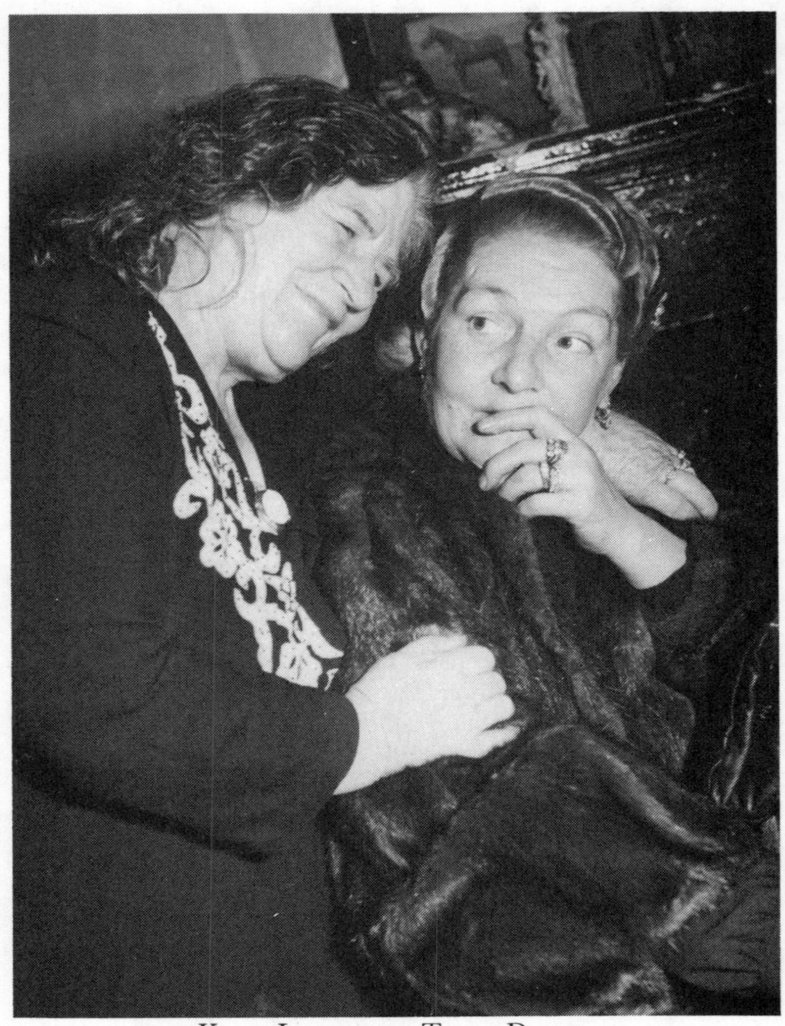

Kate Leigh and Tilly Devine

*During the 1920s and 1930s two of Australia's most celebrated female criminals, Kate Leigh (*left*) and Tilly Devine, rose to prominence amid the Surry Hills slums. Early in their careers they were deadly rivals, but in old age they forgot and forgave. Chow Hayes was a close associate of, and worked for, both women over four decades.*

they worked as prostitutes on the steps outside Mark Foys, on the corner of Liverpool and Elizabeth Streets. They charged six bob a time, and in those days that was a lot of money. If you had five customers a night you'd make 30 shillings. But they'd have more than that — and the basic wage was only about £3 a week. The prostitutes in those days were very clean — spotlessly clean both in themselves and in their homes. And they sent their children to the best schools. They were good women, not like the sheilas of today, the ones you simply pick in a pub and buy them a drink. They're tuppence a dozen."

Also, according to the *Daily Mirror*, "In her early years in Sydney Kate Leigh's principal connection with the underworld was that she lived as the mistress of a number of notorious criminals."

In 1914 her lover, the Jewish hoodlum and hold-up merchant "Jewey" Freeman (who led a group of young criminals known as the Riley Street Push), teamed up with notorious South Australian criminal Ernest "Shiner" Ryan to pull one of New South Wales's most celebrated payroll robberies, at the office of the Eveleigh Railway Workshop in Redfern. They disappeared in a stolen car with £3300 — the first time criminals had used motor transport in a hold-up. Later that afternoon the vehicle was found abandoned in an Ultimo sidestreet.

Freeman was arrested a fortnight later as he waited on Strathfield railway station for the Melbourne Express. Then Ryan's girlfriend led Sydney detectives to his Melbourne hide-out, where he was arrested as he lay in bed with his betrayer. The woman also revealed to police that Ryan had £300 from the robbery concealed in a glass jar in the chimney. That £300 was all that was ever recovered from the Eveleigh payroll hold-up.

Ryan and Freeman were duly convicted of the robbery and each sentenced to 10 years in jail. Kate Leigh testified that her lover, Freeman, could not possibly have been involved because he had been home in bed with her at the time. As a result she was charged with perjury and given a five-year sentence. "Five years for stickin' to a man," spat Kate. "I'll swing before I'll stick to another."

Chow Hayes recalls: "I later met Ryan and Freeman in jail. You hardly ever heard of an armed hold-up in those days and later Kate told me all about it."

Kate Leigh was released from jail in 1919, with Sydney hotels still operating under the 6 pm closing limits introduced during World War I. She grabbed the opportunity to make a fortune selling liquor after hours, and soon had half a dozen sly-grog shops operating across Surry Hills.

During the 1920s she married her second husband, a young Western Australian musician named Ted Barry. But again the marriage quickly broke up — after Kate found Teddy with another woman and promptly threw him out.

When well-known razor man John William "Snowy" Prendergast, accompanied by a group of fellow criminals, forced his way into one of her sly-grog dens at 104 Riley Street, East Sydney, one night in April 1930, Kate produced a rifle and shot him dead. At her ensuing murder trial she was acquitted on the grounds of self-defence. Later she told the press: "I've never been proud of shooting that chap and I've never stopped saying a prayer for the repose of the blackguard's soul. That's just because I'm religious, I suppose."

During the early 1930s she appeared regularly in the courts:

- in October 1931, she was charged with assaulting and robbing another woman at Woy Woy.
- in December 1931, she was charged with shooting at Joseph McNamara.
- in January 1932, she was sentenced to six months in jail for habitually consorting with women of ill repute.
- in August 1933, she was sentenced to two years in jail.
- in June 1935, she was fined for stealing a motor lorry tyre, rim and tube at Hurstville.

Chow Hayes remembers Kate Leigh's halcyon sly-grog days during the twenties, thirties and forties: "During the war years especially, she'd go to one of the hotels in the suburbs and buy, say, 200 dozen bottles of beer. It was 1s 2d then for a bottle of beer, and she'd give them 1s 6d. So the publican was making an extra fourpence on each bottle. Then she'd sell it after hours for three bob and double her money.

"But she also ripped off the hoteliers. She'd go and buy 200 dozen and pay cash and have them delivered to her place in Lansdowne Street. . . (Of course, the cops knew what was going on because you'd see taxis and cars lined up outside her place for half a mile trying to get served. You'd never seen cars like it. They used to queue right along Lansdowne Street, almost up to Cleveland Street. But she just paid off the coppers to leave her alone.)

"Anyway, she'd back up a couple of weeks later and buy another 100 dozen bottles from the same hotelier and again pay cash. That would go on three or four times. Then she'd run in one day and order 100 dozen and say she'd forgotten to bring her money with her and she'd fix it up next time. And they'd always say "No problem." Then when the time came to pay, she'd say she was in a bit of financial difficulty and she'd get another 200 dozen and say she'd fix him up in a couple of months' time. And of course the publican would think that she was already into him for 100 or 200 dozen so he'd have to stick with her now. She'd do this two or three times — and then she'd tell him to get stuffed and there was nothing he could do!

"She used to do that a lot. But once I remember she had to give one fellow his money back because he had a relative who was a copper, and the copper went and saw her and told her to pay the money or else. However, nine times out of ten she got away with it."

At one point Kate went to prison for 12 months following a raid upon one of her houses by a special police squad working to break Sydney's growing narcotics trade.

In her heyday Kate Leigh was also one of Sydney's leading "fences". Police said she masterminded numerous robberies — particularly, the *Daily Mirror* noted, "by young criminals just out of jail to whom she offered friendship and hospitality."

In 1937 Kate Leigh employed a hood named Henry John "Jack" Baker to stop the standover men, such as Chow Hayes, going to her beer house at the top of the hill in Lansdowne Street seeking cash handouts. Four years earlier Baker had copped a three-year jail sentence when he and Leigh were convicted on a charge of receiving stolen goods; Leigh, to avoid prison, had willingly entered into an agreement not to come within 200 miles of Sydney for five years, but then duly broke it within a matter of months.

Hayes vividly recalls Baker's return to her employment: "I was in the Lansdowne Hotel one afternoon with a couple of fellows. Baker — whom I'd never seen before, and I didn't know at that stage that Kate had employed him — approached me and said: 'I believe you're Chow Hayes.' I said: 'That's right.' And he said: 'Well, I'm looking after Kate's interests now, and I don't want you around here.'

"Well, I told him he could go and get fucked. With that we parted — I went back and had a couple of drinks with my friends and he walked out. That was early in the week. So on the Saturday night Charlie Osborne and I went to bite Kate for a tenner. In the meantime I'd checked up and found out that Baker was now employed by Kate. First I sent Charlie over. He knocked on the door and, when Baker answered, he bought a dozen bottles of beer. Then he came back and confirmed to me that Baker was there. So we went away and had a few beers and then we went back there again. But this time I sent Charlie over to knock on the door and tell Baker that I wanted to see him. So Charlie told Baker that I wanted to speak to him on the corner outside the Lansdowne Hotel.

"Baker came over and I said: 'I'm going across to see Kate.' He asked: 'What for?' And I replied: 'I want to borrow a tenner from her.' Then he said: 'You'll get fucking nothing, I told you that earlier in the week.' So, at that point, I pulled out a gun and said: 'Well, here you are, you can take this for your trouble.' Then I shot him twice, once in the stomach and once in the shoulder, with a .32.

"In those days we used to have four or five guns in certain suburbs (Surry Hills, Redfern, Woolloomooloo, Glebe and Ultimo) stored at a mate's place where you could grab one quickly. See, for example, if you found yourself in trouble down at the Loo, it was no use having to run back to Ultimo or Glebe. You wanted to be able to put your hand on a gun quickly. I even had one stashed under the old fruit barrow at the Railway — the stand owner kept it for me.

"Anyway, as soon as I shot Jack Baker — he was lying in the gutter outside the Lansdowne Hotel — Charlie Osborne and I disappeared. I went into hiding for three days. It was headline news in all the papers, of course ('Kate Leigh's door-keeper shot') but there was no inkling around as to who had done it. So then I decided to show my face again. I came out of hiding on the Thursday after the shooting and I was soon pinched at the Railway Hotel by Jack Parmeter and two other policemen.

"Parmeter approached me and said he wanted to see me outside. But I replied that I had no secrets from the blokes with whom I was drinking. However, Parmeter insisted that he'd wait until I finished my beer. Eventually I agreed to go outside and see what he wanted. But once I was outside he took me in the police car down to the CIB, in Central Lane behind Central Court — though he still hadn't told me what it was about. We went up to the third floor, where they did all the interviewing in those days. Then Parmeter asked if I knew a man named Jack Baker, and I answered 'No.' Parmeter said they were led to believe that I'd shot him last Saturday night, and I replied that was ridiculous. Then he asked if I knew anything about it, and I said nothing, except what I'd read in the papers. Then he said they were going to take me over to St Vincent's Hospital and see if Baker would identify me. At that stage I didn't know Baker well enough to guess what he might do in that situation, because he'd come from Melbourne.

"When we arrived at the hospital Baker was sitting up in bed. They took a chamber magistrate in and constituted a bedside sitting — although I still hadn't been charged with anything. But Baker immediately insisted that he'd never seen me before, and that the chap who shot him was a lot taller and darker than me. I breathed a huge sigh of relief at that stage.

"So we returned to the CIB and Parmeter said: 'I know it was you, Chow, and the only thing I can say now, is that it was a pity you didn't make a fucking good job of it.' He was really dirty on Baker, because he wouldn't identify me. . .

"Baker continued to work for Kate Leigh, but he never came after me and I became very friendly with Kate later on. Baker just copped it sweet. He must have thought I'd be too hot for him. Both he and I continued to work for Kate for 15 years afterwards. Eventually she'd ask me did I want money.

"Over the years we had a funny relationship. Originally, when I was a kid shoplifting, she liked me. Then when I started standing over people she hated me. But then, not long after I shot Baker, I was sweet again — and I stayed sweet from then on. She kept paying me regularly after that and she was very good about it. . .

"Also she footed my huge legal bills for a number of major cases, such as when I was later charged with Eddie Weyman's murder in 1945. And she bailed me out several times on consorting matters."

When she wasn't being charged, Kate Leigh was a regular in the public gallery down at Central Court. Hayes recalls they were celebrated appearances: "Whenever she went to court Kate would go to the bank first and she'd take out all her expensive rings — she had at least 30 rings in a safety deposit box. She'd put them all on, plus a big fur coat, and she always used to wear a floppy hat. Her appearance around the courts was a major event. The reporters loved her because she provided such colourful copy, and she'd pose for their photographers and so on. Whenever she arrived at the steps leading into Central Court from Liverpool Street, she'd start singing out — and you could hear her from a long way away — in her booming voice: 'Here I am! What's on today?' The reporters loved it. And she'd tick off the magistrate and every bloody thing. Then after it was over — whether she was just bailing someone out or appearing herself — she'd take all the reporters down to the hotel on the eastern corner of Liverpool Street and George Street. They'd go upstairs and she'd buy them sandwiches and drinks. And if any coppers poked their heads in, she'd call them over too and shout them. She'd spend £40 or £50 in a couple of hours. But she'd only have a glass of water herself. Then she'd head off home — but on her way she always went back to the bank and deposited her rings again for safe-keeping. And all the details about her diamond rings used to be written up in the newspapers every time."

During World War II Kate Leigh invested a fortune in war loan bonds. At one particularly memorable bond-selling rally in Martin Place she pulled £5000 in cash from her purse. Then she raised cheers from the crowd when she shouted that she'd double the amount if the principal speaker at the rally, Prime Minister Robert Menzies, would also pledge £5000 for the loan.

In January 1950, after a whirlwind romance, Kate married her old criminal mate, "Shiner" Ryan, who had been living in Western Australia for some years. Ryan joked to reporters as they left the church: "If this don't work out, I've got a good sharp razor!" And Kate, crying like a young bride, clutched her husband's arm and declared: "I'll see he doesn't get down to the bloody pub again." But within six months her third husband had deserted her and returned to the West for good. "Ryan told me he couldn't put up with her," Chow Hayes recalls.

Kate Leigh's troubles mounted during the early 1950s as the Taxation Department took an increasing interest in her curious financial affairs. She had not filed a tax return since 1942 — and in returns lodged before that date her stated income had never exceeded £100! She duly received a huge assessment for back taxes, and when she failed to pay she was quickly ordered into the Bankruptcy Court. There, in a memorable scene, she wept that she had "given away more than 10,000 quid to our soldiers between 1939 and 1945." All her houses and other assets were sold to meet the tax bill.

Leigh died following a stroke in February 1964.

• • •

Once when a reporter described Kate Leigh's great rival, Matilda "Tilly" Devine as an "Underworld Queen", she threatened to "punch him fair on the nose" if she met him.

Another time the *Daily Mirror* noted that "tough Cockney-born Tilly Devine had been known in her heyday to fight policemen...With a cyclonic temper she would swear like a bullocky...She ruled the streets of the notorious brothel area in Sydney's Woolloomooloo, where at one time she was reputed to own 18 different slum houses from which prostitutes operated."

A particularly romantic reporter from *People* magazine described her as having "a complexion of milk and roses and hair the colour of a hay-rick in mid-summer." Chow Hayes sums up with a fraction less subtlety: "When she was young, Tilly was a real good sort."

She was born in London in 1900 and worked during her early teens as a factory girl before, as the *Mirror* bashfully noted, "switching to an ancient and more profitable trade" on the London streets during World War I. Soon after, she met and married an Australian digger, James Edward Devine, and the couple came to Australia in 1919.

Unlike most prostitutes, Tilly Devine saved her money and shrewdly invested in a series of slum cottages around seedy Palmer Street, in the very heart of East Sydney's vice district. She then rented rooms to other girls at £2 per shift. She quickly amassed a sizeable fortune and purchased her own swish residence some miles away near the eastern beaches in Torrington Road, Maroubra.

In July 1929 the house was the scene of a wild gun-battle when her husband, "Big Jim" Devine, pulled out his rifle and shot dead the notorious hood George "The Gunman" Gaffney. (Gaffney, whose real name was Raymond Neill, was the leader of a Surry Hills gang of criminals). The Devines had provided a refuge for fellow criminal Frank Green. Gaffney and a group of mobsters came looking for Green, and Jim Devine shot Gaffney as he invaded the house.

Devine was acquitted of murder on the grounds of self-defence. But a bloody aftermath ensued. First another gunman, Walter James Tomlinson, was charged with shooting at Devine. Then in November 1929 Bernard Hugh "Barney" Dalton was killed and Tomlinson was shot through the chest in what the courts later heard was part of an "underworld war in William Street, East Sydney" between two gangs. Jim Devine, Leslie Gerrod and William Archer were arrested. Then Frank Green was charged witth Dalton's murder; he was acquitted after a second trial. But police subsequently charged Green with maliciously wounding both Tomlinson and Edward James Brady with intent to murder them; however the underworld's code of silence prevailed, no evidence was given by the men involved and Green was duly discharged in June 1930.

Soon after, Tilly and Jim had one of many celebrated differences of opinion. Police charged Devine with having shot at his wife. But when they appeared in court Tilly refused to give evidence and this charge was also dismissed.

Further gunfire followed at the Maroubra home in June 1931, when a group of gangsters exchanged volleys of shots with Jim Devine. Next morning taxi driver Frederick Herbert Moffitt was found slumped over the wheel of his cab in the street outside. He had died from a bullet in the chest — and the slug had come from Jim Devine's rifle. Again tried for murder, Devine argued that he had been shooting in defence against invading mobsters and Moffitt had been hit accidentally. He was again acquitted.

Meanwhile, Tilly herself was also in constant trouble with the police, with repeated charges for drunkenness, robbing clients at her establishments, indecent language and consorting. Among those splashed across the front pages were:

- in February 1930, she was remanded on a promise to leave Australia;
- in April 1931, she was sentenced to one month in jail for stealing;
- the same month she was fined for assaulting a woman who had apparently commented, upon passing Tilly in the street, "that's Tilly Devine — the Queen of the Underworld";
- in October 1931, she was charged with consorting; and
- in March 1932, she was sentenced to two months in jail on another consorting charge, and then six months for assaulting a policeman and resisting arrest.

In 1934 Tilly Devine went to Victoria for the Melbourne Cup, but was arrested and sentenced to 12 months for consorting under the name Mary Davis. She claimed she had merely stopped to talk in the street to a group of women who had previous convictions. "Twelve months for gossiping at the street corner!" she exploded upon hearing the sentence. She managed to gain bail of £100 pending an appeal. However, as soon as she was free she forfeited the money and skipped back to Sydney. Within two months she was again before the Sydney courts, for yet another consorting offence. And in 1940 she spent another six months in jail for being the owner of a house frequented by thieves.

In 1943 she divorced her husband, and moved into one of her residences (224 Palmer Street, on the corner of Berwick Lane) with ex-navy man Eric Parsons. During one drinking session Tilly grabbed a revolver and shot Parsons in the leg. But the resulting charge was dismissed when Parsons refused to give evidence against her — and in May 1945 they were married.

In 1947 the dreaded taxation Department began an investigation into Tilly's affairs. To one reporter she wailed the memorable line: "It's not taxation. It's a hold-up!"

In 1951 Tilly again decided to attend the Melbourne Cup. But at Flemington racecourse she was arrested for absconding on bail back in 1934, and was duly hauled off to Pentridge Jail. However she was released five weeks later, after her lawyers presented four doctors' opinions that she could die in jail without specialist medical treatment.

With the taxation authorities still in vigorous pursuit, she now began to claim that her cash came from "racecourse winnings" rather than the vice trade. "I backed Bernborough 16 times straight," she declared regularly." The explanation did not work, and she was initially forced to pay £20,000 for understating her income from 1948 to 1954. She acquired the necessary cash by selling off much of her real estate. "Now I've got no worries about money, " she told one newspaper. "They've left me with nought." And in later years, when facing a lonely death from cancer, she told another reporter that claims by the Taxation Department had left her with "only a toothbrush and a nail-file."

Tilly Devine eventually died in November 1970.

• • •

During the 1930s Hayes's circle of friends and acquaintances was not restricted to the underworld: he also began, occasionally, to mix in Sydney's higher social echelons.

One evening, for example, he attended a party at the Moore Park home of future New South Wales Premier and later Governor-General of Australia, Sir William McKell. It would, in later decades, become part of the folklore of the Sydney underworld. Hayes recalls: "'Paddles' Anderson took a group of us to a party at Bill McKell's house. It was out at 767 Dowling Street, opposite the park, just down from the Bat and Ball Hotel on the corner of Dowling Street and Cleveland Street. I had been drinking with a few mates including 'Kicker' Kelly and 'Toodles' Edwards and we ran into 'Paddles'. He said to come along to the party at McKell's place. I didn't know McKell at that point. By the time we arrived, half a dozen other thieves were already there. And that was also where I first met the famous medical criminal, Dr Reginald Stuart-Jones. But it was mainly a 'square-head' gathering. How 'Paddles' ever became involved I don't know.

"Anyway, a couple of hours later a bunch of heavies from the CIB walked in. They'd also been invited, and when they spotted us they gave me and 'Paddles' a dirty look and took McKell outside. They told him he had a house full of criminals and gunmen and that he should get rid of us because it would ruin his reputation. So he came back in, and he was very nice about it. He simply explained that the police didn't want us there. Then he gave us £10 each to go away. And that was the only time I ever went to his house.

"But I did see old Bill McKell a number of times after that. As a matter of fact, at one point I asked him to do a bit of business for me. It was to arrange a job on the wharves for one of my relatives, and he had no trouble doing it."

8 Gunned Down Over a Woman

By the late 1930s Chow Hayes, now in his mid-20s, was already as well known to both police and the public as any criminal in Sydney.

His record — which, of course, listed only the few matters upon which he was caught out — now became crammed with a succession of serious offences:

- 3/2/37: "stealing" charge in Brisbane. Hayes clobbered a chap named Albert Blake, who had been in the Railway Gang's "Big Mob", over the head with an iron bar. A charge of "grievous bodily harm" was laid and the police were looking for Chow. So he hightailed it up to Queensland. "I was shoplifting in Finney Isles, the big menswear store in the main shopping centre in Queen Street, when three shop detectives grabbed me," Hayes recalls. "So I copped three months' hard labour in Boggo Road Jail. . . Then when I returned, the Sydney coppers arrested me, but Blake didn't appear against me and I got off."
- 26/5/37: "demanding money by menace" and "malicious wounding" charges at Central Petty Court. "They were both discharged," Hayes explains. "I tried to stand over an SP bookie who operated from a house opposite the University, about halfway up City Road between Broadway and Newtown shopping centre. It was the first time I'd attempted to extract money from him, as a matter of fact — and he said afterwards that if he'd known who I was he'd have given it to me. Anyway, I hit him on the eye and that's how it came to include the wounding charge. Initially he went to the police. But then some mates of mine visited him and he didn't appear at the court. However, he had to give up his SP game after that, because the coppers told him that if they saw him operating they'd pinch him."
- 2/12/37: "stealing" charge at Central Petty Court.
- 10/5/38: "indecent language" charge at Glebe Petty Court.

- 11/10/38: two charges of "indecent language" and one of "resist arrest" at Glebe Petty Court.
- 3/11/38: a series of "stealing" charges at Glebe Petty Court.
- 15/12/38: "insulting words", "assault constable in execution of his duty" and "assault police" charges at Glebe Petty Court. Hayes became involved in an altercation with a uniformed policeman near the Railway. "He then placed me under arrest," Hayes recalls, "but I wouldn't go. There was a further scuffle and a few of his mates raced down to help him. I copped six months' hard labour for it all."
- 19/12/38: charge of "assaulting a constable" and two charges of "break, enter and steal" at Central Petty Court. "I was down at the Railway and I saw the same constable," Hayes explains, "and I went over and hooked him. I hooked him because I was already on appeal and I knew I could serve any additional penalty concurrently with the six months when I eventually had to serve it."
- 3/1/39: "drunkenness", "indecent language" and "threatening words" charges at Glebe. Hayes was again drunk near the Railway and, in his words, "threatening the coppers".
- 26/1/39: "consorting" charge at Glebe.
- 2/3/39: "drunkenness" and "malicious damage" charges at Glebe. "That was all to do with a policeman from Glebe," Hayes explains, "and the 'malicious damage' was to his uniform. But I said I wasn't drunk when they charged me. So they took me to the hospital, but they didn't have the proper test done on me, so the magistrate dismissed that bit."
- 3/4/39: Hayes withdrew four outstanding appeals at Sydney Queen's Square. The six-month sentence came into effect, and he duly served all sentences concurrently.

• • •

By late 1938 Hayes was 27 years old and, in his own words, "gaining quite a bit of notoriety." He enjoyed the prestige it brought among his peers and among the young females of the inner suburbs.

Hayes had his eye for some time on one particular teenage lass from Glebe. "Anyway, I took her out a few times," Hayes explains. "Then one afternoon I was having a drink in Glebe in the Ancient Briton Hotel (we knew it as Furlong's Hotel, after the then owners) on the corner of Bridge Road and Glebe Point Road, right opposite Rest Park. A bloke came in and said 'Knocker' McGarry wanted to see me outside. So I walked out and 'Knocker' said he wanted to talk about this young girl. He said I was a married man and too old for her. I said it was up to her and that I'd see her any time she wanted to see me. Then he walked away and I went back into the hotel for about an hour and a half.

"But later he returned and stood in the doorway and said he wanted to see me outside again for a minute. I walked outside and down about 10 yards [metres] to the corner of Bridge Road and Talfourd Lane, which was a little back-alley running behind the hotel. When we stopped on the corner 'Knocker' pulled out a gun and shot me in the stomach. Then he ran off across the road. I found out later that he raced to his aunty's place in Talfourd Street, where they covered him up in the laundry and he hid under a pile of old clothes and blankets.

"Well, that made no difference to me because I wasn't in any condition to chase him. I put my hand down to my stomach and it came away covered in blood. I lost consciousness for a moment as I sat down in the gutter. It was about 1.30 pm and a lot of people came rushing out from the hotel and nearby shops to see what had happened. I heard someone yell 'Get an ambulance!' and the next minute I noticed that the uniformed police had arrived. Ray Blissett was one of them, and they took me to Prince Alfred Hospital.

"I'd known Ray Blissett for donkeys' years. He used to be on the beat when the local coppers walked around the streets in pairs. He'd be one of the few fair dinkum coppers I met in my life. Everything he'd say in court would be exactly what took place — no verbals or any of that rubbish. Glebe Police Station was only a block away from where I'd been shot (and only two doors up from where McGarry had run to hide in Talfourd Street) and Blissett was in charge there at that time.

"On the way to Prince Alfred Hospital I'd lapsed unconscious for another two or three minutes. I came out of it as they were carrying me on a stretcher from the ambulance into the hospital's casualty section. There they prepared me for the operating theatre. They undressed me so that I only wore a white operating gown, white socks and one of those white caps. Blissett and two

RAY BLISSETT

"Blissett had Glebe all cleaned up from the hoods and crims. This was back in the days when the police would go around and give young larrikins a good kick up the backside if they got out of line — and Blissett had them all terrorised around Glebe . . ."

or three other police were in the room. Blissett used to call me Johnny — unlike everybody else who all called me Jackie or Chow.

"So Blissett asked: 'Who shot you, Johnny?' And I replied: 'Leave me alone, Ray, for Christ's sake.' But he kept asking and asking so I finally said: 'Will you stop asking me silly questions if I tell you?' And he agreed. Well, it was around Christmas time, about 15 or 16 December, so I said: 'Bend down and I'll whisper.' When he bent down I answered: 'Father Christmas hit me with a broken bottle.'"

This incident later became one of Sydney's best-known, if slightly exaggerated, criminal tales. At one point *People* magazine reported: "The uninspiring career of this most undesirable citizen almost came to an end in Glebe in 1938, when he was shot and badly wounded...Hayes obeyed the underworld code... He refused to name his assailant, and grinned cynically as he told detectives that he had been cleaning a gun and it had gone off. When asked the whereabouts of the weapon he said, 'Father Christmas has got it.' When the police first appeared and asked him what had happened to him, he told them, 'Father Christmas hit me with a bottle.'" Another time, *Truth* reported: "When Hayes himself was a victim of violence in a Glebe lane, he nursed a bullet wound in the arm and told Det. Sgt. Raymond Blissett: 'It's okay...Father Christmas just gave me a little present.'"

Meanwhile, at the hospital, Blissett and his offsiders left the room for a few minutes. "I was on my own," Hayes recalls. "Well, I didn't feel too bad (they'd put some padding on the wound to stop the bleeding) and I began to think that heads were likely to roll over this shooting. I also knew the police would keep pestering me over and over about it, trying to find out who had shot me. So I decided to give it all a miss and, since the window was open, I climbed out. But they'd already taken my clothes away, so I was wearing only the white operating gown and socks (I'd taken off the cap).

"I walked straight out through the hospital's front gate and over to a telephone box in Missenden Road. I immediately rang Charles 'Kicker' Kelly and asked him to come and collect me. The funny thing is, I didn't have any money for the call and I didn't reverse the charges. I don't know to this day how the call went through, but the bloke on the other end, Kelly, heard me easily enough. At first he told me I was mad and to go back into the hospital. But I insisted that I was waiting right there until he came and picked me up. He lived in Glebe and he arrived over in his car about eight minutes later.

"Kelly took me to a doctor I knew — Dr George in Glebe Point Road, whose surgery was three or four doors up from Glebe Public School. He was on the fringe of the underworld. He put me under anaesthetic in his surgery and extracted the bullet."

The newspapers trumpeted the sensational story of Chow Hayes's flight from the hospital, emphasising that if he didn't return he was liable to die within 48 hours. "It was all a load of rubbish," says Hayes, "and after about 12 hours Dr George, whom I knew well, told me I'd be alright. I was still in his surgery, but I couldn't stay there any longer so I told him I'd go. I'd been lucky because the bullet, which had lodged in my breadbasket area, hadn't hit anything vital. And it wasn't too deep either, which made it easier to remove.

"So 'Kicker' Kelly, who'd taken away the white hospital gown and dumped it somewhere, went and fetched some of my clothes from my home. I sent word to my wife that I was okay, and unlikely to die despite what the papers were saying. Kelly drove me over to my cousin 'Ezzie' Bollard's place in Cleveland Street. Then 'Ezzie' spread the word that I was quite alright, so that it would filter back to the police. Soon after, they ceased searching for me and I stayed with 'Ezzie' for about a fortnight. Then I contacted Dr George again and he wanted to take another look at me. I went back over to his surgery in a taxi with 'Ezzie', and Dr George said the wound was healing well. Then I decided I was going to have to show my face again sometime and it might as well be then.

"I went down to the Railway Hotel for a drink and the police arrived in a matter of minutes, led by Jack Wiggins, who was in charge at Redfern at the time. He said he wanted a chat — and that they knew who shot me because the bloke had given himself up. Wiggins said 'Knocker' had walked into Glebe Police Station and told them he'd shot me. So Wiggins asked what did I have to say about that? But I replied: 'No, he (McGarry) didn't shoot me. He's only making that up to big-note himself.' I added that I knew the man who shot me well, and it wasn't McGarry. So then Wiggins went away . . .

"Three or four days later I found out that 'Knocker' McGarry always went to the corner of Glebe Point Road and Bridge Road to meet a girl at 7 pm. So I went there on a Thursday evening about 6.30 with a .32 revolver and waited in Rest Park, about 50 yards [45 metres] from the corner. I sat there with a good view of the corner, and I put the .32 under a newspaper on the grass beside me, about four yards [four metres] away.

"But soon after, Ray Blissett and Norman Mijch arrived. Obviously someone had spotted me there and knew I was out to knock off McGarry. So they'd rung the police and lagged on me. Blissett asked: 'What are you doing here, Johnny?' And I replied: 'Having a bit of a rest.' He made me stand up and he ran his hands over me looking for a gun, and he was surprised when he didn't find one. But then he noticed the newspaper and he went to kick it away. As soon as he kicked it, of course, he saw the gun and exclaimed: 'Ah, my information was right. You were here to knock McGarry.' I said it was the first time I'd ever seen the gun, and he laughed and said: 'Don't give me that rubbish.'

"He told me he was going to charge me with carrying an unlicensed gun. So he took me to Glebe Police Station. As usual, he did things strictly by the book and went through all that rigmarole about my rights and so on. There were only three of us in the room and just then another young constable came to the door. I was sitting facing the doorway, Blissett was opposite me and the third copper was to the side of him. Now Blissett had his back to the door and, when the constable outside asked to see him for a minute, he stood up and turned his back to me and started to walk to the door. And at the same time the other copper sitting in the room watched Blissett walk towards the door so that his eyes were away from me.

"Now the gun had been a fully loaded six-chamber revolver. The police had already counted out the bullets and noted that there had been six in the chambers and one in the barrel, making seven bullets in all. They were laid out on the table in front of me. So at that instant, when they both had their eyes toward the door, I took one bullet and held it in my fingers up against my bottom lip — as though I was scratching my lip — because I wasn't sure whether the third copper had seen my move or not.

"When I realised he hadn't seen me, I quickly flicked the bullet into my mouth and swallowed it. It wasn't hard to swallow at all. When Blissett returned from the door, he said he was now going to charge me with being in possession of a fully loaded unlicensed gun with six bullets in the chamber and one in the breech. He took out one of the standard blue police envelopes, swept up the bullets without re-counting them and placed them in the envelope and sealed it and signed it. Then the other copper signed it too. Then they took out one of the big brown envelopes and put the gun in it, sealed it and they both signed that as well. As far as they were concerned the evidence was now sealed away.

"So they took me into the charge room and put me into the dock. They told the sergeant behind the desk my full name, address and what I was charged with. They said they'd arrested me about 6.50 that evening and so on, and handed over the exhibits. Then I had to turn out my pockets — cigarettes, matches, pen, comb, handkerchief, et cetera — and they searched me to check I didn't have anything else on me. I asked for bail and Blissett replied that he'd have to see what the magistrate said in the morning. So then I asked whether I could at least have my cigarettes and matches back, and Blissett said "Okay" and laughed to the sergeant: 'He won't burn the place down.'"

Hayes was placed in a cell at Glebe police station. Next morning he was taken across the road to the court house. "I told the magistrate I had to contact a solicitor," Hayes recalls, "and I was given a remand. When I applied for bail, the magistrate asked what the arresting constable thought about that. Blissett said he had no objection to me being granted bail considering I was so well known. So I was remanded on £100 bail, and my wife collected the money from friends and I was released later that day.

"However, when I was back in the charge room collecting my belongings Blissett happened to be there. He called me aside and said bluntly: 'Now I'm warning you: if anything happens to 'Knocker' McGarry, I won't have far to look.' But unbeknown to me, anyway, McGarry had gone bush."

Hayes sought, and was granted, a series of remands before the charge, "carrying a pistol at night", eventually came before Central Petty Court on 1 March 1939. Hayes was represented by Jack Thom, one of the leading criminal barristers of the era. "The case started about 10.30 am and Blissett was the first witness called," remembers Hayes. "He was in the box most of the morning. I noted that during his evidence he repeatedly said the gun was fully loaded and there was another slug in the barrel, making a total of seven bullets. Now at that stage I hadn't told Thom anything about the bullet I'd swallowed. So at the luncheon adjournment I told Thom I wanted him to come down to the nearby hotel for a moment and have a quiet drink. Well, he didn't want to go, but I insisted that it was very important and it'd only take 10 minutes.

"So we went to the hotel and I had a beer and he had a lemonade. I reminded him what Blissett had repeatedly asserted about there being six bullets in the chambers and one in the barrel, making a total of seven. 'Well,' I said, 'there are only six in the exhibit envelope.' Of course, he immediately wanted to know how I knew that. But I just said that I knew for certain. Then he declared that it wasn't good enough if I was only guessing. But I insisted there were definitely only six there, though I couldn't reveal how I could be so sure. Thom was worried that someone in the charge room had merely passed on a rumour to me. But knowing Blissett was so honest, I figured that even if he'd had a look in the envelope since I was charged and found out there were only six bullets, he wouldn't have added another one in its place.

"When we returned to court after lunch, Blissett was in the box again. And Thom took him back over his evidence about the gun several times, without hinting exactly what was likely to emerge. Then he took Blissett through the details of what happened to exhibits after a person was charged: how they were locked in the station safe and how the only person with the keys was the station sergeant. After a while Thom casually asked to look at the gun for a moment — and then, almost as an afterthought, at the bullets too. The magistrate joked, as Thom examined the chambers and the bullets: 'Oh, Mr Thom! Don't put a bullet in it!'

"Then Thom asked Blissett to repeat his evidence about the fully loaded gun with seven bullets being under the paper in the park beside me, and so on. Then he called the other copper into the box and he gave exactly the same story as Blissett, including the details about the seven bullets. Then Thom recalled Blissett into the witness box and was careful to ensure Blissett told the court that he had personally counted the bullets and put them into the envelope and sealed it. Then he dropped the clanger: 'Tell me this, Mr Blissett. How come there are only six bullets here? If the gun was fully loaded and there was a bullet in the barrel, there should be seven. But all you're producing in court are six bullets. Now how did that come about?'

"Blissett was dumbfounded, and said: 'No. No. There were definitely seven bullets there.' So the magistrate looked at the police prosecutor, who in turn looked at Blissett — they were all looking quizzically at each other. Eventually Thom submitted that there was no case to answer; that I denied ever having seen the gun before; and that both police officers had sworn on oath that the gun was fully loaded with one bullet in the barrel so that there were seven bullets, but only six had been produced in court. Therefore, Thom argued, there was considerable confusion somewhere and he asked the magistrate to give the benefit of the doubt to me. Well, the magistrate, with the implication that something was fishy, had no choice but to agree and the case was dismissed...

"Meanwhile, when I'd been bailed out that first afternoon

after I'd swallowed the bullet, I went home and immediately took a large dose of castor oil. It worked my bowels that night and two or three times the next day. They used to have chamber-pots in those days in the bedrooms. So I would take that into the toilet with me and check through what came out, prodding with a pencil. Anyway, on the third day I saw the bullet okay. So then I pulled the chain and flushed if off down the toilet."

Hayes still had every intention, however, of "squaring up" with "Knocker" McGarry. But McGarry had wisely "gone bush". A couple of years later Hayes received a four-year prison sentence, and during that period McGarry returned to Sydney. "So by the time I'd done four years in jail I'd forgotten all about pursuing McGarry," Hayes explains. "When I came back from prison I saw him a few times and we shook hands and let bygones be bygones."

• • •

Ray Blissett remains one of the few New South Wales police whom Chow Hayes respects. Raymond George Blissett had worked briefly as a bullock-driver dragging logs in the Dural district west of Sydney, before joining the New South Wales police force as a 17-year-old in 1928. He was a broad-shouldered lad and, of the thousands of cadets who passed through the police training college at Redfern during that era, he became renowned as the only one who could turn an old-fashioned ice-cream churn non-stop for 30 minutes — a feat of stamina upon which he won money.

From college young Constable Blissett went to Glebe where, for the next two decades, he kept the toughs of the inner suburbs under control. Years later he recalled to a *Sun–Herald* reporter that, during that era, "There were so many thieves about you could put your hand out of the police station window and pull in a thief practically any time." Many of the local villains and thieves gathered at the nearby Toxteth Hotel in Glebe Point Road. Blissett recalled one particular occasion when the well-known hood Norman Connelly took thieving to extremes: "I remember once pinching him for stealing the false teeth of a bloke who was having an epileptic fit."

As a detective-sergeant, Blissett took over duties as Chief of the CIB Consorting Squad in early 1953. Later, as a commissioned officer, he served at Paddington, before being appointed in 1960 as superintendent in charge of the Northern Division. In

1967 Blissett was awarded the Queen's Police Medal for distinguished service. He retired in 1968.

"For the first 20 or more years of his service he was stationed at Glebe," Hayes remembers. "Then they shifted him up to Regent Street, near the Railway. But the shopkeepers and factory owners around Glebe banded together and prepared a petition and, after about 18 months, they got him back. That was because Blissett had Glebe all cleaned up from the hoods and crims. This was back in the days when the police would go around and give young larrikins a good kick up the backside if they got out of line — and Blissett had them all terrorised around Glebe...

"In the old days," Hayes also recalls, "the first thing that came out for the coppers to drive around in were the old PD cars. But there were only a few of them and they went at barely 20 miles [30 kilometres] per hour. You could outsprint them if you were any sort of runner. And in the side-streets, where the cars couldn't drive through, you'd leave them for dead. The coppers in those days were mostly on foot, in pairs. Early in the nights they'd walk up and down the streets, and as they went past a house it would be nothing to see one of the neighbours come out and ask whether they'd like a cup of tea. And they'd almost always stop for a cuppa, because they knew most of the people in their area."

• • •

One of the first cars in which Hayes ever travelled was a stolen vehicle.

One day in the late 1930s he was drinking in the Grand Hotel at the Railway with two friends, Bernard "Benny" Gorman and Norman "Hoppy" Connelly, when another mate, named Leslie "Toodles" Edwards arrived. (Gorman, when charged with stealing hats in April 1933, had been described in court as a "member of an organised gang of thieves".) Edwards informed his comrades that he'd stolen a car the night before and left it parked in a Balmain lane. So Hayes suggested Edwards go back and check if the car was still there and, if so, that he meet Hayes, Gorman and Connelly at Railway Square at 9 that evening.

"The plan was to go and smash a few shop windows in the Balmain area," Hayes explains. "I said I'd have no trouble selling any merchandise we could grab. Sure enough, 'Toodles' turned up at 9 pm and said the car was still where he left it. So the four of us hopped onto a tram and headed for Balmain, where we jumped into the car. But then we realised we hadn't brought anything with which to smash shop windows. Suddenly 'Toodles' suggested there must be a jack in the boot. So we broke open the boot and took out the jack and laughed that we were in business.

"We drove to the main street in Balmain and quickly picked out four shops; one was a men's shoe shop and the other three sold general menswear. We decided the four of us would squeeze across the front seat while we filled the car's back seat and boot with the merchandise we grabbed. We hit the shoe store first and snatched all the shoes out of the windows and threw them into the boot. Then we hit the menswear stores and grabbed all the clothes upon which we could lay our hands — including the dummies because we didn't have time to stop and undress them — and threw everything onto the back seat. The whole operation only took three or four minutes and then we left Balmain in a hurry! I reckon we were back in Glebe by the time the Balmain coppers reached the shops from Balmain police station.

"We eventually pulled up in Wentworth Park Road, Glebe, and started to unload the stolen goods from the car. We hung them up beside the fence in Wentworth Park. But some old nark saw us carrying one of the dummies — dressed in a suit — into the park and, thinking it was a human, rang Glebe police. So while we were stripping suits from a couple of these dummies, Benny Gorman looked up and saw three uniformed coppers running across the park towards us. They shouted out: 'Stop! Police!' The four of us bolted, of course, but then the coppers began firing their guns. They fired half a dozen shots after us.

"Now I wasn't a bad runner in those days, so I soon hit the front as we ran out of the park into Bay Street, Glebe. I glanced over my shoulder and the coppers were 50 or 60 yards [45–50 metres] behind, but I could only see Gorman and Connelly. People began coming out of their houses to see what was causing the commotion and, as most of them knew us well, I wasn't stopping long enough for anyone to recognise me.

"Anyway Gorman, Connelly and I made it to a friend's house in Bay Street and gave the police the slip before reinforcements arrived on the scene. They were running around with torches and guns drawn, knocking on all the doors. When they came to the house in which we were hiding, the bloke who was renting it walked out onto his balcony and asked the coppers what they wanted. When they explained they were looking for three men, he angrily replied that we certainly weren't in his house, that inside were only his wife and children, and 'all you have done is frighten the life out of them with all your banging and shouting.' With that they left him alone.

"When dawn arrived the coppers were still out on the streets in force — walking about in pairs and riding up and down on their pushbikes — looking for us. Finally about 1 pm Gorman, who only lived a couple of streets away, said he was prepared to take the risk and walk home. Then Connelly left about an hour later, and not long after I decided to leave.

"I was walking up Bay Street towards George Street when I met a chap I knew well. He said it wasn't safe around there at the moment. When I asked why, he explained that 'all hell broke loose last night in Wentworth Park. The coppers shot "Toodles" Edwards. I don't know if he is dead or alive.' Well, that was the first I knew about 'Toodles' having been shot.

"Of course, the details were splashed across the front pages of the two afternoon newspapers, the *Sun* and the *Evening News*. I knew where 'Toodles' lived, so I immediately called around to see his family and find out the latest. His father said he was alive but in a critical condition in hospital — the bullet had hit him close to his spine and, even if he lived, at that stage they didn't know whether he would ever walk again.

"Then I went home to Shepherd Street, Chippendale, and it was only about half an hour before the coppers arrived and bundled me off to Regent Street police station for questioning. They had already arrested Gorman and Connelly and were holding them at Glebe police station. Of course, I denied everything. But they finished up charging the three of us with 'break, enter and steal'. The person who gave us up told the police who we were, but wouldn't give evidence in court — so to this day I don't really know his or her identity.

"The next day the police also charged 'Toodles', who finished up recovering but had to use a walking stick for years afterwards. Gorman, Connelly and I pleaded not guilty to the charges, and we were acquitted because there were no witnesses who came forward. But 'Toodles' pleaded guilty — he had no chance, since he was shot and caught with the stuff — and copped a jail sentence. However 'Toodles' insisted on oath that we were not the three men who were with him that night."

Benny Gorman later became a well-known urger around Sydney's racetracks. He was part of a gang of half a dozen crooks which worked as a team to rip off unwary racecourse types. At one point the gang moved to England to pursue their rort, but when their exploits became too "hot" in Britain, Gorman returned to Australia.

• • •

Meanwhile Chow Hayes continued to appear almost monthly in the Sydney criminal courts.

On 12 April 1939, he was charged with demanding money with menaces at Sydney Queen's Square. "That involved Jim Black, who used to be the distributor down at the Railway for the *Evening News* paper," Hayes recalls. "I was basically standing over him and I got £14 from him. But then he went and dobbed me straight in to the coppers. I was acquitted after some mates of mine 'got' at him."

Less than a fortnight later, on 24 April, Hayes appeared at Sydney Quarter Sessions to face a charge of "break, enter and steal". "That was a grocery shop in Shepherd Street, just up from where I was living," Hayes explains. "I was caught breaking in during the night by the owner, Joe Lando, who knew me well. I was by myself and I broke in through the back door. But then Lando came down and disturbed me while I was hunting around inside. So I just pushed him aside and walked back out and went on my way. He told the police. But I arranged an alibi and the jury couldn't come to a decision about it, so the case was discharged and I was remanded for another trial. . . At the retrial I was acquitted. My alibi was supported by Aunty Ninny and my wife, both of whom said I was home at the time I was supposed to have done it. Another man, Paddy Marr, also gave evidence for me; he said he was with the group at my place that night."

On 29 February 1940, Hayes was fined £2 on an "indecent language" charge in Redfern Petty Court. Later, on 15 August, a month before his twenty-ninth birthday, Hayes was charged at Glebe Petty Court with riotous behaviour, indecent language and resisting arrest.

• • •

At one point in 1940, with the War dominating world news, Hayes walked into the Annandale Recruiting Office and attempted to enlist. "I did it on the spur of the moment," Hayes recalls. "I didn't consult my wife in advance. I just went along one morning by myself. A lot of my mates did the same — and one, Billy 'Little Rot' Verney, was later killed in action. But I remember 90 per cent of the young blokes, at the beginning, thought it would be a holiday. At that point the army had erected long rows of tents for recruit training inside the Sydney Showground. They practised with broomsticks — they never had guns there.

"Anyway, I had my medical check-up, but I never made it into uniform. I received a letter about six weeks later informing me I'd been rejected because of my criminal record."

So Hayes's life continued much as before: sleeping through the day; spending most of his free time at the races and drinking in Sydney's inner-suburban hotels; and planning his evenings around a regular circuit of standover collections from the city's illegal gambling and sly-grog dens.

His wife had long since given up trying to talk him into a steady job. "She just decided I was a lost cause," says Hayes, "and then she lived more or less for the children."

"My children never discussed my lifestyle with me either. Even when I returned from a stint in jail — while they were school kids — they knew where I'd been, but they never asked me about it. If I was released from jail on a Monday, then on the Tuesday I just picked up where I left off...But I've thought since how awful that must have been for the children, especially later, having to go to school when I was so well known. And when we lived in Thomas Street, Ultimo, the Tech was only across the road. There were hundreds of students attending every day, and they'd only be there a couple of weeks before they all knew which was Chow Hayes's house.

"In the end my wife and kids settled into a routine which involved going along as though they didn't have a father — my wife was both mother and father to them — so that even when I wasn't in jail, they just lived their lives without worrying what I was up to. I simply came and went as I pleased...

"We had Dairy Farmers on one corner of Harris Street and Thomas Street, and the Tech on the other corner. They held cooking classes there, and any leftover meat and cakes were given to the locals. In addition, the markets were just around the corner, where I knew all the barrowmen — I only had to take a sugar bag down there, any day of the week, and I could fill it up immediately for nothing.

"My wife could also walk into the Tech on a Thursday and have her hair done for nothing by the students in the hairdressing classes, because they were always looking for models on whom to practise. And we could always collect some free milk at Dairy Farmers — always.

"At one point there was a carter named George working at Dairy Farmers. He lived at Rockdale and I didn't know him at all. But he saw me walking down Harris Street one day and whistled. I looked over my shoulder and spotted this bloke across the other side of the road. I glanced around and I was the only one in the street, so I looked back at him again and he called me over. He asked me: 'How are you going, Mr Hayes?' I said: 'Do I know you?' And he replied: 'No.'

"This was when butter was being rationed. He introduced himself to me — he knew my reputation — and asked whether I had a regular supply of butter. I replied that I could do with a bit; but I thought he was going to charge me for some black market stuff. However, he knew that I lived around the corner in Thomas Street. So he explained that he worked at Dairy Farmers, and he wanted to store two boxes of stolen butter in my backyard. I said that was okay, depending on what was in it for me. He said I could have half a box. So I replied that was fair enough, and he merely wanted me to leave my gate open.

"I did that, and he sneaked the butter in there, and from then on he did it two or three times each week. He was simply stealing it from Dairy Farmers. He'd carry a box out — they didn't have a gatekeeper — and then he'd just walk up the lane, which was only about 50 yards [45 metres] long, and straight into my backyard. He'd store it in the laundry and scatter some old clothes over the top. Then he'd go back and grab some more. He used to pinch about six boxes a week — and I copped half a box from each two boxes that came into my laundry...

"Talking about Dairy Farmers...late at night you could walk into their cafeteria and you'd see lots of coppers and nightwatchmen and shift workers. For just 1s 3d you could buy a terrific meal — things like soup and roast dinners and sweets and the lot."

From 1941 to 1944 the Hayes household in Thomas Street (as well as the nearby *Sydney Morning Herald* building and surrounding thoroughfares, Wattle Street and Jones Street) was part of an army camp. "The army blokes were all living in tents," Hayes recalls. "There were only seven terrace houses in our block, plus a couple of factories up the road. Their workers had to carry a special white ticket, which showed they were employed in those factories, to pass through the sentry points. And my wife and kids, and our neighbours, all had to carry pink tickets to pass through to the houses. If anyone wanted to come and visit, they had to inform the sentry box on the corner of Harris Street and Thomas Street; at the other end there was another sentry box on the corner of Jones Street and Thomas Street. So if someone wanted to visit they had to wait at the sentry box, while one of the sentries came up and knocked on your door. Then you'd have to walk back down to the corner to identify the person before they could enter with a special pass which was issued at the sentry box...

"In those years you also needed coupons to buy clothes. Luckily, a mate of mine named Eddie Stewart (not the bloke with the same name who worked at Thommo's two-up game) was working in the coupon office in George Street. When I was released from jail in 1944 I went down to the office to obtain some coupons and, lo and behold, there he was behind the counter. He gave me four lots, and told me any time I wanted more just to come back and see him. Of course, I went back a couple of times and then sold them — but they were only worth about £20."

9 An Armed Robbery Goes Wrong

March 1941 marked a turning point in the criminal career of shoplifter-turned-gunman Chow Hayes.

On 4 March he appeared in Glebe Petty Court to face charges of "assault whilst armed" and "illegally use car". Hayes, Charles "Kicker" Kelly and Leslie "Spud" Murphy had gone to Annandale to stand over a local SP bookie. "It wasn't much," Hayes recalls. "I think we ended up with £30. As for the car, it was stolen and Kelly drove it. [Hayes never learned to drive.] In those days Kelly was the only one among us who could drive. Anyway, I was the only one who was pinched over it — because I was the only one whom the SP knew. And he told the police that I had a gun — that's where the 'assault whilst armed' charge came from. But, as usual, friends of mine went and threatened him and nothing further happened about it."

Then three weeks later, on 25 March, Hayes and his close buddy Septimus Annen appeared in Number 1 Criminal Court at Darlinghurst to face a charge of "armed robbery".

Hayes recalls this matter as a watershed in determining the path of his later life. "The first time I became involved in really serious trouble," he explains, "was with this armed hold-up charge. A man named Laws operated a fruit shop in the front part of one of a row of terraces in Charles Street, Forest Lodge. And he ran an SP operation from the back of the house. Now Seppi Annen and I and two accomplices spent three or four weeks planning to rob him. But we waited for a Saturday afternoon when a lot of outsiders won at the races so that, we figured, he'd have a lot of cash on the premises. His regular customers usually walked up through the backyard and entered via a rear entrance. But we marched straight in through the front door about 5.30 pm.

"Laws's wife was upstairs and he was sitting in the back room.

I had the gun, which was a .22. When we entered I pointed it straight at him and said: 'This is a hold-up. Give us all your cash!' Laws took out notes totalling about £20 from his side and hip-pockets. But we weren't interested in that, because we knew there was a drawer hidden under the table where he kept most of his cash. So one of the others crawled under the table and found about £600. At that stage Laws suddenly made a move to stop him crouching underneath, but I pointed the gun at him and yelled: 'Get back, you bastard, or I'll blow your fucking head off!' Laws stepped back immediately, but he warned us: 'I'll remember you blokes.'

"We took the money and disappeared. Then we divided up the £600 and agreed to meet again on the following Monday afternoon at a hotel in Botany Road near Henderson Road.

"We gathered about midday on the Monday. But while we were having a celebratory drink, one of our two accomplices walked out onto the street for a minute. And right at that moment a police car drove past carrying two young coppers and a sergeant named Holmes. Well, Holmes spotted our mate (whom he knew as an associate of criminals) and, unknown to our mate, Holmes stopped the car up the road. Then he sent one of the young coppers back down to the pub to see who was drinking with our mate. Meanwhile our mate came back inside and sat down with us. The young copper took a quick peek inside — and reported back to Holmes that the bloke who'd just been pointed out to him was drinking with three others. Holmes put two and two together and decided these were probably the four gents who'd pulled the hold-up at Laws's SP joint the previous Saturday. So he radioed for reinforcements and two other police cars arrived with three or four police in each. Then the dozen or so coppers surrounded the hotel and burst in all three doors at once with their guns drawn.

"But just before they came in, our two accomplices had gone to the toilet. And they were still out there when the police raced in through the doors. Holmes did the talking, and yelled: 'Put your hands on the table, Chow and Seppi. Now where are the other two bastards?' Seppi and I looked at each other and we both replied at the same time: 'Who are you talking about?' And Holmes said: 'The other two who were with you on Saturday afternoon.' We replied that we didn't know what he was talking about. Meanwhile our mates were ready to walk back out from the toilet. But, as they opened the door, they spotted the police and ducked back inside again. Then they hid in one of the toilet cubicles and locked it. The police went into the toilet block during their search, but one of our mates was standing on the seat while the other sat down pretending to be drunk, talking to himself. The police thought it was only some old derelict and came back out.

"By this time Seppi and I had been handcuffed and taken out into the street. I didn't have a gun on me (I only carried it around the streets at night). They took us to Redfern police station and said they were charging us with armed hold-up. They asked where was the gun I'd had with me. But I replied that whoever told them all this was making up stories. Then they paraded us in a line-up, and Laws had no trouble picking us out.

"The police then left us in a room, guarded by uniformed constables, while they talked to Laws outside. I could hear them assuring him: 'Yeah, you picked the right men. There's no doubt about that.' But they couldn't drag any information (relating to the identity of our two accomplices) from either Seppi or myself. So in the end our other two mates were never charged...

"About 8 pm Holmes returned with a gun, a .32, and offered it to me and said: 'Here, Chow, have a look at that.' But I didn't want to put my hands anywhere near it. Then he just laid it on the table. But I still wouldn't touch it. So finally, in desperation, he said: 'Well, you had one on Saturday, and we can't find that, so now you've got this one instead!'

"Then they formally charged us and shifted us to Central police station in a police wagon. We appeared in court on the Tuesday morning, were remanded without bail and taken out to Long Bay Jail. We were held there on remand for over three months.

"In court, after a two- or three-day hearing, we were eventually found guilty. Judge McGhie said I was the ringleader, so he gave me four years with hard labour and he gave Seppi three years."

The *Sydney Morning Herald* reported that Annen and Hayes had been officially convicted of "being armed with a revolver" and having "assaulted William James Laws, a dealer, and robbed him of 25 shillings." Hayes was described in court by police as "a man with a violent nature."

Hayes recalls: "Later we were taken back down to the Darlinghurst cells below the courts. The crown prosecutor, Mr Kidston, came down and told me bluntly that he didn't want to bugger around, so he'd advise me not to appeal against the sentence. (We'd had alibis — which obviously hadn't been accepted — that I was at a party and Annen was home sick. I had arranged for some of my mates to lie for me; three men and two women all said I was with them.) Anyway, Kidston said I shouldn't appeal because, on the other side, the police were pressuring him to appeal against what they saw as the leniency of the sentence. He said he'd leave the matter for a few days, and see if I was cheeky enough to lodge an appeal. And if I did, then he'd take it right on from there. But he said that, for the moment, he was satisfied with the sentence.

"So he more or less hinted that if I was cheeky enough to appeal, there was a good chance that I'd actually end up with a longer sentence. And I knew myself that I was likely to cop a longer sentence. See it was armed hold-up and I thought I was very lucky. My lawyers had been warning me that I might cop 10 years — especially with my previous record. Annen had a bad record at that stage too. So, actually, I was very relieved when I only copped four years — and an appeal had never entered my head until the prosecutor came down to see me...

"With the sentences in those days, they didn't add non-parole periods. Four years meant four years, and you received two months a year off for good behaviour. So they then took us out to Long Bay — and if I behaved myself the whole time I was looking at three and a half years in jail."

• • •

Seppi Annen ended up in Parramatta Jail. And Hayes, after getting in a spot of trouble at Long Bay (he assaulted another prisoner), was transferred to Bathurst Jail and then later to Goulburn Jail.

"The fellow's name was 'Baldy' Mason and it started in the yard," Hayes recalls. "I hit Mason on the head with a 'shit tub' — it was like a hefty bucket with a lid on it, which a prisoner used as a toilet. There were about 12 or 15 of us in the yard and I picked up the tub. Mason knew I was coming — he could see me walking towards him — and I clobbered him over the head with it. Then I gave him a bit of a kicking too. We'd been old enemies — I'd been crooked on him for years, and he'd been crooked on me too. After I hit him, a brawl developed and the screws ran in and broke it up. They wanted to charge me, but Mason wouldn't lay any charge. He said it was his fault, that he threw the first punch. So they decided to split us up, and they sent Mason to Parramatta and me to Bathurst and then later to Goulburn. I definitely copped the worst end of that — gee, Goulburn was an awful bastard of a place in those days...

"It was 1941 when I hit Goulburn — I was 29½ — and it was the first time I'd seen it. They had special yards for isolating people and, for nearly four months, they kept me in one by myself. My wife and a few others came to visit once a month; that was all they were allowed. It's a funny thing — you were allowed 20 minutes per visit at Long Bay and Parramatta, but you only received the same 20 minutes at Goulburn or Bathurst and your relations had to travel all the way out to those jails...

"I knew 'Paddles' Anderson at Bathurst. We'd been shoplifting together as teenagers. He was serving a two-year sentence for assault. This was just after he'd been in a whole lot of trouble down in Melbourne, where he was charged with murder (he shot a bloke named Abrahams outside a gambling joint) but was acquitted. However, 'Paddles' definitely shot him — everyone knew he did it, and he freely admitted it to his mates."

Frederick Charles "Paddles" Anderson, one of New South Wales's most vicious criminals over five decades, was later described by crime journalist Bob Bottom as "the titular head of organised crime in Sydney" during the late 1960s and 1970s. In a notorious murder trial in Melbourne in September 1940, 26-year-old Anderson — then also nicknamed "The Big Doll" and described as a Sydney caterer — was found not guilty of murdering Melbourne thug John Charles Abrahams. "God, that's better than winning all the lotteries in the world at the same time," gasped Anderson upon acquittal as he grabbed the hand of his counsel Maurice Goldberg. Anderson told the throng of newsmen: "I got myself into bad company, but I'm finished with that after this." Anderson, who had been visiting Melbourne, shot Abrahams outside a Collingwood illegal gambling school. The bullet passed in one side of Abrahams's throat and out the other. Despite being identified by one witness as the man who then ran from the scene, Anderson produced an alibi, thereby creating enough doubt to escape conviction.

Upon his return to Sydney Anderson was, in one week, charged with having been in a house "frequented by thieves"; with having "demanded money with menace from a bookmaker" and having "assaulted the bagman"; and with having consorted with known criminals at a house in William Street, East Sydney. Thereafter Anderson, now describing himself as a machinist of Surry Hills, quickly emerged as a character of some renown among observers of the Sydney underworld scene.

"While I was at Bathurst," says Hayes, "'Paddles' was in the yard next to me. We were all segregated into single yards. 'Paddles' was about my age. Later he was shifted down to Long Bay, and I was moved to Goulburn...

"Eventually, after many applications by my legal advisers to the Comptroller General of Prisons [now called the Commissioner for Corrective Services], my wife had to pretend she'd had a nervous breakdown to try and have me moved from Goulburn. My solicitors wrote letters to the effect that my wife needed me nearer to Sydney — and Dr George from Glebe wrote out certificates that she'd had a nervous breakdown, and that she'd had to give up work and so on. Anyway it worked, and the Comptroller General, Mr Nott, agreed they'd shift me down to Parramatta — but, he warned, if I put one foot wrong I'd be sent straight back to Goulburn.

"'Baldy' Mason was still at Parramatta. And, in the meantime, 'Paddles' had been moved over there too — but only for about four months before he was discharged. And Seppi Annen was there. And so was another close mate from my teenage days, Fred 'Boonie' Smith, who'd copped five years for inflicting grievous bodily harm on a copper in Glebe. And another really close friend, Johnny Flanagan, came in a couple of times doing a 'sixer' — a six-month sentence. (Three months was called a 'drag'.) There were lots of other blokes in there whom I knew very well — probably half the blokes I knew well in Sydney passed in and out of Parramatta Jail during that period...

"Anyway 'Paddles' was released. And Seppi was released. And Mason was also released and, soon after, he was murdered by another gunman, Mick O'Hara." However, in May 1943 a court declared that William Francis Mason had been officially murdered "by persons unknown". A few years later Anderson was a little more fortunate. In June 1945 he was stabbed three times during a wild brawl in Glebe, but survived.

One incident Hayes recalls from his years in Parramatta Jail involved a hardened criminal nicknamed "Snowy". "After one visit," Hayes explains, "he was walking up and down the yard and you could see he had just received really bad news. This went on for a couple of days, before one of his mates finally asked what was wrong. 'Snowy' said he'd just found out his wife was having a baby — and he couldn't possibly be the father! His depression continued for a couple of months and he continually threatened what he was going to do to his wife when he was eventually released. Finally his mother-in-law came to visit him, and suddenly he returned all laughs and smiles. And do you know what she told him? She told him that his wife was going to have twins. And he had the idea that, by having twins, it would take 18 months for the children to be born! Now that is the gospel truth. And so he forgave his wife for everything, because he thought he was the father."

While in prison during those years, prisoners were allowed to receive what was known as a "parcel" (a type of food hamper) at Christmas, Easter and the King's Birthday. "Your family and friends could bring as much as they liked for you," Hayes explains. "They could include a case of fruit or anything, but it all had to come together. It was mostly tinned stuff (fruits, corned beef, salmon, sardines) because that lasted the longest. But I'd also receive a lot of perishables too. All my friends used to take their contributions for my 'parcel' down to my wife's place in Thomas Street, Ultimo, the day before the trip. Then one of them would provide a car — he might own it himself; if not, he'd steal the bastard. Anyway, he'd drive her up to the jail.

"One particular time Seppi Annen had only been out of jail about a fortnight, and he arrived at Thomas Street with a big wooden banana case filled with mixed fruit. Then he and another fellow accompanied my wife up to Parramatta. When it was time for my visit they naturally let my wife in, and they didn't know the other fellow by sight (he'd been in jail but he'd never been to Parramatta) so they let him in too. But when Seppi went to put his foot through the gate, they stopped him. So Seppi began swearing at one of the officers and a big commotion started at the gate. Eventually Seppi punched him and split his eye wide open and it needed eight stitches. Anyway Seppi copped 12 months and came back to Parramatta, and I ended up being released a long while before him."

Hayes's lifelong mates Seppi Annen and Johnny Flanagan lived in the same block in Glebe. Flanagan's residence was a couple of houses down from one of Hayes's favourite watering holes, the Friend In Hand Hotel in Queen Street, Glebe. His backyard ran into the yard behind Annen's house in Crown Street.

Over the next 10 years both men made numerous appearances before the courts. In August 1947 Annen relied on an alibi as his defence and was acquitted of having assaulted a man and robbing him of £12 and a bottle of brandy. Then in June 1949 both Annen and Flanagan were acquitted on charges of having stolen or received three bales of dress material. Later Flanagan was charged in July 1951 with consorting and in August 1951 with having stolen a tyre and tube.

10 Teaming up with Joey Hollebone

During his years at Parramatta Jail, Hayes spent much of his time "out on the woodheap" (chopping wood) with Eric Kelly, Billy Madden, Danny Kerry and "Face" McKeon. (Back in September 1933 William Madden had hit the headlines when shot in the chest after a fight in a Redfern billiard saloon. And Daniel Kerry, with an accomplice, James Patrick Walsh, had been sentenced in March 1941 to three years in jail — though Walsh's term was later reduced to 12 months — for assault and robbery.)

One particularly repulsive character Hayes encountered at Parramatta Jail, Albert Andrew Moss, had been charged with the murder of three men (Timothy O'Shea, Thomas Robinson and William Partley) who disappeared around the central-western New South Wales town of Narromine back in mid-1939. None of the three bodies was ever discovered, but some of O'Shea's belongings were found in Moss's possession.

Moss once told the head of Sydney CIB, Supt. M. F. Calman, in a confidential discussion that he had killed 13 people. When Moss, aged 79, eventually died from cancer in Long Bay Jail hospital in January 1958, Calman said Moss had a criminal record dating back to the age of 17. "On a number of occasions after being arrested for some crime, he pretended to be insane and he was certified insane 11 times. . . His victims were not rich. Of the three murders for which he was charged, one was committed for a horse and sulky, another for a bicycle and the third for a few pounds in money."

"Moss, whom we all called 'Old Mossie', was in his early 60s when I arrived at Parramatta Jail," Hayes recalls. "He was a real weirdo. When you came out of your cell after lunch, you might have a piece of bone or a bit of meat which you'd throw in the barrow. Well, Moss would stand beside it and pick up all the scraps, and collect them in a bucket and take them back to his cell. There he'd stash the stuff under his bed, and it really stunk to high heaven. In fact, the smell was so bad that the screws refused even to enter Moss's cell to search it.

"Anyway, at Parramatta Eric Kelly (who'd been convicted of attempted murder following the shooting of pawnbroker Nathan Segal at Redfern in 1939, but I know for a fact that the police definitely pinched the wrong man) and 'Face' McKeon used to do all the work on our work gang, and the rest of us would sit around brewing the tea and having a smoke. We were 'on the woodheap' — which meant cutting timber and so on. We were supposed to be chopping wood for the kitchen house and the prison woodpile.

"Danny Kerry used to cut the chips for the prison governor's house and his office. They didn't have a heater in those days, they had pot-belly stoves. But one day someone called out to him, and he slipped and chopped his thumb off. It fell onto the ground and, for a moment or two, it was still jumping with the nerve ends in it. So then 'Face' McKeon picked it up and ran down to 'Old Mossie' and called out: 'Here you are, here's a bit of human!' And do you know, Moss was chewing on that for about the next six weeks. And when you were close to him you could hear him chewing on the nail and bone.

"Moss was charged with three murders, but the police said he'd committed up to a dozen. He was a cannibal. He used to put an advertisement in the newspaper, asking anyone who had a horse and dray, or a caravan, to come to his address and they'd go prospecting for gold, but he'd pay all expenses. Well, off they'd go and no-one would ever see the other fellow again... But Moss was harmless in jail.

"Like that silly Darcy Dugan. He loved publicity, but he was nothing in jail to the hard-headed criminals — never was and never would be. He gave me the shits. He blamed everyone else: the screws were no good, the coppers were no good, the other crims were no good. If he'd taken the time to stop and have a good look at himself, he'd have found that, in fact, he was the one who was no good.

"Dugan wanted public sympathy all the while. I didn't worry about that: if I had admitted to every crime I committed during my life, I'd have to live five or six times over. I would, because I'd owe that much jail — I'd owe about five or six life sentences."

• • •

Outside jail a number of Hayes's friends and acquaintances were murdered during the 1930s and 1940s. They included Barney Dalton, the SP bookie at the Tradesman's Arms Hotel in Palmer Street, who was shot dead during a betting argument; William Henry "Sap" Johnson, a shoplifter and petty thief who was kicked to death in Surry Hills; Cecil Charles "Hoppy" Gardiner, who was shot dead while attempting to stand over Paddy Roach's two-up game at Erskineville; Harold Robert "Tarlow" Tarlington who was shot and killed at St Peters by fellow mobster Myles Henry "Face" McKeon during a dispute over a woman; "Face" McKeon, who was himself subsequently shot dead in Chippendale by Hayes's cousin Ezzie Bollard; and "Nigger" Fox, who was stabbed and killed on the front verandah of his sly-grog den in Alexandria.

• • •

Back in those days, Hayes is fond of recounting, a man had to "know people in jail to be able to survive. For example, you couldn't live on the tucker. So we'd band together out on the farm — while we were 'out on the woodheap' — and cook stews and things. We'd been classed as no-hopers because we wouldn't work inside the jail, so they put us way out on the farm. It had walls around it (brick walls 16 ft [5 metres] high) but they kept us out there away from the other prisoners. We'd go to the jail butcher's shop at Parramatta to obtain some meat — we had contacts in there. And we'd grab a few vegetables from where we were supposed to be working. You could put on a real good stew and you could have as much as you liked. Sometimes we'd cook a bit of steak or some chops and sausages. We'd fry them on the grill.

"Then there were the bakehouses — Goulburn and Bathurst didn't have bakehouses, but the others did — at Parramatta and 'The Bay'. They made real top bread in those bakehouses, and supplied all the hospitals around their district. They also made pies and cakes, but only for different crims who were their mates. Of course, when I first went into jail I was lucky, because I belonged to one of the pushes — and as I've said before, Gosford was a breeding ground for crims — and there might have been a couple of my own Railway Gang there, maybe from the Big Mob. And there'd always be someone inside from one of the other pushes like The Rocks, or Surry Hills, or Glebe. We'd all know each other and we wouldn't fight while inside a jail. Instead, we'd tend to team up with one another because we had something in common. But if you were a loner, then you'd have been lost. Luckily, no matter which jail I went to, there'd always be someone inside whom I knew and who would give me the 'layout' — someone to give me the tip about the rorts at that particular jail.

"So we could make stews, for example, by gathering up the titbits from the butcher's shop, the cookhouse, the bakehouse, all the places where you'd establish contacts. And that's how you'd survive.

• • •

Of all the criminals with whom he spent his time at Parramatta, the man who was to have most influence on Hayes's subsequent criminal career was a chap named Joey Hollebone.

Summing up his notorious career years later, the *Sydney Morning Herald* reported that William "Joey" Hollebone was described by police as a "gunman and well-known criminal" who had "several times been charged with violent crimes, including murder."

In 1935, aged just 19, Hollebone and two accomplices, James Augustus Charters and Edward Sydney John Smith, had kicked to death a fruiterer, Leslie Archibald Hobson, in King Street, Newtown, during a brawl. A jury found Hollebone not guilty of murder, but guilty of manslaughter and he served 10 years in jail. At Parramatta, during that sentence, Hollebone and Hayes forged the foundations of what became a lifelong friendship.

"Joey Hollebone was a silent bloke, due for release about four months before me," Hayes recalls. "He'd copped 10 years for kicking that young bloke to death in Newtown. They were stealing the bloke's bike outside a paper shop, when he ran out and tried to stop them. Apparently they didn't mean to kill him. During the fight they pushed the bloke and he fell into the gutter and they started kicking him and he died...

"So I teamed up with Hollebone at Parramatta and, right from the start, I knew he was as 'solid' as a rock. In jail we used to walk up and down the yards in small groups of three or four. Hollebone said he'd like to join forces with me, two-out, once we were outside again. The police hated him...

"Anyway, when I was released from jail, Joe Taylor [the big-punting, illegal casino boss] put me on the wages book at Thommo's two-up school for £100 a fortnight. I was running around with Joey Hollebone and we were both drinking heavily. Taylor knew I was mates with Hollebone and that we were standing over people and one thing and another. So one day Taylor said to me that his informants reckoned Hollebone was a very tough bastard. And I replied: 'You couldn't find anyone tougher, so why don't you put him on the payroll?' Taylor was wary about whether Hollebone would behave himself if he put him on. But I said he would. So then I introduced Hollebone to Taylor, and Taylor said he'd start Hollebone at £60 a fortnight.

"But soon after, Hollebone was sent back to jail for a year for carrying an unlicensed pistol. And while he was inside, Alfie Dawes went to his home and robbed it. He took all Hollebone's clothes and backhanded his wife, Hazel Hollebone. Of course, Hazel immediately went and reported all the details to Joey in jail. He advised her not to mention it to anyone else — including me — because he wanted to deal with the bastard himself. So she never told me about it and I didn't know anything of the matter until Hollebone was released from jail. And by that time I was back inside myself — serving six months — and he came and visited me and told me the details.

"Hollebone explained that he was going to fix Dawes that week. He told me to listen on my 'jigger' — in those days we called the little wirelesses which we made ourselves 'jiggers'. Hollebone said to listen to the news every morning for the next week. It was 29 August 1946 and he went to a cottage in Mary Street, Waterloo, around 9 one evening. Inside were Dawes's mother Josie, father Alf senior, Noreen Miller who was 'on' with Dawes at the time, Jimmy Graves, Lance Williams and several others. Hollebone simply strode up to the door, walked in, pulled out a gun and fired seven shots. He hit six people, killing three of them, including Dawes and Graves, and wounding three others."

Hollebone then casually walked back out to his car and drove away. The next day the newspapers tagged the shootings "The Battle of Waterloo". Hollebone remained in hiding for a couple of weeks, before eventually strolling into Redfern police station to give himself up. He was immediately charged with the murder of Alfred Frederick Dawes but, miraculously, he was acquitted.

Truth later reported that crown prosecutor, Mr R.R. Kidston, described the Mary Street house as "a squalid wooden shack." Among the dozen or so people present at the time, the three dead victims were officially listed as: Alfred Frederick William Dawes, 24, who'd died from a bullet wound above his right eye; Marjorie Naomi Nurse, 19, who'd died from a bullet in the nose; and Douglas George Graves, 27, who'd died from a bullet in the side

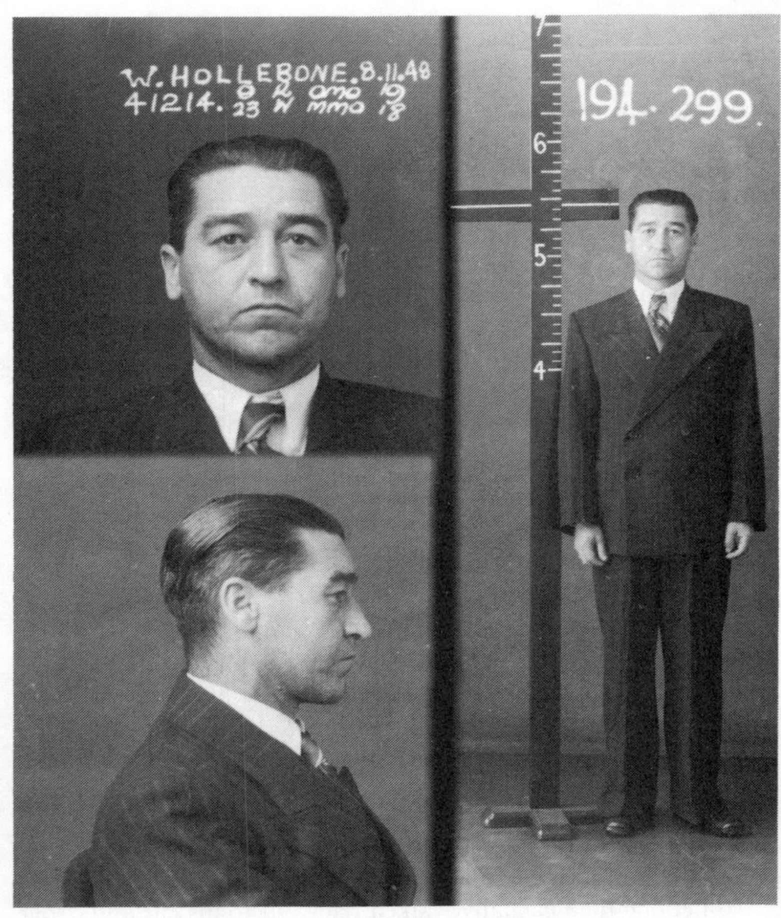

Joey Hollebone

William "Joey" Hollebone teamed up with Hayes during the 1940s to form Sydney's most feared duo. One of Australia's best-known detectives later described Hollebone as "the most cold-blooded bloke I ever knew."

of his head. Wounded were: Patrick "Blue" McMahon, 27, who was hit in the forearm; Alfred Ernest Dawes, 55, who told how, after being shot in the hand, "I got under the table"; and Noreen Miller, 23, who told the court that she lived with Alfie Dawes junior, and had been feeding their three-week-old baby when the shooting started. A bullet had struck Miller in the left shoulder, narrowly missing the infant. Others present included: Henry "Eggs" Phillips; Arthur McNamara; Lance Williams; "Pretty Vera" Riley; Colin Michell and Louis McMahon.

Asked whether Hollebone was the man who fired the shots, Noreen Miller replied: "I would not call him a man, but a mongrel." Asked the same question, Elizabeth Josephine Dawes yelled from the box: "That murderer. That dirty murderer. . . You murdered my son in cold blood." *Truth* noted that "after the witness left the box, Mr Amsberg (for Hollebone) said that Mrs Dawes was so affected by liquor that he did not want to cross-examine her."

In contrast to Miller and Mrs Dawes, Patrick McMahon, Henry Phillips and Lance Williams all told the court that they could not identify Hollebone as the man at the house on the night of the shooting.

Hayes recalls: "Hollebone had been charged, and duly remanded, and sent out to Long Bay Jail without bail. Old Mrs Dawes had identified him. But she was a notorious drunk. Anyway, in an absolute coincidence, my cousin Ezzie Bollard had met a friend for a drink in the hotel which used to stand on the corner about 50 yards [45 metres] down City Road from Cleveland Street. The friend told Ezzie that after the shootings, Mrs Dawes had no sheets to cover the corpses. So the police had borrowed three sheets from her next-door neighbour. But later Mrs Dawes went and asked the authorities for the return of the sheets, and then washed and ironed them. However, instead of subsequently returning them to her neighbour, she'd taken them around to Grace's pawn shop in Abercrombie Street, Chippendale (on the corner of Vine Street, directly opposite the Berkeley Hotel) and pawned them for about 12 shillings. Meanwhile she told the neighbours that she still hadn't received them back from the police.

(Grace's pawn shop had been one of Sydney's better known commercial sites in the era between the wars. In one celebrated court appearance in August 1929, pawnbroker Mark Abel Grace, upon being charged over stolen hats and overcoats, provided amazing details about how he handed over a large sum of cash to a Sydney detective.)

"Anyway, George Amsberg — who wasn't yet well-known, but later appeared for Hollebone and me on many occasions — was Joey's barrister. Now Ezzie Bollard had gone and told Hollebone and Amsberg about the sheets. So Amsberg asked solicitor Phil Roach to check it out; and Roach went and confirmed the dates and details with Grace...

"Now at the Coroner's Court (the old one down near Circular Quay) Amsberg would begin every day by asking Mrs Dawes how many drinks she'd already had that morning, and so on. And he kept encouraging her to repeat how sure she was that Hollebone was the man who'd murdered her son. But he saved his trump card...

"So the case eventually came before the criminal court — and that's when Amsberg first raised the matter of the sheets. He cornered Mrs Dawes so that she was forced to say that she'd collected them from the police and returned them to the neighbour. And he encouraged her to declare that she was sure of that — and she was just as sure that Hollebone was the man who'd murdered her son. Well, once Amsberg revealed all the details about how she was lying blatantly about the sheets, it added to the confusion between the witnesses about identifying Hollebone. So in the end Judge Herron directed the jury to find Hollebone not guilty...

"Of course, that case was such a matter of coincidence. You'd never have given Hollebone a million-to-one chance of beating it at the start."

• • •

While Hayes enjoyed Hollebone's quiet, unemotional company, he often found his wife, Hazel, a pain in the neck. "Hazel was forever telling Joey that someone was 'pitching for her' behind his back. She was really just trying to grab some attention and cause a bit of a fight. We called those types 'air raiders'. Hazel wanted notoriety, and she enjoyed having Joey think that other men were chasing her.

"One night a large group, including Jackie Hodder, was drinking in Hollebone's terrace in Surry Hills. Hollebone walked out into the backyard, and Hazel followed and asked if he knew that Hodder was pitching for her. So Joey replied: 'Well, why don't you give him a fuck, instead of coming to me with your troubles?' Hollebone used to treat her like that. Hollebone would never say much — he was a real quiet type, a listener. He hardly ever opened his mouth and you'd never see him smile.

"Anyway, he came back in and sat opposite me on the lounge. I asked what was up and he said that Hazel had started again. So I asked who was it this time? And he said: 'Hodder.' I said: 'You don't believe her, do you?' And he replied: 'Of course not.' We had a couple more drinks and then, all of a sudden, he turned around to me and looked deadly serious and said: 'You're the bastard!' And when I asked why he replied: 'Because everyone in Sydney's knocking Hazel off — she tells me so. The only one she hasn't mentioned has been you. So you're the one.' But he was just having a go at me.

"Anyway, I went back around to his place the next day and he'd been drinking all night. He was a funny man. He had plenty of money. And in those days the hotels were only open for a certain number of hours each day because beer was rationed. We'd go into the hotels (the Surrey or the King's Head) and we'd be served straightaway because we'd give the barmaid 10 bob. Even if there were only three or four of us we'd still sling the barmaid 10 shillings, so even if she was up at the other end of the bar serving someone, as soon as she saw that we needed refills she'd run down to serve us. But Hollebone liked wine — not good wine, real cheap wine. The hotel would be packed and the barmaid would ask him what he wanted and he'd say a wine. So she'd have to stop pulling beers and go and find him some wine.

"So this night Joey and Hazel had been on the wine. And next morning I went around there about 10 am and they'd been arguing all night. He told me he couldn't put up with it much longer. And she replied that he didn't have to put up with it at all, that he could get out. One thing led to another, and the next minute he smashed a glass and jabbed her in the face. The jagged edge slashed a huge half-moon across Hazel's cheek. She needed about 40 stitches in it. She fell to the kitchen floor screaming and Hollebone said to me to come with him and forget about her. But I said we couldn't just leave her there. So he told me to look after her. I pulled a couple of towels from the rack and put them over her face and staggered out the door with her and flagged down a passing car. I told the driver that the lady had just fallen over and seemed to have injured herself on a glass or a spike or something. He said we'd better rush her to St Vincent's Hospital. Once we arrived at the casualty ward, and the doctors and nurses were attending to her, I left. Later the police pinched Joey for it. But, of course, Hazel wouldn't give him up, even though they knew she didn't fall over. That was the only time I saw Hollebone fly off so suddenly."

Years later veteran policeman Ray Blissett recalled to a

Sun–Herald reporter: "Hollebone was the coldest-blooded bloke I ever knew."

• • •

One favoured drinking spot of Hayes and Hollebone during the war years was the Plaza Hotel. Hayes recalls: "It had four little bars, sort of corner things, and there was only one woman serving behind each. Hollebone and I were in there one day with Ernie Means, and the barmaid was about 28 years old. She kept staring over at us, especially looking at Hollebone. Means asked Hollebone whether he knew her, because she was giving him a real good look. Hollebone replied that he'd seen her out of the corner of his eye a couple of times. So we decided to go over to that particular bar and I bought a drink and handed her a quid, and she gave me the change. Then, when it was his turn to buy a round of drinks, Hollebone handed her his quid — but she gave him back the £1 note without charging him for his shout. Then on Means's round, he put his quid over the bar and received the correct change. Now this went on for three or four rounds. Eventually Hollebone asked me whether I was receiving the correct change, and I said 'Yes.' But he said she wasn't charging him whenever it was his shout.

"So then he decided to have a go at her. Means and I walked away to another bar and left Hollebone talking to her, and he bought her a drink. About 90 minutes later she was half-drunk and Hollebone called me over. Her name was Elsie, and Hollebone told her that we were going to a party — even though this was only about 3 pm. He asked her to come along and said it was starting in about an hour. Initially she replied that she had to work. But Hollebone told her to forget about working and come with us now. Then he looked behind the bar and saw an empty carton, and he told her to fill it up with whisky and we'd have a real good party.

"So she filled it up alright — with whisky and wine and so on — and there were also three or four cartons of beer. Means carried out the beer and Hollebone carried the whisky and they put it all in Means's car. Then Hollebone went back in to bring Elsie. And he told her that, while she was there, she might as well grab whatever cash was in the till. So she did that, and then untied her apron and threw it on the floor and walked out and jumped in the car.

"We all went over to 'Cossie' Dugdale's place at Maroubra. In the end Hollebone and I stayed there drinking for two days. But first he took Elsie into a room and he had her in there for three or four hours before he threw her out. Later she was arrested because they knew where she lived, and two days later the police picked up Hollebone too. They placed Hollebone in a line-up, but she didn't pick him out. She insisted she couldn't see the man involved. Instead, she just copped the rap herself."

• • •

Hayes and Hollebone had teamed up permanently and, during the mid-1940s, collected standover money and mobster-style "wages" from a series of criminal haunts around Sydney's seedy inner suburbs.

As well as being on Joe Taylor's two-up payroll, "Later I was also collecting cash from Perce Galea and Eric O'Farrell at the baccarat," says Hayes. (Galea, Sydney's legendary "Prince of Punters", was the man who, after his champion colt Eskimo Prince won the 1964 Golden Slipper Stakes at Rosehill racetrack, caused a mini-riot by throwing a roll of £10 notes over the saddling paddock fence to the cheering crowd.) "Galea had two or three clubs then; the main one was the Carlisle Club, which Taylor finished up taking over, in Kellett Street, Kings Cross...

"Over the years I saw Taylor and Galea help lots and lots of people, especially Taylor. Later on, when I copped a life sentence, for example, I thought that would mark the finish of my £100-a-fortnight payroll money. But Joe Taylor and Dick Reilly knew my wife when I was going with her as a teenager and they always had the greatest respect for her. So when I later copped a life sentence (in 1952), Taylor called her around and explained that he was keeping me on the payroll and he'd give her £20 a week. It was to look after Topsy and the kids and it was still good money in those days. Topsy was also receiving the pension then, and Reilly would give her extra money for Christmas and for the kids' birthdays. And that went on all through my life sentence — Taylor never missed with the £20 a week...

"Anyway, the two-up in 1944 was in Reservoir Street, Surry Hills. Taylor and Wally Goddard and Herman 'The Jew' Singer ran it (they eventually bought Singer out) in a terrace 100 yards [90 metres] from Elizabeth Street. They had 'cockatoos' standing on the corner of Elizabeth Street. And whenever the game was 'going off' — about to be raided by the police — they were warned in advance. So they went across into Belmore Park and rounded up a dozen drunks. They paid them £2 each to stand

Perce Galea

An illegal gambling czar, he provided Chow Hayes with weekly standover payments from his baccarat dens and seedy casinos throughout the 1940s and early 1950s. Known as the "Prince of Punters" at the racetracks, Galea mixed in elite circles; here he is seen with the head of the Catholic Church in Sydney, Cardinal Sir Norman Thomas Gilroy (on his right), and the Australian Prime Minister, Sir Robert Menzies (on his left), at the Australia Hotel in 1964.

around and be arrested. Then they'd bail the drunks out straightaway and no-one ever appeared in court the next morning. The 'Big Game' was right next to Dobson's baths in Reservoir Street, while the 'Little Game' operated 24 hours a day behind the terrace around the corner...

"I was also collecting money from people at the races and one thing and another. For example, when I was introduced to Phil 'The Jew' Jeffs I bit him for £20 straightaway. He didn't put me on the payroll, but I could always go and bite him. And I made a habit of biting him every two or three weeks — for £10 or £20 or £30, depending on how he was going. He had the 400 Club in Paris House in the city."

The phrase "as rich as Phil The Jew" had become a common

expression in Sydney during the Depression. When Phil "The Jew" Jeffs died in 1945 his obituary in *Truth*, under the headline "Phil The Jew, King Of Thugs", began: "Phil the Jew, Sydney racketeer, gangster, drug pedlar, sly grogger, razor man, alleged phiz-gig for some detectives, gunman and wealthy friend of some politicians and many police. . ."

Jeffs had emerged during the razor-gang wars of the 1920s as the first of Sydney's modern criminal patriarchs, extorting protection money from illegal SP bookmakers and prostitutes (he had a number of callgirls working for him in Kings Cross flats) and operating as one of the leading cocaine dealers. With his "girls" Jeffs operated a blackmail racket, "the badger game", whenever they could hook a well-heeled victim. Jeffs would burst into the girl's flat posing as an irate husband, rave and curse his "wife", then gradually quieten and accept a cash payment to soothe his feelings and avoid further action.

In 1925 he was charged with manslaughter but acquitted. Surry Hills identity Mrs Eva O'Grady had been killed when Jeffs capsized an eight-seater automobile near Glenbrook; without a licence, he had been driving a car-load of roistering criminals and their girlfriends to the Blue Mountains.

One of his favoured ploys of the time was the choke-and-rob game in city lavatories and lanes. Once, while they were "playing" this game in 1928, a 26-year-old married woman, Mrs Ida Mavis Maddocks, was walking home along Bayswater Road, Kings Cross, when she heard a man's voice call from the shadows near the King's Lynn flats, "Hello, dear!" She started to hurry onward, but three men seized her and dragged her down a passageway into a flat where, according to a newspaper of the day, "she was unspeakably assaulted by seven men." Police rushed to the flat and arrested Jeffs and four others, all drunk. In court the woman said Jeffs had been the ringleader and described how the others held her while he hit her repeatedly with his open hand to make her submit to the rape without struggling.

Jeffs was at the centre of the infamous "Battle of Barton Avenue" one evening in May 1929 when 20 mobsters brawled on the ill-lit roadway with fists, razors and revolvers. The fight began because Jeffs was substituting boracic acid for cocaine. Several gangsters, including Charles Sorley and James Gregory, were battered unconscious; another, William Archer, was shot in the leg. As the wounded Archer ran to jump on the running board of a passing car, Jeffs pulled him off and kicked him

"Phil the Jew" Jeffs

Razor-gang veteran and racketeer "Phil the Jew" Jeffs ran two high-profile sly-grog dens, the 50–50 Club and the 400 Club, during the 1930s. Chow Hayes collected standover payments from him every fortnight.

repeatedly in the face. Jeffs then thrust a .38 into the ribs of a terrified taxi driver and disappeared from the scene of the brawl unharmed. But early next morning two men from the rival gang kicked down the door of the house where Jeffs was living in Kensington and shot him twice, in the shoulder and stomach.

After the razor-gang wars of the later 1920s, sly grog (illegal sales of alcohol at blackmarket prices) emerged as a major source of illicit incomes and standover revenues during the 1930s. Jeffs became Sydney's most prominent sly-grog trader, and among his seediest enterprises were the notorious sly-grog dens, the 50–50 Club and the 400 Club. *Truth* tagged the 50–50 Club in Darlinghurst "a rendezvous of street walkers and a house of assignation". Jeffs didn't charge the women anything to enter, but collected five shillings every time they went out with a customer. Another racket involved serving the street girls with lemon squash and water, though the mug escorts were charged for gin and squash.

Jeffs and society doctor Reginald Stuart-Jones opened the more up-market 400 Club in the early 1930s in the historic Paris House building near the corner of Phillip and King Streets. One woman later recalled the lively evenings at the 400 Club: "It was rather racier than the other nightspots — the place where gentlemen took ladies who weren't their wives. There were lots of charming private dining rooms. If you felt like singing they would wheel in a piano. They would even wheel in a double bed if you wanted it."

During 1936 *Truth*, campaigning against such debauched venues, reported that Sydney was "humming with stories of the bacchanalian gaiety, the drink, the scantily-clad girls." In one notorious incident at the 400 Club, two opposing criminal gangs broke into a fight with coshes and razors. In the middle of the fracas an innocent customer walked between the combatants and had an ear sliced off. He was a well-known business executive, so Jeffs personally rushed him to Sydney Hospital in his car and produced the ear from his pocket to be sewn on again.

Jeffs also purchased Oyster Bill's club at Tom Ugly's Bridge in southern Sydney in the late 1930s and refurbished it as a luxury roadhouse, complete with swimming pool and top band. But in October 1942 Jeffs's 400 Club was permanently shut down by a national security order.

However, when baccarat boomed in Sydney in 1944, Jeffs came out of a brief retirement to organise several schools in the Kings Cross area with the young Perce Galea and his mentor Siddy Kelly, another survivor of the razor-gang wars. (Back in September 1930 Kelly had been sentenced to five years' jail and a whipping following a particularly vicious razor-slashing in Melbourne.) Among Kelly and Galea's most infamous early Kings

Cross sites were the Mont St Clair Club in Victoria Street and the Club Enchantment in a lane behind William Street.

Soon baccarat games sprang up everywhere and the profits were large. Since 1942, when US troops began arriving in Australia, there had been a boom in both legal and illegal gambling. It was to continue until 1947, when returned Australian servicemen exhausted their back-pay.

11 Donald "The Duck" Day and Dr Reginald Stuart-Jones

Another source of income for Hayes after his release from Parramatta Jail in mid-1944 was Donald "The Duck" Day, whom Hayes had met in Parramatta Jail during Hayes's four-year armed robbery sentence.

Donny Day was a leading figure in Sydney's wartime sly-grog and illegal drug trades. When Day was shot dead in Surry Hills in early 1945, his wife, Irene Merle Day, told the court that society-page celebrity Dr Reginald Stuart-Jones was her husband's best friend and that Day, Stuart-Jones and another criminal, Alexander McDonald "Scotty" Jowett, dealt in liquor together. The court heard that Day and Stuart-Jones used the doctor's luxury yacht, *Sirocco,* to peddle whisky, liquor and drugs to American soldiers, and that their associates in hosting these floating sly-grog orgies on the harbour included the notorious criminals Dick Reilly and Chow Hayes. At one time, the court was told, the doctor had stocked 60 cases of liquor on the yacht.

Hayes recalls: "Day had two beer houses, one on either side of Elizabeth Street just up from the Dental Hospital. One had been a hotel years before and they'd turned it into a private residence — we knew it as The Private Hotel. Day's wife, Rene, was running the operation while 'The Duck' was in jail.

"Anyway, he told me to come and see him when I was released and he'd put a few quid my way. So one Sunday, about a fortnight after I was released, I decided to go around there. I went to the place he called The Private Hotel, but 'The Duck' wasn't there. (He and 'Chicka' Reeves often used to drive up into the bush and buy beer for, say, 30 shillings per dozen bottles and bring it back to Sydney and sell it for £3 per dozen. There were many beer houses going in those days. 'Paddles' Anderson had one in Redfern and anytime I met 'Paddles' I wouldn't have to ask for money, he'd just offer it to me.)

"Anyway, I went around to Day's place and at that point, I'd never met his wife. So I asked to see 'The Duck'. But she said he was away in the country and wouldn't be back until later that evening. I went away and had a few drinks with some mates at a hotel until about 7 pm. Then I decided to go back again. This time Day was there and he was very friendly and introduced me to his wife. He added that he'd take me down to a tailor the next morning to buy me several new suits. And he gave me a couple of hundred pounds in cash straight away — and said he'd also give me £50 a week to help him look after his places. He explained one bloke in particular, Billy McCarthy, was causing him a lot of trouble at that point.

"Then this big, good-looking fellow walked in with his wife. Day took me out into the kitchen and introduced me to 'The Doc', which was Stuart-Jones. Now Stuart-Jones had changed a lot, compared to when I'd seen him out at Bill McKell's place 10 years earlier. At first, I didn't realise it was the same bloke. We had a drink and he asked me: 'How are you travelling?' Well, I'd only been out of jail for a fortnight so I said I didn't have much money. He replied that he didn't have much on him, but he'd give me a grand tomorrow! Well, I immediately thought to myself that he was a big dope for promising such an outlandish amount, and we kept on drinking. But after he and his wife left, Day said to me: 'What time do you have to come tomorrow?' So I asked: 'What for?' Then he explained that this was Stuart-Jones — and that 'The Doc' was always fair dinkum. Day went on to explain that 'The Doc' was running the abortion rackets and all sorts of other bits and pieces, and that he was a very close friend of Day's. So Day said to be back there at 11 the next morning like the Doc had said, and I'd receive the grand for sure.

"I returned at 10.30 am and 'The Doc' duly arrived and, sure enough, he gave me £1000 in an envelope. I didn't count it out, I just whacked it in my side-pocket. We had a few drinks and he said that any time I was short of money I could contact him. He said he'd rather I didn't ring him, but just to contact Day. He said Day would then let 'The Doc' know about my problems and he'd give Day something for me. 'The Doc' was a very nice fellow — not just because he gave me money. He had style. The wife with him at that stage was Kath."

Legendary playboy, punter and nightclub-proprietor, Dr Reginald Stuart-Jones was probably the most colourful medico Sydney has known. The flamboyant abortionist and sly-grog

DR REGINALD STUART-JONES

Legendary playboy, punter and nightclub proprietor Dr Reginald Stuart-Jones operated a series of sly-grog dens during the 1940s in partnership with leading criminal Donny "The Duck" Day. The Doc handed Chow Hayes £1000 in an envelope when Hayes left jail in 1944 and thereafter Hayes received a weekly retainer to act as a hired gun for their illegal beer houses and "residentials".

trader was born in London and his family, then bearing the uncomplicated surname Jones, migrated to Ausralia when he was nine. After graduating in medicine from Sydney University in 1929 he returned to Britain and married his first wife, Shena, heiress to a chain of theatres. There too, to aid his rise in British society, he combined his middle and last names. He returned to Australia in the mid-1930s and in 1935 set up in Macquarie Street as a specialist in gynaecology.

During the 1930s Stuart-Jones was a partner in a succession of seedy nightspots, including the Lido in Ramsgate Avenue at Bondi Beach and, with Phil Jeffs, the 400 Club in Phillip Street. He also gained a reputation as a colossal gambler and racetrack punter, who owned horses, trotters and greyhounds.

In 1936 he divorced his first wife. Over the next few years he consorted with all the most infamous mobsters of the day, revelling in the notoriety and headlines. He always carried a revolver, which he would sometimes fire into the ceiling of crowded hotel bars in Woolloomooloo and Surry Hills while drinking with his criminal associates.

During the late 1930s he gained a reputation as the man to see if you were female and had an embarrassing problem requiring urgent treatment and discretion. It was through the expanding abortion rackets that he met the young standover man Richard Reilly, who later became his partner in this lucrative trade. In 1944 Stuart-Jones was charged with having "unlawfully used an instrument for a certain purpose" on a young woman after police raided one of his Macquarie Street rooms and found the patient (who had paid Stuart-Jones's secretary £40) "lying on a bed covered with a sheet".

That year Stuart-Jones married his second wife, Mary Kathleen, a much younger woman — but within four months he sued for divorce on the grounds of her adultery with the criminal Clifford Thompson (alias Cliffie Thomas, the name under which he fought as a welterweight boxer). Stuart-Jones had found his new wife in Thompson's pyjamas in a room in Leichhardt. However, husband and young wife were reconciled before the decree nisi became absolute.

Then followed one of the most sensational underworld sagas Sydney has seen. Just before midnight on 31 October 1944 Stuart-Jones was approached outside his luxury Moorish-style mansion, *Casa Clavel*, in Drumalbyn Road, Bellevue Hill, by two criminal acquaintances and asked to "look at a fellow in their car who was not too good." When he reached the car Dr Stuart-Jones suddenly found himself the prisoner of "Scotty" Jowett and Clifford "Cliffie Thomas" Thompson and was taken at gunpoint on a car trip to Maroubra designed as a ride to death. While two accomplices sat in the front seat, Jowett and Thompson told Stuart-Jones they intended to shoot him and throw his body over the Maroubra cliffs. Just after midnight their car reached Marine Parade at Maroubra, and Jowett put his gun close to Stuart-Jones's chest and pulled the trigger. Miraculously, Stuart-Jones was not fatally wounded — the bullet passed right through his body severely damaging a lung. Stuart-Jones then talked the confused "hit squad" into leaving him on the footpath outside the Vassilia private hospital in Frenchman's Road, Randwick. From there he was rushed to St Vincent's Hospital at Darlinghurst, where an emergency operation saved his life. The four men were subsequently charged with attempted murder. Thompson and Jowett were found guilty and sentenced to death — sentences which were later commuted to life imprisonment.

The court case hogged Sydney's headlines for a month. At one point *Truth* summed up the proceedings as containing "the most astounding evidence related in a *cause celebre* for a decade." Later *Truth* reported: "The trial was almost a fiesta for Sydney's underworld. Each day they arrived in cars. On one occasion nine handsome limousines parked outside the court were owned, according to a detective, by reputed gunmen. Their women, flamboyantly dressed, predominated in the galleries. They had changes of costumes each day in the manner of the society divorcee, and they obviously delighted in the abashed stares of ordinary citizens who also attended."

During the case, evidence was given of Dr Stuart-Jones's activities as a sly-grog trader, dope-pedlar, abortionist, partner of notorious criminals and wife-basher. The court also heard the sordid details of the criminal Thompson's love for Stuart-Jones's wife, Thompson's own wife's love for Jowett, and numerous other tidbits about love-affairs between society big-wigs and underworld figures. It also heard that the accused Thompson had shot and wounded himself in Long Bay Jail because his co-accused were "standing over" him.

Hayes recalls that incident clearly: "Cliffie Thomas shot himself — and the screw who brought in the gun got the sack over it. See, the OBS [observation unit] was for people on capital charges, and others who weren't the full quid. But they had so many prisoners in there at that point, that Superintendent Harold Vagg came around one day and said he was going to move some of us over into A Wing (that was the remand centre for anything). So over there they put Thomas and Jowett, along with 'Big Percy' Neville, 'Skinny' Brett, myself and another bloke who'd killed his girlfriend (she used to work on the Railway).

"Now Jowett was in Thomas's ear all the time, urging him to

make a statement that he shot Stuart-Jones and leave it in his cell, because they had no chance of beating it. Jowett was geeing him up, trying to talk Thomas into copping the lot. So Thomas told me one day that he had arranged for a gun to be brought in the next morning — he told me and 'Skinny' Brett while we were walking up and down the yard. I thought it was all part of some plan for a break-out. But then he explained he was going to pretend to commit suicide, in order to clear Jowett.

"Well, the next day he received the gun alright. A screw sneaked it in, and Thomas carried it with him all that day. Then he wrote a suicide note that night and brought it out into the yard and showed it to us the next morning. I immediately thought to myself: 'This is going to blow this place wide apart!' Anyway, Thomas said he was going to shoot himself at dinner-time, but he wasn't really going to try and kill himself. He showed us where he was going to aim the gun at his right shoulder. But 'Skinny' Brett told him not to do it there, but to do it on the left side instead — Brett actually wanted him to kill himself!

"Anyway, his cell was two doors along from mine. The 1 pm bell rang, and then the next one went at 1.10 pm, which signalled for prisoners to come out from their cells again. 'Big Percy' Neville had the cell between us. Just as the screw opened my cell and I walked out onto the ramp (the verandah outside my second-storey cell) we heard this almighty bang. It was only a .32, but the screw jumped and yelled: 'What was that?' I said it must've been a shit-tub falling or something. Then I went straight downstairs. Meanwhile they opened Neville's cell and then Thomas's cell and found him lying on the floor bleeding. The stupid screw thought he'd stabbed himself with a fork and sang that out to the other screws downstairs. The gun was on the floor. Anyway, they took Thomas over to Long Bay hospital until the ambulance came, and then they transferred him to Prince Henry.

"At one point we heard he was dead. Then we heard he wasn't dead but was in a serious condition. Meanwhile they found the suicide note, and they wanted to know how he got the gun. No-one would say anything, so we were locked in our cells for five days. The police came down to me and insisted I'd been in the yard with him and knew he had the gun. But I said: 'Don't be silly! If I knew he had a gun I wouldn't have even been in the yard!'... Anyway Jowett and Thomas were eventually convicted. But in the end they only served three or four years."

Meanwhile, in 1947 Stuart-Jones was forced to sell *Casa Clavel* to pay a huge bill for income tax evaded over the previous seven years. He maintained he had won the money on racehorses — and he was certainly involved in some spectacular punting during those years. In 1949 he and Mary Kathleen ended their stormy relationship, and, soon after, he married his third wife, Adeline Claudia, an Adelaide beauty queen less than half his age.

Stuart-Jones's wild living, reckless punting and murky involvement in the abortion rackets had by now earned him a sensational reputation. After a series of racing scandals during the 1950s he was eventually disqualified from racing by Queensland Turf Club stewards in 1958 after his horse Kingperion contested a race at Bundamba. By that time Chow Hayes's buddy, Dick Reilly, had become his personal driver and partner in the abortion rackets. Stuart-Jones died suddenly of a heart attack in 1961.

• • •

When Hayes took the job on Donny Day's payroll in mid-1944, one of his first duties involved ridding his employer of the unwanted attentions of well-known criminal Billy McCarthy. "He was trying to stand over Day," Hayes recalls, "and he was causing the business a lot of trouble. So Day said he wanted me to deal with McCarthy — to have a talk with him or whatever. Well, barely half an hour later McCarthy came and knocked on the door and Rene Day, 'The Duck's' wife, answered. She walked back inside and said McCarthy wanted to see Donnie. I asked Day if he had a gun on the premises, but he said "No." Well, at that stage, I'd have had to run a mile to grab a gun, so I said I'd go and talk to McCarthy first. I went to the door and told him that Day had just stepped out the back way and he'd be about half an hour. So I asked what did he want? McCarthy said he wanted £100 from Day. But I said I didn't think he'd be able to squeeze £100 because Day was 'going bad'.

"Then I suggested we go and have a drink while he waited for Day. We walked down to the Aurora Hotel run by Jack Lewis (directly opposite the Dental Hospital in Elizabeth Street) and had a few drinks. I really went there hoping to spot someone I knew and grab hold of a gun quickly. But there was no-one there. So when we left, I suggested we hop on a tram as it went past and catch it back up to 'The Duck's' place. We hopped on, but my intention was to grab the hook which the trams used to change over. I picked up the hook, and McCarthy asked what I wanted it for. I said a bloke had asked me to grab one for him, because his drain was blocked and he wanted to lift it up. Anyway, when we stepped off the tram, I suggested we walk around and use the back way into 'The Duck's' place. But as soon as we entered the laneway outside 'The Duck's' backyard I gave it to McCarthy. He needed about 80–90 stitches. But he was the toughest man I ever met. I hit him everywhere I could — all over the head and arms. As a matter of fact I thought he was dead. Of course he had it coming, in a way, but my intention was to kill him. But he didn't die. (A few years later he copped another 70–80 stitches after he was bashed at the Bookmakers' Clerks Club, alongside the Plaza Theatre. And another time he was ambushed by my mate, 'Kicker' Kelly, and another very good friend of mine, 'Greyhound Charlie' Bourke. Bourke shot McCarthy three times in the stomach and chest, while Kelly drove the car. McCarthy fell down and then he got up and chased them along Palmer Street. Of course they then drove away, and McCarthy collapsed in the gutter and was eventually taken to St Vincent's Hospital.)

"When I gave it to McCarthy, they took him to Prince Alfred Hospital. After that he never went near 'The Duck' again. But he was the hardest man I ever saw."

A decade later William Joseph "Billy" McCarthy, 38, was found by an air hostess lying face-down in Flood Street, Bondi, at 2.15 one morning in March 1957. His clothing was saturated with blood and an empty cartridge shell lay on the ground nearby. McCarthy had been shot in the back at almost point-blank range and later died in St Vincent's Hospital.

The *Sun–Herald* reported McCarthy was "a Sydney criminal who was hated and feared in the underworld of three States", and that he was "the State's most shot at and beaten up man". Four previous attempts had been made to kill McCarthy, and at the time of his murder a bullet was still lodged near his spine from a shooting in 1944. In that incident "Greyhound Charlie" Bourke had pumped three .45 slugs into McCarthy at Woolloomooloo after he'd attempted to hold up a two-up school. Police then took his dying depositions, but he survived. On another occasion, the newspaper noted, McCarthy had been beaten unconscious with an iron bar (this was, in fact, the beating with the tram hook) in a street a few hundred metres from the headquarters of the Sydney CIB. Later McCarthy was attacked in Brisbane with a butcher's knife and had his throat slashed. He recovered after hovering between life and death for a week. In Melbourne he was stabbed in the chest, but again survived.

After his murder, police said McCarthy, whose record for stealing offences spanned more than 20 years, had a "multitude of enemies but very few friends"; that he "was a man subject to a number of violent acts, at times with guns and at other times with other instruments — once in connection with chains and a mattock handle"; that he was regarded as "one of the worst types" of the Sydney underworld; and that "he had a reputation of being a standover man and had been in considerable trouble with police."

A notorious Sydney criminal, Charles Edward "Chicka" Reeves, then a 30-year-old painter, was quickly charged with McCarthy's murder. At Reeves's trial, Crown Prosecutor R. R. Kidston, QC, alleged Reeves shot McCarthy after a quarrel over a woman at the Avalon Sports Club at Bondi Junction earlier that night. Kidston added that Reeves had previously had possession of a .45 Colt automatic pistol, and that a cigarette lighter found at the scene of the shooting was one given to Reeves by a female friend, Miss Faye Payton.

McCarthy's mother and brother both told how McCarthy, shortly before he died in hospital, had said he'd been drinking with Reeves. And the nightclub proprietor told how McCarthy had been drinking in the Club with Reeves, another man and a woman. McCarthy was "fairly drunk and kept singing." At one point Reeves yelled at McCarthy: "She's not going with you. You're an animal!" The proprietor told how McCarthy later left the club before Reeves and the others.

The Crown case was that after McCarthy made insulting remarks to Reeves's female companion, McCarthy was challenged by Reeves to a fight. The two later met at Waverley Oval where Reeves shot McCarthy in the back with a .45 calibre revolver.

Miss Payton, who admitted she had worked as a prostitute in East Sydney, told how "almost every day for seven days a week" she gave Reeves £20 to £30. She said Reeves drank heavily and that "he was a madman in drink". She told a shocked courtroom how Reeves had once inflicted wounds on her face with a tin-opener — and boasted that the wounds were "the Reeves brand". She told how, on another occasion, she was going to shoot Reeves but her gun jammed.

Justice Manning eventually directed the jury to acquit Reeves of McCarthy's murder due to "insufficient evidence". He said that, according to the law, the only evidence that was admissible had been insufficient — although he noted that it was a case which "aroused the greatest suspicion".

Chow Hayes asserts: "'Chicka' Reeves definitely shot and killed McCarthy. Reeves pulled up in a car and jumped out and shot him in the back. But Reeves was able to produce a fake alibi . . . Reeves was also on Donny Day's payroll for years."

• • •

"Greyhound Charlie" Bourke, who shot McCarthy in 1944, was one of Sydney's better-known thugs during the early 1940s. A standover man and part-time greyhound trainer, he accumulated a long list of police-station and courtroom appearances, including: acquittal for the attempted murder of Jordan Eastaughffe in May 1939; refusal to speak to police after he was shot in the back in October 1943; charges involving sly grog offences in October 1945; charges of housebreaking, stealing and receiving at Leichhardt in March 1947; and two charges of shooting with intent to murder in December 1952.

Chow Hayes knew Charlie Bourke well. "I liked Bourke," he explains, "and I dealt with him over many years. But one night in late 1944 I remember particularly clearly. Some of my mates were up at Donny Day's place in Elizabeth Street, The Private Hotel. 'The Duck' was away and Harry 'Bronze' Monsetti, Arthur Bedford and Jackie Walsh were having a bit of a party, and they had three or four sheilas with them.

"Well, Charlie Bourke pulled up in a taxi, and he wanted to see Donny Day. He wanted to bite Day for a few quid (Bourke was pretty sweet with Day and could bite him for £50 or £100 any time he wanted it). But when Bourke knocked on the door, Monsetti answered it. Bourke said he wanted to see 'The Duck', but Monsetti replied that he wasn't there. So Bourke asked when Day would be home. Monsetti answered that he didn't know. However, Bourke could hear singing and the party in the background and he demanded to know: 'Who's in there?' Monsetti replied: 'What's it to do with you?' Then Bourke said he thought 'The Duck' was inside, but Monsetti said he wasn't and insisted that it was a private party.

"Bourke said he was coming inside to have a look. But Monsetti retorted: 'No, you're not. You'll have to take my word that he's not here.' Then Monsetti added: 'Tell me your name and I'll give him a message when he comes back.' (Monsetti, at this stage, didn't know who Bourke was — and, as a matter of fact, he shitted himself the next day when he found out!) Bourke then moved to barge his way in and 'Bronze', who wasn't a bad fighter, king-hit him. When Bourke went down, Bronze also gave him the boot. Then Walsh walked out and, though he knew Bourke slightly, he didn't know what was going on. He was followed by Bedford, who didn't know Bourke and joined in with Monsetti by also putting in a bit of boot.

"Just then I pulled up in a car with a sheila. I walked into the hallway and saw them giving this fellow a kicking. For a minute I couldn't see who it was because their victim was covered in blood. Finally I looked down closely and realised it was Bourke, whom I'd known very well for years. Then I yelled: 'Oh, jees, what are you blokes doing? Cut it out, he's a good fellow!'

"Then 'Bronze' started to tell me the story. But I pulled Bourke, who was half-unconscious, out onto the footpath. I said to him: 'I'm very sorry this happened to you, Charlie.' He said: 'So am I. I'll be back, Chow!' I asked whether he wanted to come in the car and I'd take him to hospital. But he insisted that he'd be alright if I could just hail a taxi for him. So I said I'd do that, but he shouldn't wait outside 'The Duck's' place; rather, he should struggle down to the corner about 50 or 60 yards [45–55 metres] away. Then I sang out to Walsh to order a taxi for down on the corner and I took Bourke down there. When the taxi arrived I put Bourke in it and asked if he'd be alright. He said yes. Then I returned to Day's place where 'Bronze' told me the whole story.

"He insisted that Bourke was a cheeky little bastard who'd tried to barge in. So I told 'Bronze' that, in fact, Bourke was a vicious gunman and that 'Bronze' had better be very careful from now on. I advised him that, after he'd had another drink, he'd better go, because Bourke mightn't recognise Bedford and Walsh again, but he'd certainly recognise Monsetti. I thought Bourke was going to come back that night with a gun, maybe accompanied by two or three offsiders. So Bronze went (he was living at Balmain at the time) and I stayed there until 6.30 the next morning. Walsh had already gone, but Bedford stayed on with me. Finally I left Bedford at the Railway, and went home to Thomas Street, where I had a shower and breakfast before heading for bed.

"Now my wife would never wake me in the mornings. I always

told her not to wake me unless it was very urgent. But about 10.30 am Donny Day and Rene Day came over. Rene had been at the house during the party the night before, and she knew Bourke. Donny told my missus that he had to speak to me urgently. She said she wouldn't wake me herself, but if they wanted to risk it they could go into my bedroom. So Don and Rene came up into the bedroom and woke me and I received the shock of my life. Day said Bourke wanted to see me and I asked: 'What for?' Day said he didn't know, but Bourke wanted to see me straightaway. Well, I told Day that Bourke might want to see me straightaway, but he could go and get fucked! I said I'd meet Day at 3.30 that afternoon at 'The Duck's' place. Bourke was living down the Woolloomooloo end of Palmer Street at the time, and Day explained Bourke was home in bed. So 'The Duck' went off to tell Bourke that I would meet Day at 3.30 pm, and then we'd head down to Bourke's place in Palmer Street.

"Later in the day I left Thomas Street about 3 pm and arrived at 'The Duck's' place at 3.30 pm. We had a drink and then Day said we'd better head off because he'd told Bourke we'd be there by 4 pm. Bourke lived at 286 Palmer Street and, at one point, he and Nellie Cameron lived there together. When we arrived a woman opened the door, and Day explained I was the bloke Charlie wanted to see. I walked upstairs to his bedroom, where Mick O'Hara was sitting in a chair beside the bed. (O'Hara had previously knocked off 'Baldy' Mason.) Bourke looked an awful mess — eyes all puffed up so he could hardly see, and lumps and bumps everywhere. Later I found out the reason Bourke hadn't returned to Day's place the night before was because he was so knocked around and sick that he couldn't.

"When Day and I walked in Bourke immediately asked if I had a gun. I said no, I'd come down to see him. He could only see out of one eye and then he asked me: 'Who was that bastard I had the stink with?' I replied: 'A fellow I work with, why?' He declared: 'I'm going to kill the bastard!' And I said: 'Do you think you should?' Bourke replied: 'Fucking look at me!' And all the while he had his right arm under the sheet. Then Bourke inquired: 'Do you know Mick?' I replied I did — that I'd been in jail with him. Then Bourke insisted he wanted to know the name of the bloke who'd beaten him up, but I said I didn't know it. Then he added: 'He's a mate of yours.' To which I answered: 'Yeah, I work with him, so you could class him as a mate.' Then he asked: 'Well, why did he do this to me?' So I answered: 'Well, why did you barge your way in?' Then he demanded: 'Are you going to tell me his name?' But I replied: 'No, I'm not going to tell you his name.' Then he said: 'No, of course you're not. So I'll tell you his name. It's 'Bronze' Monsetti!' Bourke knew he came from Balmain and everything else about him. He knew every detail: that Bedford and Walsh were the other blokes, and even the names of the sheilas they were with. Rene Day had obviously already told him, and I think Donny Day might have told him too.

"Then Bourke said: 'There's no doubt about you, Chow, you're fucking solid. Anyone else would've told me.' And with that he threw the sheet back and he had a .38 pointed right at my guts. So I told Bourke we had no argument between us, but 'Bronze' was a good bloke and I wouldn't like to see Bourke kill him. I added that, if he looked at it fairly, he would see that 'Bronze' was in the right. It had been a private party and Bourke was the one who barged in, and Day was not there — he'd been up in the country collecting beer.

"Bourke knew all that, and he said he'd think about it. He asked if I'd bring Monsetti down to Palmer Street in a couple of days. But I had no intention of taking 'Bronze' down there, because I knew they'd knock him off. So I replied: 'No, Charlie, I won't bring him down here. But I'll tell you what I'll do. When you get better we'll arrange a meeting. It could even be at 'The Duck's' place. But I'm telling you he's a good fellow. He's even been in jail and he's never given anyone up. But he's not a gunman and, if the truth be known, there'd have been no trouble if he'd known who you were or that you were there to bite "The Duck". He'd have asked you to come in, without barging your way in.'

"Then Bourke laughed and said: 'You're not going to lecture me, are you?' And I answered: 'No, I'm not going to lecture you. But I wouldn't like to see you knock him.' Well, of course, I couldn't have stopped Bourke if he wanted to knock Monsetti, unless I really wanted to stick my own head into it. Not that I was afraid of Bourke, because as far as I was concerned Bourke was nothing. But I didn't want to see 'Bronze' knocked off.

"I didn't see Bourke again for about 10 days. Then he sent another message and I met him in the Tradesman's Arms Hotel. I went down with 'The Duck' and I didn't have a gun. But as soon as I walked in, Bourke said: 'I'll see you in the shithouse.' Well, I thought this looked nice — why did he want to corner me in the shithouse? Why not speak to me out here? And I was a bit more cautious after he'd had a gun under the sheet the last time. But I knew I couldn't show any weakness, so I had to go. However I kept my wits about me and I was very wary. If Bourke had put his hand in his waistband or went for his coat or hip pockets I'd have jumped him. But he merely explained: 'Look, Chow, I've been talking to a few of the boys and they say that bastard's not a bad fellow. It was my fault so I'm prepared to forget it. But will he back-up?' Well, I insisted: 'No, he won't back-up! Not in a fit! He's not into that sort of thing.' So then Bourke asked whether I'd arrange a meeting. I replied: 'Yes, but only on my terms.' Bourke asked what were they. So I insisted I'd meet Bourke somewhere and we'd travel by car and I'd take him to Monsetti. But I added that, before he entered the car, he'd have to let me frisk him for a gun.

"So I met Bourke in the Tradesman's Arms the next day. I'd arranged for Monsetti to be sitting on a seat in Belmore Park waiting for us. And I explained to 'Bronze' that Bourke just wanted to meet him and hear 'Bronze' apologise for the bashing he'd given him. So Bourke and I jumped into the car and, as we were driving back to the park, he said: 'I don't have a rod. Do you want to search me?' I replied: 'No, you gave me your word you wouldn't have a gun — and, anyway, it's broad daylight and you'd only be giving yourself up if you did anything.' Then he asked where we were going. I merely replied that I'd tell him when we arrived there. We left the car in Pitt Street, near the Tivoli Theatre, and started to walk to Belmore Park where Monsetti was still waiting on the seat. Bourke didn't really recognise him. He looked at Monsetti closely and then asked: 'Are you sure you're the bastard who went on with me?' Anyway, they had a talk and then we went to the Hotel Sydney and had a few drinks and they shook hands and that was the end of it.

"I liked Charlie Bourke. I think the main reason he left the Monsetti incident at that was because he was collecting quite a few quid at the time from one thing and another. He figured that if he knocked off Monsetti he might find himself out at 'The Bay' on remand for three or four months and he'd lose a lot of business and contacts. Bourke was protecting a large number of people around that time. One was Thommo, the bloke they said committed suicide many years later in Anzac Parade. He had half the Loo tied up in SP betting at that point and Bourke and O'Hara and Frank Green were all looking after him." (Big punter

William Joseph Thompson had run a gambling school in Palmer Street, East Sydney, until he was shot dead in a car outside his Kensington home in July 1960. Over £1000 in cash was found on Thompson's body.)

Bourke's career in violence and the underworld dated back to the 1920s. "Charlie had escaped from Boggo Road Jail in Brisbane during his younger days," Hayes recalls, "and that's how he came to Sydney. After 18 months they knew where he was, but they didn't bother to extradite him... He shot several people over the years. One was a taxi driver, whom Charlie said was on with his missus. Charlie shot him in bed down at Woolloomooloo...

"Bourke was particularly sweet with Stuart-Jones and Day — until the time he conned Stuart-Jones for £10,000. He told Stuart-Jones he needed the cash because he was in trouble with the police — which he wasn't — and he had to pay £10,000 to settle the matter. So Stuart-Jones gave it to him. But later Stuart-Jones found out (he had very good contacts inside the police force) that Bourke wasn't in trouble. From that point he'd done his dash with Stuart-Jones."

Charlie Bourke became one of the principals behind the Club Enchantment when baccarat boomed around Kings Cross at the end of the War. Later he became a prominent standover collector from the city's Greek clubs, and trained greyhounds for many of the other baccarat school bosses of the 1950s and early 1960s.

"Greyhound Charlie" was executed late one evening in February 1964. The coroner declared Bourke had been "ruthlessly and viciously exterminated", and police commented that they regarded it as "a particularly vicious killing, carried out with callous determination."

Bourke usually left his home each Sunday between 9.30 pm and 10 pm to travel to the city, ostensibly to visit people with whom he was associated as an owner and trainer of greyhounds. On the night of his murder he arrived back home at Norton Street, Randwick, around midnight following visits to several of his clients at the Kings Cross baccarat schools. He parked his car in the street and walked about three metres up a grassy slope to his front door. A brick wall and garden shrubs divided Bourke's home from the house next door, and from this hiding place a gunman fired 10 shots at Bourke with a semi-automatic .22 calibre rifle. Bourke fell, the gunman jumped the wall and, pausing to reload, approached Bourke's slumped body. Standing over it, he emptied another 10 slugs into Bourke's neck and back.

Two men were seen running from the house. (Two of Sydney's wildest gunmen of the 1960s, Raymond Patrick "Ducky" O'Connor and John James Warren were both later mentioned in police investigations as likely participants in Bourke's murder.) Rumours swept Sydney that the murder arose from trouble over betting transactions involving greyhounds. At the coroner's inquest — in the understatement of the decade — the police evidence was that "because of Bourke's activities in past years we feel he may have made some enemy who would have liked to see some harm come to him."

• • •

Meanwhile, Donny "The Duck" Day's activities became a central part of Hayes's life during the War. "Donny Day had two or three things going during the war years," Hayes explains. "When an American ship came into port, Day would drive down to the wharves and ask to see the captain. He was a good talker and he'd explain to the captain that he had two beer houses, and he had women there and so on. And he'd emphasise that he didn't want to see the sailors running around the streets being ripped off, and that at his places they'd be well looked after. (On the street corners the conmen would sell whisky bottles which were half-full of tea and rip off the Yanks, but Day wouldn't do that.) The visiting captains got to know Day well — and he'd make sure to arrange that the Yanks were driven back to the ship at the end of the night by car or taxi, and he'd sling some cash to the captains too. And often he'd also take them down half a dozen bottles of whisky or something.

"One racket Day and Stuart-Jones had going was to encourage a moll to find out how much money a sailor had in his bank account. The sailors had to keep a certain amount for their wives, mothers and families back in the USA. Some of them had $US4000 or $US5000. So Day and Stuart-Jones would take a moll down to the ship, where they'd talk to the captain. They'd quietly explain that the serviceman was with this young lady last night, and a couple of nights before that and, as a matter of fact, over the last two or three weeks. Then they'd emphasise that they didn't want any publicity about it; but she was pregnant. And 'The Doc' would say she had to have an abortion and she had to be looked after. If they knew the sailor had $US6000, they'd ask for $US4000. And the Yank would only be too pleased to pass over the $US4000 because he didn't want his relations back in the United States to know...

"One day Jackie Walsh and I were at Day's beer house and Day asked us to drive two negroes down to the wharves and see they were returned to their ship. 'The Duck' gave them a bottle of whisky between them. On the way down they said they'd give us some cartons of cigarettes. So when we reached the ship we went aboard to pick up the cigarettes, and it was like a palace. We walked into the storeroom and they told the storeman that they wanted half a dozen cartons of Camels for us. But while they weren't looking, Walsh pocketed one of the official stamps with 'US Navy shipments' on it. A package bearing that seal meant it hadn't been opened."

That official seal became the key to a veritable goldmine for Hayes and his cohorts. Hayes sums up bluntly: "We made thousands of pounds out of it — and I mean thousands! When we used the seal, we'd stick a piece of paper about five inches [12 centimetres] wide across the top of a box and then stamp it three times — once on each end and one in the middle — to show the box hadn't been opened...

"In one incident I ran into my old mate, Benny Gorman. He had this box which was supposedly full of cigarettes. It was done up with string. I took him to John Maggs's grocery shop in Shepherd Street, Chippendale, where I'd been dealing for years because I lived nearby. Gorman told me the box contained cigarettes and I had no reason to disbelieve him. I went in and asked Maggs if he wanted to buy a carton of American cigarettes — Gorman waited outside in the car — and Maggs said, "Yes." There were 50 cartons in each box and Gorman wanted £1 a carton. Maggs agreed and Gorman carried the box in and put it on Maggs's kitchen table. Maggs gave Gorman £50, and then we went down to the Broadway Hotel and had a drink and Gorman gave me £25. (Normally, Maggs would then have sold each carton for 25 shillings.) But a couple of days later I heard that Maggs wanted to see me. When I went back he told me the box had been full of sand and waste paper. So I made sure he received his money back. But it put an idea into my head — and soon after we started on something we called 'the cabbage leaves rort'."

12 The Cabbage Leaves Rort

The caper that Hayes and his mates tagged "the cabbage leaves rort" involved Hayes, Jackie Walsh (who had actually stolen the official 'US Army' rubber stamp from the ship), Arthur Bedford, Harry "Bronze" Monsetti and Eddie Weyman. For six months in 1944 it provided them with more cash than they were ever likely to see again in their lives.

"The five of us would go down to the fruit markets near Chinatown," Hayes explains, "and collect all the loose cabbage leaves from the gutters. The street-sweepers used to push them into piles at each corner. Cabbages were just the right weight for our plan. We took them back to Jackie Walsh's place and weighed them. Then we took a genuine box of cigarettes and weighed them — and they were exactly the same weight. So once we became organised, we paid the street-sweepers with the big brooms £5 a day to keep all the cabbage leaves for us. We'd drive down with a truck and load all the cabbage leaves. Then we'd go away and pack them up in cigarette boxes. And after the seal went on them, you'd swear blind the boxes had never been opened. Then we started selling them.

"We were picking up the cardboard cigarette boxes from Palmer Street in Woolloomooloo, where Anthony Horderns had a warehouse. The Navy took it over, and that's where they stored all their cigarettes which weren't on the ships. We bribed a couple of American blokes down there to keep the best boxes for us. We were slipping them whisky, not cash.

"We sold the cabbage boxes all over Sydney for £50 a box, and that was supposedly for 50 cigarette cartons in each box.

"One day I was having a drink in the Surry Hotel. A chap walked in and told me Jackie Finnie — the former boxer who was mixed up in a couple of shootings — wanted to see me. I didn't know what it was about, but the message was to go and see him at the Australian Hotel, just down from the police station in Newtown. So I said, 'Okay,' but then it slipped my mind and I forgot about it. A fortnight later, Finnie himself came and saw me at Eddie Weyman's house. He explained that a well-known copper, Detective Sergeant Jack 'Long Tack Sam' Harrison (a really tall bloke), had been "half in" with a barber–tobacconist from King Street, Newtown, to whom we'd sold eight boxes of cabbage leaves for £400. Finnie warned me that Harrison wanted his half of the cash back. But I explained we couldn't return it because it was already spent.

"Eventually, I said I'd talk to the others and see what they thought. But I knew then that we wouldn't be returning any of it, because once you gave one sucker his money back, then they'd all be demanding it back. So I mentioned it to the others and, a few days later, I went back and saw Finnie and confirmed that £200 of it belonged to Harrison. Finnie reckoned he wasn't being paid anything himself — that he was only doing a favour for 'Long Tack Sam'. So I arranged to meet Finnie that night in Union Street, Newtown, where I said I'd give him the money.

"Jackie Walsh drove me up there around 8 pm. When I stepped from the car Finnie was already waiting outside a fruit and vegetable shop. I stopped about five yards [five metres] from him and said: 'Here you are. Here's your money!' I fired a shot (I had a .32) but it only hit him in the shoulder. It wasn't much of a wound, it went straight through. Finnie started to run and I fired again but missed him. I left him in the gutter. He never went to a hospital for treatment, but instead visited a doctor he knew. So that fixed him up — he never came back again.

"But some time later I was at Central Police Court appearing on a minor matter, when I felt a sudden tap on the shoulder. I looked around and it was 'Long Tack Sam'. He said: 'That was a nice thing you did to Finnie.' Then he warned me: 'If you ever put your foot inside Newtown, I'll load you up so tightly you'll be in jail for years!' And I knew he was fair dinkum, because in those days the senior police in places like Leichhardt and Newtown — unlike the men from the CIB who had a roving commission and could go everywhere — stayed in their districts and literally ruled their areas. So, from that point, I made sure I stayed away from Newtown."

"Long Tack Sam" Harrison was a tough, much-feared detective of the old school. Years later former policeman Ray Blissett recalled to a *Sun-Herald* reporter an incident involving Harrison and fellow detective Jack Healy, who was nicknamed "The Crusher". The two policemen were cruising along Cooks River Road one day in an A-model Ford when Harrison spotted a criminal named "Chocolate" Gordon, strolling along the street. The lanky detective jumped from the car and emptied his pistol at Gordon, who was running so fast, according to Blissett, that he left both shoes behind. By this time "The Crusher" had wheeled the car around, ready to give chase, and called out: "Come on Tack, we'll catch him!"

". . . . him, let him go," Harrison leisurely replied. "That'll teach him to swear at me in pubs."

• • •

A decade earlier Jackie Finnie had been involved in a celebrated fracas involving Chow Hayes's long-time friend, Dick Reilly. The episode reached its violent climax with the murder in 1937 of fellow hood Clarrie Thomas.

Hayes explains: "Clarrie Thomas was one of the youngest men in New South Wales ever to go to the First World War. He was only about 15½ at the time, but he was a big man. When he came out of the Army he became a standover man and I knew him pretty well. At one point he even arranged for a friendly priest to preach a sermon about how the police were unjustly booking people for consorting.

"Clarrie Thomas was also a gunman and standover man. One evening he and Jackie Finnie went to the Ginger Jar nightclub (which later became the Ziegfeld Club). My mate Dick Reilly was the doorman and bouncer at the time. Thomas and Finnie tried to stand over Reilly. They basically wanted money from the nightclub owner. But Dick's job, as the doorman, was to protect the owner from blokes like Thomas and Finnie. So Reilly grabbed a gun and followed them up Castlereagh Street and shot Clarrie Thomas dead outside the Windsor Hotel. Reilly was charged with murder, but he pleaded self-defence and was acquitted . . .

"Ironically, both Jackie Finnie and Dick Reilly later worked for Dr Stuart-Jones."

• • •

Meanwhile Hayes and his mates continued to con half of Sydney's shady characters with the cabbages rort.

"One time I was in the bar at Randwick racecourse and spotted this fellow who had a mixed business," Hayes recalls. "We'd conned him for £1200 from the cigarettes two months earlier. He was with two other fellows and I noticed him continually looking at me. He kept staring and I knew I'd seen the face somewhere before. Finally he gave me half a smile, but I took no notice. When we'd finished our drinks, we had to pass them to leave the bar. As I walked past, he said: 'How are the cabbage leaves going?' And I replied: 'What do you mean?' He just smiled and said that, obviously, he couldn't go to the police. And that was the beauty of the cabbages rort — none of our victims could go to the police, because they thought they were buying stolen goods and the police might charge them with receiving. As the old saying goes: 'If there are no receivers, there are no thieves.' Anyway, the bloke at the races just laughed and said: 'Forget it. I was a fool and I fell into it.' He was very nice about it, though I kept pretending I didn't know what he was talking about. Eventually I just walked away.

"Another bloke, named Harry Barker, ran a hotel in Harris Street, Ultimo. We'd arranged to sell four boxes to Barker. But he said not to bring them to the hotel. He arranged to meet us with the £200 at 2 pm outside the White Bay Hotel at Balmain. When we arrived Bedford and I walked in and had a drink at the bar, while Walsh stayed over on the other side of the road with the truck. Barker arrived and said he was too busy for a drink. He had another couple of blokes with him. We walked over to the truck and he glanced in to see the boxes, and you'd swear blind they'd never been opened. So he said: 'That's fair enough. But I can't give you £200. I'll give you £40 a box.' That was £160 in total. But I insisted: 'No deal, because we're selling to everyone else at £50 a box.' However, Barker remained firm and declared: 'Take it or leave it.' Finally, as he began to walk off, I said: 'Okay, we don't want to lump them back to the city. Give us the £160.' But of course, while he thought he was touching us for £40, we were actually touching him for £160.' And later when Barker came to see me, he laughed about it and said: 'We were both in the same boat — I tried to do you, but you did me.'

"Another time, 'Bronze' Monsetti strolled around to a barber shop in Elizabeth Street, just off Reservoir Street, for a haircut. But he bumped into two Greek fellows we'd done with the cabbages a few days earlier. Monsetti immediately ran off, but they chased him all over Surry Hills. They'd have killed him if they'd caught him. Luckily he eventually made it to Weyman's place, and by that time he was as white as a ghost.

"Over a period of months we sold the cabbages to everyone. I remember the first time I met Perce Galea, was when we sold him 12 boxes of cabbage leaves. He was running a gambling club in Pitt Street, just down from the corner of Park Street. It was upstairs, opposite Lowes, on the same side as the Lyceum Theatre. Monsetti and I fronted him, after 'Paddles' Anderson put us onto him. ('Paddles' had a beer house in York Street at the time.) Later I became good friends with Galea, and collected money from him for years and years."

• • •

One day during that time Jackie Walsh and Hayes were driving down Park Street in central Sydney as the USA Military Police were picking up deserters. "Right in front of the Town Hall, where Park Street meets George Street, the traffic began to bank up behind them," Hayes recalls. "Two MPs had run over and grabbed a bloke and thrown him into the back of their wagon. But they replaced the bolt on the outside without locking it. Then the MPs walked back around and hopped in the front beside the driver. Walsh and I followed them down George Street in our car, until the traffic was held up again. Then I told Walsh I wouldn't come back to our car but I'd meet him at the Railway. I jumped from the passenger's seat and walked up to the wagon and looked in. There were four deserters inside. So I said: 'Righto, boys. Out you go!' I pulled the lock open and, of course, they nearly trampled me in their hurry to jump out. They raced off up the road and I just kept walking and turned into King Street and went back to the Railway!"

• • •

Meanwhile Hayes and his team were pocketing astronomical amounts of cash from the cabbages — between £8000 and £10,000 a week at its height, which divided into £1500 to £2000 each.

Eventually however, greed soured their lucrative operation. Hayes recalls: "Just down from the Clare Inn Hotel, Balfour Street runs off Broadway into City Road. There were about 30–40 flats there. But if you walk through a side-doorway — seemingly into one of the ground-floor flats — you actually walk into the back-lane. But anyone who didn't know the layout would think you were going into a flat. So we had a bloke lined up to buy 24 boxes — that was £1200 worth of cigarettes. We had them in the truck in the lane. Bedford was the front-man this time. He was out in the street. I was on the truck with Jackie Walsh, and Monsetti and Weyman were together near the door.

"After a while the bloke and Bedford began arguing about whether the cigarettes or the money would be handed over first. Bedford kept insisting that he only lived inside the 'flat' (which was really the doorway into the lane but looked like a flat front door) so he wasn't going to run away or anything. Eventually Bedford told the bloke to wait while he went inside and discussed it with his brothers. So he pretended to walk into the 'flat', and came into the lane. Then Weyman said he'd deal with it and went out and told the bloke that, though they lived in the 'flat' there, they'd been taken the other day and weren't handing over the cigarettes first. Then the bloke suggested his two mates would come into the 'flat' and carry the boxes out. But of course Weyman said they weren't coming into his 'flat', that he had three or four workers of his own inside and they'd carry the cigarettes out.

"Eventually they agreed that while we carried the boxes out and put them on his truck he'd pay over the money. So, as each box was placed on the truck, he paid Weyman £50. When the last two boxes were loaded, we went back through the door, making out that we were returning inside the 'flat', and we jumped onto our truck and drove away. The rest of us went back to Weyman's place in Surry Hills to split the money, but Weyman never showed up. After a couple of hours, I walked across the road to Thommo's two-up game. I was talking to Eddie Stewart when I suddenly saw Weyman coming up Reservoir Street into Mary Street where he lived. But he went in via the back gate.

"I gave him about five minutes and then I walked back over. They were all in the kitchen: Weyman, Bedford, Walsh, Monsetti, Weyman's wife Edna and her sister Violet Walsh. (Edna was a Walsh before she married Weyman. Monsetti was on with Violet.) They were all staring at one another and there was drink on the table. I asked why they were all down in the dumps. Weyman replied that he didn't have the cash. He said that as soon as we all disappeared into the laneway, they'd grabbed him and taken the money back. Well, I believed him, we all did, and we just forgot about it. Anyway we earned more that night...

"About three weeks later Bedford walked into the London Hotel in Reservoir Street, just up from the two-up game. We were all drinking in there: Weyman, Walsh, Monsetti, Lawrie McKeon and a few others. Bedford said he wanted to see me outside. We went and sat in his car and I asked: 'What's going on?' Bedford explained that one of the blokes whom Weyman claimed had taken the money (not the bloke who'd originally paid over the money, but one of his helpers) was not a bad sort of a chap. And he'd told Bedford that they'd had a laugh that we'd done them for the £1200. So it seemed obvious that Weyman had been lying and had kept our money for himself.

"I went back into the pub, and then later that night we conned someone else for £600 worth of cigarettes. Afterwards we returned to Weyman's place in Mary Street (he'd bought the house for about £900 with some of the cash from the cabbage rort). Whenever we went there for a drink, after the pubs had closed, we'd buy some sly grog in a sugar bag. A dozen bottles in a sugar bag cost about £3, and we'd buy a dozen sugar bags at a time — we'd never buy one or two — and we'd have a party.

"But when I was dividing up the cash this time, instead of splitting it five ways I only divided it into four lots of about £150 each. I handed the others their money, and put my own share in my pocket. Then Weyman asked: 'What about me?' And I snapped back: 'Your share comes off the £1200 you owe us!' He went white. So then I accused him and he asked what did we mean? I told Bedford to tell him. At first Weyman denied it. Then Bedford suggested the only way to determine who was telling the truth was to go and front the blokes we'd conned. Weyman agreed, and he stood up, put on his coat and headed for the kitchen door with Bedford. 'Bronze' and Walsh and I were going to stay there. But Weyman only made it as far as the kitchen door before he admitted that he did pinch the money. But he made the excuse that there was a good reason. It was that one day, when we were going bad, he planned to pull out the cash and say: 'Well, there's the £1200!' Now, of course, he had no such intention, the bastard! However, he insisted he was only minding it for us. But I repeated he was an out-and-out bastard and the others agreed.

"The next day Jackie Walsh was pinched for the army. He'd been called up before, but this time they went to his home in Glebe and grabbed him. They locked him in a detention centre down at Circular Quay near the old Coroner's Court. Well, this was playing on my mind, and I was thinking about Weyman robbing us. But, while Walsh was in the detention camp for about 10 weeks, it only left four of us. (However, we were still giving Jackie's cut from the rort to his wife Vera.) So even though we'd found Weyman out, we kept operating every day and night. And we continued to give Weyman his share too. But I knew we were going to squeeze the £1200 back from him eventually. There was no doubt at all in my mind that I was going to take it back. But, for the moment, I didn't want to bust up our team...

"Now Edna Weyman, she was a mad sex woman. Bedford said to me one day that Edna wanted me to knock her off. Bedford had already fucked her. So eventually I did fuck Edna Weyman, and I asked her where Eddie kept his bankroll. She told me it was in the toilet out in their backyard. It was in a tin box up in the cistern. But she said she didn't know how much might be there. She was a low bastard. Anyway, I said I was coming back that night to have a look. So Bedford and I returned to Eddie's backyard around 2.30 am. I put my hand in the cistern and found the tin box and it contained £3800. So I said: 'That'll do for the £1200!' We took the lot and we included 'Bronze' in the split-up, but we didn't put Jackie Walsh in for that one, mainly because Walsh and Weyman were fairly close mates and spent a lot of time together because Edna was Jackie's sister.

"Naturally, Eddie Weyman put on a real tantrum when he found out the money had been stolen. But he didn't think anyone knew about it except his wife. So he blamed Edna and gave her a bit of a hiding. And, as a matter of fact, I was glad he gave it to her."

• • •

On Christmas Eve 1944 Chow Hayes was drinking in the London Hotel when in walked Eddie and Edna Weyman, "Bronze" Monsetti and Violet Walsh. Weyman still did not know who had stolen his £3800 (Edna had never told him). "Weyman announced they were going to have a party at his place that night," Hayes recalls. "Of course, parties in those days were only sandwiches and beer. Anyway, he asked did I want to come. I replied by inquiring whether he was going to spend the £1200 he owed us? He answered: 'No. That's still alright. That's still in the bank whenever you blokes want it.' Well, I said I wanted it now.

"Soon after, I walked up to 'The Duck's' place, because I had a gun (a .38) hidden there. I took it to Weyman's house in Mary Street, Surry Hills. At the front, you walked up four steps from the street to the front room. But there were also six stairs which led down to the floor underneath the footpath. It was actually a three-storey terrace and the four steps up into the front room led into a sort of lounge–dining room on the middle storey. But I walked in the back way, because we always used to enter via the back door. Some were in the kitchen ('Face' McKeon was sitting there with a girl and another bloke) and the rest were drinking in the front room.

"Now it had started to prey on my mind that Weyman was a real bastard for touching his mates for £1200. So I decided I'd give it to him tonight. After a while I told them I was leaving and I walked out into the backyard. Then I went into the yard next door, where you could lean over the fence and see right into Weyman's kitchen. 'Face' McKeon was sitting there with the female and Weyman was now sitting beside them. I took aim and fired — but I didn't allow for the jump in the gun. It was a shot of about eight yards [7 metres], and I hit Weyman in the shoulder. The female screamed, but I calmly walked down the backyard without running and strolled out into the laneway. Then I walked around the corner into Reservoir Street and jumped on a tram to Railway Square.

"I went home first. My wife was up ironing and I told her that I'd only dropped in for 10 minutes to inform her that I wouldn't be back home for a while. I said I was going away to Gosford on some business. Then I went up to 'The Duck's' place and told him what had happened. He wanted to know if Weyman was dead, but I said I didn't know. Then Day put me into hiding with one of his girls, Judy, who worked there. Day told her I'd had a row with my wife, who was taking out a court writ against me. Judy took me to her flat in South Bondi and I stayed there for five days.

"Meanwhile I found out Weyman was only wounded in the shoulder, though he'd been admitted to St Vincent's Hospital. Everyone knew I was the one who'd shot him — and of course Bedford, Monsetti, Walsh and Weyman knew it was over the £1200 — so I came out of hiding. The first bloke I ran into was 'Face' McKeon. He said he wished I'd warned him, because he nearly had a heart attack when the shot came through the window. It just missed him and, at first, he thought it was meant for him. Then I contacted Bedford and found out Weyman's condition, and the two of us went for a drink at the London Hotel.

"Pretty soon half a dozen coppers barged in with their guns drawn. They put me in a car and took me down to the CIB." The police later told newspaper reporters that Weyman had said to them: "You know as well as I do who shot me. There is only one person who wants me dead."

Hayes says that at CIB headquarters the police immediately declared they knew he'd shot Weyman, but they had no witnesses and Weyman wouldn't help them. "Initially the police interviewed Weyman in hospital," Hayes explains. "They said to him that he was shot at his place, but he insisted he'd been shot over at Leichhardt. He said he was with some other bloke's wife and the bloke came home and found him there and shot him. And, of course, he said he wouldn't reveal the woman's name because he didn't want to bring her into it. But the coppers knew he was telling lies...

"Since the police had no witnesses, all they could do was warn me that, if anything else happened to Weyman, they'd know exactly where to start looking.

"The next day Weyman came out of hospital. A group of us were drinking in the London Hotel, and Monsetti walked in. (Walsh was still in the Army detention centre.) Then, soon after, Weyman came in and said to me: 'Let's be friends and forget about it all. I'm going to the bank right now and I'll withdraw the £1200. And I don't want my share — so you can all have £300 each, including Walsh.' So I agreed, and extended my hand to shake on it. But he didn't put his hand out. He just walked away. About two hours later he returned with the cash. But while he was away Bedford warned me: 'He hasn't forgotten.' And I knew that was right, because Weyman had told his missus he was going to 'back-up' [get back at me] — and, naturally, she told her sister Violet, and Violet told Monsetti, and Monsetti told Bedford, and Bedford told me. In addition, I knew he was going to back-up. He was a man with a criminal record, who'd just come out of jail himself.

"So I knew I was going to have to jump in first — and make darn sure of it next time."

13 Eddie Weyman's Murder

On New Year's Eve 1945 Donnie Day threw a big party at Paddington Town Hall and invited all his friends. Eddie Weyman announced he was not going because he'd been invited to another party in Newtown. However, Weyman's wife Edna went to the Paddington celebration, with Don and Rene Day.

"I arrived at Paddington about 9 pm," Hayes recalls. "But my wife would never attend any of these functions — she wouldn't associate with those people. Two hours later, around 11, Lawrie McKeon (he was 'Face' McKeon's brother) walked in and whispered to me: 'Weyman's going to knock you, you know.' And I replied: 'Yeah, I know.' McKeon added that he'd just been at the Newtown party with Weyman and, as a matter of fact, he'd just dropped Weyman back home to his house in Mary Street barely 20 minutes ago. Then McKeon had continued straight to Paddington.

"I immediately thought this was my chance because there was no-one else there. Arthur Bedford drove me to a place in Surry Hills — but we made out we were just walking outside for a smoke — and I collected a .38. Since Bedford was driving his own car I told him not to park outside Weyman's place. This all happened on the spur of the moment, otherwise we'd have stolen a car.

"I went in via the back entrance to check that Weyman was there, while Bedford parked on the corner of Mary Street and Campbell Street. Weyman's back gate was always open and I walked into the backyard, and then straight into the kitchen. I didn't turn on any lights, but kept walking through to the front downstairs bedroom where Weyman was lying on the bed, wearing only a singlet, having a smoke. I told him he'd brought the whole drama upon himself by robbing us of the £1200. And I added that he couldn't really think for one minute that I believed he wasn't going to back-up. He insisted: 'No, I'm not going to back-up.' But I simply replied: 'Here.' I fired and hit him five times with the .38. The last I saw of him he fell down alongside the bed. I knew he was badly wounded and I thought he was dead — but he wasn't. . .

"I left via the front door, put my handkerchief over the knob so as not to leave fingerprints, and walked to Bedford's car. We drove straight back to Paddington Town Hall. Then the coincidence which eventually saved me occurred. You wouldn't believe it in a thousand years, but my cousin Ray Bollard happened to drive past with his wife Josie, just as Bedford and I had stepped out of the car. So it looked like we were merely standing outside having a cigarette. In the car with Ray Bollard and his wife were a well-known boxer of the era, Jackie Day, and his wife Kitty. (Day fought Sands and all those types. He was a good fighter, but a foul fighter — you'd go down to back him and, if he was losing, he'd knee his opponent in the balls or butt with his head so he'd be disqualified. Then all bets were off. But if he had a chance of winning he'd try fair dinkum.) Kitty and Josie were sisters.

"Bollard pulled up and asked what we were doing. We said we were at a party inside. Then he asked if we wanted to go with them down to his house in Cleveland Street for a drink. I hadn't seen him for 18 months, so I replied: 'Okay, but I'll just pop back inside and inform the others first.' When I returned inside, the others hadn't even noticed that we'd been outside at all. Only 'The Duck' seemed to have any idea that I was outside. Basically they were all either half-drunk or too busy dancing. So I said I was going, while Bedford decided to stay at Paddington. I jumped into Bollard's car and we headed off to Cleveland Street. But before I left I made an arrangement with Bedford to contact me at Bollard's place and let me know if something developed about Weyman. However, I didn't tell Bollard anything about what had happened.

"I stayed drinking at Bollard's place until 6 am. Then I decided to walk over to a mate's place in Glebe. I left an instruction with Bollard that, if Bedford came around looking for me, to send him over to Glebe.

"It was a Saturday morning and I arrived in Glebe about 11 and the 'cable editions' of the papers, which came out early, were on the streets. Weyman's murder was all over the front page. So there was no doubt he was dead. But back when the party had finished at Paddington Town Hall, Edna Weyman and her sister Violet Walsh, and Bedford and Monsetti had returned to Weyman's place. In the meantime Lawrie McKeon had informed

Edna at Paddington that he'd dropped Eddie home. But she'd decided to stay on without him until after 2 am. Then they all went back to Mary Street and, as usual, walked in via the back door. Bedford cunningly sat down on the settee and proposed a drink, because he wanted Edna to find Weyman. He suggested that she go and see if Eddie wanted to join them all for a nightcap. So she went into the front bedroom — but then returned and announced he wasn't there!

"Bedford, naturally, was alarmed, because he knew I'd shot Eddie five times. But now the body wasn't there. So Bedford went in but, after a cursory glance around, couldn't see any body either. He came back out in shock and poured another drink. Then he thought further about it, and suggested he'd have a look on the other side of the bed. So he returned to the bedroom — where he knew I'd shot Weyman — and on the other side of the bed he quickly spotted a pool of blood. Then he noticed a trail of stains leading to the front door. Bedford opened it and found Weyman lying on the steps. He'd apparently staggered out from the downstairs bedroom and crawled up three or four steps. Bedford raced back in and called out that Eddie was on the front steps, and he thought he was asleep. They all immediately walked through to the front door and found the body. The police were contacted straightaway."

Truth informed its readers: "The first light of New Year's Day, 1945, revealed the bullet-riddled body of Eddie Weyman, clad only in a singlet, lying sprawled on the front steps of his home in Mary Street, Surry Hills. Weyman's body was discovered by his pretty blonde wife, Edna Weyman, after she and other people from her house had returned from an all-night dance at Paddington Town Hall."

The police duly carted Edna Weyman and Violet Walsh, "Bronze" Monsetti and Arthur Bedford, down to the CIB. They were questioned in separate rooms and asked where they'd been that night, and when was the last time they'd seen Chow Hayes. They all replied at the Paddington Town Hall. The police eventually let them leave about 8 am. Bedford immediately contacted Ray Bollard and found out where to rendezvous with Hayes in Glebe. Then he drove across and met Hayes and told him what had happened. Bedford assured Hayes all the statements to police were consistent, because they'd all told what they thought was the truth: that Hayes had been at Paddington Town Hall all night. Then to double-check, Hayes telephoned a policeman he knew well and asked him to find out exactly what had been said in each of the statements. The policeman told Hayes to ring back in two hours. When Hayes returned the call the police contact confirmed that none of the statements implicated him. But the policeman also warned Hayes that the detectives were looking for him, and they were sure Hayes was the murderer.

Hayes recalls: "I was immediately the number one suspect. I had a talk to a few close friends and I decided to show myself. It was about midday, still on the same day as the murder. I was walking over to 'The Duck's' place in Surry Hills, and I passed through the subway from Railway Square to Elizabeth Street. Just as I reached the top of the steps, I spotted some mates in a car so I jumped in. I intended to drive down and have a peek at what was happening at Mary Street, see who was there and so on. But then I spotted Edna Weyman walking up Elizabeth Street. So we drove about 50 yards [45 metres] past and stopped the car. I stepped out and waited for her. I said I'd heard Eddie had been killed, and asked what had happened. At that stage she definitely didn't know I'd done it. I suggested we sit down in Belmore Park, next to the subway in Elizabeth Street. But I hadn't seen an old police sergeant over on the corner who knew me by sight. He rang the CIB and three car-loads of reinforcements arrived. They crawled across the grass on their hands and knees with their guns drawn and arrested me — they looked like Indians creeping up. Norman Mijch was the leader, and sang out: 'Don't move your hands, Chow, or I'll blow your head off!' They quickly bundled me into a car with Mijch, and they pushed Edna Weyman into another car. We drove to the CIB and they took us into different rooms for questioning.

"Mijch immediately declared that I had murdered Weyman. But I replied that I didn't know anything about it until I'd read the story in the cable editions of the newspapers that morning. Then Mijch took me down to the Coroner's Court to look at the body. The attendants pulled it out on one of the drawers which fit into the wall. And while we waited, one of the other coppers offered me a cigarette. Now viewing the body didn't have any effect on me at all, because I'd seen them often and they never affected me in any way. But when I took the cigarette one copper commented: 'Look at the bastard smoking, he's not shaking in any way.'

"Then they took me back to the CIB. In the meantime they'd let Edna Weyman go. Regulations then required that they take me to the police station nearest where the body was found, which was Darlinghurst. There they charged me with murder and took me to the cells. They had a uniformed copper outside the cells in those days to see you didn't commit suicide. They took my belt, cigarettes, matches and so on, but after about half an hour I was given back the cigarettes and lighter. Then my wife came to see me and I told her she had nothing to worry about. Around 10 that night they took me back to the CIB and into the cells at Central Police Station. Next morning around 10.15 I was paraded before Number 1 Court and formally charged with murder. I was remanded, refused bail and taken out to Long Bay Jail.

"Out at 'The Bay' I started worrying about a few things. Edna Weyman had a new baby and I was doubtful about what she might say. I figured that if the coppers applied enough pressure she might tell them anything — and they were visiting her almost every day. They kept telling her there was no doubt I'd left the party and committed the murder. And they were insisting that she knew all about it. But she stuck to the story that I never left the party as far as she was concerned. So while I was definitely worried that she might weaken under the daily bombardment, the key factor in my favour was simply that she didn't know the truth. I also sent my wife to visit her a couple of times. And one day when Bedford came to see me I suggested that it would be a good idea if he went back and threatened her, just to make doubly sure that she intended to stick to her story. (Bedford and Lawrie McKeon were still the only ones who knew the real story. Lawrie was subsequently shot dead in Petersham.) I also asked Bedford to bring Edna out to Long Bay to visit me. I thought that looked good. From then on she used to come out twice a week until my trial began."

The matter first came before the Coroner's Court (sitting in the old Coroner's Court building in George Street north) where Hayes was represented by leading barrister Bill Dovey and his usual solicitor, the city's busiest criminal practitioner, Phil Roach. "I sat in the room directly behind Roach," Hayes recalls. "Back at the CIB I'd explained to Mijch that they had nothing on me because I had a perfect alibi: Bollard, Day and their wives. But when he asked for their names, I said I wouldn't tell him. The simple reason I wouldn't tell him was that I thought I might find an even better alibi before the case came on. Of course, Bollard, Day and their wives knew that, as far as they were concerned, I didn't do it. But I was afraid Bollard, who was my first cousin, had a few convictions and mightn't be a good witness. However, when I explained all that to Dovey, he disagreed. He insisted that, in his opinion, it would be all the better because, if I didn't put Bollard in the witness box, they could think it was a false alibi. But if Bollard appeared they'd think the other way — that I wasn't even afraid to put a criminal in the witness box to confirm my alibi...

"At the Coroner's Court I still hadn't revealed to the police the identity of the person or persons upon whom my alibi rested...

"During one lull in proceedings, this big chap walked in. I didn't know him from a bar of soap. I thought he was a copper. He walked straight past me and began whispering to Dovey. I thought to myself: 'Why's this copper whispering in Dovey's ear?' So I tapped Roach on the shoulder, but he told me to be quiet and he'd fill me in later. I tried to insist that he tell me there and then. But Roach was adamant that he'd tell me at the lunchbreak. I spent the next one and a half hours wondering what was going on. At lunch the coppers took me into an adjacent room. I was handcuffed, because they didn't have a cell there. I signalled to Roach that I wanted to talk to him. I asked: 'What was the copper talking to Dovey about?' Roach started to explain that it wasn't a copper. Then he called Dovey across and told him what I wanted to know. And Dovey laughed that it was 'my son-in-law' — which, of course, was Gough Whitlam."

Hayes was eventually committed for trial. At that stage he'd still only revealed the identity of the witnesses for his alibi to Roach and Dovey.

"Ray Bollard came out to see me at 'The Bay' and I asked him whether the boxer Jackie Day had any convictions," Hayes recounts. "He said definitely not, that Day was a cleanskin [had no criminal record] and so was Day's wife. And I knew Bollard's wife was a cleanskin. Bollard said they'd all be okay in the witness box because they'd tell the truth — which, of course, he thought was that I was with them and had nothing to do with Weyman's murder."

However Hayes, left with time to consider all possibilities, wanted to send a detailed and highly confidential message out from Long Bay. But he was worried that "the screws" (the prison officers) might be listening in. At the time Arthur Bedford was making the trip out to see Hayes almost every day. So during one of those visits, Hayes asked Bedford to tell Monsetti to taunt the police until he was arrested on some minor charge such as bad language or drunkenness. Then he'd be sent out to Long Bay, where Hayes could deliver the important message in detail. "Because Bedford came out almost every day," Hayes explains, "the screws had begun to know him. But not many of them knew much about 'Bronze'. So Monsetti abused a cop in Pitt Street for nothing at all — he'd come out of a café and called a copper a dirty big fat bastard, or words to that effect. So they pinched him and fined him £5 or 10 days and he took the 10 days. He came out to 'The Bay' and saw me the morning after he arrived. He didn't mind doing it for me; in fact, he was pleased to do it, because I was a much better mate of his and of all the others than Weyman had been, and that was very important. I asked Monsetti to tell Bedford to go and see Edna Weyman. Bedford was to tell her to say that two days before New Year's Eve, just after Eddie had returned from hospital following the first shooting, they were walking up Reservoir Street on their way home, when a car pulled up and a tall blond bloke jumped out and wanted a word with Eddie. She was to say that she moved about five paces away but could still hear clearly. The blond man had said to Weyman: 'I missed you the other night, you bastard, but I won't miss you next time!'

"So Edna duly received that message. And I also ensured that my wife went and visited Edna several times."

Eventually the criminal trial began. The *Sun* newspaper later called Hayes a "shoplifter turned standover man, standover man turned gunman, gunman turned killer." It declared that "the 'Chow' Hayes murder trial was the nearest thing wartime Sydney could turn on that would have passed for a social event... Like the gangster heroes of the popular film melodramas of the time, there was a baleful fascination about a man like Hayes."

At the trial, the Crown presented basically the same evidence it had previewed at the Coroner's Court. "Then when Edna Weyman was giving her evidence," Hayes recalls, "Dovey asked her all about what happened soon after Eddie had come out of hospital. So she told the yarn about the tall blond man. And when the Crown Prosecutor stood up and asked why she hadn't spoken about the incident earlier, she replied: 'For the simple reason that I wasn't asked!'

"The Crown didn't have much, and Dovey advised me that since my witnesses were telling what they thought was the truth, I should call them to give evidence. I stood up first and made a statement from the dock denying everything — I hadn't even told Dovey or Roach the truth. Then my witnesses were called. Ray Bollard entered the box first and, a funny thing, they never asked him about his criminal record. Then Bollard's wife was called, followed by Day, the boxer, whom Dovey led through his evidence. Then the crown prosecutor stood up and started rattling papers and pretending to go through court records or something similar. He suggested to Day: 'You've been in trouble before.' And Day replied: 'Yes.' When he appeared to succeed with that tactic, he went a bit further and kidded to be looking again at his papers and he asked: 'You've been in trouble a few times, haven't you?' And Day answered: 'Yes.' Well, at that stage I thought: 'What's Bollard done here? This will bring me undone.' So I looked over at him and he was astounded too. Meanwhile the prosecutor said to Day: 'Tell us what serious trouble you've been in.' And Day replied: 'That was the night I fought Dave Sands at the Sydney Stadium!' With that, the court burst out laughing. Even a flicker of a smile came over the judge's face, and he pulled out the lace handkerchief which he had up his sleeve and covered his mouth briefly, pretending to be wiping it . . .

"The case was so weak that, following Dovey's address on my behalf, the crown prosecutor would normally speak after him and then the judge delivers his final address. But in this case, Dovey talked for about half an hour and sat down. Then everyone expected the crown prosecutor to speak. But he declined. He didn't want to address the jury — you'll only see that about one in a thousand cases. That's how weak their case was. Finally the judge summed it up and virtually told the jury the case wasn't good enough with all the doubts. The jury was only out about 20 minutes before returning with a 'Not Guilty' verdict."

Truth reported: "Extraordinary scenes followed the trial. Kate Leigh, who had occupied a seat in the front gallery throughout the trial, called out: 'Good on you, Jackie'."

The *Sun* later reported, with a touch more hyperbole, that "when the moment of acquittal came Kate Leigh, whose notoriety matched Hayes' in the world of bullets and booze, let out a cheer. 'Good on you Jackie,' she cried. And to the jury: 'Good on you too, jurymen. You're worth your weight in gold'." Then, the paper noted, Hayes himself declared from the Central Criminal Court dock: "God almighty! If Eddie Weyman could come in here now he would tell you that I am as innocent of this crime as any man in this court. Eddie Weyman was my friend."

Hayes explains: "Kate Leigh had paid Dovey's costs for me. She paid all the legal expenses of my whole case. Joe Taylor and a few others offered to put in their whack, but Kate wanted to do it all. And while I'd been on remand for 11 weeks (in those days you could 'keep' yourself while you were on remand) Kate made sure my meals were brought out to 'The Bay' every day. So I never had the prison food, but only the best stuff. The fellow that I'd previously shot, Jack Baker, used to drive the food out. Kate had Baker in her Lansdowne Street beer house as a 'backstop' [strong-arm man]. She sent everything I could possibly want: pork, sweets and so on.

"After the verdict, we went straight around to Kate's place in Lansdowne Street for a couple of drinks. But then I had to go home for a while because my wife was very upset about the whole thing. But she wouldn't go to old Kate Leigh's place in a fit. So I'd left my wife in a coffee shop with Kitty Day and Josie Bollard while I was away at Kate's place for about an hour. Then I returned to the coffee shop (it was opposite the Court House Hotel) and my wife and I caught a tram home to Thomas Street, Ultimo. I stayed home that night, and it was the first for a long time."

• • •

During the trial the crown prosecutor had asked Edna Weyman: "Are you familiar with Hayes?" She had replied no, that she only knew him as a friend, and that he was more an associate of her husband than herself. *Truth* reported: "Police gave evidence that on the afternoon of January 1 — the day of the murder — Hayes and Mrs Weyman were seen sitting together in Exhibition Park. Mrs Weyman said that she was very upset over her husband's death. While she and Hayes were in the park, Hayes was trying to comfort her. She was crying and he gave her a handkerchief. Mrs Weyman denied that she and Hayes were kissing. She said that her feeling for Hayes was nothing more than a normal friendship, and that Weyman had never made any suggestion that he thought Hayes was paying attention to her."

Now, the day after his acquittal, Hayes met Arthur Bedford and "Bronze" Monsetti in the London Hotel. After a few drinks, Monsetti said he had to pick up Violet Walsh from the Weyman household, where she was staying with her sister Edna. Bedford and Hayes decided to go along for the walk with Monsetti. Hayes added that, while he was in the area, he'd stroll across the road and have a chat to Joe Taylor at the two-up school.

"Taylor was inside the game at the time," Hayes recalls, "so I asked Wally Goddard, his partner, to tell Joe I wanted to see him. Wally congratulated me on beating the charge, and then Taylor came out, all smiles. I explained Kate Leigh had paid for everything at the trial and I had no money at all. I said I appreciated what Joe had done for my wife — she was still receiving my wages while I'd been at 'The Bay'. But, I explained, neither Bedford nor Monsetti had any cash they could lend me — the cabbage business had fallen apart without me there. So I asked Taylor if I could have a grand. He replied: 'No trouble at all. Wait there for a moment.' Then he walked inside, grabbed it in cash and came back outside and handed me £1000.

"I put the money in my pocket and walked about 15 yards [13 metres] up the street to where Bedford was waiting. I asked whether 'Bronze' had returned from the Weyman house yet. Bedford said he hadn't. Now, from where we were standing we could see across to Weyman's place in Mary Street. I suggested we ought to walk over there. We went in the back way and Edna was there with her baby, and so were Violet and Bronze. We were sitting around talking and, suddenly, in rushed the police.

"Mijch led them through the door. He gave me a glance but didn't speak to me. But he addressed Edna Weyman: 'You weren't familiar with the bastard yesterday, but you're bloody familiar with him today!' She protested that I'd just arrived. But Mijch said they were going to search the house anyway. It was a big place, a three-storey terrace with 11 or 12 rooms. Finally he asked what I was doing there. I replied that I'd just dropped in to offer my condolences. Then he ordered me and Bedford to leave — and we disappeared pronto. I think someone had spotted me talking to Taylor and telephoned the coppers to say I was in the area. The police didn't find anything in the house and they never searched us personally."

• • •

While Hayes had been preoccupied by the Weyman trial, his part-time employer, Donny "The Duck" Day, had been gunned down in one of his "residentials" on the corner of Crown and Foveaux Streets, Surry Hills.

Upon his death Day was described by police as "one of the leaders in Sydney's underworld" and by the *Sydney Morning*

Herald as "a notorious underworld character...well and unfavourably known to police in every State".

At 2 o'clock one morning in January 1945 a woman telephoned Darlinghurst Police Station to report that Day had been shot. Police found Day lying on a bed in an upstairs room with a bullet hole through his cheeks and nose and two bullet wounds in his chest. One of the latter slugs had passed through Day's heart and killed him instantly. Police also found two American soldiers, said to be absent without leave, and three women (including Day's long-time de facto Irene Merle "Rene" McCormick) in the house. In the room where Day's body had been lifted onto a bed, women's clothes were scattered about. Police found two revolvers, alleged to have been stolen, in a house next door. Day had arrived at the house, at 428 Crown Street, in a car he'd recently purchased from his sly-grog partner Dr Reginald Stuart-Jones.

Keith Kitchener Hull, a 27-year-old salesman, was charged with murder but pleaded self-defence. Chow Hayes recalls: "After they charged Hull and brought him out to 'The Bay', they wouldn't put him in the same yard as us. There were 'Skinny' Brett, Percy Neville and I, and the four blokes (Jowett, Thomas and co.) who'd been pinched over the Stuart-Jones shooting. We were all in the special yard at 'The Bay' for people charged with murder. But because Day had been a mate of ours, they kept Hull in a separate yard."

Hull was eventually found not guilty, even after US Army private George Miller told the court how he heard shots, went downstairs and saw Day lying on a bedroom floor with Hull and another man standing over him. US merchant seaman Bill Simpomis told how he was woken by banging on a door. A few minutes later he heard shots. When he came downstairs Hull was standing over Day's body with a gun in his hand. Hull had said: "He was going to get me." There was another gun lying on the floor near Day's body. Hull told the court Day had a gun and fired it at him, but it didn't go off. He said he then fired back at Day in self-defence. Well-known underworld figure Edward Herbert Reeves said he'd been in the car with Day when they'd driven to the house. Irene Day had opened the door and Donald Day went into a bedroom. Two minutes later three or four shots rang out.

The *Sydney Morning Herald* summed up Day's life: "Day was a racketeer in black-market liquor and other commodities. Recently he was sentenced to six months imprisonment for having been found in unlawful possession of tyres, and he was on bail pending appeal against the conviction. He was also awaiting trial on a conspiracy charge over black-market liquor at Lithgow. In his younger days he was a licensed jockey, but was disqualified for life for improper practices."

• • •

Another murderer Hayes knew very well, Cyril Norman, also grabbed the headlines during January 1945.

Norman, alias Thomas Couldrey, held up the King Street shop of Sydney gunsmiths Cowles & Dunn Pty Ltd. But during the attempt Norman shot and killed store manager Maurice Joseph Hannigan, before fleeing with six revolvers, a large quantity of ammunition, and £164 from the cash register.

Hayes recounts: "Norman was mainly a petty thief until he killed the gunsmith. He was only a little fellow, about 8 stone [50 kg] and 5 ft 6 in [168 cm]. He went to the gun shop and asked Hannigan to show him some guns. Hannigan obliged and Norman then asked if he could have some bullets to fit a revolver. Norman put two or three in the chamber, then shot Hannigan dead. He scooped up half a dozen guns and took them to a house in Woolloomooloo, where he was boarding. His intention at that stage was to sell the guns to the underworld. But then he decided to go up to Central Railway Station and knock off passengers' luggage, which was one of his capers. He'd done it many times.

"So the day after shooting Hannigan, Norman went to Central Station and picked up two bags and carried them back to his room in Woolloomooloo. When he opened them he found they belonged to an American Army officer. Cyril tried on the uniforms, but they were too big for him. Also in the ports he found a wallet with several thousand American dollars. Norman took the clothes, including the officer's uniform, to a shady tailor he knew and had them altered to fit him. Then he began passing himself as an officer in the US Army."

A few weeks later, however, Norman, dressed in the American service uniform, shot Constable Eric George Bailey outside the Exchange Hotel in the central western New South Wales country town of Blayney with a Colt .32 stolen from the King Street shop.

"Norman made history by being caught by the man he killed," Hayes recalls, "and he always used to insist how unlucky he was to be doing a life sentence. It happened this way. Norman went up to Blayney and booked into a hotel. After a wash, he came down to the bar and met a few locals. He shouted them a drink and told them he was an American officer, and they believed him. Then he went out and strutted up and down the main street and all the locals were pointing him out. Later he returned to the hotel and decided to have a shower. But when he walked along the hall to the bathroom, he left open his hotel room door. One of the maids was walking past, and she saw all the guns on the bed. She was terrified, and went downstairs and told the publican. He said it was alright because that man was an officer in the US Army. She believed that until she was having lunch, when she saw Norman walking out the door. She thought he was too small to be in the Army, so she went to the local police station and informed them about the guns in the room. Now, at that time there had been big write-ups in the newspapers about the gunsmith murdered in King Street in Sydney. So the police made a routine check.

"They went to the hotel room and saw the guns still on the bed. Then Norman returned. They asked him for some identification, and he produced the American Army officer's wallet from the stolen bag. He later told me: 'I had the bastards convinced, until one copper went to the telephone and checked.' One constable went off to do that, while the other stayed in the room with Norman. After some time, the copper said: 'We'd better go down to the station and check all this out.' Norman replied: 'That'll suit me.' So they walked downstairs and out into the street. But as they were heading toward the police station, Norman thought to himself: 'Once I arrive there I'm a goner.' So he started to run. But he'd only gone about 15 yards [13 metres] before the constable low-tackled him like a footballer and brought him to the ground. Within seconds the copper had snipped one handcuff over his own wrist and one onto Norman's wrist. But during that period Norman fired two shots and fatally injured the policeman. However, the copper slumped on top of him, and was still lying over him when the crowd and other police arrived.

"Norman later told me: 'There I was lying under the bastard that I'd shot.' He was then taken to the police station and charged, and later convicted of murder. It's the only case in Australia where the person who was killed arrested his own killer. That made very big headlines. Norman spent most of his sentence (he finished up doing about 24 years) in Parramatta Jail, where I saw a lot of him."

14 Joe Taylor and Thommo's Two-up School

In February 1945, a month after Donny Day's murder, another of Hayes's employers, Joe Taylor, was shot.

Joseph Patrick Taylor, the perennially popular boss of Sydney's best-known illegal gambling site, Thommo's two-up school, was a former prize-fighter who fought under the pseudonym 'Joe Black'. After being knocked out in four rounds by the great Fred Henneberry in 1930, Taylor turned his hand to promoting bouts at the old Newtown Stadium.

Just two years younger than his boss, Chow Hayes had known Taylor as a teenager. "We used to call him 'Limerick'," Hayes recalls. "He started out managing The Hub theatre in Newtown. Later he took over Thommo's two-up game, with Wally Goddard and Herman 'The Jew' Singer. . . I remember talking to Taylor once outside 'The Game', when a woman came down. She was a 'squarehead' and asked which one was Mr Taylor? She explained that her husband came to 'The Game' every Friday and lost his wages (Friday was payday in that era). She said it had been going on for months, and now she couldn't pay the bills, and the children had nothing to eat. She was really sincere. So Taylor told her not to worry anymore. He said her husband wouldn't be allowed into 'The Game' again — and he handed her £200 to pay the bills. That's the sort of bloke he was."

Over four decades Taylor would become known as one of Sydney's most fearless and leviathan racecourse bettors. When he was shot in the chest outside his legendary two-up game in Surry Hills at 3 am the *Sydney Morning Herald* described him, first and foremost, as a "spectacular punter".

Joseph Dudley Prendergast was charged with the shooting, but the charge was later dismissed. Hayes explains: "Taylor was at Hawkesbury races one day early in 1945. He became involved in an argument with Prendergast, who was a petty thief and a 'bludger', which meant he lived off the earnings of prostitutes. Fair dinkum knock-around men in those days didn't like 'bludgers'. They wouldn't have anything to do with them. 'Bludgers' were looked down upon, even among the criminals. . . Anyway, Taylor and Prendergast had a fight at Hawkesbury, and it was a real good stoush. But the following evening Taylor was standing in Reservoir Street outside 'The Game' and a car drove slowly by and two shots were fired. One hit Taylor in the chest and the other missed altogether. Then the car sped away. The ambulance rushed Taylor to St Vincent's Hospital and he was okay.

"Half of Sydney would have willingly knocked off Prendergast for shooting Taylor. The only reason it didn't happen was because Taylor wouldn't allow it. Joey Hollebone and I went and saw Taylor and offered to do it immediately. The very next day we went and saw Goddard about it — and we didn't want any money. But Goddard insisted that Taylor didn't want Prendergast murdered. I argued that if Prendergast was allowed to shoot Joe, and Joe didn't back-up, then every silly mug in Sydney might start taking pot shots at Taylor. But Goddard explained Taylor's reasoning was that, if Prendergast was killed, the authorities would step in and close 'The Game' altogether. Taylor reiterated that rationale to us when he was discharged from hospital a fortnight later.

"The authorities duly arrested Prendergast for the shooting. But when he appeared in court, Taylor said he wasn't the man who shot him. So Prendergast was discharged — and then fled to Melbourne for a few years before he was game to return to Sydney."

The original Thommo's — a dingy gambling den hidden among the warehouses and terraces of Surry Hills — had been started in 1910 by George Joseph Guest, a gambler, boxer and racehorse owner. Guest had worked in a Melbourne boot factory, before pursuing a brief boxing career in New Zealand under the ring name Joe Thomas. He returned to Sydney in 1908 and, after several local bouts at the old Gaiety Theatre (later to become the Tivoli), he spent two years operating pie stalls in Castlereagh Street.

Thomas's Surry Hills game boomed between the wars. Green baize was stretched over the bare floorboards to form the ring, which was surrounded by a narrow bench. By the start of World War II Thommo's employed a permanent staff of 40 ring-

JOE TAYLOR

He was the boss of Sydney's best-known illegal gambling site, Thommo's two-up school in Surry Hills. Taylor and Hayes had been friends as teenagers and he subsequently made weekly cash payments to Hayes over four decades — in return for Hayes's services as a "heavy" whenever his gambling operation required them.

keepers, cockatoos, bouncers, doormen, clerks and cashiers.

The 1940s and 1950s were Thommo's heyday. In the early 1940s American soldiers were the biggest bettors, and single wagers of £1000 were not unusual. During that era Thommo's became a popular nightspot for Sydney's smart set — a sort of after-dinner "must" for politicians and the legal profession, businessmen and their guests, as well as wharfies, labourers and criminals.

Chow Hayes stopped in at Thommo's, for at least some part of the evening, almost every night of the year. He knew all the regulars well. "Punter and sporting entrepreneur Rufe Naylor lost a fortune at Thommo's over the years," Hayes recalls. "Many of the Sydney celebrities of the era — men like Dr Reginald Stuart-Jones, Dr George from Glebe (the man who took my bullet out), and the lawyers George Osborne, Jimmy Kincaid, Phil Roach and George Amsberg — went there often. I had to laugh a few years later when Amsberg was heading the Reg Doyle/Joe Arthur Royal Commission in 1953. [The Commission examined whether Joshua George 'Joe' Arthur, New South Wales Minister for Mines, had been guilty of any 'improper, wrongful or corrupt act' in any dealings with convicted confidence trickster and racing identity Reginald Aubrey Doyle. Judge Amsberg eventually found Arthur's financial dealings were 'improper for a Minister of the Crown'.]

"Amsberg had become a judge by then, and during cross-examination Doyle referred to 'a grand'. But Amsberg, feigning naivety, asked: 'A grand? What's a grand?' Well, I laughed my head off at that, because Amsberg knew everything there was to know about gambling and sly grog around Sydney. I know, because sometimes Joey Hollebone and I used to drink with him in old Kate Leigh's place and other dives. And the police knew all that too. But to see him up on the Bench later on, you'd think butter wouldn't melt in his mouth. In addition, of course, over the years we'd touted a few crims for him (that is, we sent them to him to defend them). He won the big murder charge — the Dawes case — against Hollebone at Waterloo. And he won the Weyman case for me. So if an ordinary crim was pinched for something like house-breaking and sought Amsberg's representation, old George would send for me or Hollebone to check him out first — that is, to ensure he was a good fellow who knew how to mind his own business. Then, if he was okay, Amsberg would charge him £50. But he wouldn't officially acknowledge income of £50 — he'd only give the customer a receipt for £20. The idea was to touch the Taxation Department, and most of the solicitors did that in those days. In other words, Amsberg and the others would charge you £50 to appear for you, but only give you a receipt for £20...

"John Harper, the radio man, also lost a couple of fortunes down at Thommo's. It wasn't unusual to see him arrive at the game at 1 am in his dressing gown, pyjamas and slippers. And fellow radio star Jack Davey was the best of the lot: if he won a quid, everyone won a quid, because he used to hand his winnings around among the other players. Another regular was Peter Lawford, John F. Kennedy's brother-in-law. Even Diana Barrymore (who was the big American entertainer at Joe Taylor's Celebrity Club in York Street) visited once, when old Joe Thomas took her along to show her around. But that was in the daytime, not the night...

"I asked Joe Taylor one day: 'Why do you bar crims from the Celebrity Club?' And he said: 'I'm not barring them, Chow. It's the coppers. They'd close me down if I let crims in. If it was up to me, I'd much rather let in the crims — rather than these old 'Sirs' and so on who buy half a bottle of wine and sit there for hours. In contrast, the crims would come in with £50 or £60 and spend up big...

"Bill McKell, when he was a politician, used to visit 'The Game'. But that was before he became Premier, and later Governor-General. And Eddie Ward, the firebrand ALP politician, was also a regular. 'The Game' was in his electorate. Thommo's often supplied hecklers to stir things up at the political meetings oganised by Ward's opponents. Eddie Ward would do anything for anyone. I knew him very well, and if I wanted anything done he'd do it, within reason. For example, if I wanted to help have someone shifted from one jail to another, then I'd go and see Ward and I'd take the man's relation with me. He'd be only too pleased to make representations on their behalf. Little things like that were never any trouble to him. He was also a great friend of Joe Taylor's. Ward was a regular player too. But I think that, on the way out, he was reimbursed for whatever he lost.

"Other big-name regulars included jockeys like Neville Sellwood and Andy Knox (who rode Old Rowley to win the 1940 Melbourne Cup) and young kid Billy Lappin who was killed in February 1940 in the sensational fall at Randwick. Most of the jockeys visited regularly. And of course all the big bookies and punters, like Tom Powell and 'Grafter' Kingsley, came to Thommo's. And many of the boxers were regulars too — men like Jack Carroll and Jack Haines and Sid Godfrey. So were the entertainers, after their own shows finished — people like Roy Rene and Mike Connors and Jim Gerald."

Hayes recalls the system which operated between Joe Taylor and the Sydney police whereby Taylor paid large cash bribes so that Thommo's would be left alone — except for the occasional "dummy" raid for the benefit of official records. "Each Monday morning, between 10 and 11 am, a young plain-clothes copper from the CIB would arrive at The Game in his own private car with a briefcase," Hayes explains. "He'd hand the briefcase to Taylor personally and Taylor would take it into his office. I don't know exactly what amount of cash went into it — but it would have to be massive because, in those days, both games (the Big Game and the nearby Little Game, known as the 'Snake Pit') were operating 24 hours a day.

"Taylor told me there were only two keys to that briefcase. Taylor had one himself (he kept it on his personal key chain) and the top copper on the receiving end back at police headquarters had the only other one. Taylor would put the cash in the briefcase, lock it again and then walk back out from his office and hand it to the young copper. He'd then take the case back to the top police in town, where it'd be split up between the head cops. I was there many times when the briefcase payments were made. I'd simply walk away, down to the corner of Reservoir and Elizabeth Streets and talk to a cockatoo while the young copper was there. This payment method went on for years and years.

"Meanwhile, local uniformed coppers would also arrive at The Game in pairs from surrounding police stations at Darlinghurst, Regent Street and Central. Those police would receive 10/- or £1 each. But it often caused arguments among police on the beat, because they'd all want to be rostered on to that shift so they could each grab their share of the bribes."

Whenever Thommo's was due to "go off" (be raided by the police) the organisers would round up a bunch of derelicts from Belmore Park and take them over to 'The Game'. "They were paid £2 each to stand inside and be rounded up in the fake raid," Hayes laughs. "There'd be 30 or 40 of them, and as soon as they were taken off to the police station, the real game would start up again...

"I didn't have much to do with the gambling clubs, because their customers were mostly squareheads. Galea and the blokes running those clubs didn't want obvious criminals like myself and my mates being seen around them. Many of their best customers were doctors and lawyers and businessmen. That was also half the reason we were paid by Galea and his partners — so we'd stay away from their clubs. But, of course, Thommo's was different. That was the working man's gambling spot."

• • •

Joe Taylor had been shot by Prendergast in February 1945, and then Chow Hayes had been in court over the Weyman matter during March. But the following month Hayes was back to his old habits.

On 10 April 1945, Hayes appeared at Central Petty Court charged with being "found in a disorderly house." The police had raided Donny "The Duck" Day's "private hotel" in Elizabeth Street during the day. They'd already placed a notice in the *Sydney Morning Herald* and other newspapers announcing that it had been declared a disorderly house. Hayes recalls: 'They pinched Jackie Walsh, Arthur Bedford and me with a sheila named Daphne (she was a prositute who worked there) and one of her relations. We were all charged. We started an all-in brawl with the police when they arrived, which led to further charges: consorting, indecent language and two counts of assault police. Two car-loads with about eight police arrived. We were taken down to Central and charged. I eventually copped six months' hard labour over it, though I was out on appeal for a while."

Some months earlier, upon his release from jail following the Laws SP robbery, Hayes had gone to Donny Day's two brothels in Elizabeth Street. Day had about 10 molls working there at the time. The woman named Daphne also worked for Day as a cleaner. "Since I'd been in jail for nearly four years between 1941 and late 1944," Hayes explains, "'The Duck' said I could have any woman I wanted. So I chose Daphne. We went out on the town and then returned to 'The Duck's' place, where I fucked her. But when I woke up in the morning the bed was soaked. I thought I'd wet myself. I was really embarrassed, so I sent her off to the shower and quickly changed the sheets. I hid the dirty wet ones under the bed. Later I told 'The Duck' and Rene Day about it. But the same thing happened the next morning: I slept with Daphne and then woke up with wet sheets. However, it didn't happen the following morning, because I hadn't slept with Daphne. But then I slept with her again on the fourth night and, sure enough, I woke up with wet sheets. I thought there was something wrong with me. But then Daphne explained that it wasn't me, it was her. I was really relieved."

Three days after the "disorderly house" matter Hayes

appeared, on 13 April, in Redfern Petty Court charged with "indecent language" and "assaulting police". A fortnight later, on 26 April, he appeared in Central Petty Court on charges of "assault", "offensive behaviour", "resist arrest" and "indecent language". These followed a fight with another drinker outside the London Hotel in Elizabeth Street.

Then on 21 May 1945, Hayes appeared at Sydney Quarter Sessions to face the serious charge of "assault occasioning actual bodily harm".

He had been working as an illegal bookmaker at Sydney Stadium, taking bets on boxing matches. He always sat in the same spot, three rows from the ring and about four seats along from the aisle. "One night a young chap named Cahill, whom I never took to be a copper, walked down toward me," he explains. "He leaned past a couple of people to speak to me and asked: 'What do you think you're doing? Well, I replied: 'I'm taking bets. Which fighter do you want to back?' But he ordered me not to accept any more bets. He wore a hat with a little feather, which was a favoured style among detectives at the time. But I thought he was an usher. So I ignored him and continued to accept bets. A preliminary fight was in progress, and when the round ended he asked if he could speak to me for a moment. I stood up and thought we were going off to see Harry Miller senior, who was running The Stadium at the time. I was pretty sweet with Miller. So I walked into the aisle and asked what was the trouble. He said he was a police officer, and I replied: 'Don't give me that!' Many of the senior coppers were regulars at the fights, and I'd never had any trouble before. But he continued: 'I'm a police officer and I'm arresting you for betting.' I said: 'You're not arresting anyone!' He put his hand on my shoulder, but I pulled away. I attempted to return to my seat, but he pulled me back. With that I turned around and punched him on the lip. Then we fell into a scuffle. He was on the ground and I was on top. Everyone stood up cheering — it was a better fight in the aisle than in the ring. They were all geeing me on because I was very well known and he wasn't. . . Eventually a few other police raced in and they carted me off to Paddington Police Station."

But *Truth* reported a different story when the matter came to court. Detective Sergeant Norman Mijch told the jury that Hayes "is somewhat of a braggadocio among criminals" and that he was "a violent man" and an "associate of the worst criminals in this State. He is a man of peculiar temperament insofar as, when he is in the company of criminals, in a form of bravado or in an effort to show himself as a big man, he will act violently. Yet if you converse with him on his own, he seems to be quite reasonable-minded. I think drink plays a big part in his violence."

Police told how Constable Ernest Cahill of the Vice Squad had been "on special duty regarding betting" at the Stadium in plain clothes. He was standing near Hayes at the end of a preliminary bout "when he was suddenly felled to the floor by a terrific punch in the mouth that put his teeth through his upper lip and broke his dental plate. Five stitches were inserted in the lip." Cahill, who identified Hayes as his assailant, said he heard Hayes say: "You mug copper." Then he was felled. The Crown said the attack was "as unheralded and as violent as it was unprovoked." Cahill said he was helped to his feet and saw Hayes standing a few feet away. He "caught hold of Hayes, who struggled violently." Several other police rushed to his aid and Hayes, "still struggling violently, was handcuffed."

The jury found Hayes guilty and Judge Kirby sentenced him to three and a half years in jail, commenting: "You have been found guilty of a savage, unprovoked and cowardly assault on a man you knew to be a policeman who was on duty at the time."

• • •

"Back in those days," Hayes recalls, "the patrol wagon used to tour the police stations and pick everyone up and take them to Darlinghurst Jail — not the courthouse, Darlinghurst Jail — where they'd bundle you all into one big cell. Then the prison tram drove into the yard, inside the police station, and you'd walk out from the cells and step on board. Then they'd drive you out to Long Bay. At 'The Bay', the tram didn't enter through the main gate. It went in via another entrance and continued right into the jail itself. Then you stepped out into a big birdcage. As you alighted, the prisoner governor, prison doctor, a male nurse, the chief warder and half a dozen other warders would be there to meet you. Then the chief warder would order those on remand to step forward, and he'd tell them to turn left and proceed into the reception room. Meanwhile the sentenced prisoners would wait outside for about 10 minutes and then they, too, would march into the reception room.

"One day Hollebone and I were sitting in the prison tram, on our way out to Long Bay, and travelling on the same trip was

David Stewart Dawson. His family was very wealthy. They owned the Strand Arcade, and various other business interests." In the mid-1940s Stewart Dawson had shot George Rankin McKay, formerly a lieutenant commander in the Royal Navy. The ensuing scandal shocked Sydney society. Stewart Dawson was charged with maliciously wounding with intent to do bodily harm. The shooting occurred after an altercation at a party described as including music, dancing and "considerable drinking", at his father Stuart Stewart Dawson's palatial Palm Beach house.

About 11 pm the radio had been switched on and the national anthem began. David Stewart Dawson made insulting remarks about the British King, and McKay took exception. McKay later explained in court: "As the anthem came on, David Stewart Dawson walked over and flicked off the radio, saying in a sneering manner, 'To hell with the ——— King!' I was furious with him. I admit I was drunk. I lost my temper, stalked over to the radio, pushed him aside, and turned on the national anthem again." When McKay pushed Stewart Dawson away, he spilled a couple of glasses of liquor which were sitting on the radio. McKay replied to David Stewart Dawson: "To hell with you! We will have the King." Subsequently, a heated argument developed between McKay and several members of the Stewart Dawson family. Eventually Mrs Jean Stewart Dawson suggested McKay should leave.

He went out to his car, removed his coat, but then returned to demand an apology. McKay claimed: "Stuart Stewart Dawson came through the door brandishing an empty gin bottle. David Stewart Dawson came out behind his father. Stuart Stewart Dawson said: 'Get off my property, you swine! You English Reserve ———!' He kept on calling me names for about five to 10 minutes. I told him that I was not an 'English Reserve ———!', but that I was a Royal Naval officer. Stuart Stewart Dawson then said: 'Get out or I will hit you on the head with this bottle.' The next thing I heard was the sound of two shots. I felt a shock in my stomach. I slumped down on a flower vase on the porch."

Amid the exchange of heated insults and threats of violence on the entrance porch, David Stewart Dawson had apparently taken a pistol from his pocket and fired a bullet which struck McKay in the groin and lodged at the base of his spine. McKay was in hospital for 14 days. He admitted in court that he wanted to fight

David Stewart Dawson if he did not apologise, and that was why he returned to the house. McKay also admitted insulting Mrs Jean Stewart Dawson, so that her husband Stuart Stewart Dawson called him "a swine, a cur and a blackguard".

At one point during the headline-grabbing court hearing, crown prosecutor Mr C. V. Rooney suggested their son David Stewart Dawson was known to his associates as "Trigger" Dawson, and that he associated with gunmen. The defence denied both assertions.

David Stewart Dawson claimed McKay had picked up a ginger-beer bottle and threatened his father. "McKay was drunk, very white in the face and terribly menacing," David Stewart Dawson said. "When he moved his hand I shot at the ground." He said he aimed to miss McKay, but must have jerked the revolver when he pulled the trigger. He insisted that he had shot at McKay's feet and, at the time, did not think he hit McKay.

Police said that during questioning David Stewart Dawson added: "A man should have pumped five bullets into his guts. He screamed like a woman. I shot at McKay's feet to protect my father."

In his address to the jury, crown prosecutor Rooney described the accused's father, Stuart Stewart Dawson, as an "emotional old pantaloon" who provoked McKay and behaved like a "drink-maddened commando". In return, the defence barrister said McKay was nothing but a drunken lout who, "inflamed with drink", tried to take charge of the Stewart Dawson household.

After the guilty verdict was delivered against his son, Stuart Stewart Dawson collapsed in the vestibule of the court. He had to be carried, gasping for breath, onto the grass outside Darlinghurst Quarter Sessions. He sat there for 15 minutes before friends assisted him to his car and he was driven away. The following week, when the judge pronounced a sentence of 10 years with hard labour upon David Stewart Dawson, his step-mother, Jean Stewart Dawson, wept openly in court.

"This particular day when Hollebone and I were travelling out to 'The Bay'," Chow Hayes continues, "we were on a big tram with about 17 compartments. There were six to eight prisoners crammed into each compartment (if it wasn't a busy day there were usually only four in each compartment). In our compartment at least one fellow was standing up. The coppers used to patrol up and down the corridor — the coppers were still in charge of you at that stage, and right up until you arrived inside 'The Bay', where the screws took over.

"There were a couple of old methos in our compartment, along with David Stewart Dawson, who'd already been out there a couple of times. He always used to take some cash inside with him — £20 or £30, which was a heap of money inside jail in those days. On this particular occasion he'd already been warned not to try and bring any money or tobacco inside with him. He was very worried about it. So while we were in the tram, I told him to give the tobacco and cash to me and I'd smuggle them inside for him. He handed me four packets of tobacco and £40. Hollebone wanted to grab the cash, but he told Hollebone: 'Oh no! You're too well known. They'll give you the strip search for sure.' Then Hollebone suggested it'd be safer if he gave the cash to one of the old methos. But the metho didn't have a tie on, so Stewart Dawson took off his own tie and put it on the metho. Now the screws wouldn't search the methos — they'd always refuse, because the methos were picked up around Belmore and Hyde Parks and were always filthy.

"We arrived at 'The Bay', and the remand prisoners stepped out. We were still waiting around, when the next minute this old metho jumped out and — I'll never forget it — called to the chief warder: 'Mr Irwin, I want to pay my fine. And I want to pay so-and-so's fine. And I also want to pay so-and-so's fine!' With that, he pulled out the £40 from under his collar, where Dawson had hidden it when we'd arranged the tie around his neck. That caused a great laugh — especially a couple of days later when everyone found out it was Stewart Dawson's money."

• • •

After prisoners arrived at Long Bay, and those on remand had been separated from those about to begin a sentence, the groups would proceed to the reception room. There they would take part in a routine medical parade, during which prison doctors would examine all male prisoners for signs of venereal diseases, particularly syphilis and gonorrhoea.

"Syphilis was obvious to everyone because of the scabs and sores on the outside of the penis," Hayes explains. "But gonorrhoea involved pus inside the urinary tract, and so you had to squeeze the tip to show whether anything oozed out or not. And if a remand bloke was discovered to have VD, then he'd have to front a visiting chamber magistrate inside the jail first thing next morning — and he'd be immediately detained without bail until he was cured. Moreover, the authorities refused on such occasions to inform relatives why the bloke had been detained — so he had to tell his family himself that he had VD and that was why he'd been locked up without bail.

"Now the treatment for syphilis involved a needle in the arm and two in the backside each week. And for gonorrhoea it was a 'washout' every day: that involved using a bucket of Condy's crystals and a piece of thin tube running from it and inserted into the eye of the penis. VD was very prevalent from the end of World War I until the 1940s. And what made things worse was that many people who caught it decided to 'break even' — that is, they'd decide to spread it recklessly to others, taking the attitude: 'Some bastard gave it to me, so I'll give it to some other sheila!' "

• • •

After serving his sentence for the Sydney Stadium assault, Hayes was released from Long Bay in 1948.

He went to visit his old friend Richard Reilly, who was now running a booming baccarat school on the first floor of the building opposite the fire station at the top of Kings Cross.

Two days after he was released, Reilly happily handed him £2000 to help him "regain his feet".

"The £2000 was already waiting for me in an envelope," Hayes recalls. "There was nothing mentioned about money or how much I wanted or anything. He just said: 'Here, Chow. This will kick you along for a while.' And, to tell the truth, there was a lot of money around then and I thought I might even receive a bit more.

"However, soon after, they closed up Reilly's baccarat operation and he was out of business on that front for about eight years.

"I 'bit' Reilly many times over succeeding years. It wasn't for much — only £200 or £300 at a time. But whatever I asked him for, I received. And I was also receiving money from him while I was in jail. I never bit Joe Taylor or Perce Galea while I was in jail, because they were looking after my wife, especially Taylor, who saw her every week, whereas old Perce was more birthdays and Christmas. But if I wanted anything while I was in jail — say I wanted a couple of hundred dollars — I'd tell my wife during a visit and then I'd write a letter to Dick Reilly. Then she'd take the message up to Kings Cross to Reilly and the cash was always there for me if I needed it."

As usual, it was not long before Hayes made his next court

appearance. On 27 August 1948, he appeared in Central Court of Petty Sessions charged with "assault and rob", following the robbery of an SP bookie in Foveaux Street, Surry Hills.

"Leslie 'Spud' Murphy and I took all his money," Hayes elaborates. "There was no evidence to offer later because we threatened him and the matter was discharged. We went to his place, initially, to stand over him. But we finished up robbing him. We grabbed about £1800. But he knew us, so he went to the local cop shop and they subsequently arrested us. But in the meantime, before it came to court, we arranged for someone to threaten him and he dropped off."

Hayes's mate from childhood, Leslie William Murphy, had earned a particularly violent reputation by this time. Back in February 1939 he and Stanley Arthur Dayment had been charged with murder after Constable Lionel George Guise was fatally shot; Murphy was eventually sentenced to three years in jail for manslaughter. Later, in November 1947, he had been acquitted on a charge of stealing 14 bags of sugar.

• • •

During the late 1940s and early 1950s, Chow Hayes and Joey Hollebone were the two best known and most feared gunmen in Sydney. The newspapers followed their deeds with a constant fascination. But their notoriety instilled instant fear into ordinary citizens who crossed their paths. "Often, if we walked into a hotel for a drink, we'd only be there five minutes before the coppers would arrive to book us for consorting," Hayes recalls. "The squareheads would telephone them and report where we were, because they were afraid of trouble. At that stage six o'clock was always closing time. Then half a dozen of us would pitch in and buy a dozen bottles of beer in a sugar bag and head off to someone's house to drink it."

One incident Hayes and Hollebone were involved in around this time concerned the former boxer Billy Madden, who fought under the name "Sailor" Madden. Hayes had first met him in Parramatta Jail, when Madden was serving 10 years for a manslaughter conviction.

"Madden was a nice little fellow, only a bantamweight," Hayes recalls. "But by the time he left jail he'd ballooned out to about 10 stone [64 kg]. Early in 1948 he walked into the London Hotel in Foveaux Street. He had a young bloke, aged about 19 or 20, with him. He was a big lump of a lad, and Madden told me and Joey Hollebone that this kid was a good fighter — which turned out to be a load of shit! Madden boasted that he'd made arrangements for this young bloke, whom he called 'The Duke', to fight at Leichhardt Stadium. Madden told us to go and bet on him because he was a sure thing.

"The Leichhardt fights were staged on Thursday evenings. Hollebone and I gathered some cash together and went over and backed him. In addition, Madden had assured us that, if his bloke was losing, he'd knee his opponent in the balls so he'd be disqualified — and then all bets would be cancelled. But his opponent walked out and hit him straight on the chin and the big bastard lay down and wouldn't budge.

"After the fight Hollebone and I bought some beer and went back to Hollebone's place in Surry Hills, with 'Cossie' Dugdale and Madden and 'The Duke'. Hollebone was complaining that 'The Duke' was nothing more than a big wimp, but Madden kept insisting he wasn't, that he'd hurt his head. In that case, Hollebone suggested, he should take a whiff of gas from the oven to clear his head. Hollebone said he did it himself every morning when he woke up to clear his head from the beer. So 'The Duke' bent down on his knees and put his head inside the oven door. I turned on the gas, and Hollebone instructed: 'Now be sure to take a good whiff.' And with that Hollebone pushed his head right in and slammed the door.

"Madden soon began yelling not to kill the poor bastard. His head was inside for about half a minute, and he was unconscious when we pulled him out. We carried him down to the corner of Elizabeth Street and Kippax Street, and left him there. When he was found, the coppers didn't know what had happened. The newspapers initially suggested that a man had tried to commit suicide by gassing himself. But the police found out later that Hollebone and I were involved. Nobody was charged with anything, though it made things pretty hot for us at the time.

"Madden was later hit over the head with a couple of bottles in Alexandria and killed. It was just a fight. They charged a bloke over the incident, but he beat it."

15 The Wig and the Pianola

Hayes and Hollebone regularly became involved in high-spirited, all-night drinking sessions. They would fill a couple of sugar bags with blackmarket bottles of beer, round up a few mates and settle down for a timeless drinkathon. But in August 1948 one of their informal "parties" turned decidedly nasty.

Hayes and Hollebone, accompanied by Leslie "Cossie" Dugdale and William "The Kid" O'Connell, trooped over to Herbert "The Wrecker" Warner's home in Surry Hills. (In March 1947 Warner, described in court as a "dealer", had been convicted of using a standing vehicle for selling peaches; two months later, this time described as a "barrowman", he'd been found not guilty on a charge of having stolen or received a wireless set. A Sydney court would later hear that Warner had a criminal record including 117 offences involving barrows, and 15 other convictions. The same court was told Dugdale's record included 42 convictions, including breaking, entering, stealing and assault. Later Dugdale, described as "well-known in Sydney's underworld", was found shot through the stomach and shoulder after a brawl during a party at the rear of a Woolloomooloo house in November 1951; he was rushed to St Vincent's Hospital with a bullet embedded in his pelvis. O'Connell's record included convictions for breaking, entering and stealing.)

Hayes and Hollebone arrived at Warner's place with several of the tell-tale sugar bags slung over their shoulders. But Warner, though glad to see his mates, confided that he was "having a blue with the missus". Rather than miss out on a rowdy drinking session, however, he quickly suggested they all walk down the road to the nearby home of Philip and Adelaide Great in Raper Street.

"We were sitting there having a drink," Hayes recalls, "when 'Wrecker' suddenly said to Philip Great: 'That's my pianola!' So he and Dugdale picked it up and carried it out the door and over to Warner's place. Hollebone and I simply sat there watching from the lounge. It wasn't 'Wrecker's' pianola at all, and Great was complaining loudly. Then 'The Kid', Warner and Dugdale went upstairs and pinched some jewellery and money. Hollebone and I honestly didn't know anything about what they were up to — we just sat there on the lounge drinking.

"Meanwhile their daughter came home with three young fellows (they were about 21 and she was about 19). She went into the kitchen to talk to her parents and then they continued what was a heated discussion out in the backyard. Now from the yard they could see Warner, Dugdale and 'The Kid' upstairs — they'd turned on the light up in the bedroom — and they could also still see, through the kitchen window, that Joey and I had remained seated downstairs on the lounge. The daughter came back into the loungeroom and asked us why we'd let Warner take their pianola. We replied we knew nothing about the pianola dispute. But when we stood up to leave, the daughter stopped us and said she wanted the pianola back. In the meantime, her old mother had gone upstairs and found the place ransacked and the jewellery and money stolen. She screamed out and ran back down the stairs. So Hollebone and I decided we didn't want to become involved in this, and I said: 'Let me through the doorway.'

"Now I never hit women. But I had to move them away from the door. So I grabbed the mother by the hair to pull her away and, you wouldn't believe it, off came her wig and she was as bald as a new baby's bum! She grabbed her hair and ran outside screaming at the top of her voice, with her husband chasing behind. I fell back onto the lounge laughing, and the three young blokes took off after the Greats. Hollebone and I were left there with Warner, Dugdale and 'The Kid'. About 20 minutes later an old police sergeant arrived, accompanied by a young copper. As they walked along the hallway the sergeant, who knew Hollebone and me, took one look into the loungeroom and declared: 'Oh! You have a house full of murderers in here!' And with that he walked straight back out again. He didn't want to become mixed up in this argument at all.

"We all headed off home: Hollebone and 'The Kid' to their nearby houses in Surry Hills, Dugdale to his place out Bondi way, and me to Thomas Street. But about 2 am a loud banging started on my door. It was the police. I was convinced I'd done nothing, so as I was walking down to the door, I really thought someone must have been shot. Whenever anyone was shot in those days the first people the police would come and question were Hayes and Hollebone.

"The police took me down to the CIB by car. I walked past one room and Hollebone was sitting there with two or three coppers talking to him. They marched me into another room and, after about 20 minutes, said they were going to charge me with armed robbery. They didn't even ask me any questions — they just said I was at Great's place that night and had robbed it. I said I didn't have a gun, neither did Hollebone nor anybody else who had been there. But they gave Warner a gun — they said one they 'produced' was his — and they kicked the shit out of him. They also beat up Dugdale and 'The Kid'. But they never touched me or Hollebone. Then they took us down, charged us and split us all up into different cells. On the way down the stairs I passed a senior copper on his way up. He asked the coppers who were taking me down: 'Did Chow make a statement?' And they all laughed and one replied: 'Yeah, he made a *verbal* statement!' (All my life I've never made a single written statement.) Then he added Hollebone had made a verbal statement too, and they all laughed again."

Hayes, Hollebone, Warner, Dugdale and O'Connell duly appeared in Central Court charged with having assaulted and robbed the Greats. Warner was also charged with carrying an unlicensed power pistol at night. Police Prosecutor Sergeant Whelan said it was alleged that while the men were at the Greats' home "they tied neckties around the throats of Great and his wife" and, reported the *Sydney Morning Herald*, "threatened to choke them and shoot their son. They then threw them into the street and ransacked the house." The *Sun* noted Whelan told how the five men, plus several others, arrived at the Greats' house with "two bags of beer" and, after a meal and some drink, the men had tied neckties around the throats of Mr and Mrs Great, threatening to choke them if they "squealed to the coppers".

Hayes and Hollebone engaged their friend and regular defender, George Amsberg, to represent them in court. From the outset, Amsberg insisted it was impossible for the armed robbery charge to be sustained against Hayes and Hollebone because they had never moved from the lounge.

Nevertheless Hayes appeared in Central Court of Petty Sessions on 7 September 1948 — two days after his thirty-seventh birthday — and was duly committed for trial on a charge of armed robbery involving £619 (the value of the pianola, jewellery and cash) and a separate assault charge which related, among other things, to his action in pulling off Mrs Great's wig. Two

John Frederick "Chow" Hayes

Chow Hayes as he looked in his prime as Sydney's most feared gunman in the late 1940s.

months later, on 2 November, the trial began in Sydney Quarter Sessions.

Truth reported how Kate Leigh "resplendent in a new-look fawn frock, large picture hat and silver fox fur, and with a couple of diamond rings glittering on her fingers. . .had a dress circle seat in the public gallery" during the hearing. "Kate listened intently to police evidence. . . At the luncheon adjournment she dashed over to the boys in the dock and advised them to 'go to the cells and have a good feed'."

Philip Great told the court how nine men and a woman barged into his house around 8.45 pm as uninvited guests. Trouble had begun when he found a picture had been taken from a frame on the mantlepiece. At one point Hayes walked over to him, kicked him on the leg, and said: "Go out and get some glasses, you silly old ——." Great added that Hayes "manhandled me through the door, saying 'bring in four glasses, you silly old ——.' I brought in six glasses, and Hayes said, 'You old ——. Are you trying to be funny? You ought to be dead.' He put a tie around my neck, and pulled the two ends until I almost went out to it. I got the tie off, and Hayes said: 'You old ——, I'll bite your ear off,' at the same time grabbing my ear. My wife raced in, and Hayes said: "You old ——. You ought to be dead too.' He then put the tie around our necks. Warner was singing out: 'String them up to the highest rafter. The pair of ——s should be dead. They don't enjoy their money. Let's put their heads in the gas oven.'"

Adelaide Great told how she was in her nightdress and dressing gown when there was a knock at the door. When she opened it, Warner entered, followed by other men and a woman. "I was pushed back against the wall as they came in," she said.

Despite Amsberg's assurances the five were convicted, and then Judge Stacey classed Hayes as the ringleader. As a result, he sentenced Hayes to five years with hard labour, Hollebone and Dugdale to three years each, Warner to two years and O'Connell escaped with a bond.

"After we were sentenced," Hayes remembers, "a copper came down to see me in the cells. He reminded me that I was also charged with assault (over the wig). He said that if I went back upstairs immediately and pleaded guilty to the assault charge, I'd receive the maximum, which was two years, but that I'd be able to serve it concurrently. He guaranteed that would be the arrangement. Since I'd already copped five years on the robbery charge, it meant I wouldn't effectively receive any more time for the assault. But he also warned me that, if I mucked them around, and went before another judge in two or three weeks time, then I would cop the sentence accumulated rather than concurrent. Well, since I'd already received five years, and it had never entered my head to appeal, I went straight back upstairs and pleaded guilty to the assault charge as the copper had advised. The judge gave me two years, and he made it concurrent. But Amsberg told me later that the assault would have had to go back to the lower court if I'd waited — and it would only have involved a fine or, at most, a three-month sentence!"

Upon conviction and sentencing, Hayes and Hollebone were taken back to Long Bay Jail. After four or five days, Amsberg came out to visit and said he wanted them to appeal. "Amsberg still maintained that we should not have been convicted," Hayes recalls. "Of course, he knew the law, but I hadn't taken much notice of what he'd been saying about it throughout the case. So, initially, I simply said I wasn't appealing because I couldn't beat it. However, he insisted that we would beat it. Then he said we had nothing to lose. But I replied: 'Of course we do. We could wait up to 17 months in the Long Bay appeal yard, when we could be serving some of our sentence at Parramatta or Bathurst or wherever.' Eventually, however, we gave in and agreed to appeal."

The appeal began in the New South Wales Court of Criminal Appeal in King Street, Sydney, on 17 December 1948. "And you wouldn't want to know," Hayes recalls, "they were only in court about 10 minutes — there were three judges — and Amsberg won his point. It all turned on the fact that the witnesses said they could see inside the house and, while the other three were upstairs, Hollebone and I never moved from the downstairs lounge during the whole incident.

"After the hearing I walked down to the court reception room with Hollebone. But as I went to leave, an official knocked me back and said: 'No. You still have two years to serve.' I knew it — but I thought they might've overlooked the wig matter long enough for me to slip out. So then I was sent to Maitland and served the two years for the assault."

• • •

Soon after Hayes arrived at Maitland, his daughter Topsy junior celebrated her ninth birthday. Her mother therefore took her "up country" to Maitland Jail to visit her father.

Hayes recalls the occasion: "Family visits at Maitland — which were only permitted for a maximum of 40 minutes — took place in one of the two small visiting boxes inside the jail. During such visits, the prisoner was kept separated from his family members by a wire partition inside the tiny visiting boxes. And it was a strict rule that absolutely no physical contact was permitted between the prisoner and any family member. But I couldn't resist trying to kiss little Topsy 'Happy Birthday' through the wire — and it immediately cost me three days in solitary confinement on bread and water!"

• • •

Hayes was released from jail in 1950. He immediately re-established himself as one of Sydney's most feared gunmen. *Truth* later summed up: "By the early 1950s, Hayes had graduated to a peak where he was able to 'stand over' with regular success the hardest men in town. He extracted regular weekly tribute to keep away from one big two-up school."

"When I left jail in 1950 I was running real wild," Hayes recalls. "I was standing over everyone. I was collecting £150 a week 'wages' from Joe Taylor; £100 a week from Perce Galea and his partners at their baccarat school in Bayswater Road; between £30 and £50 each week from old Kate Leigh, who was still in Lansdowne Street, Surry Hills (her payments varied depending on how she was going, but it was never less than £30); and £50 a week from a Glebe bookmaker named Larry Daley, who ran the SP in the Vulcan Hotel in Wattle Street, Ultimo. I was also standing over many other people. I used to 'front' a large number of bookies, both SP and at the racetrack. One in particular was giving me £50 and £60 every time I went to the trots or the dogs.

"I'd made up my mind to 'go for broke' and collect money everywhere. I was pocketing up to £1500 a week. It was huge money in those days — but I was spending it just as quickly as I was collecting it...

"One day Hollebone and I went around to collect our 'wages' from Joe Taylor. Taylor spoke to me rather than Hollebone... Taylor started going on and asking: Didn't we think we'd both already spent too much time in jail? Then Taylor put a proposition to us. He said we'd still receive our 'wages', but he'd also put us into a beer house in Crown Street — it was just down from Crown Street Hospital — on Thursday, Friday and Saturday evenings. We were only to sell the beer to taxi drivers sent there by Taylor. He started by supplying us with 300 dozen bottles of beer in sugar bags. But Taylor's stipulation was that we were to stay off the grog ourselves.

"So the beer was delivered on the Thursday to start at 8 pm, and we had good intentions at that stage. However, during the evening Hollebone kept going out to the toilet, and I later discovered that he had a sugar bag there with beer in it. So then I decided to have a drink too. Meanwhile the taxi drivers arrived and produced a card from Taylor to collect their beer. They paid £3 a dozen — Taylor was buying for about 25–30 shillings per dozen. Some of the booze came from the London Hotel in Foveaux Street.

"By about 1 am Hollebone and I were blind drunk. As a result, customers were simply knocking on the door and then carrying sackloads out without paying for them. We finally started to sober up again at about 8 on the Friday morning. But we only had £460 — and there were barely eight sugar bags of beer left. So we went and saw Taylor about 4 that afternoon (another delivery was due at 6 pm). He told us we were real no-hopers, and he suspended us from the 'payroll'. It had cost him £600–£700.

"Then on the Saturday we were in the Newmarket Hotel, on the corner of Campbell and Elizabeth Streets (champion swimmer Fanny Durack's father had owned it) and 'Big Itchy', one of the ringmen at the two-up, walked in and said Taylor wanted to see us. So I went to see Taylor, but Hollebone didn't come. Taylor said it would only be hurting Topsy and the children if I wasn't on 'wages' anymore. He said that if I sent them along on Monday at 6 pm each week they could collect my money. And the same applied for Hazel Hollebone to come and collect Hollebone's money."

Meanwhile Hayes and Hollebone continued to lead the proverbial life of Riley.

"There was a moll named Victoria," Hayes recalls, "and her brother was a police sergeant out in the southern suburbs. All the heavies in the police force, especially all the 'jacks' at the CIB, knew her well. But Hollebone didn't know her, and one day he took her up to 'Wrecker' Warner's place. He was there for about three hours fucking her. But then she said something to him and he backhanded her. So she threatened that she'd 'tell the boys on you'. When Hollebone asked who 'the boys' were, she named all the important detectives.

"Anyway, Hollebone and I were pinched later on for consorting. At Central Court they had four or five cells and then one big cell — if they didn't know you they'd put you in the big cell. Anyone they knew they split up and divided among the little cells. On this occasion I was lying on the board in one cell and Hollebone was over in another cell, when I heard someone inquire: 'Where's Hollebone?' And Hollebone, who was looking out through the peep-hole in his cell, asked; 'What's up, sergeant?' Then this copper replied: 'Who's Hollebone? He's been fooling around with my sister.' Well, you wouldn't want to know, Hollebone pointed over to my cell and said: 'He's over there!' So this old sergeant came in with another uniformed copper and gave me an awful kick in the ribs and yelled: 'Stand up, you bastard, and fight like a man!' Then he said: 'I'll give it to you for going on with my sister, you bastard!' And all the time I was copping a dreadful kicking, Hollebone was across the passage laughing his head off. I finally managed to stagger to my feet and smother up, and I was lucky the sergeant couldn't fight much."

• • •

The late 1940s and early 1950s were years when Sydney's gunmen roamed the streets with what often seemed, to ordinary citizens, to amount to virtual impunity. More often than not, however, he who "lived by the gun died by the gun" — and few of the most notorious gunmen survived into the modern era.

Chow Hayes was one of the lucky few. "The only time I was ever shot was that one occasion in the stomach involving 'Knocker' McGarry," he recalls. "However, another time in 1950 Lawrie McKeon pulled a gun on me one night in Belvoir Street, Surry Hills. But he only threatened me. He had no intention of shooting — the bastard was too weak. I was half-drunk myself, and I was more or less geeing him into firing the shot. But after a lot of talking he didn't, he just walked away."

One particularly cold-blooded gunman of the period, however, died by rather different means. He was Lionel Charles Thomas, whom Hayes met in jail during the 1950s. He was once described by the *Sunday Telegraph* as 'a swarthy beetle-browed underworld lothario", who lived by violence and the gun and faced trial for murder four times.

A baker by trade Thomas had served his first jail sentence (four years for shop-breaking) in Melbourne's Pentridge Prison at the of age 26 in 1931. Upon his release he moved to Sydney and attempted to hold up department store messenger George Oakman in Oxford Street, Darlinghurst, while he was returning from a bank with a payroll. Thomas threw pepper in Oakman's eyes, grabbed the money bag and jumped into a waiting car. But Oakman staggered after him and tried to wrench open the car door. Thomas then thrust a revolver through the window and shot Oakman as the vehicle sped away. Thomas was arrested two weeks later and charged with attempted murder. But at his trial he called a Victorian prison warder as his alibi. "I saw the accused on the verandah of his parents' home in Melbourne at the time of the hold-up," the witness testified. The jury accepted the alibi and Thomas was acquitted. However, the warder later admitted to Sydney detectives that Thomas had bamboozled him about dates and he had not really seen Thomas on the day of the hold-up. But the admission came too late: a man cannot be tried twice for the same crime.

Buoyed by his success, the arrogant Thomas attempted the same pepper-throwing caper in a lane off William Street in Kings Cross in August 1935. Thomas snatched a bag containing £600 from elderly victim John Wilson, and then hauled himself over a two-metre fence and escaped. He was later arrested with a loaded revolver in his pocket and sentenced to four years in jail.

When he returned to the streets, Thomas lived largely as a shop-breaker and burglar until the morning of 7 December 1941, when he and an accomplice pulled off a daring robbery from a railway car which made a fortnightly run to Goulburn to pay railway workers along the line. Outside the village of Yanderra the two criminals set a huge gelignite charge beneath the track. The explosion hurled the car 15 metres along the line, where it rolled over an embankment. Two of the crew were killed instantly, and a third died in hospital the following day. Meanwhile, the explosion scattered hundreds of banknotes around the scene. But by the time police arrived the two crooks had vanished into the bush with most of the £12,000 payroll.

Soon after, Thomas joined the army under the alias Fred Stephens and, somehow, one of the nation's most vicious criminals arranged to serve with the military police. But within a matter of months an army canteen was robbed. The official investigation uncovered some of the stolen goods in Stephens' possession. He was duly convicted of theft by court martial and dishonourably discharged.

Thomas moved back to Melbourne and in 1945 shot and killed a ticket office attendant who tried to slam down the window as Thomas held up Carnegie railway station. At this murder trial, the prosecution produced a confession allegedly made by Thomas when he was first questioned. But in court Thomas repudiated it, alleging detectives had forced him to sign it. "They tortured me," he cried to the jury. "They suspended me outside a second floor window at Russell Street police station and threatened to let me drop. When that didn't work, they tightened a wire band around my head until I fainted." The jury failed to agree on a verdict. Thomas was subsequently tried a second and third time with the same result. The Victorian Government then abandoned the prosecution.

Thomas again ventured north to Sydney, settling in Bankstown under his favourite pseudonym, Fred Stephens. While working as a baker he befriended an attractive middle-aged widow of significant fortune named Phyllis Page. Inevitably a newspaper headline would later record: "Ruthless Romeo wooed and slew widow for her cash."

Thomas had initially moved into Mrs Page's home as a boarder. Eventually he persuaded her to sell her house, cash in two insurance policies and buy a panel van so they could undertake a long camping trip through New South Wales, Victoria and South Australia. They set off in February 1950, but the last her relatives ever heard from Phyllis Page was a letter dated 19 February and postmarked from the southern New South Wales border town of Eden. In June, worried by her silence, they contacted police. Investigations showed Thomas had disposed of Mrs Page somewhere near the Towamba River. After selling the van in Melbourne, Thomas had continued on to Adelaide and then Perth, where he had become engaged to a 19-year-old girl. But late on the wedding eve police broke into Thomas's hotel room and found a collection of bank books with total deposits of more than £5000.

Thomas was brought back to Sydney and tried for Mrs Page's murder in September 1950. Although her body had not been located, he was convicted and given a life sentence.

"Thomas worked in the bakehouse at 'The Bay'," Chow Hayes recalls, "and I became friendly with him. Every Friday afternoon and Saturday morning they'd bake cakes and pies for themselves and he'd make some extras for me. But one morning I came out of my cell and there was a big commotion. Thomas had hanged himself during the night."

A few days later Thomas was cremated at Rookwood Cemetery in the presence of police and reporters. The *Sunday Telegraph* noted that, as the body slid from view, a veteran detective uttered the grim epitaph: "The only decent thing he ever did for the community was to hang himself."

• • •

In November 1950 Hayes appeared in Redfern Petty Sessions, charged with "offensive behaviour", following a roadside brawl in Cleveland Street with a good mate, Eddie McMillan. At the height of the ensuing mêlée the police arrived. The following month, Hayes was convicted of "indecent language" at Newtown Petty Sessions. Then in January 1951 he was convicted of "offensive behaviour" at Central Court of Petty Sessions. He was fined on each occasion.

A fortnight later, Hayes appeared in Paddington Petty Sessions to face charges of "indecent language", "resisting arrest" and "taking liquor into a public hall". He recalls the incident vividly: "I was going to a party at Paddington Town Hall with a group of mates, but the organisers said I couldn't take liquor inside. I told them to go and get fucked. So they rang the police, who rushed down — and I told them the same. The police arrested me and I resisted arrest." Hayes was again convicted and fined for each offence.

February 1951 brought the hanging of some of Hayes's criminal acquaintances: the infamous Jean Lee and her associates.

Jean Lee, Norman Andrews and Robert Clayton had been convicted of the murder of 73-year-old SP bookmaker William Kent at his room in Carlton, Melbourne, in May 1949. Police later told the court that Kent had been "trussed, strangled and robbed of a roll of notes." After a headline-grabbing trial and a series of appeals, they faced the gallows 21 months later.

The *Sydney Morning Herald* reported the following morning that: "Jean Lee was hanged at 8.01 am — the first woman to hang in Victoria since 1896. She could not walk to the gallows. The hangman and his assistant had to carry her from her cell about 20 feet [6 metres] away. She was hanged while sitting in a chair. Lee appeared to be unconscious, and would have fallen from the chair if the hangman's assistant had not held her. The Governor of Pentridge, Mr J. Edwards, said later that Lee had been given a mild sedative last night, but nothing this morning. She wore a grey skirt, whitish blouse and a white mask. At 10 am prison warders led Clayton and Andrews, already masked, to the gallows. Their hands were manacled behind them, but their gait was steady. Two chairs had been placed side by side on the trapdoor but they were not needed. The two men's ankles were manacled just before the trapdoor was released . . . the murderers (Andrews and Clayton) said goodbye to each other in muffled voices a few seconds before they were hanged. With his face covered by a white mask and the noose around his head, Norman Andrews said to Robert Clayton: 'Goodbye Robert'. Clayton, who was standing about two feet away, replied: 'Goodbye Charlie'..."

Hayes recalls: "I'd been in jail with Norm Andrews, who wasn't a bad bloke. But Jean Lee was a real moll. She was the ringleader...It was never revealed in the newspapers, but the whisper was that they'd cut off their victim's penis and stuffed it in his mouth."

• • •

Around this time Hayes and Hollebone became involved in a bizarre series of events while attempting to help sort out the love-life of fellow criminal George "Bombardier" Williams.

A dozen years older than Hayes, Williams had been one of the "Big Mob" at the Railway back when Hayes began selling newspapers. In December 1931, he was sentenced to six months in jail, with hard labour, for carrying razor blades. The court was told that police knew Williams to be "a dangerous criminal" and "close associate of notorious gunmen", and that his criminal record dated back to 1913. Later, in November 1940, he was sentenced to another 18 months in jail for assault and robbery.

Williams had now turned 52 — though from the day he reached 35, he always claimed still to be that age. However, despite his advancing years, Williams had fallen for a shy 17-year-old lass named Junie, from Cleveland Street in Surry Hills. She, naturally enough, was terrified by his advances.

One Thursday, while drinking in a pub down at the Railway, Williams informed Hollebone and Hayes that he was heading off to fight the girl's brother. The brother, Williams explained, worked at a factory in Cleveland Street. Williams asked Hollebone and Hayes to accompany him, ostensibly to ensure a fair fight.

"We agreed we'd go along," Hayes recalls. "Williams knew Junie's brother took his lunch break at 1 pm, and he was planning to confront him in the street. Now old 'Bombardier' was always frightened of guns and iron bars — he'd fight anyone, anytime, with bare fists, but he was afraid of weapons. So Hollebone wrapped an iron bar in brown paper and concealed it in his own back pocket. We caught a taxi across to Cleveland Street and, during the trip, Hollebone offered Williams the iron bar and suggested he hide it in his back pocket just in case he needed it. But Williams refused to take it. Then Hollebone looked at me and whispered that, if Williams started being beaten, then Hollebone would jump in with the bar and whack the other bloke himself.

"When we arrived, we waited about 20 yards [15 metres] up a side-lane outside the factory. Now Williams had been telling us how big this brother was; and how he might prove hard to beat; and how he'd been insisting that Junie not marry 'Bombardier'. So we thought we were about to confront a big strapping young bloke, 30 years younger than 'Bombardier' and fit as a mallee bull. But when half a dozen of the workers walked out for lunch, this tall thin fellow was among them. He would only have been 19 and, in fact, if I hadn't known his age I'd have taken him to be barely 14 or 15. As soon as we realised Williams was only talking about a young kid, Hollebone said to leave the poor bugger alone. But by that time the kid had reached us, and Williams grabbed him and pushed him up against a wall. Williams threatened that he'd better stop attempting to dissuade Junie from marrying him. The poor kid was as white as a ghost. He protested that Junie was his sister. He said he was only telling her the truth and advising what was in her best interests. Then I began to walk away, and Hollebone went over and pulled Williams off and the young fellow disappeared."

Soon after, Williams had an operation on his bowels in North Shore Hospital. In the adjacent bed was a country chap from Tamworth. "One night Hollebone and I went to visit," Hayes recalls, "and Williams kept telling us what a champion fellow this bloke from Tamworth was. After that, every time we went to visit Williams told us about his Tamworth mate and we became quite friendly with him. Meanwhile, young Junie visited Williams daily — he used to threaten her with violence if she didn't keep coming.

"But one night Hollebone and I walked in and Williams suddenly began telling us what a rotten bastard the Tamworth bloke was! Apparently, the Tamworth man had made the mistake of complimenting Williams on his daughter — and Williams had flown off the handle, thinking the bloke was implying that he was an old man!"

Not long after, Hollebone, Hayes and "Cossie" Dugdale were with Williams when he suddenly decided at 10.30 pm one Friday that he was going to marry Junie. "We didn't think he was fair dinkum," Hayes remembers. "But there was an old parson in Harris Street, Ultimo, and Williams went and woke him up and said he wanted to get married immediately. The parson replied that he needed 48 hours' notice. So Williams arranged to return two days later, on the Sunday evening.

"Junie was terrified of Williams. But she didn't ask me what she should do or I'd have told her not to marry him. I'd have advised her to move right away from the area. But instead of asking me, she asked Hollebone. She told Joey she didn't want to marry Williams because she didn't love him and, she added, he was old enough to be her father. But Hollebone stupidly advised her to marry George because he had plenty of money.

"So they were married. Her parents were against it, but she ignored them and ran off with 'Bombardier'. Later the authorities pinched him for marrying a minor and they gave him a year. For a while she would go out to Long Bay Jail to visit him two or three times a week. And by this stage Hollebone and I, and 'Skinny' Brett and Seppi Annen were all in there too. We knew whenever she was coming for a visit, because Williams would go to endless trouble to spruce himself up.

"She always came at 1.30 pm. But one day she hadn't come by 2 pm and Williams began to pace uneasily up and down the yard while he waited. Hollebone and I were sure she'd given him the flick.

"Now between 16 and 17 Yard at 'The Bay', there was a big bell which the screws would ring. That was where you went to be admitted through to the official rooms for your visit. The sweeper usually brought the news that a visitor was waiting. But this day, when Junie hadn't fronted by 2.30 pm, Hollebone persuaded the sweeper to come out in 10 minutes' time and inform Williams that a visitor had arrived at the gate for him. And the sweeper did it alright.

"Then Williams went over to where the screws let you through and said he had a visitor. But the screws insisted that they knew nothing about it. So Williams started to become agitated, because visits ended at 3.30 pm. Finally it was approaching 3.15 pm and Hollebone, pretending he didn't know, asked Williams what the matter was. When Williams explained, Hollebone advised him to start ringing the bell — adding that, when the first screw came over to stop him, Williams should flatten the screw and then, no matter what, he should continue ringing that bell until he grabbed the attention of higher authorities.

"So Williams did just that and warders came running from everywhere. Eventually, when they couldn't stop him, the boss,

Superintendent Harold Vagg, arrived. Only then did Williams finally stop ringing the bell. Vagg walked down to the gate and then came back and confirmed there was no visitor for Williams. Therefore, he said, they were going to charge Williams with misconduct. But soon after the word circulated that Williams had been set up.

"Junie, meanwhile, didn't come out to Long Bay anymore. She'd taken up with another bloke."

16 The Murder of Danny Simmons

The climax of Chow Hayes's criminal career came on the evening of 29 May 1951.

People magazine tagged the sensational happenings "a chain of events that exploded into the gun killing of ex-boxer William John 'Bobby' Lee at Sydney's Ziegfeld nightclub." The events would certainly explode across the newspaper front pages the following day, and continue to do so for much of the ensuing 12 months. And during the subsequent police investigation and eventual courtroom drama, the messy, sordid details of life in the Sydney underworld would be displayed publicly as never before. *People* later summed up the lengthy saga: "Shots rang through a Sydney nightclub. A man slumped to the floor, dying. And the underworld fought to save a ruthless murderer from justice."

People's correspondent depicted Hayes, the murderer, in almost demonic terms: "John Frederick 'Chow' Hayes, man of violence who spat curses at the detectives responsible for his downfall when he was sentenced to death by Mr Justice McClemens in the Sydney Criminal Court...in the course of an Inquest and three trials the evidence was unswervingly of underworld hatred and suspicion, of smouldering rage and finally sordid murder." In a dramatic overview of the whole lurid affair, the magazine added: "Police say that in recent years Hayes has been a feared and hated figure in the underworld...as a 'stand-over-man' who used threats, intimidation and violence for extortion from fellow crooks. But the common criminal combination of an uncontrollable temper with an overweening vanity and a taste for liquor has always made him a potential menace to any man who might get in the way of his ruthless gun or his savage ambitions."

The trigger that ignited the eventual powder keg came some months earlier, in the dimly lit Surry Hills street outside Joe Taylor's legendary gambling den, Thommo's two-up school.

Earlier, two of Hayes's close mates, Seppi Annen and Johnny Flanagan, had been arrested and charged for some criminal offence. Taylor, as usual, put up their bail. Hayes explains: "Taylor used to give the bail money to the old boxer 'Nigger' Reeves — father of 'Chicka' Reeves (a notorious gunman and murderer during the 1960s). On this occasion it was a serious charge and Annen and Flanagan sought several remands, and each time 'Nigger' went down and bailed them out afterwards with Taylor's money. Now the night before they were again due to appear in Central Court, they went and saw Taylor to check that the bail arrangement would continue the following morning. And Taylor, as usual, said yes. So they appeared and were granted another remand and Taylor gave Reeves the money to go bail them out. But Reeves had a few drinks on the way, and he was several hours late. When they were eventually released Annen and Flanagan went around to see Taylor. But they ran into Taylor's partner, Wally Goddard, and he took their visit the wrong way. They tried to explain that they were thankful for the bail, but there'd been a hitch. However, Goddard thought they wanted to be bailed yet again — and they'd only just been bailed. So Goddard began ranting and raving that they were coming around there too often, always wanting bail.

"Meanwhile, Hollebone and I were on the 'wages book' from Taylor and Goddard. We'd collect our money on a Monday, and have nothing left on Tuesday — I'd give my wife half and spend the rest overnight. So we'd walk up the hill from Elizabeth Street and old Wally would be sitting on the verandah in Reservoir Street. (The small game, known as 'The Snake Pit', operated in the house behind the verandah where Goddard sat, in the Mary Street back-lane; while 'The Big Game' was opposite the verandah, behind Dobson's baths.) We'd walk up Dobson's side of the street on Tuesday or Wednesday and make sure Goddard realised we had nothing left. He'd call us over — he loved doing this — and he'd stand there telling us we were no fucking good and never would be and so on. Then he'd put his hand down into his big trouser pocket and pull out a roll of notes and give us another £30 or £40 each and declare: 'Now don't go and drink that!' And of course he knew that's exactly what we intended to do with it...

"Well, Annen and Flanagan were confronted by Goddard and he misunderstood their purpose. Now at that point Bobby Lee, who knew Annen and Flanagan very well, walked out of the house and asked what was going on. Wally replied that these bastards wanted bail again and Lee said: 'Don't bail them!' Annen, of course, immediately told Lee where to go. So Lee, who was one of half a dozen boxers employed as bouncers at 'The Game', walked back inside the house and then returned with three or four other enforcers. They took Annen and Flanagan round into the Mary Street lane and gave them a terrible hiding. And it was all over absolutely nothing.

"When I heard the details the next day, I was really dirty — especially because Bobby Lee and I had never hit it off. My mate Fred 'Boonie' Smith told me. He said: 'You're on the payroll at "The Game"?' And I replied: 'Yes'. Then he said: 'That's a nice thing they did to Seppi and Johnny.' And I asked: 'What was that?' So 'Boonie' told me all about it. He said it wasn't anything to do with Taylor; that old Wally had misunderstood; but then Lee, who knew Annen and Flanagan well, had put on a brawl. Well, the first thing I wanted to know was whether Annen and Flanagan were going to 'back-up'. Naturally, they weren't, because they weren't gunmen — they were good thieves but not particularly violent men. So I decided to talk to Lee and see what it was all about.

"I met Hollebone around 5 that afternoon and he already knew about it. I said I was going down to 'The Game' to confront Lee. So Hollebone and I went there, but Lee wasn't around. I saw Taylor first and he was very upset about everything — and by this time old Wally was upset about it too. Taylor tried to convince me not to do anything to Lee because it was all a misunderstanding. But I insisted it wasn't a misunderstanding at all, that Lee knew exactly what he was doing. I said Seppi and Johnny would never try to stand over 'The Game' because it was always too good to them — for example, if they needed to borrow £20 to pay the rent or something, they knew where they could go to borrow it. Then Taylor agreed that, if I came back at 11 the next morning, he'd have Lee there and we'd straighten everything out.

"Then I went over to where Annen and Flanagan lived next door to one another in Queen Street, Glebe. They looked awful — bandages and stitches everywhere — and they could hardly talk. We drank a couple of dozen bottles of beer (though it was mainly Joey Hollebone and I doing the drinking) and they told us the whole story. I asked what they were going to do about it and they said they planned to give the same style of beating back to Lee. Well that was fair enough as far as I was concerned, and Joey and I left them.

"Next morning I rose about 9 and couldn't stomach any breakfast. I felt crook because Joey and I had stayed at a beer house until 4 am. Around 10.45 am I headed for 'The Game' and met Taylor, Goddard and Lee. We went into the house opposite, which they used as their office, and Taylor attempted to explain how it had all been a mix-up. But I maintained Lee knew Annen and Flanagan wouldn't stand over 'The Game', and that he was a real bastard for bashing them. Even if he thought they were trying to stand over 'The Game', I insisted, he should have taken them aside and talked them out of it. But I knew he didn't misunderstand their purpose at all...

"Well, six weeks passed, and Seppi and Johnny had done nothing about it. They'd decided to just forget the whole episode. They were still out on bail, and Taylor continued to put up the money. And, basically, Taylor didn't want them doing anything more about it because it would only create problems at 'The Game'. Then one Saturday evening I was drinking in the London Hotel. I'd just come back from Randwick, where I'd backed a winner in the last race. It was a real wet day and I can still remember that I was going to put my £300 on the favourite. But it started at 6–4 on, so I decided instead to punt on an 8–1 chance. I had a bet of £2400 to £300 and it won.

"I walked into the London Hotel about 5.45 pm. A lot of people whom I knew were there, including Bobby Lee. After about half an hour I asked him what had triggered the trouble with Seppi and Johnny. He replied that they'd gone to 'The Game' and tried to stand over Joe Taylor. But then I retorted: 'They'd never do that! You only wanted to big-note yourself and gain favour at "The Game".' However Lee insisted he was simply doing his job. Then I declared: 'Simply doing your job! But Seppi and Johnny are mates of yours!' And he replied: 'They were mates.' Then he asked why I was sticking my head into it, and I said because they were mates of mine too. He said he was also supposed to be a mate of mine. But I replied: 'You don't go around knocking down blokes who are supposed to be your mates!' Finally we told each other to get fucked, and so on, but a few bystanders broke it up before it flared out of hand.

"Soon after, we walked outside with three or four other blokes. Before Lee knew what had happened I king-hit him. He fell down and I immediately swung the boot into him. The whole episode had been playing on my mind in the pub, so when we happened to walk out at the same time I just hit him. Of course, he was a boxer so it was important that I landed that lucky punch first, otherwise he'd have beaten me for sure in a fair fight. There were quite a few onlookers standing around as I charged into him, but they didn't interfere — although one did call out: 'Give him a go, Chow.' I glanced over my shoulder and stared menacingly at him and replied: 'You get fucked!'

"I gave Lee a decent serve, and he never landed a single punch. Once he went down I started kicking, and all he could do was try to protect himself. The other drinkers took me back into the hotel afterwards, while a couple bundled Lee into a car. They wanted to take him to Prince Alfred Hospital, but he didn't want to go. So they took him home. Later he told his relations and close friends that he was afraid of what I might do next. He explained that he wasn't afraid of me if it came to fisticuffs, because he could smack my arse. But he was frightened I'd kill him. And apparently a couple of his mates advised him that, if that was indeed the case, then he ought to make sure he 'jumped in first'."

• • •

The next event in the saga involved a relation of Topsy, Hayes's wife.

Years earlier, when Hayes's future wife Gladys Muriel "Topsy" King was 14, she had left home to go and live at her married older sister's house in Wentworth Street, Glebe. The sister was Mrs Elizabeth Simmons. She eventually bore eight children, of whom three were under four years of age when Topsy moved in. Topsy, while living there, provided a much-needed helping hand with the youngsters' upbringing. The tribe at that point included Dolly, Margaret, Betty and Jackie; later Harold, Shirley, Pattie and Danny Simmons followed. (Chow Hayes had originally met Topsy just before the move and then, after a break, resumed their relationship when she was 17.)

The perky youngster Dolly Simmons was about nine years of age when she first met Uncle Chow, himself then about 20. Dolly quickly established herself as Chow's favourite. "She was a bit of a scallywag," Hayes recalls, "and sometimes wouldn't go to school. When Topsy and I married, and moved to Thomas Street, Ultimo, Dolly practically lived at our place. It was about a mile and a half [2.5 kilometres] from her home in Glebe across to our place in Ultimo. I used to spoil Dolly. I always gave her sixpence or a shilling when I saw her. Sometimes when she was around I'd say: 'Gee, the soles of my feet are hurting.' She'd immediately rub them, because she knew she'd receive sixpence or a shilling for doing it. Dolly's mother, Mrs Simmons, always maintained that I spoilt her too much. When I first used to go to the Simmons house I would give each of the kids a sixpence, but then I always pulled Dolly aside later and gave her an extra sixpence. At one point, when Dolly started missing school regularly for about six months, her mother asked me to talk to her. The truant inspector visited her home looking for her, but the authorities never actually took her to the children's court over it. Then all of a sudden things clicked, and she returned to school again and she loved it from then on.

"Dolly came everywhere with Topsy and me during those years. For example, if I took Topsy to the pictures, Dolly would come along too. Topsy said to me: 'She's more like a sister to you than a niece.' From then on Topsy called her 'Sis'. Later Dolly looked after our second child, Paddy, while my wife went to work (Dolly had turned 14 by then). And while she was 14, 15 and 16 she used to come with my wife to visit me in jail. On those trips, Topsy always wrote her down as my sister (in the jail visitors' book), and most of the police and all the screws thought she was my sister. (Years later, after my wife died, Dolly more or less took over looking after me. She did more for me than any sister could. She followed me to every jail, and so on...)

"Dolly's youngest brother was Danny Simmons; we used to call him 'Boy'. He was my wife's favourite, and he wasn't a bad-looking kid. He often used to bring a girl with him when he dropped around to our place. I'd have a go at him (when Topsy couldn't hear) and I'd say: 'After you're finished with her, are you going to leave her with me?' He'd laugh and reply: 'Alright, Uncle.' That's how he'd upset me, because he knew he could always call me Uncle, even in the street, and he knew I'd be dirty about it, especially if he had a sheila with him. He'd say: 'I want you to meet my uncle'...

"On Friday, 28 April 1951, 'Boy' Simmons brought a sheila over to our place in Ultimo. I went out on the town for the evening and Topsy went up to bed, leaving Danny on the lounge with his girl. They stayed for a couple of hours...

"Now we never used the front door at that Ultimo house. There was a laneway, about two and a half yards [2 metres] wide, running off Thomas Street right opposite the Dairy Far-

Danny Simmons

Dennis James "Danny" Simmons was shot through the back window of Chow Hayes's home in Thomas Street, Ultimo on 1 May, 1951.

mers building. During the war years the army had their tents running from Wattle Street to Thomas Street and everyone who lived in our row of seven houses had to carry a special pass to enter the area. So that was why everyone had developed the habit of entering our place via the backdoor.

"But on the Monday evening, 1 May, I didn't go up the back way. For some reason I went to the front door. I jumped out of a car on the corner of Thomas and Harris Streets, and instead of walking another 15 yards [14 metres] to enter the backyard through the lane, I walked straight to the front door. We lived in the middle house, 93 Thomas Street. I strolled in and my wife Topsy, my daughter Little Topsy and 'Boy' Simmons were having tea. I sat down with them and, during the meal, we drank a couple of bottles of beer — though 'Boy' never drank very much. I told him I was intending to take my wife and daughter to the pictures that evening..."

Earlier that day Hayes had bumped into Lenny "The Black Orphan" Wright in George Street near the Plaza Hotel. "I tried to 'bite' him for £200," Hayes recalls. "But he said he was sick and tired of giving me money all the time and that I'd receive nothing. So I grabbed him by the tie and pushed him into a doorway of a little shop and hit him on the eye. He fell over and his glasses fell off. Then he struggled up and ran away down George Street. There was a fruit barrow a little further down the road. I picked up his glasses, walked over to the bloke running the barrow and said: 'That bastard might come back. These are his glasses.' Then I headed over to City Tattersalls Club in Pitt Street. I used to collect a lot of money there on Mondays from the bookies. I had a couple of drinks while I was there, and then I returned home. I forgot all about Wright—he was the house manager at a baccarat game at Joe Taylor's Carlisle Club in Kellett Street, Kings Cross, at the time—and that was the end of the incident as far as I was concerned...

"So on the evening of 1 May 1951, I took my wife and daughter to the Lyceum in Pitt Street. My son Paddy was working in a milkbar on the railway ramp opposite the Plaza Hotel, just down from the Town Hall. Meanwhile Danny Simmons, who didn't have to leave to meet his girl until 9 pm, decided to stay at our place on the lounge. As we left the house, my wife said to him: 'When you go out, "Boy", don't forget to turn off the lights.'

"Now, unknown to me, Bobby Lee was sitting watching our house at this stage, from a car parked up the road in Thomas Street. I found out later that when we walked out the front door (my wife, my daughter and I) Lee, half full of grog, thought it was my wife, my daughter and my son, rather than me. So we went off to the pictures, but Lee thought I was still at home. We left around 7.15 pm in a taxi. Five minutes later Lee jumped out of the car and tiptoed down to our backyard via the laneway. Lee was by himself, but he had a bloke driving the car (it was stolen, naturally) named Ray Griffiths. Lee looked through the lounge-room window. The light was on and he could see the outline of someone on the couch. He thought it was me, so he fired two shots using a .38. The lounge was right up next to the window and both bullets hit 'Boy' Simmons in the back of the head."

People magazine summed up the cold-blooded assassination:

> *An unknown murderer crept along an alleyway beside Hayes' house, and shot dead ex-boxer Danny Simmons, apparently in mistake for Hayes. Simmons was the nephew of Hayes, and a one-time featherweight champion of NSW, latterly a Brisbane bookmaker's clerk, and only recently returned to Sydney. He had no police record in Queensland or NSW, and was a floridly handsome, long-haired, drape-suited member of the mainly adolescent milk-bar clique of bodgies and widgies . . . Hayes was to say that jealousy had been the cause of that shooting, "for Danny was a bit of a ladies' man" . . . Early in the investigation into the death of Simmons, Hayes told the police that four bullet-holes in a nearby wall had nothing to do with the case—they merely resulted from an earlier outburst with lethal weapons!*

While Danny Simmons lay bleeding on the Thomas Street couch, the Hayes family had been enjoying the film *Annie Get Your Gun*. "When we came out of the theatre," Hayes remembers, "my wife suggested walking down to the milkbar near the Plaza Hotel and meeting our son Paddy. But it was only 10.30 pm and I said he didn't finish until midnight — it was no use going down there and waiting around for an hour and a half. Instead, we hailed a taxi and returned home. It was just on 11 pm by the time we alighted from the taxi. Now we both had keys to the house and I generally let my wife open the door. But she remarked: 'That silly "Boy" didn't turn off the lights.' So for some reason I used my key to open the front door.

"I opened the door and walked along the hallway. Meanwhile, my wife and daughter followed me in and then turned to the left to enter the dining room. There was one big dining room at the front, then a middle room which we used as the loungeroom — this was where "Boy" Simmons was lying — and then came the kitchen. There was no bathroom inside the house in those days; it was out in the backyard.

"As soon as I entered the second room I looked over and saw blood down Danny's face and clothes and everywhere. But at that stage my first thought was that he'd been in a fight and had come back to lie down. Then my wife called out: 'Is "Boy" there?' On the spur of the moment, I replied: 'I don't think so.' Then I returned back up the hall to where my wife was removing ribbons from my daughter's hair. I told them both to walk back out into Thomas Street with me for a moment. I explained 'Boy' had been in a fight and he'd been cut up pretty badly. Immediately Topsy wanted to run back in, but I stopped her. At that stage I still thought he was merely unconscious — I didn't realise he'd been shot and killed.

"I made them both stay outside and I walked back into the loungeroom. This time I could immediately see that 'Boy' was dead. There were large bullet holes in the top and back of his head. I also realised he'd obviously been shot through the window in mistake for me. But, funnily enough, later on that night I had my doubts, because he was running around with so many different girls. I thought it might have been a jealous lover or a husband.

"As I started to walk back outside, I began wondering what was the best thing to do. I knew a squarehead would immediately contact the police — but I was another matter. And I knew I had to tell my wife something. So I told her Danny was unconscious and looked pretty badly hurt, and that we'd better go up to Regent Street police station, which was only about 400 yards [370 metres] away. We walked up the hill and an old sergeant named O'Keeffe, who knew me, was on duty with two young constables. O'Keeffe had lived in the district for 30 or 40 years, and I'd known him when he was only a constable on the beat. When I walked in he looked up from his work and his first words were: 'What are you pinched for, Chow?' My wife was three or four yards [2½–3½ metres] behind, and he thought other coppers would be following me in. But then my wife and daughter walked in and he knew them too.

"I said my nephew had been hurt down at our place and there was a bit of blood. I couldn't tell him everything — my wife and daughter were right there and would have become hysterical. O'Keeffe asked what had happened and I said I had no idea because we'd been at the pictures. Then I winked at him and asked could I see him about something out in the passageway. When we walked out there, I told him that Simmons was dead and it looked like he'd been shot, but I didn't want my wife or daughter to know yet. Then we returned to the charge room and O'Keeffe told my wife he was going to send a constable down to our place to check things out. Meanwhile, he insisted both my wife and daughter ought go with him and have a cup of tea. At the same time another old sergeant and a young constable, who didn't know me, pulled up outside the station in what they used to call a PD car. They came in and we all sat around the little room where the police made their own cups of tea. O'Keeffe introduced me to this other sergeant and said he wanted him to go down to Thomas Street and see what had happened. I gave him my keys and the old sergeant and his constable headed off. And when he returned, I've never seen a sergeant so white in all my life. He'd left the constable down outside the house, and he didn't bother about the PD car. He'd just run back and was puffing furiously. Instead of running into the station and calling O'Keeffe outside, he blurted it all straight out in front of my wife and daughter: 'The young bloke's dead and has been dead for some time!' Of course my wife immediately screamed. But when she looked at me I gave her the nod that it was true. Then they said they'd have to contact the heavies at the CIB."

The following morning's *Daily Telegraph* reported: "Constables Somerville and Paddock went from Regent Street police station at 11 pm to investigate a report that a man had been injured. When they found Simmons dead they called in Det. Sgt. McLachlan, Detectives Prentice, Krahe, Rea, Baldwin, Strachan, and the Eastern Wireless Patrol."

A bevy of Sydney's best-known detectives of the era descended upon Regent Street police station. Hayes continues: "When Jack Aldridge arrived he took me outside and said: 'Come upstairs and tell me the whole story.' So we went upstairs (there were only two floors at Regent Street) and all the others followed. At that stage I was surrounded by 10 coppers. I told them everything that had happened that evening. Then they asked if I knew who'd shot Simmons. Well, at that stage I didn't — though I had a very rough idea who it might have been. So I replied: 'No.' But then Aldridge immediately mentioned that I'd had a stink with Bobby Lee on the Saturday evening, 29 April, and I said: 'Yeah.' Then he added that he also knew I'd had another blue earlier that day with 'The Black Orphan'. But I insisted that was nothing. Then he asked did I mind if he questioned Topsy to verify my story? I said: 'No.'

"In the meantime it was approaching midnight. Soon after, my son Paddy arrived home at Thomas Street and found the uniformed copper standing guard. Paddy naturally thought I was in some trouble. He moved to go inside, but the uniformed copper stopped him and informed him that the rest of the family was up at Regent Street police station. He rushed up the hill and had arrived just as I walked upstairs with Aldridge. At that stage I hadn't mentioned to the police that I believed Simmons might have been shot because someone thought it was me on the lounge.

"Aldridge returned downstairs and left me in the upstairs room while he talked to Topsy. She told him exactly the same story. Then he made himself a cup of tea and we all sat there quietly. He explained he'd have to take my keys and lock the house, and that he couldn't do any more until the coroner arrived. Then Aldridge inquired: 'In the meantime, Chow, can you take Topsy and your daughter and son to stay somewhere else overnight?' I replied: 'Yes, they can stay with Ninny at Marrickville.' So I took them out to Ninny's place in a police car. Then I returned to Regent Street, where Detective Sergeant Ray Kelly had arrived while I was away.

"Kelly boomed at me straightaway: 'You fucking done it!' And I answered: 'What are you talking about?' He said I was the only one who had a chance to do it, and he didn't believe my story about the pictures. I simply told him to get fucked. Then he said he wanted me to walk back down to the house again to identify the body. I replied that I'd already identified it, but he insisted that he wanted me to go down again, accompanied by police. At that stage, Kelly had taken over the whole investigation.

"Then he told Ray Blissett and one of the others to go down with me. He wanted Blissett to go because Blissett knew 'Boy' Simmons. Kelly gave Blissett my keys and we headed off. The house was still locked up with a young constable standing out the front. The coroner's people still hadn't arrived, and they didn't come until about 5 am. It was now about 2 am. I walked inside with Blissett, and he immediately commented that whoever had shot Danny had made a good job of him. We both knew it was Danny, so we returned to Regent Street station. Then Kelly said he was going down there, and several other detectives went with him. They were away at least three-quarters of an hour. When he arrived back, Kelly said to me: 'No, Chow, I was only joking when I said those things to you earlier.' Then he explained he knew I didn't do it, but he wanted me to come down to the CIB at 10 the next morning, the Tuesday. When I asked why, he said to make a statement. I replied that I'd make one on the spot, there and then, but Kelly insisted: 'No, we're too busy and we have lots of other things to attend to down at your place first.' Well, I knew what they were going to do down there — they were going to ransack the place, looking for guns and so on! Then he added that I'd better bring my wife, daughter and son with me in the morning and the police would take statements from them too.

"It was now about 5.30 am. I went back out to Marrickville and had a shower. But I couldn't change my clothes because all the others were still locked up at Thomas Street. I never went to bed. Later, over breakfast, I told Topsy what had happened. Then around 10 am we went to the CIB, where Kelly was waiting for us. I went into a room with Kelly and repeated the same statement I'd already made to Aldridge the night before. My wife, followed in turn by my daughter and son, did the same. After the statements were taken Kelly said we could all go. But we couldn't return to Thomas Street yet, because the scientific police weren't finished there. So I asked about our clothes and Kelly said they'd make the appropriate arrangements. A policewoman went with my wife and daughter to Thomas Street, where they collected the clothes they needed and then returned to the CIB. Danny's body had been taken away and all they could see in the lounge room were the blood and some glass from the broken window. Then my son and I were taken down and we grabbed the clothes we needed. Kelly wanted to know where we intended to stay, and I said Topsy and my daughter and son would remain with Ninny and I'd be staying with various friends. They then took the others to Marrickville in a police car and I went straight around to 'The Game'.

"The murder, of course, was the talk of the town, and at that stage I only had an inkling that it might have been Lee. But soon after I arrived at the two-up I was sure, because I was given the complete details of how it took place. Over the next couple of days I stayed at Hollebone's place, and checked and rechecked what I'd been told. There was no doubt it was Lee."

In essence, Hayes was informed that Simmons was indeed shot by mistake; that the bullets were meant for him; that Ray Griffiths and Lee had been sitting outside the house in the car; and that Lee thought it was Hayes whom he'd killed. "So Lee had gone into smoke," Hayes continues, "and Griffiths had also gone into hiding. Then I heard a whisper that 'The Orphan' was in it too. So about 3 pm on that same Tuesday afternoon I went and fronted Wright up at the Carlisle Club, and he shitted himself when I told him his name had been mentioned. He denied it completely and said he was sorry he hadn't given me the £200. And he gave me £500 on the spot. I knew he was completely innocent. So I left him on good terms and went back and talked to Hollebone. Meanwhile, Joey had also heard from several people that it was definitely Lee who'd shot Danny.

"Over the next few days we were tipped off about two or three false trails in our attempts to find Lee's hide-out. We burst into several houses with guns drawn, looking for him — one in Surry Hills, one at Stanmore and one at Rosebery (where 'Cossie' Dugdale came with us). We were loaded up very heavily, but they were all false alarms. And to tell the truth I still don't know where he was hiding out. But a lot of people knew that either I was going to kill Lee or Lee was going to finish me, and so they were trying to jump into my good books by giving me information. However, we didn't hear any reliable information until Monday, 29 May, exactly four weeks later.

17 Bobby Lee — Gunned Down in the Ziegfeld Club

Sydney's media had a field day covering the immediate aftermath of the Danny Simmons murder.

First came the funeral. *People* magazine, noting that Simmons was the nephew of the notorious Chow Hayes, described proceedings as "an event which seemed a minor imitation of gangster burials in the prohibition-time Chicago tradition." But the *Daily Mirror* reported: "The human side of Chow's make-up — so rarely seen — was strongly evident at Danny's funeral. Although his role forbade tears — and there were quite a few shed at the graveside — his white, strained face showed that he was greatly moved. It was Chow who arranged taxis for those who couldn't fit into the mourning coaches, and his hand went deep into his pocket to tip lavishly the sweating gravedigger when the last shovelfuls of earth were placed on the grave of his ill-fated nephew."

Then came the police investigation, accompanied by daily updates; the latest theories; and numerous investigations into the colourful background of the unconventional world frequented by Simmons and his companions.

The *Daily Mirror* recalled:

Dennis James "Danny" Simmons . . . Girls could have been the cause of Simmons' murder. They found it hard to resist the 26-year-old boxer with his black hair and his charming smile. Danny Simmons was also what was known at the time as a bodgie — a cult which was noted for crew-cut hair, velvet jackets, jeans and flash ties. Just after the War, Simmons won the NSW Featherweight Title and the success went to his head. He continued to fight, mainly at Leichhardt Stadium, with moderate success, but with far greater fame as a lady-killer . . . Outside [the Thomas Street murder scene] two neighbours, Mrs Kathleen Border and Mr Kevin Lowe, heard the sounds of the shots. They also heard the noise of two people running up the narrow laneway which ran at the back of Hayes' home. Then they heard the sound of a car moving off. The neighbours discussed the incident briefly, but did nothing more . . .

The *Guardian* of 6 May 1951 reported:

Girls were the chief curse of bodgey-boy boxer Danny Simmons who was shot dead Tuesday evening . . . Girls found it very hard to resist Danny Simmons, with his glossy black hair, high Irish coloring and charming smile, and many of them don't seem to have tried their best. Danny was a curious and unusual mixture — a natural bodgey and a natural boxer. He fitted perfectly into the bodgey world of Sydney. A bodgey is a teenage boy or a young man who generally wears jeans, a velvet jacket and brilliant shirts and ties. The wealthier bodgies wear suits cut in the full American drape style. All bodgies affect peculiar hair cuts — the most popular being the crew cut in which the hair on the top of the head sticks up or is brushed back . . . Sydney police say that bodgies are a menace and that they produce idleness, violence and crime. Many clergy say that bodgies and their widgies (girl friends) are shockingly immoral and that in public they kiss and dance in a most suggestive manner . . . They call their special girl friends "cherries". To be a "cherry" is a kind of super order of bodgey womanhood . . .

Danny Simmons fitted perfectly into the bodgey picture — he loved the bright clothes, the moving in gangs, and the widgies . . . Simmons was a lad of 16 when the War broke out. Two years later he joined the Army . . . Military training toughened him and he decided he would like to be a professional boxer. One day in 1943, while on leave, he drifted into the office of stadium manager Herb McHugh and said he would like some fights . . . He appeared occasionally in the ring in Sydney for the remainder of the War, and more regularly after it ended, first as a preliminary fighter, then in main bouts . . . Just after the War Simmons won the NSW featherweight title and the success went to his head rather badly . . . Wearing full American drape suits, blazing ties and two-tone shoes, and favoring a crew haircut in approved bodgey style, he was a familiar figure in the milk bars, restaurants and dance halls of Oxford Street and Paddington. Milk bars are the very hub of Sydney bodgeydom. Bodgies and widgies meet in them, dally over chocolate malteds and talk about each other in a language that is quite foreign. Pretty girls are "keen" and attractive youths are "sharp". Love is a word they never use. They shudder at it.

Simmons became a bodgey leader . . . Many bodgies looked up to

Simmons with something like awe . . . He developed the habit of approaching girls — total strangers to him — in the dance halls of East Sydney. He would roughly edge a girl's partner out of the way in the middle of a dance and say simply. "I am Danny Simmons." The flashing smile appeared and Danny set out along the familiar path to conquest . . .

About two years ago Danny Simmons quit the fight game. He went to McHugh and said that he was going to give up fighting. "I'm going to bow out now, while I'm as near the top as I'll ever be," he told McHugh. "I'm not going on fighting until I'm punch drunk. I've seen too many of them." Privately — and not unreasonably — Simmons confessed to some of his bodgey friends that he didn't want his face to get knocked about. Two years ago he went to Brisbane where he became a bookmaker's clerk . . . About two weeks ago Simmons came to Sydney for a holiday . . . But Sydney friends persuaded Simmons to return to the ring and, at the time of his death, he was considering a challenge to fight featherweight Keith Francis . . . Five days after his last dance, aged only 26, he was to die . . .

A few days later one newspaper reported, with huge headlines, that detectives had learned

murdered boxer Danny Simmons recently knocked out members of a gang who tried to waylay him. About a week ago the dead man thrashed four men who attacked him on his way home from a dance. Detectives said they knew several men were jealous of Simmons because of his popularity with women . . .

Detectives believe the murderer scaled a six-foot [180-centimetre] galvanised-iron fence dividing the tiny backyard of the Thomas Street house from a narrow lane off Mews Street. They found bags over the top of the sharp edges of the fence. Detectives said that the killer had then climbed over a stack of boxes near the window to avoid knocking over a group of empty beer bootles . . . Chow Hayes told detectives that several bullet marks in the living room wall were made during an earlier shooting . . .

Lance Young, who lives next door, said he heard a crash about 8.15 pm, followed by two shots. "A man ran up the alley into Mews Street and jumped into a car, which a mate was holding there with the engine running," he said.

Eventually City Coroner Mr A. N. Bott found that "Simmons was murdered by a person or persons unknown."

• • •

Danny Simmons's Funeral

Chow Hayes and his wife, Topsy, at the funeral of their nephew, the good-looking womaniser and bodgie-boxer, Danny Simmons. He was murdered in the Hayes home in Ultimo, mistaken for his uncle, Chow Hayes. The mix-up triggered a series of sensational events which culminated in a volley of gunshots beside the crowded dance floor of the Ziegfeld Club.

Four days after Simmons's murder the Hayes family returned to their home. But Joey Hollebone and Chow Hayes continued to search around Sydney's underworld hide-outs for Bobby Lee. Eventually, on 29 May, while Hayes was drinking at the London Hotel (where he'd earlier flattened Lee) a friend named Jackie Hodder walked in.

(Years later John Charles "Jackie" Hodder would be sensationally stabbed through the chest on the municipal dance floor during a wild party at Waterloo Town Hall in March 1965 attended by several dozen car-loads of leading criminals, stand-over men, spivs and touts, pimps and prostitutes. The astounded trial judge subsequently remarked that Hodder's death had almost no effect on several hundred guests at the debauched party — the band went on playing and the guests continued to dance around the crumpled, badly bleeding Hodder. Notorious gunman Charles Edward "Chicka" Reeves, a man Sydney police were extremely eager to see behind bars, was charged with murder. Reeves always insisted it was a "frame-up" but, knowing he had no chance before a jury against Her Majesty's constabulary, he agreed to plead guilty to manslaughter and was duly sentenced to three years in jail. However, eyewitnesses within the Sydney underworld have always laughed that, in fact, another prominent underworld thug, Ronald Albert Feeney (whose nightclub sobriquet was 'Ronni Royal') was actually the man who plunged the knife into Hodder's chest.)

Jackie Hodder discreetly informed Chow Hayes that his brother, Wally Hodder, had arranged to meet Bobby Lee later that evening. Jackie Hodder explained that he didn't know where the meeting was to occur, but he did know that his brother and Lee were eventually dining at the Ziegfeld Club.

The Ziegfeld Club, in King Street between Pitt and Castlereagh Streets, had previously been known as the Ginger Jar. It was then a dance hall of sorts, with Chow Hayes's mate Dick Reilly working as the doorman. But after a shooting on the premises (following which a man and a woman were each sentenced to 10 years in jail) the name was changed from the Ginger Jar to the Ziegfeld Club.

The information about Lee's imminent appearance in public at the Ziegfeld Club was the break for which Hayes and Hollebone had been waiting. "I asked Jackie Hodder to contact Wally," Hayes recalls. "Jackie said he would do it, and that I should come to his home in Riley Street later that evening around 8.30. So Hollebone and I did that, and Wally Hodder was there with his brother, Jackie. Wally also had his wife Betty with him. Wally confirmed that he had indeed arranged to meet Lee at the Ziegfeld that night, and that Lee would be accompanied by a seaman and two sheilas. Wally didn't mind helping me — he wanted to be on my side in any 'blow-up' because he thought I'd be much more dangerous than Lee.

"We left Jackie Hodder's house about 9 pm. Hollebone had a .22, but he felt it was too small. So he suggested that he return to his home and grab a .38. But I had a .38 with me, so I said: 'No, you can take this.' Then Hollebone headed off and I said I'd meet him later at a mate's house in Glebe — that was where I had to wait for a telephone call from Wally Hodder to confirm that Lee had arrived. Then I returned to my own home, where I had a .45. Now a .45 is about eight or nine inches [20–23 centimetres] long and it's a real heavy bastard, weighing about 1½ lb [700 grams]. You couldn't carry it in your outside coat pocket because it was too big. And you couldn't conceal it in your hip pocket because it was liable to balance over and fall out. So the only way to carry a .45 was in your waistband.

"Now this is where fate came into things. My wife liked Hollebone — she enjoyed his company compared with that of most of my other friends — but she didn't like his wife, Hazel. About 10.15 pm Hollebone arrived at my place and he had Hazel with him. I immediately called Joey out into the kitchen and asked: 'What's Hazel doing here?' And he replied: 'Oh, she put on such an act I couldn't get rid of her.' Hollebone had told her that he was going to a party and she'd insisted that she wanted to come. Now I knew Hazel was 'solid' and would never say anything. But at that point I had no intention of actually shooting Lee at the club — I thought it'd be outside later.

"Anyway, at 10.30 pm I went across to the Glebe house by myself. By the time I arrived they'd already received the telephone call from Wally Hodder to confirm that Lee was at the Ziegfeld Club. So I rushed straight back to Thomas Street. But in the meantime Hazel had informed Topsy that we were going out to the club and there were likely to be other women present and all that sort of thing. Now Topsy usually let me do what I liked. But when, earlier, she saw me take out the .45, she knew I was up to something and she didn't want to see me end up in trouble. So when I arrived back home, she insisted that she was also coming with us. I said she couldn't, but she kept insisting that she was. Eventually she had her way — mainly because I didn't want to be stuck there arguing and miss Lee.

"It was my son Paddy's night off from work, and my daughter was also at home. So my wife took them down to Mrs Haywood, who lived in another terrace two doors along the block, and asked if they could stay there for a few hours. Then the four of us headed off to the Ziegfeld Club, which Eric O'Farrell (who operated a series of illegal gambling clubs with Perce Galea over the years) was running at that point.

"There must have been 80 people inside the Ziegfeld that evening. A band featuring half a dozen musicians playing guitar, piano and so on was performing on a little podium-style stage. As we walked in and started down the stairs, I spotted Lee straight away. He was with the seaman, two sheilas and Wally and Betty Hodder. He spotted me, too, and he watched our group walk across and sit at a table about three away from where he and the Hodders were seated. Soon after, O'Farrell strolled out from the kitchen, noticed us and immediately walked over to say hello. He had no idea I was there looking for Lee. He commented how surprised he was to see us all there, because Hollebone and I didn't usually take our wives out to this type of nightspot. We replied that we'd just walked in for a drink, and O'Farrell said he'd fix us up. My wife didn't drink, so I asked O'Farrell if they could arrange a cup of tea for Topsy. He said "Certainly," and a waitress went and made it for her.

"All this time I hadn't told Topsy that it was Lee who killed Danny Simmons. Whenever she asked me, I'd reply that I didn't know, but that maybe it was a stranger, such as an ex-lover of one of his girls. Topsy didn't even know that I thought it was supposed to be me at whom the bullets were aimed...

"After a while I happened to glance over to Lee's table, and I noticed he was staring back at me. So I informed Hollebone that I was going to walk over to Lee's table. Joey advised me not to do it; he wanted me to be patient and wait, instead, until Lee left the Club. But then a new dance began and Lee stood up and commenced dancing with one of the sheilas. Shortly after, Wally and Betty Hodder walked over to our table, and bloody Betty Hodder asked me: 'What about a dance?' So we stood up to dance. But as we reached the dance floor, Lee and his sheila returned to their table and sat down again. I continued to glance around and glare at him and, when the dance eventually finished, we stopped right beside Lee's table. And, of course, there were now two vacant seats, left by Wally and Betty.

"So I sat down at Lee's table, right opposite him. But Betty walked back to Wally at our table. Then Lee asked: 'Are you going to let bygones be bygones and we'll have a drink?' But I replied: 'Have a drink? You bastard!' To which Lee retorted: 'It was just a mistake.' Now by this time Hollebone had strolled over and I'd decided to go along with Lee, for the moment, and pretend I was going to let bygones be bygones. Lee introduced his seaman mate to Hollebone when Joey arrived at the table. And Lee told Hollebone that he and I had patched up our differences. Hollebone said that was alright, but Lee had still done the wrong thing by bashing Seppi Annen and Johnny Flanagan. Lee retorted that they deserved it. But Hollebone began to argue the point. He insisted even Joe Taylor now agreed they did not deserve it, and that Lee had raced out with a few other ex-pugs, itching for a fight, without checking what was really going on.

"Hollebone declared: 'I think you're a bastard for that!' But Lee stupidly replied that it wouldn't have made any difference if it had been Hollebone himself. Well, at that comment, Hollebone told Lee he was talking shit. And Lee, now that he'd swallowed a couple of beers, was becoming a bit cheeky. In addition, he assumed we wouldn't do anything as outrageous as shoot him in the middle of the club. And, of course, at that point I had no intention of shooting him while we were inside.

"Then Hollebone threatened Lee: 'Come out into the shithouse and I'll give you more than Chow gave you.' Of course Lee replied that he wouldn't walk into any shithouse with Hollebone. Then I tried to calm things down a bit, because I knew Hollebone was liable to fly off the handle and shoot Lee at any moment. So I interjected: 'Oh break it down, Joey. He doesn't mean it.' But Lee butted in again: 'I mean it alright!' And he repeated his boast that it would have made no difference if Hollebone had been the one up at 'The Game' that night. Then he added that it would have made no difference even if it had been me. Well, I immediately snarled: 'You're fucking joking!' But he snapped straight back: 'I'm not joking.' So then I said: 'Look, I want to have a talk with you — we'll go outside.' But he replied: 'Don't be fucking silly! I'm not going outside.' Finally I said: 'You'll have to leave sometime.' But he quipped: 'No, I won't. I'll just stay here.' Then he added: 'I'll ring up and arrange some protection.'

"Then one of the sheilas poured out some drinks. But I had no intention of sharing a drink with the bastard. And Hollebone kidded to spill his glass, because there was no way he was going to drink with Lee. Again I suggested to Lee: 'Now look, come outside for two or three minutes and we'll have a talk. We can't talk here in front of strangers.' But he replied: 'They're not strangers, they're my friends. And I'm not going out because I know why you want me out there.' So I asked him: 'Why do you think I want you outside?' And he replied: 'To go on with it, of course!' Then I insisted: 'No. I told you it's all forgotten.' But he said he definitely wasn't walking outside with me.

"Then Lee said: 'You wouldn't do it in here, with the lights shining and all the people around.' So with that I pulled out the .45 from my belt and held it just above the table. I wasn't really hiding it and other people did see it. And said: 'I'll fucking give it to you here, don't worry about that!' But he said: 'No you won't. There are too many witnesses.' Then I said: 'Are you going to come outside, and we'll talk things over and I won't do anything to you?' But he replied: 'You get fucked!' So then I just said: 'Well, here's yours!' And I fired and hit him twice in the chest.

"He fell over and out the back of the chair. Then I stood up and walked around the table, because he'd fallen out of sight. When I arrived above his slumped body I pumped another slug into his side and two more into his back. I fired three more times — and by this point the band had stopped playing and people were running everywhere, screaming at the tops of their voices...Of course, after the first two shots, everyone in the Ziegfeld Club — there were many squareheads, as well as a few crims — had seen me walk around the table and pump the other three shots into Lee...

"Meanwhile Hollebone had run over and grabbed Hazel and Topsy. He knew we had to disappear from the scene as quickly as possible. He led them towards the door, as I also headed for the bottom of the stairs. When I reached the stairs, a bloke about 55 years old from Melbourne (I found that out later) grabbed my arm and hit his hand on the railing and said: 'That's the most cold-blooded action I've ever seen in my life — and I've been to the war and...' But I cut him off by telling him to 'go and get fucked' and pointing the .45 at him, pretending that I was likely to shoot him too. (He was 'playing up' on his wife and was visiting Sydney with a young sheila, his secretary, whom he'd brought to accompany him on a business trip.)

"Then, at the top of the stairs, the doorman attempted to stop us leaving. But I thrust the .45 into his guts and declared: 'Do you want the same?' And he gasped: 'Oh Jesus, no!' So I ordered: 'Well then, out of the way!' He'd initially attempted to stop Hollebone and the women running up the stairs — and Joey said

The murder scene inside Sydney's seedy Ziegfeld Club after Chow Hayes pumped five bullets into two-up club bouncer Bobby Lee late one night in May 1951.

afterwards that he was about to give it to him. But then when I arrived and pushed the .45 into his guts he let us all rush past...

"We hurried out into the street — the Ziegfeld Club was in King Street between Pitt and Castlereagh Streets — and I suggested to Hollebone that we'd better split up. I said I'd contact him the next morning at 'Bronze' Monsetti's fish shop in Cleveland Street. Then I headed off down the hill toward George Street with Topsy, and he went up the other way toward Castlereagh Street with Hazel. When we reached George Street, I put Topsy on a tram and told her to go back to Thomas Street, pick up the kids and take them over to Ninny's place. At that stage, she still hadn't asked me what the shooting was all about. I said I'd contact her later. Once Topsy was on a tram heading for the Railway, I jumped aboard another tram travelling in the opposite direction along George Street, towards the Quay. I stepped off down at Circular Quay and walked up onto the Harbour Bridge. Then I threw the .45 over the railing, assuming it would land in the water. But I mistakenly thought I was further over the water than I actually was and, you wouldn't want to know, the gun landed in a grassy patch on the water's edge. If I'd walked another 10 yards [9 metres] further along the bridge, there'd have been no problem."

Edward Patrick McCudden, a truck driver who lived in North York Street, later told the Coroner's Court that at about 5.30 am on 29 May, while exercising greyhounds in Hickson Road, Miller's Point (immediately below the Harbour Bridge's southern pylons), he found a pistol, which he handed to police. Detective A. F. Clarke, from the CIB Scientific Bureau, said he considered that six cartridge cases found in the Ziegfeld nightclub were fired from this pistol.

Hayes continues: "Then it hit me that all the heavies in the CIB already knew that Topsy and the kids had stayed at Ninny's place in Marrickville when Danny Simmons was shot. And now I'd made an arrangement to meet Topsy there. So I jumped in a taxi and headed straight for Ninny's place. In the meantime Topsy had picked up the kids and caught another taxi to Marrickville. Well, she'd no sooner arrived there in her taxi, than I arrived in mine. I told her to leave the children there, but I wanted her to come with me. She asked: 'Where to?' And I replied: 'Ezzie's place.' I explained it was necessary to go to Ezzie Bollard's house because the police would come straight to Ninny's home looking for us. We took a taxi to Ezzie's place in Cleveland Street, Redfern, and arrived in the middle of the night. I explained to Ezzie what had happened (I'd already informed him previously that it was Lee who'd shot Danny Simmons). By this time I'd also explained to Topsy that Lee was the bloke who'd murdered 'Boy'. It was now about 3 am and I told Ezzie that, in the morning, I wanted him to take Topsy down to Phil Roach's office. Then Roach, as her solicitor, should take Topsy to the CIB.

"Bollard arranged all that for me and Roach duly took Topsy to the CIB, where she made a statement that she was at the club with Hazel and me and Hollebone. She said she saw a man shot, but it wasn't me who fired the gun. I had told her what to say, because I didn't want her to end up in any trouble. Meanwhile, the police pinched Hazel over at the Hollebone household in Surry Hills. But Hazel wouldn't make a statement — she wouldn't say anything at all. Hazel was so uncooperative that she wouldn't even give her name, and simply told all the detectives to get fucked!

"In the meantime, Bobby Lee actually lived for another 12 hours after I shot him. We thought he was dead when we left the club — no doubt about that — because he had five bullets in him and they came from a .45. But after I arrived at Monsetti's fish shop in the morning and met Hollebone, we listened to the 10 am radio news. It said Lee was alive and we couldn't make it out. Then we saw the cable edition of the newspaper, which came out just before lunchtime, and it reported the same thing. Later, during the afternoon, we followed the news bulletins on the radio, and they all advised that Lee was still alive. But he eventually died around 7 that evening."

18 Sydney's Most Infamous Manhunt

When, mid-morning on 30 May 1951, the cable editions of Sydney's afternoon newspapers hit the streets, the Lee murder was splashed across both front pages. The papers reported two people, Wally and Betty Hodder, had been escorted by police from the club. The Hodders, the papers explained, had been in the company of two other unnamed couples. It was also reported that: "Walter Dennis Hodder, 36, clerk, of Clayton Street, Balmain, was charged in Central Court with having shot at William John Lee with intent to murder him at the Ziegfeld nightclub. Police prosecutor Sgt. E. Cahill said police alleged that Hodder was a member of a party at the nightclub when a man was shot three times at about 3 am. . . Solicitor Mr J. Thom appeared for Hodder. . . Hodder was remanded by Mr Beavers SM to June 6 on £400 bail."

"Now you are not granted bail on a murder charge," Hayes recalls. "So I immediately said to Hollebone: 'This stinks' — meaning there was something wrong here. . . Apparently back at the Ziegfeld Club Eric O'Farrell hadn't seen what happened, because he was out in the kitchen. When he heard the shots, he raced in and spotted us all running up the stairs. But he hadn't seen the actual shooting. So he'd rushed over to Hodder and asked: 'What the hell's going on?' And Hodder had replied: 'I don't know.' Then O'Farrell had gone whack, I was told, and knocked Hodder right out. And Hodder was still out when the police arrived two or three minutes later. So the police revived Hodder and took him to the police station."

The *Daily Telegraph* provided a less dramatic version of events: "The club manager, Mr Eric Farrell [*sic*] was locking up the night's takings when Lee was shot. When he heard the shots he said to an assistant: 'Some mug is letting off crackers. Come on and we'll put him out.'. . . An attractive young woman, a friend of one of the club staff, rushed to Lee's aid when he fell. A devout Roman Catholic, she muttered a blessing for Lee and pressed her handkerchief against the wound in his chest."

Back at the police station, Detective Sergeant Ray Kelly quizzed Betty Hodder over the shooting. "I know almost the exact words he used," Hayes claims. "Kelly said to her: 'We're going to charge your husband with murder — and we'll charge you, too, unless you tell us the whole truth.' So she told them everything that happened. Then they said, 'Well, we'll let Wally go on £400 bail, but we still have to charge him. But they never charged her...

"In the meantime they pinched Hazel Hollebone. But we didn't know that until later in the day. They refused Hazel bail and charged her with murder. Then when Topsy accompanied Phil Roach down to the CIB and made a statement they charged her too, and refused her bail. But none of that was in the cable editions — the only details they carried were in relation to Hodder. So I insisted something was wrong about Hodder being granted £400 bail. But Hollebone maintained Hodder wouldn't say anything to the police, because he'd be too frightened. (However, his evidence, both in his statement and subsequently at the coroner's court, was that we were all at a table and he bent down to tie his shoelaces. It was a sure way of 'lagging' us, because you don't say that, you say that you saw everything and Chow was not the man. But he said he bent down to tie the laces and, while he was looking down, he heard shots like crackers going off. And later when my lawyers asked him if he looked up, he replied 'No', that he was too frightened.)

"Anyway, the police charged Topsy and refused her bail. So I sent for Ezzie Bollard and asked him what on earth Topsy had said. He told me she said we were there, but that I hadn't done it. Nevertheless Ray Kelly charged her. Ezzie said it was a holding charge for me. They knew I'd come to light for Topsy — and I would, I had to, I'd have pleaded guilty...

"So Bollard and Hollebone and I were at 'Bronze' Monsetti's place, and I was going to turn myself in. But Ezzie warned: 'No, wait a bit until we can find out a few more details.' Then he went back down to Roach's office and asked why they'd charged Topsy with murder. Roach told him it was definitely a holding charge. Roach had known me for 30 years, and he told Ezzie: 'They want Chow.' Roach explained that the police reckoned they had witnesses willing to testify that Chow had shot Lee.

Roach explained the police were taking Topsy to court on Friday and she'd then be allowed bail — no doubt about that..."

Topsy and Hazel duly appeared in court, where Mr Justice Maxwell granted each £1000 bail. The newspapers reported: "Two women, described as the wives of notorious gunmen, were charged in Central Court today with the murder of William John 'Bobby' Lee in the Ziegfeld Cabaret, King Street, City, early Tuesday morning...Gladys Muriel Hayes, 38, of Thomas Street, Ultimo, and Hazel Hollebone, 31, of Albion Street, Surry Hills...Mr P. N. Roach for both women...Police prosecutor Sgt. Rex Hamilton said...'Hayes and Hollebone are notorious gunmen.'"

Hayes recalls: "So I didn't have to give myself up after all, because Topsy was granted bail. But, in the meantime, those four days in Long Bay nearly killed her. The only consolation was that the authorities rushed her straight into the prison hospital, because they knew she was a squarehead. Joe Taylor put up the £1000. Kate Leigh also went down to bail her, but by the time Kate arrived Topsy had already been bailed. So then Topsy went home."

Meanwhile, Bobby Lee had died in Sydney Hospital at 7 o'clock on the Tuesday evening, about 16 hours after the shooting. One newspaper reported that "doctors had fought all day to save Lee's life by operating and giving him blood transfusions." The *Daily Telegraph* noted that Lee, 38, had worked as "a 'strong-arm' man at a city two-up school" and reported that "Lee's sister, Mrs Dolly Carr, said that Lee played the role of boss of a two-up school in the Maureen O'Hara film, *Kangaroo*, recently made in Australia...Friends said he earned up to £50 a week at the city two-up school and spent lavishly." Somewhat incongruously, the newspaper also reported that "Lee's sister, Mrs Dolly Carr, who described herself as a 'fat lady model', poses for advertisements for a firm specialising in outsize women's dresses..."

After a service in St Vincent's Catholic Church, Redfern, where Lee was once an altar boy, Lee's funeral cortege left for Rookwood Cemetery. Newspapers reported that "about 600 people lined the street outside the church" and "a police car followed the cortege to Rookwood."

Hayes stayed at Monsetti's place on the first night after the shooting. The following morning he contacted his mate, "Wrecker" Warner, who worked as a barrowman. (During those years

Warner and his fellow barrowmen were chased around the city, from one street to another, and fined £2 at a time if the authorities caught them selling from their unofficial fruit stalls.) Hayes asked Warner to go to Thomas Street on Friday afternoon, once Topsy was home from Long Bay Jail, and, in case the police were watching his house, knock on each door in the row of terraces. When Topsy came to her door, Warner was to pass on a message that Chow was okay.

Meanwhile, after the night at Monsetti's place, Hayes and Hollebone had gone into hiding at Jackie Day's house. (Day was the man who'd given evidence for Hayes during the Eddie Weyman murder trial six years earlier.) At that point Day was living in the Rockdale–Kogarah area, away from his wife Kitty. The fugitives stayed with Day for about a week. "Day was alright about it," Hayes recalls. "But he didn't really explain who we were to the sheila with whom he was living. And she was a bit of a squarehead and didn't want us around. You could feel the tension. Then one evening about 5.30 pm Hollebone and I walked up to the local hotel at Kogarah to buy some beer. We were in the bottle department and from there you could see out into the lounge area. Well, you wouldn't believe it, but Les Gastle, the well-known detective, was sitting at a table having a drink with his wife. So we hightailed it out of there very quickly!"

From Day's place Hollebone went back to Monsetti's fish shop in Cleveland Street and Hayes returned home to Thomas Street. "I simply decided to go home," Hayes explains, "hoping it was the last place the police would look for me. I had to stay out of the way of the kids, so I hid in the back room and locked the door. I'd come out when the kids went to school."

In the months before Lee's shooting Hayes had been betting heavily, on credit, with Larry Daley, the SP bookie at the nearby Vulcan Hotel in Wattle Street, Ultimo. Hayes, loaded with more cash than he knew how to spend, was plunging £200 or £300 at a time on horses, and settling his account with Daley each Friday. "Daley also owned a few houses around the district which he rented out," Hayes recalls. "He was a very nice fellow and you could go and 'bite' him for £1000. As a matter of fact I bit him one day for £1500. I told him I was going bad (at that stage I already owed him about £2200) and that I owed another bloke £1500. Well, he said he'd lend it to me, which meant that I owed him almost £4000...

"When I returned to Ultimo from the Kogarah hide-out,"

Hayes continues, "I started betting with Daley again. And a couple of months later when I was eventually captured by the police, I thought he might have caused it indirectly — though I later found out he had nothing to do with it. See, I had been betting big, but paying him on the Friday. And while I was in hiding my wife, Topsy, would take the bets down to the pub for me (it was only around the corner) and she'd have five bob each way on something for herself. I was betting up to £1500 and £2000 a week. So at first I thought Daley was the only one who knew that I had to be in constant touch with Topsy to decide my bets and, therefore, I must be hiding out at home...

"I was living at home for six weeks. On different occasions various detectives such as Jack Aldridge or Ray Kelly would drop around to the house. Aldridge would knock on the door and tell Topsy that he knew she would have been in touch with me, and that I should give myself up to him and everything would be alright. She'd duly reply that she hadn't seen nor heard from me. Of course, at the time Topsy was out on £1000 bail herself and she had to report to police twice a week.

"I remember one day Aldridge and another detective arrived and I was sitting on the lounge. There was a knock at the door and, as Topsy answered, she gave me the hint by immediately exclaiming: 'Oh, it's you, Mr Aldridge!' But there was no place I could hide. Anyway she was positive that they'd never come inside, so she asked if they would like a cup of tea, and they replied: 'No.' But by doing that she knew they'd think there was no way I was there at the time. And so they went away..."

During the two months Hayes and Hollebone were on the run, a policewoman (unaware Hayes was, in fact, living in his own home) used to follow Hayes's young daughter to and from school, on the off-chance Hayes might contact her with a message for his wife.

On 1 June police asked Sydney's newspapers to publish large pictures of the fugitives Hayes and Hollebone. On 24 June, nearly a month after the massive manhunt had begun, one newspaper dramatically reported: "Detectives say two gunmen they are hunting have boasted to friends that they will 'shoot it out'. Detectives describe the police search as one of Australia's most intense 'undercover' manhunts... Detectives estimate more than 200 underworld members have been questioned on the wanted men's movements. They believe many have remained silent because they fear reprisals from the men's associates.

Police also have raided homes, guest-houses and even country shacks in their search for information." A week later another reported: "Crack members of the Shadow Squad have been called in on the search, and police in every State have been alerted. Hundreds of underworld identities have been closely questioned, but fear of violent reprisals is believed to have caused most of those interviewed to keep silent."

Eventually, on 10 July 1951, the police nabbed Hollebone hiding under an upstairs bed in "Bronze" Monsetti's fish shop on the corner of Cleveland Street and Vine Lane. A newspaper the following morning dramatically recounted events:

> *Detectives, with drawn revolvers, surrounded the Hasty Tasty fish shop in Cleveland Street, Darlington, last night and arrested William Hollebone . . . Det. Sgts. Ray Kelly and D. Hughes, with Det. Souter and Const. McDonald, have been visiting every man and woman known to have been associated with Hollebone. Last night they went to the Hasty Tasty fish shop. Det. Souter and Const. McDonald went to the back of the premises and Det. Sgts. Kelly and Hughes went to the front. When the front door was opened after a delay, the detectives questioned the proprietor Harold Vincent Monsetti. Monsetti is alleged to have said that only his father was on the premises. Detectives Kelly and Souter ran up the stairs to a bedroom. They looked under a double bed and it is alleged that a man called out, "Don't shoot. I haven't got a gun." By this time four detectives were in the room, with their revolvers drawn. They called out and a man crawled from beneath the bed. The police kept him covered with their revolvers until he was handcuffed.*

Hollebone appeared in court later that morning, and the newspapers reported:

> *. . . Hollebone, 35, described as a labourer of no fixed address . . . Monsetti, 42, . . . was charged with receiving, harbouring, maintaining and assisting Hollebone, knowing that he had murdered Lee. Mr J. Beavers SM remanded both men and refused Hollebone bail after police prosecutor, Sgt. W. Maizey, said police feared witnesses might be intimidated if Hollebone were allowed bail . . . "Hollebone was only out of jail for about a fortnight when this offence was committed," said Sgt. Maizey. "His last conviction was for carrying an unlicensed pistol at night . . . Hollebone is an associate of Hayes in other crimes of violence. If he is allowed bail, witnesses might be intimidated".*

Hayes recalls: 'Hollebone had been at the fish shop all that time. But someone tipped off the police. The trouble was that 'Bronze' had a lot of blokes and sheilas running in and out of the place all the time, and it could have been anyone. But the police still had no idea where I was. . . However, I found out later that, within a matter of days, my old friend Monsetti gave me up."

Hayes's capture soon after was a major Sydney event. Under large headlines the *Daily Mirror* reported:

> *Shortly before dawn on July 13, 1951, three carloads of picked detectives, some armed with machine guns, set out from the Criminal Investigation Branch courtyard on a vital mission. It was to bring in John Frederick "Chow" Hayes, Sydney's toughest hoodlum. He was wanted for the killing of two-up school "bouncer" and ex-boxer Bobby Lee, eight weeks earlier in the notorious Ziegfeld's night club. Day and night detectives had scoured Hayes' underworld haunts. Now the rendezvous was the least likely place — Chow's own home in Thomas Street, Ultimo. The* Daily Mirror *car followed at what was regarded as a safe distance. The detectives slipped quietly from the cars and front and back of the house were quickly covered. Det. Sgts. Denis Hughes and Ray Kelly burst in through the front. "Come out, Chow," they shouted. "You haven't got a chance. . . " Other police, guns drawn, had rushed in through the back. Hayes, sitting imperturbably on a bed, looked as if he'd been expecting them. He dressed, and showed scarcely a flicker of interest as they handcuffed him and then showed him the gun they found hidden in a wardrobe. He walked quietly into Thomas Street. Then the change was quick as there was a flash from the* Mirror *photographer's bulb. Like a panther Hayes leaped forward, almost throwing the hefty Hughes and Kelly to the footpath. The boot, which was such a dreaded weapon in underworld "kickings", lunged out at the photographer. Abuse poured from his contorted lips, as he struggled, in maniacal frustration, to maim or kill. This was the Hayes the crooks hated and feared. Here was the unchallenged lion of the underworld jungle, in all his startling and ungovernable fury. This was the man whom very few policemen would venture to handle singly.*

People magazine later recalled the event, describing Hayes as "a trimly-built, 5 ft 8 in [173 centimetre] man, who did not at first glance look much like a killer. But. . . when he was arrested, press photos showed a different aspect of him — struggling fiercely between two detectives, mouthing oaths with snarling lips and resisting violently."

A newspaper the next day summed up events:

. . . Hayes, 39, labourer, was charged in Central Court yesterday . . . Hayes was arrested by armed detectives at his home in Thomas Street, Ultimo, early yesterday morning . . . Three car loads of police left the C.I.B. at 5 am and surrounded Hayes' home in Thomas Street. Det. Sgts. Ray Kelly and D. Hughes, with Det. Chowne, went to the front door. Det. Sgt. Jupp and Det. Souter, with drawn revolvers, stood back in Thomas Street and covered the balcony of the two-storey house. Det. Sgt. G. Davis with Detectives Day, C. Abbott, S. H. Duff and Randall went to the narrow lane at the back of the house, where they found the gate barred. Det. Sgt. Kelly banged on the front door and shouted, "We are police. Let us in." Mrs Hayes looked over the balcony. Then she went downstairs and opened the door. The police ran upstairs and found Hayes sitting on the side of his bed. Hayes, who was dressed in a pyjama coat and street trousers, said: "You must have had the good oil and followed me in. I came home only a few minutes ago and was about to go to bed." Police searched the room, watched by Hayes' two young children. After Hayes had dressed he was handcuffed, taken to Central Police Station and charged.

Hayes's own version fills in a significant number of suspiciously overlooked details: "The police arrived about 4.45 am and first they roped off Jones Street, and then they roped off Harris Street. Then they moved into Thomas Street (my place was number 93) and they took up positions across the road behind a brick wall. They focused big searchlights on the house. Then Aldridge did the talking, using a loudspeaker. I was awake and my wife was asleep beside me. I heard Aldridge call: 'Come out, Jack. We know you are in there. We don't want any trouble. This is Mr Aldridge. Send Topsy to the balcony.'

"Now the kids didn't even know I was in the house. And my niece, Pattie Simmons (Dolly's sister), had been staying at our place that night and she didn't know I was there either. I had a peep out the window and could see there were lights everywhere. I wasn't going to escape, so I told Topsy to walk onto the balcony. I had a gun but I wasn't going to use it. Topsy called out: 'I'm coming onto the balcony, Mr Aldridge.' Then she went out, and he told her: 'Tell Jack we don't want any trouble. Think of the kids.' Well, first she replied: 'He's not here, Mr Aldridge.' But he called back: 'Oh, we know he is, Topsy, so just come downstairs and let us in.' Then she answered: 'Wait a minute.'

She came in and asked what I wanted to do, and I said: 'Yeah, let them in.'

"By this time all the neighbours, plus half the staff from the Dairy Farmers factory, were out in the street watching. And a big crowd had gathered in Harris Street too. But before Topsy let the police inside, I sat down on the bed and put my son Paddy on one knee and daughter Little Topsy on the other — they'd woken up by now — with my arms around them. That way the police could see I didn't have a gun, and there wouldn't be any shooting if there were kids in the room. Then Topsy opened the front door and Aldridge came upstairs first, with the others following. They all had their guns drawn as they raced up. Ray Kelly was the fifth man into the room. All that rubbish in the papers later about him leading the capture, it was all bullshit! He was the fifth man in and then, of course, once he knew it was safe, he took over control of the case.

"We went downstairs and sat in the loungeroom. I knew I had to go with them, so I asked Kelly if I could have a shower first. Kelly said: 'Yeah, that's okay. But go and open the kitchen door first.' Now there's no doubt Kelly wanted me knocked off there and then — because if I'd opened the kitchen door his men outside would've shot me straight away, pretending that I'd tried to make a run for it. But Aldridge heard what Kelly said, and he shouted to me: 'No, no, Jack. Wait a minute!' Then he appeared to glare at Kelly and, before he opened the door, he sang out: 'This is John Aldridge and I'm about to open the door. Everything's under control.' If I'd opened the door I'd have been shot. So Aldridge opened it and walked out into the backyard and told the other police that I was coming out to have a shower and not to fire. Then I walked out and had my shower.

"Finally out the front of the house, as they were taking me away, a team of reporters had assembled. One of them pushed the camera right up into my face and almost hit me in the teeth with it. So I kicked out and he jumped back. Then they loaded me into the police car.

"When we reached the main CIB building in Liverpool Street, we jumped into the lift and went up to the third floor. There must have been 15 or 20 coppers there — so many they couldn't all fit into the room. Kelly told them they could all write their names in the book, indicating they were in on the capture. Then he turned to me and said blatantly, in front of everyone: 'Now look, Chow. You know and I know that you killed Lee. We both know that.'

And I replied: 'That's only your opinion.' But he began again: 'Well, look, forget that because we know you did it. I am going to charge you the same as I charged the others. And I will tell as many lies as I can to convict you, and you tell as many lies as you can to beat it. Is that fair enough?' (Now that's the gospel truth. What would I gain by telling silly fibs now? It was years and years ago and I've served my sentence and everything. That's on an oath on the dead bodies of my children. He said it in front of everybody.)

"So I said: 'That's fair enough. Let's go downstairs again.' Now if we went downstairs, I'd have been okay, because he couldn't 'put the verbal' on me since we hadn't been up there long enough — we'd only been there about 10 minutes at that point. But Kelly replied: 'Oh no. We'll have a drink.' He walked over to his desk and pulled out a bottle of whisky and we had a few drinks. Then he sent for my breakfast, and some of the coppers went and ate their breakfast. And when they returned the others went and had their breakfast. It was eventually 2 in the afternoon before they took me down to the court and charged me.

"In the meantime I asked Kelly bluntly: 'What about Topsy?' And he replied: 'That's what I was going to talk to you about. We're going to hold her over your head.' I asked: 'What do you mean?' He explained: 'She passed the gun to you from her handbag.' At that point I almost exploded: 'Oh, don't give me that shit! Look Ray, she only had a little bag — much too small to carry a .45.' But he replied: 'I know that, but read this statement.' With that, he handed me a copy of Betty Hodder's statement. He even admitted he didn't believe it. The other police were still all there, walking in and out while Kelly was saying all this to me. They all knew it was a great set-up — but they also knew that I did it. So they thought they were justified in nabbing me whichever way they managed it...

"Eventually they took me down to the court and charged me. Then when I came out I again asked Kelly: 'What about Topsy?' Kelly reiterated that they intended to hold her over my head. He boasted: 'The others will all have their charges withdrawn at the coroner's court. But Topsy isn't going to beat it there.' So when the day came for the inquest...Wally Hodder and I, and Joey and Hazel Hollebone and my wife all fronted up. In the meantime Hollebone and I had been held at Long Bay, while the others had been allowed out on bail."

Chow Hayes lashes out at a Daily Mirror *photogragher as he is led from his Ultimo home, handcuffed to Detective Sergeant Ray Kelly, just after 5 a.m. one morning in July 1951, on his way to police headquarters to be charged with boxer Bobby Lee's murder.*

On 11 September Mr Justice Kinsella formally refused Hayes bail. The Crown said it feared shootings would occur if Hayes was released. The Crown also opposed bail on the grounds that Hayes might abscond — the court was told he had "hidden from the police for six weeks before his arrest in July", and that "he might intimidate or prevent witnesses giving evidence."

19 "Verbal" Kelly and the Coroner's Inquest

The lengthy legal saga, which would eventually encompass three murder trials, began at the City Coroner's Court on 10 October 1951. *People* magazine summed up:

> *Hayes' first appearance after his arrest was in the cold, shabby Sydney Coroner's Court. There he faced City Coroner A. N. Bott, assisted by Police Sergeant D. G. Goode . . . Charged with Hayes were his wife, Gladys Muriel Hayes (38), William Hollebone (35), Hazel Hollebone (31) and Walter Dennis Hodder (36). Three of these, enjoying bail, came to court unescorted, but Hayes and Hollebone were brought in handcuffed to detectives.*
>
> *Kate Leigh, a notorious Sydney character who is popularly supposed to be rivalled only by "Tilly" Devine in power in her city's underworld, was an onlooker at the inquest. Mrs Leigh, who dresses with a sort of loose and comfortable flamboyancy, favouring wide, floppy hats, diamonds and fur pieces, came on the first and most other days in a taxi, accompanied by a retinue of friends. She took advantage of most adjournments and halts in the proceedings — when she would not be committed for contempt — to hurl more or less amiable jibes at the police. She also encouraged Hayes with hopeful cries from time to time, and once went so far as to slip a bottle of liquor into his pocket while talking to him during a recess. Sharp-eyed officials saw this move, pounced on the bottle, and told Kate Leigh bluntly of some of the things that would happen if she tried it again . . .*
>
> *Large, boyish-faced solicitor J. Thom was looking after the interests of Walter Dennis Hodder. Lean, saturnine-featured P. N. Roach was keeping a shrewd and disillusioned eye on anything that might concern Hayes and his wife. And prominent barrister George Amsberg, a slight, mentally and physically quick-moving man with a thin, good-humoured face was retained by the Hollebones . . .*

THE BOBBY LEE MURDER TRIAL

Kate Leigh attended the trial daily. During the adjournments she hurled amiable jibes at the police. Amid one halt in proceedings she covertly slipped Hayes a bottle of liquor, but sharp-eyed court officials spotted it and pounced immediately.

Expert police witnesses . . . produced a plan of the Ziegfeld nightclub, later qualified as a "disorderly house", thus not requiring a police warrant for entry. Factual testimony came from a doctor as to the cause of Lee's death, and from men of the C.I.B.'s scientific, fingerprint and ballistic bureaus . . .

The first witness who had been one of the nightclub party in which, allegedly, drunken resentments and suspicions had flared into murder, was Kenneth Paul Russell, a large, well-built, fair-haired seaman . . . He had been with Lee, and they had been joined later by the other, larger party, he said. Lee and Hollebone had withdrawn for a few minutes to discuss something privately, after which they had shaken hands and appeared to be friendly. Soon he heard Lee say, "I flattened him", and Hayes had said to Mrs Hollebone, "Give it to me." Mrs Hollebone had pushed "a small flat object wrapped in a handkerchief" across the table, and Hayes had put this in his pocket. Sgt. Goode then produced for Russell's inspection the large ugly automatic pistol which had been identified as the one with which the crime was committed, but the witness was positive that the object passed by Mrs Hollebone had been much smaller. Shortly after the incident, he said, he had adopted a strategic position under the table, because "I thought there was going to be a fight"...

*Eric Farrell [*sic*], proprietor of the Ziegfeld Club, well-fleshed, smartly-dressed, smoothly-laundered citizen, entered the box. He said he had told the Hayes–Lee party at one stage, "If you want any blues, have them outside". Later, when in the kitchen, he had heard five explosions and had come back to find Lee groaning on the floor and Hodder and Russell standing nearby. He had asked "Who shot Bobby?" and somebody — Hodder, he thought — had answered, "I don't know. He's gone through." He had kept Hodder and Russell on the premises until the police and an ambulance had arrived. His evidence was corroborated by a couple of Ziegfeld employees. One, Arthur John Clarke... one of those young men who manage to be barrel-shaped without much fat... stated the words of Farrell's inquiry after the shooting more dramatically and less grammatically as, "Who done this?..."*

Det. Sgt. John Henry Aldridge told in a clear, precise, metallic voice of having been called to the nightclub. Hodder, he said, had at first claimed to have been asleep at the time of the shooting, but had later said, "Well, I didn't shoot him. I won't make a written statement, but I will tell you, off the record, what happened. You realise my position — I don't want to be shot." Hodder, according to Aldridge, told him of the development in the party of an argument over the murder of Danny Simmons... "I heard Lee say that he had flattened Simmons, and Hayes said, 'What do you think of him now?' Lee said, 'I still think he's a ———'" Then the shots were fired. On who fired the shots, Hodder had said, "Hayes did, he's mad. The gun was passed to him, but I don't know anything about that." Hodder had denied an arrangement with Hayes that was designed to end in the shooting of one Lenny Wright, but had admitted knowing that Hayes was armed, and had said, "I know Hayes is a dangerous man to knock about with. The ———'s mad."

A morning newspaper report on 17 August 1951 recorded dramatically that the coroner had been:

... told yesterday that in his dying deposition... Lee refused to say who shot him... Mrs Florence Kathleen Carr, of Pitt Street,

THE BOBBY LEE MURDER TRIAL

*The key figures leave court during Chow Hayes's trial for the murder of boxer Bobby Lee. Hayes (*front left*) is handcuffed to a detective. Immediately behind him (*left*) is his wife, Topsy. Further behind Hayes (*right*) is his partner-in-crime, Joey Hollebone. In the background (*to the left of the detective and partly obscured by his hat*) is Hollebone's wife, Hazel. In the foreground (*extreme right*) is Hayes's mortal enemy, Detective Sergeant Ray "Verbal" Kelly.*

Redfern, a sister of Lee, said she saw Lee about 6 pm on May 26. "He told me he had a fight with some man," she said. "He said the man was a mate of Chow Hayes. . . ."

Kenneth Paul Russell, of Goodwood Street, Kensington, was asked by Sergeant Goode, "Do you remember leaving your chair?" He replied, "Yes. I dived under the table. I thought there would be a fight." Goode asked, "While you were on the floor, did you hear something?" and Russell replied, "I heard a number of shots fired . . ."

Asked if it was right that he arranged with Hayes to go to a game at Kings Cross and let him know when Lenny ["The Black Orphan"] Wright arrived, as Hayes was going to shoot Wright because he believed Wright was connected with the shooting of Simmons, Hodder replied, "I won't say anything about that but I know Hayes is a dangerous man to knock about with . . ."

EDWARD LEE AND FLORENCE CARR

The brother and sister of murdered boxer Bobby Lee, outside the Coroner's Court. Mrs Carr claimed Lee, on his deathbed, had told her about a fight with a man who was a mate of Chow Hayes.

People magazine devoted a lengthy report to Betty Hodder's sensational testimony:

> *Elizabeth Annette Hodder. . . hesitated for long, miserable periods that underlined her reluctance to admit such things as that her husband had, on the night of the killing, been far too drunk for murder or anything else, and that she, too, had had considerable liquor. Mrs Hodder, a short, neatly-built brunette, who wears glasses, appeared in a tailored suit with a fur across her shoulders. Tears seemed never far from her eyes. . . She eventually whispered that before the shooting Mrs Hayes had told her that Hayes had a gun and that it had previously been in her handbag. She had seen Hayes holding the gun between his legs, she affirmed. . . She had been talking to Hollebone when she had heard the explosions. Hayes had then had his right hand by his side, slightly bent at the elbow and just*

Betty Hodder

Elizabeth "Betty" Hodder told the court she had seen Hayes holding a gun between his legs just before Bobby Lee was shot. Soon after, she swayed in the witness box and nearly collapsed. After she finished her testimony she broke down in tears and had to be consoled by friends in a room behind the court.

touching his hip. At this point Mrs Hodder seemed to sway in the witness box and detectives and policemen jumped forward as Hayes rose from where he and the other accused were seated on a bench. Hayes mumbled an explanation that he had thought she was going to fall. Mrs Hodder continued her movement which, it seemed, had been made to demonstrate the position in which Hayes had held his hand immediately after the shots had been fired. He had been "more or less grinning" she said.

Her tears finally came when she had finished her testimony and she had to be consoled by friends in a room behind the court . . . Soon afterward, the Coroner dismissed the charge of murder against her husband.

A fortnight later, on 28 August, Coroner Mr A. N. Bott similarly declared that there was "no evidence which could possibly connect the Hollebones with the crime." He convened a Court of Petty Sessions and discharged William and Hazel Hollebone. *People* recorded:

A lean, greying individual with a strong face which was mostly expressionless, Hollebone spoke deliberately, taking time for thought before answering questions. He denied having taken any part in the shooting and, on the advice of his counsel, declined to say whether he had seen who shot Lee . . . Apart from the people already mentioned as having been at the Ziegfeld, he had seen another man there, a stranger, about 10 minutes before the shooting, and this resulted in an adjournment of the inquiry for two days, to August 30, so that all witnesses could be recalled. The Coroner said, "Hollebone's evidence is so important that it must be thoroughly investigated." Hollebone described his "stranger" as a man of fair complexion, wearing a dark suit . . . A few minutes before the shooting Lee had knocked this man out in the lavatory of the club and Hollebone had seen the stranger holding a gun just before Lee had been killed.

A newspaper reported: "Hollebone . . . said . . . Lee hit him on the face and left him lying on the floor. Back at their table, Hollebone said, he asked Lee why he hit the man. Lee replied, 'He's a no-good ———, and he has been looking for it.' Later he heard an explosion and saw the man standing about a foot [30 centimetres] away from Hayes and holding a pistol or revolver. The man ran out."

People continued: "When Farrell, the nightclub proprietor, was recalled, he agreed that one member of a second party of

Joey Hollebone

William "Joey" Hollebone is led handcuffed into the court early in the Lee murder trial. He and Hayes had looked all over Sydney for Bobby Lee before eventually cornering him at the Ziegfeld Club.

three men and a girl had disappeared after the shooting. . . Sgt. Goode said, with an air of bored disbelief in the 'stranger', 'We can explain the identity and activity of everybody who was in the club at the time.'. . ."

Hazel Hollebone

She was also charged with Bobby Lee's murder but was acquitted.

Hayes recalls the events of that time: "The police put me in half a dozen 'line-ups' — they couldn't arrange for all the people who'd been in the Ziegfeld Club that night to come down to the CIB at the same time. So I stayed at the CIB for three days while the line-ups were going on. But you wouldn't believe it — especially knowing my court record and so on — but they all came in and looked up and down the line and said no, they couldn't see the man who shot Lee. I thought at least a dozen would identify me — after all, they were all squareheads. And they all knew it was me. But every one of them refused to pick me out for the police. The coppers must have gone through 60 or 70 people and not one identified me, simply because they didn't want to become mixed up in the case. Even the band members said they couldn't identify me. However, the police didn't bring in Betty Hodder (I'd dismissed her in my mind anyway) and they didn't bring in the Melbourne bloke who'd grabbed my arm...

"But throughout the lead-up to the court proceedings, I kept hearing about this mysterious witness the police had up their sleeves who was going to identify me. So the day the coroner's inquest began, I said to Amsberg: 'They have two mystery witnesses who are going to identify me.' And he replied: 'I know.' I asked: 'Who are they?' But he said he didn't know either. Of course I feared the bloke who was going to identify me was the Melbourne chap. But apparently he'd returned to Melbourne and, when they tried to contact him, he took another holiday. So that left them with their mystery witness as Betty Hodder, and she was the only one who identified me."

The media had a field day when Ray Kelly appeared in the witness box at the Coroner's Court. *People* magazine summed up:

> *Det. Sgt. Ray Kelly . . . had helped arrest Hayes and had interrogated him almost immediately . . . His evidence was to tell heavily against Hayes, and Hayes' loathing for him (Kelly) was eventually to reach a level of hysterical hate. Even at the Coronial Inquiry with a constable on the stand, Hayes was soon protesting angrily that Kelly . . . was "telling him what to say" . . . Showing great excitement Hayes continued to talk, and when the Coroner warned him sharply of the consequences of contempt Hayes cried, "You can do what you like. You can do what you like." Said the Coroner, "I will not be talked to like this. He can go back to Long Bay." The seething court was then adjourned for seven minutes, during which Hayes was persuaded to apologise.*
>
> *Kelly's evidence was to the effect that Hayes had admitted the killing . . . saying . . . "Do you know he was the bloke who got the car they used the night Danny Simmons was shot in mistake for me?" In reply to a direct question as to whether he (Hayes) confessed to the murder, he had said "Yes. What else can I do? There were a lot of*

people there, and they saw me shoot him. I think I was entitled to shoot him. What would you do if you knew a mug who had got a car to shoot you? He has been running around with Martin Goode, Len McPherson and the Black Orphan. I thought he might have had a gun. You never know what a ——— like that will do, so I got in first." He had later added, "The police didn't catch anyone for the shooting of Danny Simmons, so I decided to do it my own way".

A newspaper report of 29 August 1951 read:

Kelly . . . told Bott . . . that he interviewed Hayes after Hayes was arrested. Kelly said he asked Hayes if he admitted having shot Lee. Hayes answered, "Yes. What else can I do? There were a lot of other people there, and they saw me shoot him, but I think I was entitled to shoot him. What would you do if a mug had got a car to knock you off?" . . . Kelly asked Hayes if he had ever heard it suggested that Lee carried a gun. Hayes replied, "The ———'s been running around with Martin Goode, Len McPherson and the Black Orphan and I thought he might have a gun. You never know what a ——— like that will do, so I got in first." Kelly said Hayes had explained a man called Len Wright was known as the Black Orphan . . .

Kelly said he told Hayes, "We have been informed that you . . . intended to go to the baccarat and shoot Len Wright as soon as he arrived, as you blamed him for shooting Danny Simmons. Is that correct?" Hayes had answered, "No, but if I had run into the Black Orphan I would have had to shoot him, or he would have shot me." . . . Kelly added that he said to Hayes, "You told me and other detectives that Martin Goode, Len McPherson, Jacky Riley and a man named Griffiths shot Danny Simmons in mistake for you, as you had been standing over Len Wright for money and assaulting him." Hayes had replied, "You know as well as I do they intended to shoot me, and not Danny Simmons." . . . Hayes had continued, "Do you know Lee is the ——— who got the car from up at the game for Martin Goode and the others the night they knocked Danny Simmons off in mistake for me?"

Kelly added that when asked if he'd told Det. Sgt. Aldridge that he had received information that Lee was responsible for shooting Simmons, Hayes had said, 'No. The police didn't catch anyone for shooting Simmons, so I decided to do things my own way.'

Hayes recalls those tense days in court: "Kelly said that when he interviewed me, he told me he was going to charge me with murder, and he asked me: 'Did you do it?' And he said I replied:

'Yes, I did it. And I only wish a bastard like you was alongside him and I'd have done it to you too.' That was absolute rubbish. Now that was his main verbal. I didn't see the statement. I never saw the verbal statement which they are supposed to give you. It was an unsigned statement — I've never signed a statement in my life."

Eventually, on 11 October 1951, Coroner Bott announced his finding that "Lee, aged 38, of Pitt Street, Redfern, died from the effects of a bullet wound in the stomach feloniously inflicted by Hayes and his wife." Bail of £1000 was allowed to Mrs Hayes (subject to her reporting daily to the CIB) and she was also granted a separate trial.

Hayes recalls: "So Topsy and I were committed for trial. They were only keeping Topsy so they could hold her over me. I was taken back to Long Bay. We sought two or three remands, and Joe Taylor paid all the legal costs for both Topsy and my defences."

The first trial began before Mr Justice Clancy in Central Criminal Court on 26 November 1951. Barrister Simon Isaacs KC (later Mr Justice Isaacs) and solicitor Phillip Norman Roach headed the Hayes team, while the Crown Prosecutor was Mr C. V. Rooney KC. *People* magazine summed up:

> *Hayes' first appearance in the Criminal Court was enlivened by an unsworn statement from the dock . . . and by spirited clashes between Simon Isaacs KC, who then appeared for Hayes, and Det. Sgt. Kelly. Hayes said that he had seen the man referred to by Hollebone approach his party, with a gun in his hand. He went on, "I heard a loud explosion as the man with the gun was standing right beside me. I grabbed my wife and we got out of the club as quickly as we could, for we did not want to be mixed up in this business." The motive for the killing of Simmons had been jealousy, "for Danny was a bit of a ladies' man." He had not admitted to Kelly that he had shot Lee, but Kelly had threatened him with the words, "I'll put the verbal on you." This is a common term in the underworld for alleged verbal confessions.*
>
> *In cross-examination of Kelly, Isaacs made considerable play on this last allegation by Hayes, and asked the witness if he were known as "Verbal" Kelly. The Det. Sgt . . . denied this. When Isaacs asked, "Did you not tell Hayes you were the best liar in the police force?" Kelly answered firmly, "That is a figment of your mind, not his." He scornfully repudiated the suggestion that the alleged confession had been a "concoction".*

The *Sydney Morning Herald* of 28 November reported: "Hayes said the killer was a man who suddenly appeared beside him, and fired the shots. Hayes gave his defence to the charge of murder in a statement from the dock. He said that he went to the Ziegfeld Club with his wife, Mr and Mrs Hollebone and Mr and Mrs Hodder. Lee invited them to his table, they were drinking together when a man approached with a gun. 'I heard a loud explosion,' Hayes said. 'The man with the gun was standing right beside me. We got out of the club as quickly as we could, as we did not want to be mixed up in the business.'"

Chow Hayes recalls his first trial: "The only witness they had was Betty Hodder. She said that she didn't see the gun in my hand but she saw flames coming out. Now a .45 is so big you can't hide the thing, especially out in the open. But she said she couldn't see me with the gun, only flames coming out of my hand. Now without her testimony Kelly had nothing, because the rest of the police case was only backing up what Betty Hodder said...

"Then I made a statement from the dock. I couldn't call Topsy because that would only have jeopardised her chances — she'd have been a very good witness, being a squarehead and everything. But also prosecutors tell the jury that you can't take any notice of a wife anyway, because what else would you expect them to do but defend their husband?

"The only other witness I had was Hollebone, so I called him. Well, he nearly buggered up the whole case! When he was being cross-examined they asked him: 'You know a bit about guns, Mr Hollebone?' But he replied: 'No.' So the prosecutor said: 'Come on, Mr Hollebone, you've been convicted of carrying guns.' But Joey replied: 'Oh, I've been convicted.' And so he was asked: 'Well, how do you load one?' And he kept going on with really silly answers, making out he wasn't familiar with guns, instead of just admitting straight out that he was familiar with them."

Eventually the jury deliberated for four hours on what they had heard. Then they requested that the 30-page typed transcript of Kelly's evidence be read to them. After another hour they had still not agreed. Mr Justice Clancy then discharged them, and Hayes was taken back to spend his Christmas in Long Bay Jail.

The *Sydney Morning Herald* of 29 November 1951 recorded:

The jury yesterday failed to agree on a verdict... Mr Justice Clancy discharged the jury and remanded Hayes for retrial. The jury retired to consider its verdict at 11.34 am. At 3.40 pm the Court reassembled and the jury asked if Det. Sgt. Ray Kelly's evidence could be read to it. A 30-page typed transcript of Sgt. Kelly's evidence was then read in turn by the court shorthand writer and Mr S. Isaacs KC. . . and Mr C. V. Rooney KC. The reading of Sgt. Kelly's evidence took 80 minutes. The jury again retired, and returned to the court at 5.30 pm, still without a verdict . . . When Mr Justice Clancy asked whether the jury required further time for deliberation, the foreman said: 'If we stayed all night I don't think we would agree.' His Honour then discharged the jury.

Hayes recalls: "When the jury disagreed, they should've then charged Topsy and put her case on. But they didn't. They postponed it so they'd still have her hanging over me. . . Meanwhile, Hollebone came out to see me, and I told him he'd nearly brought me undone. He admitted he was half-drunk at the time. So for the next trial I decided not to call him as a witness."

20 The Cause Celebre of the Decade — and the Death Sentence

The second trial, again in the Central Criminal Court before Justice Clancy, began on 10 March 1952. George Amsberg appeared for Hayes, with Crown Prosecutor Rooney presenting the police case.

People magazine reported that, after Ray Kelly had again told of Hayes's arrest and of his alleged admissions about having shot Lee,

> *Amsberg made strenuous and clever efforts to discredit Kelly's testimony. Kelly answered "Yes" when he was asked, "Can the jury take it that when Hayes made his alleged confession he was neither drunk nor mad?" He uttered a determined "No" when the question was, "You didn't coax or persuade Hayes or anything like that?"*
>
> *Kelly agreed that a confession was "out of character" for Hayes, and said that the accused had given as his reason for disappearance after the shooting, "I knew I would be picked up, and I wanted enough dough for a mouthpiece before I fronted."*

The *Sydney Morning Herald* of 12 March reported the following exchange. "Amsberg: 'Did Hayes say, as a reason for his disappearance after the shooting, I knew I would be picked up and I wanted to get enough dough for a mouthpiece before I fronted?' Kelly: 'Yes.' Amsberg: 'Did you take it from that that he intended to defend the matter?' Kelly: 'I did not know how to take it.'"

The newspaper also reported the evidence of a hitherto unheard witness: "A new witness told the Central Criminal Court yesterday that he had seen a man run from the Ziegfeld Club on the morning Bobby Lee was shot. . . William Edgar Franklin, waterside worker, of Rose Street, Darlington...said that about 3.15 am on May 29 he was about to enter the Ziegfeld Club to buy some beer. 'I saw a bloke coming out of Ziegfeld's and going hard towards George Street. A few seconds later I saw some men and women running out of the club. I thought it was a police raid so I cleared out.'"

Hayes recalls the second trial: "Kelly arranged to have a newspaper bloke brought in. They told us before the new trial that they were going to bring another witness in, and naturally I thought it was finally going to be the bloke from Melbourne. But it shows how desperate they were, that they brought in this newspaper bloke. He said in the box that he went to Thomas Street three days after Simmons was killed and knocked on the door and Mrs Hayes answered. He said he asked if I was home and said he'd like to talk to me. Then he said that Topsy had gone away to find me and come back and said I'd talk to him. He said he then came inside and sat on the lounge and chatted to me. He said he'd asked me: 'Simmons was murdered in mistake for you, is that correct?' He said I had replied: 'So I believe.' Then he said he asked me: 'Aren't you afraid of staying here?' And he said I'd replied: 'No. Why should I be? It's my home.' He said he then repeated: 'After people come here to kill you, and they didn't kill you but they killed your nephew, you still stay here?' And he said I replied: 'Yeah. I'm well protected.' He said I then lifted up a pillow and showed him a .38 revolver and I'd said: 'And that's what I'll use.'

"Well, according to his statement that was on the Thursday, and that's how I gained the second jury disagreement. See Topsy and I were never given back the keys to the house until the Friday — so I couldn't have been there and talked to him on the Thursday as he said. Well, that proved he was a ring-in. And when Amsberg went through it all with him, and asked if he was sure about all his testimony, he replied: 'Oh yeah, it's all in my notebook.' And he gave the date as the 4th, and of course Topsy never went back there until the 5th. And when he said he must have made a mistake, Amsberg asked: 'How could it be a mistake? You're trained as a reporter, trained to go into all these details, get the dates right, and so on.'"

The jury retired at 1 pm on 13 March 1952 and returned twice during the afternoon to obtain further guidance from Mr Justice Clancy. This time the jury was locked up for more than six hours, but again no verdict was reached. At 7.15 pm the foreman announced that "No agreement was likely."

Again Topsy was remanded, to keep her fate hanging over Hayes's head.

The case had now become the *cause célèbre* of the decade. Much speculation arose as to whether Hayes would be tried a third time. Attorney-General Mr C. E. Martin said the decision would be made after reports had been received from the senior Crown Prosecutor Mr Rooney and the Solicitor-General Mr Weigall. After a 10-day wait Martin announced Hayes would indeed stand a third trial in May.

The *Sydney Morning Herald* reported: "Only once in Australia in recent years has a person been tried a third time on a charge of murder after two disagreements by juries. This was in Melbourne on September 8, 1950, when John Bryan Kerr, radio announcer, was found guilty of having murdered a girl at Albert Park in December 1949."

Hayes sums up bluntly: "I've no doubt there would never have been a third trial if my name was Tom Jones or Tom Brown or Tom Smith."

However the third trial duly commenced before Mr Justice McClemens in Sydney's Central Criminal Court on 26 May 1952. Hayes challenged 19 jurors and the Crown challenged seven.

From the start His Honour took a tough line. The *Sydney Morning Herald* noted: "The use of nicknames resulted in the oblique glorification of crime, Mr Justice McClemens said...at the beginning of the third trial...Crown Prosecutor, Mr C. V. Rooney, referred to 'Bobby' Lee and 'Danny' Simmons. Mr Justice McClemens said Lee and Simmons should be referred to as Robert Lee and Daniel Simmons. 'This use of nicknames results in the oblique glorification of crime,' he said. 'It is done in newspapers and broadcasting but I am not going to have it done in my court.'"

The highlight came when Kelly clashed with Hayes's counsel, George Amsberg, and alleged the nickname "Verbal" Kelly had been manufactured by Simon Isaacs and carefully copied by Amsberg. *People* magazine reported: "The indefatigable George Amsberg still strove to inject into the minds of the jury doubt about what Kelly had told them. When Amsberg asked if he had been known as 'Verbal' Kelly, Kelly told him, 'I have been known by that by Mr Isaacs and Mr Amsberg.' Said Amsberg, seemingly greatly pained, 'You are suggesting that an eminent barrister has manufactured a piece of evidence?' 'Yes, that is what I say,' Kelly agreed. 'That is rather a serious charge to make against a barrister,' said Amsberg, and Kelly responded 'I have no hesitation in making it. I say it was manufactured, concocted, imagined, or whatever you please.'"

Hayes recalls: "For the third trial, the police had even dropped Betty Hodder as a witness. Basically she wasn't any good in the witness box — and they'd lost twice already when they'd used her. But they still used her statement, which she'd made at the two previous trials. Then Kelly walked into the witness box and he gave his verbal. And they wouldn't have convicted me — even though I did it — except for Kelly's verbal."

During his summing up to the jury, Justice McClemens said Amsberg had conducted the defence "with great vigour and great brilliance". However, the jury deliberated for just over an hour before finding Hayes guilty.

People magazine graphically described the climax:

The atmosphere of the court was tense. Mrs Hayes . . . was present, and when the foreman of the jury pronounced the word "guilty" she moaned loudly, sobbed, and later beat with despairing fists against friends who were trying to console her.

The grating voice of Hayes himself said, with slow ferocity, "I hope I live to see Kelly die of cancer of the tongue." He told Mr Justice McClemens, with insolent defiance, "I did not expect any other verdict after hearing your summing-up."

As he was removed he swung himself around to face Det. Sgt. Kelly . . . He spat viciously in his direction and shouted, "You lying bastard!" Almost simultaneously, his wife screamed, "May God forgive you. No one else will" . . .

What bitter suspense and moments of hope and despair he experienced only he can know, but he showed no sign of remorse. If it had been, as the third jury decided, his hand that aimed the heavy Colt .45 automatic pistol which thundered in the nightclub, pouring its big slugs into the grovelling body of Lee, he apparently thought of it as a simple, justified act of revenge.

The sentence of death was pronounced at 4.15 pm on Wednesday, 28 May 1952. After a three-day session, the proceedings concluded one day before the anniversary of the death of Bobby Lee.

People summed up:

Though anybody who had sat through all three trials had formed the same conclusion at each, it took the third jury only 75 minutes to reach unanimity on the guilt of Hayes. In the electric atmosphere created by

DETECTIVE SERGEANT RAY KELLY

After he charged Hayes with Bobby Lee's murder, Kelly said to Hayes: "I will tell as many lies as I can to convict you, and you tell as many lies as you can to beat it." When he was eventually convicted after three trials, Hayes shouted from the dock: "I hope I live to see Kelly die of cancer of the tongue."

the moans of Mrs Hayes, and by the fainting of a woman in the body of the court, the judge called for the reading of the convicted man's record . . . Then Mr Justice McClemens told the jury, soberly, "I think it may be some solace to you to know that record." He said the jury had returned the only verdict possible on the evidence and that its decision had relieved the community of a man whose record had been one of defiance of the law.

Hayes was savagely resentful when, after the guilty verdict, Mr Justice McClemens made the unusual move of having his record read to the jury. The list of nearly 90 convictions showed that he had been a hardened criminal for 20 years. His first conviction was for indecent language at the age of 15.

Hayes bitterly recalls the dramatic events: "Mine was the only capital charge in history where the judge read out my previous record. When I was found guilty, he instructed the court recorder to read out my record. And it hasn't been done since either . . .

"So then McClemens put the black cap on his head for sentencing. But I wasn't listening to him because I was yelling at Kelly from the dock — all that stuff about 'I hope I live to see the day you die of cancer of the tongue' and so on. Three uniformed coppers raced up the stairs from below and threw me down the stairs behind the dock — about 12 stairs — quick smart. I fell straight from the top to the bottom. So I never actually heard the death sentence announced.

"Naturally I knew I'd been sentenced to death. But I also knew it was very unlikely to be carried out, because Labor was in power in New South Wales — though I also knew that if the Liberals had been in they'd have hanged me."

People magazine summed up Hayes's demeanour in the dock:

During the long sequence of court proceedings, he sat mostly without concern, wearing an expression of intelligent interest. But he made occasional outbursts and he signalled when they were on their way, like a boxer whose rage overcomes his caution. At such times his normally swarthy complexion seemed to darken a shade, his thin lips stiffened and his brown eyes took on a fixed intensity. Watchers felt glad that Chow Hayes had no lethal weapon in the dock.

The magazine recorded the dramatic final scenes inside the court with its usual extravagance:

When Mr Justice McClemens ordered "Remove the prisoner" those in court saw Hayes' face distort . . . he spat and cursed at Det. Sgt.

Kelly . . . Its expression of unbridled and murderous fury possibly did even more than the reading of his dreadful record to convince the jury that they had done the right thing in removing him from the society of lawful men for the longest possible period.

Thus ended the career in crime of a man who, whatever his virtues, must be summed up as a menace to the community, and the victim of vanity, temper, drink and dishonesty . . .

• • •

On the second day after judgment was passed, barrister George Amsberg journeyed out to Long Bay Jail to visit Hayes. He told Hayes bluntly that he didn't think they had much chance of overturning the conviction upon appeal, essentially because honest men were far more likely to believe a distinguished policeman such as Kelly than a notorious criminal like Hayes. Then Amsberg turned to the worst part: "They're going to go on with Topsy next Monday if you appeal." Hayes remembers: "So Amsberg explained it was up to me. I replied I couldn't take the risk so I wouldn't appeal. But then Amsberg added: 'Don't let me persuade you one way or the other. You either appeal and take the risk that they might convict Topsy, or you don't appeal and cop it sweet yourself.' But I reiterated that I'd already made up my mind and there'd be no appeal.

"Now through it all I hadn't told Amsberg the whole story. But I didn't have to, because everyone knew I was guilty — even the paperboys knew I did it. Anyway Amsberg went and informed the authorities that I wasn't appealing. So on the Monday they asked for another adjournment on Topsy's case (that was because you had 10 days to appeal and I still might have changed my mind). Then when they knew I couldn't appeal, they decided to discharge Topsy — she was only in there 10 minutes, because they offered no real evidence."

Mrs Hayes appeared in Darlinghurst Criminal Court on 24 June 1952, on a similar charge of having murdered Lee. The following morning the *Sydney Morning Herald* reported: "The Crown alleged that Mrs Hayes had aided and abetted the crime by handing her husband the pistol with which he shot Lee. At the close of the Crown case Mr Justice Kinsella said there was no evidence that Mrs Hayes had anything to do with the actual shooting and directed the jury to acquit her."

People magazine described her as a person "of whom many people inside and outside the underworld report, 'There's no real harm in her. Her big mistake was in marrying Hayes.'" The magazine's court correspondent reported: "She stood quiet and alone in the dock, making no statement and listening to only three witnesses. A detective gave evidence that initially she had denied implication. Mrs Hodder...said that Mrs Hayes had told her she had carried the fatal gun. The young seaman, Russell, said that it had been Mrs Hollebone who had passed an object to Hayes. The whole hearing took only 55 minutes before the jury, instructed by Mr Justice Kinsella, found Gladys Muriel Hayes 'not guilty'."

Years later, looking back at the whole affair, Hayes explained to a *Daily Mirror* reporter: "It was a gangland affair and I claimed innocence for many years afterward. But one day I thought to myself 'What the hell' — and I told the truth to an interviewer... It was a case of first up, best dressed. If I hadn't got Lee, he'd have got me. And I had no intention of letting that happen...I'm sure Lee knew I would be after him — and I bloody well knew he'd try to get me first."

• • •

For the Sydney public, however, the saga had not yet finished. In February 1953, Danny Simmons's murder officially came before the Coroner's Court.

The *Sydney Morning Herald* reported that:

> *Hayes had named three men as responsible for the fatal shooting of Danny Simmons... One CIB detective told the court that when Simmons' death was being investigated Hayes told him: "I've been told that Martin Goode, Lenny McPherson and Jack Riley did the shooting, that McPherson and Goode went to the back lane and shot Danny through the window and that Jack Riley was driving the car." The detective said Hayes also told him: "If you don't get enough on them I will square it up in my own way."... The detective said Hayes told him at Regent Street police station on May 2: "This was meant for me and not Danny." Later that day, the detective explained, Hayes repeated to him what he had been told about Goode, McPherson and Riley and added: "They were put up to it by Lenny Wright, who is Martin Goode's partner in the Bookmakers' Clerks' Club. I don't know which one actually did the shooting."*
>
> *The detective also told the court that he had spoken to Goode on May 17 and told him: "We've also been told that Hayes has been standing over Lenny Wright and demanding money from him, and when Wright refused Hayes bashed him. The last occasion was on*

April 30."... The detective said Goode replied: "I know of 50 people who would like to see Hayes shot, but I don't know who would shoot him."

The detective then told the court that on May 20, when McPherson was told of Hayes' statement on the shooting and also told that Hayes was said to have been "standing over" Lenny Wright, McPherson replied: "Are you serious?" The detective said McPherson added: "From what I hear Chow had it coming to him, but I'm not a particular friend of Wright's and those fellows haven't got enough money to pay me to do a thing like that. I may do it if I had a particular grudge against him if it was big enough, but I had nothing against him."...

Asked if he knew of anything concerning McPherson, Riley, Wright and Goode, which would assist in the inquiry, Hayes said he did not know McPherson. He said he knew Riley, Wright and Goode, but did not know of anything which would help the Coroner.

Soon after, the newspaper also reported: "Chow Hayes... said in the City Coroner's Court yesterday that he knew nobody, except perhaps a policeman, who could help the Coroner find the murderer of Danny Simmons... Hayes was brought from Long Bay Jail under strong guard to give evidence... Lindsay Gordon Wright told the Coroner Mr A. N. Bott that he did not want to give evidence..."

Hayes sums up that whole episode: "All that stuff about Len Wright and Lenny McPherson and Martin Goode and Jack Riley... I want to set the record straight on that: McPherson, Goode, Riley and Wright had as much to do with killing Danny Simmons as the man in the street.

"I didn't even know McPherson at that point. I'd never met him in my life. The first time I encountered him was in Long Bay Jail in 1953, when he came in serving a three-year sentence. We were in 17 Yard — 'Skinny' Brett and me and dozens of well-known criminals. And I was introduced to McPherson there by Brett. Then I was transferred to Maitland Jail at the end of 1953, and I didn't see McPherson again until I was released on parole in the mid-1960s. Then I ran into him with Jackie 'Ratty' Clarke at the Town Hall Hotel at Forest Lodge. McPherson was with Clarke and we had a couple of drinks. Afterwards I remember I saw McPherson again in Pitt Street near the Marble Bar of the old Adams Hotel. And then later I bumped into him once in the Prince Alfred Club in Missenden Road, Camperdown. And that was the last time I saw McPherson. So I just never had anything to do with McPherson and his mob.

"But I'd known Martin Goode since he was a teenager. I knew him well. We were almost the same age and had been teenagers together.

"As for Jack Riley, I'd never even heard of him. But I did know Len Wright, of course, because I had bashed him."

• • •

Hayes now recalls the end of the whole saga bluntly: "Most people don't understand what a strain it is to go through three murder trials. It took a hell of a lot out of me. And when it ended I thought, 'Well, that's it. I'll never see the outside world again.'"

21 From Long Bay to Bathurst to Maitland

Out at Long Bay Jail, Hayes mixed with a number of other murderers who'd been convicted around the same time. Among them were three Maltese nicknamed "Peter", "George" and "Mary" by the other inmates. They had murdered the female owner of a Wollongong hotel while robbing it. Each of the trio duly received the death sentence.

At the time a warder named Tom worked in the 'OBS' (the observation ward) at Long Bay. Tom was something of a practical joker.

"Part of the *Sun–Herald* back page each Sunday was left vacant as a Stop Press for late news," Hayes recalls. "There were about 12 or 15 'lifers' in the OBS at that point, and one Sunday Tom came over with the *Sun–Herald* and he'd arranged for their full names (those of 'Peter', 'George' and 'Mary') to be printed in the Stop Press, along with the news that the Executive Council sat the day before and decided that they were to be hanged on such-and-such a date. Tom showed it to me, but revealed quietly that it was part of a prank. However, he asked me to let 'George', who was the weakest of the three, read it.

"So I took the paper and sat down near 'George' and pretended to be reading the first two or three pages. Then I flicked over to the back page and acted startled. I gave 'George' a glance and then looked back at the newspaper. I continued to give George a series of quick looks, to make sure he knew I was thinking about him without saying anything. Finally he asked what was up. I whispered that, if he promised not to tell anyone I'd given him the paper, I'd leave it there for him to read while I strolled back inside. But as soon as I walked off, he grabbed the paper and let out an unmerciful scream. You'd have heard him at Circular Quay! Then he fainted and fell backwards, smashing his head, which needed nine stitches.

"Now 'Daddy' Kerr was the chief warder in the OBS, but we never saw much of him because he always stayed in his office. However, this time Kerr came out, and he quickly sent for the prison governor (today they call them superintendents), who was named Harold Vagg.

"Meanwhile, another 'screw' picked up the newspaper and 'George' informed this warder that Chow Hayes had shown it to him. But Tom had quickly taken me back to my cell. He told me to insist that I'd been sick all day and that he (Tom) had locked me back in my cell earlier in the morning. Eventually Vagg, and then later even the Comptroller-General of Prisons, arrived at my cell. Tom had told them I'd reported sick at 8.30 that morning and he'd locked me in my cell. And when they came to see me I repeated that I'd been there since after breakfast that morning, about 8.30 or 8.45. Well, they knew Tom was lying — but they couldn't accept 'George's' word against a screw.

" 'George' remained in hospital for about a week. However, the other prisoners kept the joke going, by hinting to 'Peter' and 'Mary' that it was all true, that they were definitely going to be hanged. Of course, eventually the Labor Party commuted their sentences, just as they commuted all life sentences."

Indeed, about four months after his own arrival back at Long Bay following the lengthy trial, Hayes was summoned to Governor Vagg's office. Vagg informed Hayes that he had some good news: his sentence had been commuted to life imprisonment.

The formalities of the procedure require the Executive Council to commute the sentence and then convey the decision to the prison superintendent. Hence, on 16 October 1952, the following official minute from the Under Secretary of Justice was conveyed to Vagg and officially inscribed upon Hayes's criminal record: "His Excellency the Governor, with the advice of the Executive Council, has approved of the sentence death in this case being commuted to penal servitude for life."

Hayes recalls: "I replied to Vagg: 'That's lovely news, that is!' And I'll tell you truthfully, if I'd been game enough at that point I'd have 'necked' myself. I thought about suicide a couple of times while I was in the OBS. I figured I had nothing to live for — that I'd never be released again with my awful record.

"Having your sentence 'commuted to life' still meant a minimum 20-year stretch for a murderer in those days. And there were plenty of blokes who'd been convicted on lesser charges and yet still served at least that period. Old Les 'Wolf' Kennedy copped a life sentence for manslaughter and he served 21 years (mind you, he nearly took a screw's head off during that sentence). Similarly Simmonds and Newcombe were only convicted of manslaughter (killing a screw at Emu Plains) and they served around 20 years. And Tony Martini was only charged with attempted murder, but he served 21 years."

In October 1959 Kevin John Simmonds and Leslie Allan Newcombe escaped from Long Bay Jail. A few days later, while on the run, they beat Emu Plains warder Cecil Mills to death with a baseball bat while searching for food and clothing. Newcombe was recaptured soon after at Wyong Showground. But Simmonds, cunning and strong, headed into the bush and was still on the run five weeks later. In what was then the largest and most expensive manhunt in New South Wales history, a staghound and alsatian tracker dogs were brought in, snipers in a navy helicopter swept over the mountains and valleys and 500 police armed with machine-guns, high-powered rifles and tear gas searched for Simmonds. Hiding by day and fleeing by night, Simmonds crawled through the rugged bushland around Wyong, where the scrub and swamp were infested by leeches and snakes. Eventually, at dawn on a Sunday, in the bush near Kurri Kurri, the barefoot Simmonds, bleeding and tattered, living like an animal, threw up his hands and surrendered. Newcombe and Simmonds were then charged with the manslaughter of Mills and duly sentenced to life imprisonment.

Antonio Martini had originally been sentenced to four years' jail in November 1937 for armed robbery. Then in February 1946, following conviction on a "firearm in possession" charge, he had attempted to break out of his cell at Darlinghurst Jail using a hacksaw. Five months later, in July, he succeeded in escaping from a cell at Queen's Square courts. The subsequent manhunt included a sensational police search inside nearby St Mary's Cathedral, where police moved cautiously among the silent worshippers. Martini was on the run for two months before being spotted near Sydney's Taronga Park Zoo. During the subsequent gun-battle both Martini and Detective Sergeant W. A. Hargrave were wounded, before Martini was eventually recaptured. Two accomplices, Edward Garland and Royce John Garland, were also charged after the shoot-out. Martini and Edward Garland were eventually sentenced to death for wounding Hargrave, while Royce Garland received a 12-year jail sentence.

"Martini was only about 5 ft 5 in [165 cm]," Hayes recalls. "While he was on the run he would dress up as a sheila, with high heels and a blonde wig and so on. But when you saw him coming, even from 50 yards [45 metres] away, you'd know immediately it was a bloke and not a woman..."

When the news came that his death sentence had been commuted to life imprisonment, Hayes was 41 years old. "I knew I was still facing a sentence of at least 20 years," Hayes says, "and, at that stage, I was convinced that I'd probably never be released, especially with my reputation and my previous convictions. As a result there were several occasions when I considered suicide during my first 12 months back inside. But I suppose, in the end, I never had the guts to do it...

"Now sometimes you hear politicians and judges and others promising that a notorious criminal will 'never be released from jail'. But the reality is that you can't simply tell a 'lifer' that he has no hope of ever being released. If you do that, there's no incentive for him to behave himself. And as soon as that happens you pave the way for prisoners and screws to be murdered and there'd be bodies all over the jails. If you tell a 'lifer' that he'll never be released, then he has nothing to lose. So he'd rather try and go over the wall — and he won't care if he's killed in the attempt because he'd be better off anyway...That's why you have to offer a crim that glimmer of hope...

"Also, you often hear stories about child molesters and sex-crime blokes being beaten up and kicked by their fellow prisoners. Well, that's all shit — honest it is! Because when one of them arrives inside, the prison authorities immediately inform the leading crims that if anything happens to this bloke there'll be charges following. So you say to yourself that it isn't worth it. Why lose remission time over a child molester or whatever? And you tell that to your mates. The authorities always did that, because they knew everyone was watching what happened to those type of prisoners. A good example was that bloke Bradley, who murdered the little schoolboy Graeme Thorne. He ended up in charge of the hospital at Goulburn Jail."

(Stephen Leslie Bradley kidnapped schoolboy Graeme Thorne from a Bondi street in July 1960. His plan was to seek a ransom from Thorne's parents, who had recently won a substantial prize in a State lottery. The plan backfired, the youngster was murdered and Bradley attempted to flee from Australia. However, he was captured in the city of Colombo in Sri Lanka and brought back to Sydney to stand trial.)

• • •

Though the Lee trial had ended 18 months earlier, Hayes was still big news on 9 May 1954, when the *Daily Mirror* reported:

> *Criminals and police both heard with relief that Hayes had been refused a pardon and the right to appeal against his conviction for the murder of Bobby Lee. Detectives and the underworld have this in common — both believe the right and safest place for Hayes is jail, where, surprisingly enough, he is reputed to be a model prisoner. On the morning of Hayes' arrest the photographer who took the on-the-spot picture escaped serious injury by inches. In the underworld are men whose scars and limps show they were not so fortunate. Chow Hayes has been given grudging admiration, even by policemen, his implacable foes, for his toughness. One veteran detective commented: "You could hit Chow on the skull with a baton, but he'd still come up fighting. He neither gives nor asks quarter." Nuggety, slant-eyed Hayes loves his tough-guy reputation. News through the prison grapevine that no-one has yet replaced him as Sydney's toughest hoodlum comes as music to his closely-set ears.*

Out at Long Bay Hayes had indeed settled into the daily routine. "When you first went inside and stepped off the prison tram," he describes, "you looked straight over and saw the governor's office, and the clerk's office. On the left were 10 yards (what they called special yards) and the prisoners on remand were taken in there. Murderers and serious criminals on remand like 'Skinny' Brett or myself, were placed on our own in Number 9 yard. Just up from it was 1 Range, for ordinary prisoners serving up to 18 months or two years. They used to call the yards 'Ranges'. 1 Range and 2 Range were for the youths. Next to 2 Range were the workshops (the motor mechanic shop and one thing and another). Then you came to A Hall, which was for remand prisoners only. Next to it was 16 Yard, which had some workers and some non-workers. Then came 17 Yard, which was for the no-hopers (convicted criminals like Hollebone and 'Skinny' Brett and myself). Next door to 17 Yard was B Hall, which was for long-timers (people serving 10 or 15 years, such as murderers who'd had their sentences commuted). And that's where the gallows were.

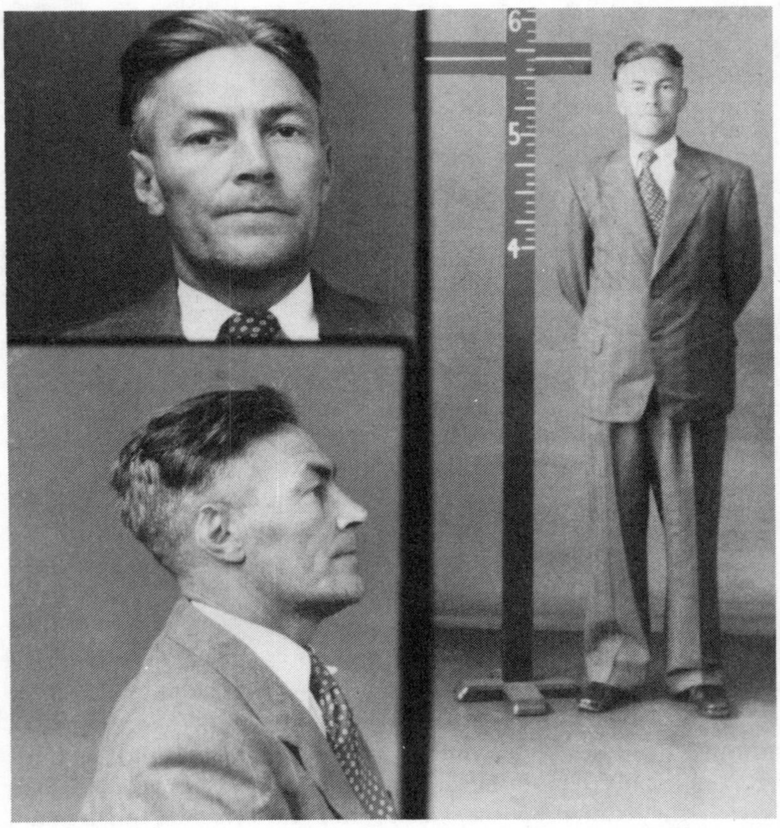

Chow Hayes as he appeared in official police photographs in the early 1950s.

"Down at the botton of B Hall was the condemned cell, in the last cell on the left-hand side on the middle landing. If you were charged with murder, they'd put you in the OBS, along with anyone not the full quid. Between B Hall and the OBS was a yard known as the 'wash-house', where they used to keep the shit-tubs. After B Hall, you came to 3 Range (for ordinary prisoners) and then 4 Range, which was the bakehouse. Then you had the hospital on the other side...

"When you first arrived at Long Bay, you'd proceed into the reception room. Of course there'd be a couple of sweepers there whom you'd know and, unbeknown to the screws — you'd have to be quick — you'd pass to the sweepers anything you wanted to sneak in, tobacco or money or whatever. Then you took a shower, before being marched to the kitchen where you received what they used to call 'grey ghost'. It was water with a bit of onion or something, which was supposed to be soup. Well, you wouldn't take that. But they'd also give you a loaf of bread, and then they'd lock you in your cell. If you were a long-timer they took you into B Hall. But if you were only there 12 months or less, they'd put you into 2 Wing if you were a boy (that was the boys' Wing or 'Range') or 1 Wing if you were a man.

"Everything was done by bells. In the morning the bell would ring at 6 o'clock. You'd tidy your cell, fold away your bed and carry it out and place it on the landing. Bed consisted of two dirty old blankets which were so thin you could look through them — and I'm not kidding about that! Sometimes, if you were lucky, you received a pillow. But if you didn't, you'd use the jacket from your uniform. You'd also receive a hammock which, slung between two hooks on one wall and two hooks on the other wall, slumped right down in the middle so it was useless. During the daytime you'd wet it to make it tighten a bit. But that would only last for two hours in the night and then it'd sag again. Most prisoners slept on the floor in those days. But if you were serving at least two years you'd be given a bit of mattress, which was about five inches [13 centimetres] thick and only made of rope. (The inmates used to roll up the rope for the mats in the yard at 'The Bay' and then send it over to the workshop where the mats were made up.) However, if you were serving less than two years, you just had to sleep on the floor. And in winter the walls would be damp, because they were all stone.

"At 6.30 am they'd open the door and you'd walk down to the yard, have a wash and clean your teeth. Then another bell would ring at 7 am and you'd line up for breakfast. It was just a plate of hominy [porridge-like oatmeal] with no milk or sugar or anything. Then you returned to your cell to eat it. There was another bell at 8 am and you came out again. I used to work in the rope yard, where you were supposed to wind up rope for the mat shop, but I wouldn't really work. You were supposed to wind the rope into big balls, but you'd always be looking to sneak down to the shithouse for a cigarette. However, if the screws spotted you they'd lock you up. That went on until 11.30 am, when another bell would ring, signalling knock-off time. Then you'd return to your yard and wash your hands and face. At midday, the bell would ring again and you went to the barrow and collected your lunch (they called it dinner then). It came in a dixie with a lid on it — half cold, because it had been cooked about an hour before.

"All the crims were on rations in those days. If you didn't work you were on a 4 ration. If you were doing a light job, you received a 3 ration. And if you were doing heavy work, or working in one of the shops, you received a 1 ration. The 1 ration was a little bit more than the 2, 3 or 4 ration. But the 1 ration was still only shit — you received two little slices of fatty meat and, if it was a baked dinner, you also copped a baked spud and a bit of cabbage and pumpkin. That was your midday meal and you took it back to your cell to eat. If you were a Catholic — like I was — they used to give you fish on Friday. But they'd only give you a rotten bit of tail or something. And the only drink available at lunch was water.

"The bell would ring again at 1 pm, though they wouldn't let you out until about 1.10 pm. Then you'd walk back to your yard or your shop or wherever you worked and do the same thing over again. At 3.50 pm another bell would ring. During the afternoon — before that bell — you'd have a shower. But you had to fight for one. They'd march you over sometime between 1.10 pm and 3.50 pm. Sometimes there was hot water, sometimes it was lukewarm, and sometimes there'd be no water at all because the showers were broken or something. The soap wasn't really soap. You'd rub and rub it for about five minutes, and even then you could barely work up enough lather even for your hands. Then you'd have to rub and rub again to create a little more lather for your face.

"At 3.50 pm the bell would ring and you'd return to your yard and pick up your evening meal, which we called tea. That was hominy again, with no milk. But at least in the evening you received an ounce [30 grams] of brown sugar. However, you didn't really receive the whole ounce, because it was in a little cup and those working in the store wouldn't put in a whole ounce. They'd leave some out for themsleves and sell it later on. After the brown sugar had been measured — and those in the store had taken a teaspoon out — it'd be sent over to the Wing and the head sweeper would also take out a teaspoon. So by the time it reached the prisoners, there was about half an ounce left. Then you'd have to keep that in your pocket to avoid the 'peter' thieves [prisoners who stole from other prisoners' cells].

"In the evening you also received a loaf of bread to last the night. After you'd served three months you were also entitled to a cup of tea at this meal. And after 12 months you received tea three times a day. There was no milk or sugar in that, it was just black tea.

"In jail in those days you couldn't survive on the meals you received by legitimate means, so you had to arrange extra helpings by trading tobacco and so on. Or, if you had a mate in the kitchen, every so often he'd make you a steak sandwich or a sausage sandwich. To do that, he'd have to chop down on the other meals a bit — but all the butchers did that for their mates. Similarly at the store, you could go and collect half a pound [225 g] of sugar. But you'd have to buy it — usually with tobacco, which was the currency and which was supplied to you in small amounts. After 12 months you received two ounces [60 grams] of tobacco a week, which made about 80 cigarettes. But the tobacco we received at 'The Bay' was called Western, and it was bloody awful stuff. You couldn't smoke it.

"At 4.30 each afternoon the daily search began. But they only used to select one or two prisoners to search in any fair dinkum manner. In theory the warders might have 72 cells to search. But if they started at 4.30 pm, and there were only four warders to do it, they'd never finish in time to knock off by 4.50 pm. So they only ever picked out a few cells to search properly.

"At 8.45 pm there would be another bell to warn you that 'lights out' was at 9 pm. You might be lying on your bed reading, or secretly writing a letter — what we used to call a 'slip'. Then at 9 pm the lights went out for the night. And that routine went on every day of the year.

"We always had a 'track' inside the jail. That was a screw who'd [illegally] go out and visit your home and collect tobacco or whatever else your family wanted to send inside to you. For example, before I was put onto the payroll at Joe Taylor's two-up game, I'd always stored a few pounds away for my wife in case I was pinched. So I had about £200–£300 in savings whenever I went to jail. And I'd never ask my wife for stuff; instead I'd write a letter to friends, and give it to a 'track'. Then, for example, if you wanted £5 brought inside, he'd take 30 bob as his commission. And when, for example, that screw brought the gun in for silly Cliffie Thomas, he received £500 from Donny 'The Duck' Day.

"You could spend money in jail, but the currency was mostly tobacco. However, if you had money, then you could arrange to receive a little bit extra in your meals. Say you wanted 2 lb [900 g] of meant from the kitchen. If you bought it in tobacco, it would cost you about four packets — that amounted to about 10s in those days. But if you gave a 'caser' (five shillings) you could also receive 2 lb of meat. See, they wanted cash more than they wanted tobacco, especially because the tobacco was no good."

• • •

From Long Bay in Sydney, Hayes was sent off to Bathurst Jail in the central west of New South Wales.

"I wouldn't accept a job in the workshop there," Hayes recalls, "so they gave me a job sweeping. But after I'd been there about five months a young fellow named 'Digger' Evans, who was working in the prison boot shop, went mad and grabbed a knife and attacked a 'screw'. Now he'd taken the knife from my bench — I still had a bench even though they'd given me another job sweeping. Anyway, I was quickly 'shanghaied' back down to 'The Bay' while they decided what to do with me. They alleged I gave the knife to Evans, which was garbage. If it was true I'd only be too happy now to say that I gave it to him, but I didn't. I didn't even know he'd taken it. Anyway I was transferred back down to Long Bay and remained there for another 14 months."

The authorities then decided to send Hayes north to Maitland Jail, where he spent the next 13 years mixing with some of the most notorious murderers in New South Wales history: men like Clarrie French, who strangled and then cut the throat of a female cook working with a railway gang; and Billy Finch, who shot dead a young woman in an Ultimo Street.

"I've often been asked who was the worst killer I ever met, in jail or outside," Hayes says. "I've met some bad ones, but I'd have to say Mervyn 'Skulls' Garvie. He was nicknamed 'Skulls' because he had a tattoo of a skull in the middle of his forehead. He became known as the 'Bulli Pass Rapist' because he'd been working in the bush outside Bulli, cutting timber, with three or four other chaps." Garvie had been convicted of the murder of Cecil John Kelly at Bulli in August 1946. Subsequently, at Maitland, Garvie was pointed out to Hayes by an old friend of his, Les Kennedy.

Hayes recalls: "When I was sent to Maitland Jail, one special fellow whom I knew very well was Les 'The Wolf' Kennedy. I used to run around with him back in the late 1930s. He was also at Maitland serving a life sentence." Leslie Ernest "The Wolf" Kennedy had been given a life sentence in March 1940 for the manslaughter of Alexander Robert Henry Miller (also known as

Arthur Wilson) in the Covent Garden Café in Sydney's Chinatown precinct.

Hayes continues: "Kennedy went to the Covent Garden Hotel and walked upstairs to the café area looking for a bloke named Billy Scully. Kennedy fired several shots at Scully, which missed him but hit a bystander (Miller). Kennedy was charged with murder, but the jury found him guilty of manslaughter. However, the judge — who'd instructed the jury that they had to find either murder or nothing — then declared that since they'd found manslaughter despite his direction, he'd show them what he thought of that and sentenced Kennedy to life imprisonment. Kennedy went on to serve 21 years.

"So when I arrived at Maitland 'The Wolf' was there, and he pointed Garvie out to me. I didn't know Garvie from a bar of a soap at that stage. Kennedy warned me that Garvie would be dying to tell me his story — that he told crims, screws, anyone who would listen, and that he never strayed from any single detail of it.

"One day I was strolling from the kitchen and I ran into Garvie in the laneway. He called out to me and we walked down into the yard and, sure enough, he insisted on telling me his story.

"He used to sneak around at night among the parked cars, full of teenage lovers, at the top of Bulli Pass. He boasted that he'd attacked several couples and raped the females, but they'd never reported it to the police. One particular night around 1 am, he spotted a bloke screwing his girl in the backseat. Garvie said he became 'real horny' and couldn't wait till they finished. So Garvie flung open the back door and declared: 'Right oh, mate, get off! It's my turn!' The startled young bloke threatened to fight Garvie as soon as he'd pulled his trousers back on. But before he knew what hit him, Garvie smashed him across the head with a piece of timber and killed him instantly. The girl began screaming, and Garvie boasted that he immediately smacked her across the mouth. Then he jumped in on top of the young bloke's body and fucked the girl several times and made her do all sorts of other things. And, he boasted, all the while he knew he had to kill her. So when he was finished with her he attempted to strangle her with his bare hands.

"Eventually she pretended to be dead. Then Garvie pushed the car over the cliff. But, in a miracle, the young girl somehow managed to roll out of the car as it was sliding over the edge. It finished up about 100 feet [30 metres] down the cliff, but luckily she landed on a small ledge only about 8 feet [2.5 metres] below the top. Garvie thought she'd fallen to the bottom and went back to the timber camp. He was covered in blood, but told the other workers he'd been in a fight in Wollongong that night. So they took no more notice of it.

"However, when the female regained consciousness she began calling for help. Eventually some passing motorists pulled her back up from the ledge and contacted the police. Garvie was tried for murder and given the death sentence, which was duly commuted to life imprisonment. The ALP was in government in New South Wales at the time, and they always opposed hanging. But I know for a fact that there were two or three in the Cabinet at that point who were so appalled at Garvie's case that they wanted Garvie to hang for that murder.

"Garvie was the worst murderer I ever knew, because he gloated over it — over every detail, all the things he did to her and so on. He even laughed because he was fucking her on top of her boyfriend's corpse. Garvie couldn't read, so at Maitland he always grabbed the copies of magazines like *Australasian Post* and *People* — the ones full of sexy photos of young girls.

"Garvie eventually committed suicide. He stabbed himself in the chest and then cut his own throat. That was also at Maitland, after he'd served about eight or nine years of his life sentence."

Another particularly despised killer at Maitland was William Ernest McDonald. He'd grabbed the headlines way back in July 1931 when, after copping a bullet in the thigh in Johnston Street, Annandale, he'd declined to name his assailant to investigating police. McDonald was subsequently convicted of the gruesome murder of his own niece, June Florence Peisley. She was just 11 years old when her tiny corpse was found "outraged and strangled near Leichhardt canal" in Febrary 1942.

Hayes recalls: "Billy McDonald was one of the biggest whingeing bastards I ever met in jail. He was never satisfied with what he received. He always wanted to know why another prisoner had received more of something than he had. No one at Maitland liked him. He was an out-and-out bastard, and he was treated as such — not by the screws but by the crims.

"McDonald had been in the army during the war years, and in early 1942 he was staying at his sister's place at Leichhardt for a while. One afternoon his sister sent her daughter, June, up to the shop to buy some groceries. Meanwhile Billy McDonald was in the backyard. His sister didn't see him leave the backyard, but he walked up to the shops and met his niece on her way back. He took her into the old cemetery near Leichhardt canal, where he sexually assaulted her and murdered her. Then he snuck back home and stayed in the backyard.

"A couple of hours later his sister, worried about her daughter, walked out into the backyard and asked Billy to go up to the shops and scout around the streets and see if he could find little June. After a while he came back and reported that he couldn't find her. The police were called in to investigate but, after several days had passed, they had not uncovered a single lead. However, one of the neighbours, who'd gone away for a few days, then returned home and the police interviewed her. She had seen McDonald walking back from the shops with his niece. When the police heard that, they re-questioned Billy. He was convicted and sentenced to life imprisonment. After being at Maitland with him for four or five years, he was sent to 'The Bay' and that was the last I heard of him."

• • •

While Hayes sat confined in his prison cell, his former partner in crime Joey Hollebone continued with his nefarious ways.

Back in 1950, he had been sentenced to 12 months in jail for carrying an unlicensed gun at night after the court heard him described as a particularly "violent type".

Then three years later the law for carrying an unlicensed gun was changed and new penalties introduced, and Joey Hollebone found himself the first case under the new law.

Hayes recalls: "Hollebone attempted to gain a remand, but his barrister told him he had no chance. So the night before the court appearance, Hollebone shot himself in his inside thigh in Missenden Road and then walked into Prince Alfred Hospital and said he'd been shot by an unknown man. He was granted the remand the following morning. But when he appeared in court soon after, he copped the maximum three-year sentence."

Back on the streets in 1957 Hollebone, described as a "notorious gunman", appeared in Glebe Court on charges of habitually consorting with criminals.

Then in May 1960 police raided a home in Beaumont Street, Waterloo, at 1.30 am and charged seven men and six women with having been found in a house frequented by thieves. Detective Sergeant A. G. Clark of the CIB told Redfern Court that police found 13 people sitting in a small loungeroom. "I spoke to

Maurice Bernard Ryan and told him we had received information that Charles Edward 'Chicka' Reeves was on the premises," said Clark. "I told him Reeves was a wanted criminal and that he was wanted on a charge of theft and breaking and entering. Ryan replied: 'Well, you've missed him. He just left.'" Clark went on: "I then said: 'We have been told you people are making arrangements for Hollebone to shoot Leonard Arthur McPherson over some trouble recently and that Nancy Brown [one of the women present] had offered £1000 to Hollebone.' Nancy Brown said: 'What a lot of rot.'"

This time Hollebone never made it to court. He died in St Vincent's Hospital soon after suffering a cerebral haemorrhage.

• • •

More than anything else, Hayes remembers vividly the endless regulation and routine of jail life during his life sentence.

"If you were serving two years or more," he recalls, "you were classed as an A Division prisoner. They'd put a number on you with a red A in front of it to notify all the screws that you were serving two years or more, no matter what the charge had been. For their first three months, A Division prisoners were put into a special yard (except at Parramatta, where you went into 'The Circle') and you were only allowed out for two hours in the morning and two hours in the afternoon. Then after you'd served the first three months, the A would be taken off and you'd be given a C on top of your number. That then signified an ordinary crim.

"At one point, someone had a bright idea. He'd just been sentenced to two years in jail, and he asked Judge McKell to give him only 23 months and three weeks. He explained all about 'The Circle' and the other similar special yards to the judge, and the judge agreed and changed the sentence to 23 months and three weeks. Then other judges began to do likewise, particularly if they didn't think the sentence should be as severe as to include a non-association period.

"Also, if you were under 25 years of age you were classed as a boy; over 25, and you went in with the men. Now if you were a boy, you were placed in 'The Circle' or a special yard, no matter how long the sentence you were serving (even if it was only a fortnight) until they found a job for you. Then they'd let you out and you'd join the prison workforce. If you didn't work, you received threepence a week — and the only reason for that was so it wasn't classed as slave labour.

"Many of the people running the jails were sadists. I say that because, if you were arrested in Sydney, then you'd expect to serve your sentence somewhere close like Parramatta or 'The Bay'. But, for example, if you were a local from Goulburn, and you had been pinched there, they'd send you to Bathurst or Maitland or somewhere, instead of keeping you at Goulburn so you could see your family and relatives. They were always trying to send you in the opposite direction.

"What we used to do was go to the governor and, say I wanted to go to Bathurst, I'd explain that if he sent me to Parramatta or Goulburn I had enemies there and they'd stir up a real stink. So he'd decide therefore to send me to Bathurst. But the authorities eventually woke up to that rort. So we had to go and arrange for a local shopkeeper (like a grocer or someone) and bring him down to Central Court to take out a warrant at the Small Debtors' Court. Then they'd send the warrant up to Bathurst, for example, to be served on you. As a result you'd be brought back to 'The Bay' on the next available returning escort. Well, then when you went to the court, you'd make sure you received a remand, or the shopkeeper would ask for a remand, or someone would be sick or something. So you'd eventually do most of your sentence back down in Sydney at Long Bay. Then they woke up to that — and to stop it, they would only bring you down to Sydney on the day before you were due to appear. And if you were granted a remand for, say, a fortnight, you'd be sent back to the country jail that night or the next day."

Hayes reckons that, all things considered, Parramatta was the worst jail of the lot — especially with its hated feature, 'The Circle'. "It had a catwalk at the top," Hayes explains, "where the screws could watch you in every yard."

However, the remand conditions at Long Bay were equally despised. "At 'The Bay', when you were on remand, the only piece of cover in the whole yard was a bit of old tin," Hayes explains. "When the rain came, it leaked all over and there was no chance of the screws allowing you to return to your cell. So you just stood there in the rain and soaked. It was a real bastard of a place. At least if you were on remand at Bathurst or Goulburn or Parramatta, they'd let you return to the cells. And at 'The Bay' there were often many squareheads — who eventually beat the charges — among the hardened criminals. But the squareheads would also spend three months out there, unable to return to their cells during the day and exposed to the elements."

In jail Hayes and his contemporaries used to smoke coir mats or tea-leaves, rolled inside newspaper or pages from the prison Bibles. "The Bible was the best," Hayes recalls, "because it was the thinnest paper!"

During those years, prisoners were often sent on "an escort" into Sydney to the Courts or between the various jails. "You'd be handcuffed in groups of 22 or 24," Hayes explains, "and a long chain ran through one of the handcuffs attached to each prisoner so that you were all chained together. Then they'd put you in the escort tram, which drove right inside the jail, and took you to Central Railway Station. That's where, on top of the old ambulance station in Lee Street, they'd walk you up to an area where most of the luggage was stored. They had two box-cars waiting, and they'd load us into them like cattle. And the number of prisoners determined the number of accompanying screws required. If there were 16 prisoners, then there'd be four accompanying screws. But there'd be a couple of uniformed coppers on hand as well, and they'd take you to whatever jail you were destined to reach. For example, if it was Parramatta, they'd meet you at the train and put you into police wagons and take you to the jail. But if you were travelling to Bathurst or Goulburn or Maitland, you just stepped off the train with the chains still on you, picked up your canvas bag which had your clothes in it, threw it over your shoulder and walked to the jail."

The standards of hygiene within the jails in those years were almost non-existent. "It's a wonder to me that very serious social disease never broke out inside the prisons," says Hayes. "You received a 'shit tub' — and it wasn't even as big as a bucket — with a lid on it. It had your cell number marked on it, so that you received the same tub back each night. But the blokes who were assigned to wash them out didn't really wash them at all. So when you walked into the yard you went upstairs and picked up your own tub and made sure you washed it out again as best you could. The problem was that there was nothing with which to wash them properly. All you had was a little bit of water in the bottom. As a result, it ensured that you cleared your bowels before you returned to your cell in the afternoon — because otherwise it'd sit there stinking all night in your cell. However, there were some dirty bastards who wouldn't go outside. They'd want to go in their cells. So one of the best things about being a 'lifer', was that 'lifers' and other hardened criminals didn't have to associate with fellow criminals. That meant you had a cell to yourself and didn't have to put up with anyone who was a dirty grub.

"Of course, if someone arrived at the jail whom you knew well, then you wouldn't mind sharing a cell with him for two or three days until he found his feet. But the main reason, of course, was so that you could hear all the latest news from outside. Anyway, most prisoners tried to make sure they went to the toilet in the afternoon, so they'd only have to piss in their shit tubs during the night. And you didn't receive toilet paper; you had newspaper chopped into little pieces.

"But the OBS was worse still (that was the Observation Unit for people on capital charges and those not the full quid). All the cells were padded in there, with stone ceilings and the floor made of wood or concrete. In the OBS, your toilet was between four and six inches [10–15 centimetres] deep, and about six inches across. It was like a very small saucepan with no lid on it, and it was made of rubber (the other shit tubs were made of tin). The rubber OBS tubs were not marked, so you might cop anyone's tub the next night. Those rubber tubs stunk so badly you couldn't even piss in them. When you went into your cell, you immediately turned it over and left it there, because you didn't know who'd had it the night before. You'd almost bust yourself rather than have to use it during the night."

• • •

Among the hardened criminals he encountered inside Her Majesty's prisons, Hayes felt genuine compassion for a few wretched souls. "Some killers do it hard in jail," he explains. "I felt sorry for people like Billy Surridge and his wife Phyllis, and 'Skinny' Jones (who came from Melbourne)." William Charles Surridge, his wife Barbara Phyllis Surridge and one James Harris (alias George Wilson) had been found guilty of the murder of a chef named Ernest Hoffman in East Sydney in June 1942.

"I knew Phyllis and Billy Surridge well," Hayes recalls. "He was a bludger and she was working the streets in the Woolloomooloo area. And the names Harris and Wilson were both aliases used by 'Skinny' Jones. The three of them worked as a team. They'd 'lumber' a drunk: he'd think he was going to a house to get it off with Barbara, but when he arrived they'd beat him up and take his money. Anyway, a racing chap was one of their victims, and they gave him a decent kicking and he died. The three of them received life sentences. Now at that time the men's jail and the women's jail were next to one another, and they only used to let them have one visit a year, in the men's part of the church. Well, I reckoned that was doing it tough — being in jail and knowing your wife's in the jail next door."

A similar case involved Joycie Williams and her son, Ronnie. "The two of them and a young Pommie fellow kicked a watchman to death out at Newtown. They all copped life sentences. The authorities used to let Joycie see her son every three or four months. That would be very hard — for a mother to be in jail while her son was also in jail."

• • •

Like most prisoners, Hayes quickly realised that, once inside, a criminal — however notorious his past — is forgotten after about 12 months. Then it is the man's family members who carry the burden.

"Every time I went to jail," Hayes explains, "the ones it hurt most were the members of my family. They had to walk down the street with people staring and pointing and commenting 'That's Chow Hayes's wife or son or daughter.'"

22 SP Bookmaking at Kirkconnel

The 1950s passed, the 1960s were in full swing and the notorious Chow Hayes had been replaced in the headlines by a new generation of hoods and thugs who lurked around the Kings Cross baccarat dens.

In what seemed little more than the blinking of an eye, Hayes had spent a decade at Maitland Jail. Then he suddenly began suffering severe stomach pains. At first he dismissed them as indigestion, but finally he was struck down, unable to walk, with what turned out to be a burst ulcer. In 1964 Hayes was rushed to nearby Maitland District Hospital, where six prison guards were assigned to stand guard outside his door, two for each eight-hour shift.

At that time the Comptroller-General of Prisons (a position now known as the New South Wales Commissioner for Corrective Services) would visit Maitland Jail three times each year. In the early 1960s the Comptroller-General was John Morony and, as chance would have it, about four days after Hayes was rushed to hospital Morony was due for one of his regular tours encompassing Maitland.

"Morony had known me years earlier," Hayes recounts, "when he was still a clerk at head office in Sydney. So he knew my whole story. Anyway he decided to come over to Maitland Hospital and visit me. He asked how I was going and I replied not too bad. Then he said Topsy (whom he knew fairly well) would be up to see me the following day, because he'd given her a special pass to spend two or three days at Maitland, during which time she would be allowed to see me whenever I liked.

"Then Morony asked, what about giving my word that I wouldn't try to escape from the hospital? Well, I assured him that I wasn't intending to attempt any escape after I'd already served 12 years. He explained that they were short-staffed over at the jail. In addition, Morony added, it was costing a lot for all the overtime involved for the guards to look after me, because that meant six less at the jail. So he promised that if I gave my word I wouldn't escape, he'd remove the guards from outside my hospital room. Well, I gave my word and he duly took them off straightaway. So from that point I was treated just like any other ordinary patient, able to roam around the hospital and do whatever I liked.

"Topsy arrived the following morning and remained for at least five hours during the day, before returning again in the evenings. She stayed at a nearby hotel in Maitland. And all this time Joe Taylor was still looking after Topsy, paying over my weekly wages from the two-up game. Also Dick Reilly and Perce Galea continued to give her extra money twice a year (at Christmas time and birthdays for the kids) but Kate Leigh wasn't involved anymore."

One fellow patient whom Hayes befriended inside Maitland Hospital was Joe Darcy, brother of legendary Australian boxing champ Les Darcy. Joe Darcy was in hospital to have his gall bladder removed. He gave Hayes a large bag of fruit soon after his arrival and the two became mates.

Eventually the good life inside Maitland Hospital ended, Hayes was discharged and returned to the jail. But some months later Mr Morony arrived again at Maitland on a regular inspection check. He spotted Hayes in the yard, walked over and asked Chow how he was feeling.

"Then he asked how I liked it at Maitland," Hayes recalls, "and I replied that I'd been there long enough to become used to it. We chatted for a while, and he informed me that, because I'd done the right thing when he took the guards away from the hospital, and not tried to escape, he'd decided to trust me again. He asked — and, to tell the truth, I thought he was having me on — whether I would still give my word not to escape if he now sent me to a prison camp. Naturally I said 'Yes,' because I knew that move meant I was almost home now. See, once they sent you to a prison camp, you were on your way out. And, of course, the camps had everything a prisoner considered comforts.

"Morony asked which prison camp I'd like to go to. I'd heard that Kirkconnel, out near Bathurst, was the best so I chose it. Morony returned to Sydney and apparently convinced the other 'heavies' in the department that, though they didn't usually send a man with my record to a prison camp, he was prepared to take a chance with me. And he convinced them that, if it proved a success, it might open things up a bit and provide an incentive for which many of the other prisoners might aim.

"A fortnight later, on Tuesday, Morony returned to Maitland yet again. He explained that he was going to send me to Kirkconnel, but on the Thursday I'd have to go down to Long Bay first to be examined by the doctors. If you went to a prison camp you had to be physically fit because, unlike the jails, the department did not employ medical officers at prison camps. So I was transported down to Long Bay, passed fit — of course, that was all arranged — and then I was off to Kirkconnel."

Hayes had been at Maitland 12 years by this time. But within a matter of weeks he was virtually running Kirkconnel. "I was the SP bookmaker there," he explains, "and I had everything sewn up. I was having a terrific time. You could walk out into the bush, because there were no iron bars, only forests. And I quickly became a talking point for all the visiting dignitaries. I was so well known that whenever anyone of note visited the camp (for example, the local mayor or a group of important visitors from Sydney), they were all brought over and introduced to me. The prison bosses would describe how I was in charge of the garden — when I didn't know a weed from a flower — and continue to boast how well prison farms worked, and how this notorious gunman was now running the garden and so on."

After he'd been at Kirkconnel 22 months, however, Hayes suddenly developed cancer in one of his kidneys. "I'd been suffering sharp pains in my lower back," Hayes explains. "But I didn't want to go and report it, because I thought it would hold me up — add more time to my sentence. For a while I convinced myself that I'd probably just strained a muscle. But, over a period of about six weeks, the pains became much worse. Finally, when the pain increased alarmingly, I decided to leave it until the next morning and see how I felt. But every time I went to the toilet the following day, this horrible black blood came out in my urine. So I went to see the camp superintendent, Ray Shirlaw.

"Shirlaw said that, next time I wanted to go to the toilet, I should come back to his office and we'd collect a specimen in a bottle. That was about 3.30 pm, and he finished his shift at 5 pm. But at about 5.30 pm I wanted to do a piss again, so I went and saw the second-in-charge and he knew all about it. They took a sample and quickly said they'd have to contact head office.

Eventually they rang John Morony in Sydney. He told them to take me to the hospital inside Bathurst Jail, and I finally arrived there about 8 pm that night. The doctor took one look at another sample and said I'd have to go to Bathurst District Hospital. There they took further tests, and the next day they sent me down to Long Bay. (When we were transferring between all these prisons we went by car, not train.) From Long Bay I was ushered straight over to Prince Henry Hospital, where I had the kidney removed."

Suddenly the gunman most of Sydney had forgotten was back in the tabloid headlines. The Sydney *Sun* of 9 May 1966 reported: "Hayes...is now a patient at the Prince Henry jail hospital. Hayes became ill last week at Bathurst Jail and was transferred to Sydney." The *Daily Telegraph* trumpeted on 3 June: "Chow Hayes is dangerously ill in Prince Henry Hospital...Hayes was transferred to Long Bay Jail after he became ill at a prison farm near Bathurst. He had been at the farm as a trusted prisoner for about two years." And the *Daily Mirror* added on 11 June: "Chow Hayes, 53, is recovering in Prince Henry Hospital today after a serious kidney operation...Hayes was transferred from a prison farm near Bathurst last month to Long Bay Jail when he became ill. He told relatives that doctors had found a cancer in his right kidney. Doctors yesterday removed the kidney... Hayes served more than 10 years of his sentence at Maitland Jail, where he was regarded as a model prisoner. He was transferred to Bathurst about two years ago."

Hayes recalls: "I was in Prince Henry about four days, having tests, and then they told me I had cancer in one kidney. But at least they didn't think it was malignant or that it was spreading. They said I'd be okay as long as they removed it immediately. I thought they meant in about a week, but then they explained they meant the next morning. I was in the operating theatre four and a half hours, but it only seemed like five minutes. In fact, when I came out I was in the post-operative room and I woke up and saw all the doctors and nurses around me and I asked one of them: 'How long is this operation going to take?' And she replied: 'You've already had it!'

"Then they shifted me into the main ward at Prince Henry. For the next three weeks I had a tube in my penis, attached to a bottle which you carry around on your hip. But then when I recovered from that I used to give them a bit of a hand, going around emptying the bottles and shit pans and so on. And, honestly, I think I could have still been there if I'd wanted to stay. They didn't want to lose me. I did more work there of my own choice than I ever did in jail. I went outside and cleaned the hospital windows for them. I was really enjoying it, and I was very appreciative of what they'd done for me. At one point a reporter from the *Sun* came out and wanted an exclusive interview at my bedside. But I wouldn't give it to him.

"While I was in Prince Henry Hospital, Perce Galea and Eric O'Farrell came out to visit me. During our chat O'Farrell asked me: 'I hope there are not any hard feelings between me and you?' He meant over the Lee shooting taking place in his club. Well, I replied: 'Certainly not. It was my fault.' And, in fact, the Ziegfeld Club was later closed up by the authorities, largely due to that incident...

"Meanwhile, the administrators back at 'The Bay' wanted to know why I was leading such a merry life over at Prince Henry Hospital and why I didn't have a guard on me and so on. It all bred a lot of jealousy. But I remained at Prince Henry for four months. Finally the doctor informed me I'd have to return to 'The College' the following weekend (all the doctors and nurses at Prince Henry referred to Long Bay as 'The College'). But the doctor also wrote out a special diet for me. And, of course, in those days you'd never heard of things like eggs and milk in the jails, only in the hospital. So what I took back, on doctor's orders, was a real luxury menu.

"Once I was back inside 'The Bay' they put me straight into the prison hospital and my menu was sent to the superintendent. But then the following morning the prison doctor and chief male nurse arrived and immediately moved me out of the hospital and back into a cell. However, as soon as Topsy came out to visit me, she told the doctor at Prince Henry what had happened. The doctor contacted Morony and there was a big stink about it, because I wasn't supposed to be in a cell, I was supposed to be in the prison hospital. The 'heavies' in the Department were onto the superintendent like a ton of bricks and I was quickly shifted back into the hospital."

Hayes remained in Long Bay's prison hospital for another fortnight, and then returned to Kirkconnel prison farm for another 12 months.

"Then one weekend in late 1967 Morony came up to visit," Hayes recalls, "and it wasn't an official jail inspection. It was more like a Sunday afternoon drive, with his wife, and no-one knew he was arriving. Suddenly Shirlaw called me to his office. Morony announced he was sending me down to 'The Bay' the following Thursday, because the Parole Board was sitting there on the Monday after that. Morony told me to keep my fingers crossed and I might have a chance. Well, this was the first I'd heard about it — I hadn't been expecting anything for at least a couple more years yet."

Eight days later, Chow Hayes, Tony Martini and several other long-serving criminals appeared before the parole board. When Hayes took his turn, Mr Morony did most of the talking. He outlined Hayes's crime, and explained it was part of a gangland-style vendetta between Hayes, Bobby Lee and co. Morony emphasised that, although it was still murder, the shooting had not involved any innocent bystanders. Then he described Hayes as a model prisoner, emphasising the responsibilities involved in running the garden at Kirkconnel and so on. Morony also produced a letter from Hayes's wife, Topsy, explaining that, even after all these years, she still visited her husband regularly and had never sought a divorce nor become involved with other men while Hayes had been in prison.

Then the judge heading the parole board handed Hayes a piece of paper. "I want you to look at that and read it," he said. Hayes looked at both sides of the sheet, but it was blank. The judge asked: "Do you see anything on that?" Hayes replied: "No." Then the judge explained: "That's a clean sheet. Do you think, if we recommend you for release, that you could keep your sheet as clean as that?" A startled Hayes immediately retorted: "Yes." Then he was told to leave the room.

Hayes recalls: "I didn't know what had happened, because after you appeared you simply waited to hear one way or the other. Finally, about four days later, Morony came and had a yarn with me. I should've known what was in the wind, because whenever they knock someone back for parole, they tell them: 'We'll see you again in another six months.' But they didn't say that to me. Anyway, about four days later Morony came back out to Long Bay. I was in the hospital and he wanted to talk to me privately before he left. So I was called over to the governor's office, where Morony told me he had good news. He said the parole board had recommended my release. But he added, as he winked at me, that didn't guarantee it would be granted, because the final decision rested with the New South Wales Governor, who had to sign the release. However, that was really a formality.

"But then suddenly, about a week later, I was called over to the prison governor's office again, and told I was returning to Kirkconnel the next morning. I protested that I hadn't yet heard the results from my parole bid. But the superintendent told me to forget that because I was going back to Kirkconnel tomorrow, and it was already 5 pm. I complained that I wouldn't have time to pack up my belongings, but he replied they'd pack them for me and send them on.

"The next morning I boarded the big prison bus with about 22 people. So I knew it was definitely going back to Kirkconnel. I was dumbfounded, but once the trip started I resigned myself to the explanation that my parole must have been knocked back after all. I sat behind the driver. All the other prisoners, except me and one other bloke, were heading to Bathurst. We were the only two heading for Kirkconnel.

"On those trips the driver always stops the bus a couple of times along the way for a cup of tea or a toilet break. And at one point on this trip, someone came up to the driver and said: 'A car has been following us all the way.' But the driver replied: 'Yeah, that's all right. I know who that is.' The driver explained that the car would drop off once we reached Kirkconnel. So I immediately began wondering who was in the car, and whether it was connected with either myself or the other bloke who was travelling to Kirkconnel.

"On the main highway between Lithgow and Bathurst, the bus turned off as usual at Sunny Corner. From there, we drove back down a dirt road about 17 miles [27 kilometres] until we came to Kirkconnel. Then they unloaded the two of us from the bus. I looked over my shoulder and there was the car, with two blokes inside. They stepped out and went into the office, while we waited outside until we saw the superintendent. They talked to Shirlaw, and then he called me inside and asked if I knew these chaps. Then he announced that he had good news — I was going home!

"The car had followed me up from 'The Bay' because, to avoid all the media attention, they never simply released you at Long Bay. Instead, they sent you back to the prison from which you'd come, and then released you from there."

The *Daily Mirror* reported on 27 July 1967: "Chow Hayes, freed after 15 years in jail for a gangland murder, today warned Australia's youth not to follow his example by bucking the law. 'I led a bad life and look at the price I had to pay,' he said. 'Anyone who bucks the law must end up a loser.'. . . The advice comes from a man who is renowned as one of Australia's toughest mobsters."

The following Sunday, 30 July, amid much speculation that Hayes had only a short time to live due to "the cancer eating away his one remaining kidney," Australia's largest-selling newspaper, Sydney's *Sun–Herald*, declared: "Severe restrictions have been placed on the movements of convicted murderer John Frederick 'Chow' Hayes, released from prison last week. Hayes, 59, who has been given 18 months to two years to live, is under a 7.30 pm curfew. He cannot go into Kings Cross, must not leave the metropolitan area without the permission of the Comptroller-General of Prisons and must report to his parole officer once a fortnight. . . 'The doctors have told me not to drink. But I like a beer and I don't care if it cuts my time in half, I'll die happy,' Hayes said. . ."

The *Sun–Herald* interview with Hayes continued:

"I was a gunman — there's no sense denying it. I have too many convictions to deny it. But none of it was worth it. You don't appreciate your freedom until they take it away from you — and take it away for 15 years. I can't describe how it felt walking through the gates of the State Penitentiary to freedom last Thursday. They told me 48 hours before that I was going out and for the next two nights I couldn't sleep because I was frightened I might sleep through freedom time."

Hayes said the monotony was the worst part of jail life. "They gave you your last feed for the day at 3.30 in the afternoon and locked you up in your cell until 7 the next morning," he said. . . He said lying alone in his cell gave him plenty of time to reflect what a fool he had been. "It's true," he said. "I suppose it was about 10 years ago I saw the light. I don't mean in the religious sense. I have no time for religion. But I thought to myself, 'It's not me they're punishing, but my family.' Being in the stir, out of circulation, didn't make that much difference to me, but I knew that outside my wife, my son and daughter were suffering. I know when they walked down the street people would point to them and whisper behind their backs: 'That's the family of Chow Hayes, the gunman'. . ."

Hayes was asked if he had his life over, what he'd do? "I'd be a mug, go out and swing a pick, do anything to stay outside," he said. "It's pitiful to see them inside, the young blokes who try to associate with you because you're a lifer in for murder. They think there's some glamour attached to it and some of it might rub off on them. It's happened since I've been out, too. It makes me sick, blokes coming up to me in the pub wanting to know me because they think it's big time to be seen with me."

• • •

A few years earlier, while Hayes was still in jail, all the residents had been evicted from their humble terrace houses in Thomas Street, Ultimo, to make way for the building of Sydney's new technical college. Hayes's wife, Topsy, moved into the Sir John Northcott flats in Surry Hills. But she soon disliked the new environment, mostly because without access to a yard she was unable to sit in the sun.

So when Hayes returned to Sydney from Kirkconnel for his kidney operation, he told his daughter, Little Topsy, to go and see Perce Galea about the problem. "Joe Taylor was still giving them my wages, so I couldn't put another bite on him," Hayes explains. "Galea and Eric O'Farrell duly came out to Prince Henry Hospital and I explained I was on my 'way out', now that I was in Kirkconnel. Galea told me to have Little Topsy arrange another house and he'd pay the rent each week. She found one in River Street, Earlwood, for $40 per week plus $300 bond. Galea and O'Farrell paid the rent two months in advance as well as putting up the $300 bond...

"Eventually I came home from jail and Dolly Simmons [the woman Hayes had for years conned the authorities into believing was his sister] was living in Park Street, Campsie. She told me that a flat opposite was available, which would allow Dolly and Little Topsy and I to share the load in looking after my wife, who was very sick. Then I went and told Galea and offered his $300 bond back — but O'Farrell told me to keep it. The new rent was only $32 per week, but they kept giving me $40 per week. Each Saturday at the races they gave the money to a mate of mine who worked as a clerk for one of the leading bookmakers. I'd pick it up from him. You could never bite Perce Galea at the track. Afterwards he'd give you anything, but he was very surreptitious at the races."

23 Joe Borg and the Vice Rackets

By the early 1960s Chow Hayes's long-time friend Dick Reilly had risen to become one of the most feared and influential baccarat operators in Sydney.

Born in 1909, Richard Gabriel Reilly was two years older than Hayes. As a youth Reilly had prided himself on his natural strength and physical fitness, working out daily at Storey's Gymnasium in Surry Hills. During the 1920s he briefly attempted a boxing career as a middleweight, while working at night as a bouncer at a series of popular dance halls, including the Palais Royal and the Savoy at Central Railway. It was during this period that Reilly and Chow Hayes established the foundations of a lifelong mateship.

In the early 1930s Dick Reilly and his brother Gerald worked as doormen at the popular Ginger Jar nightspot, before moving on to similar employment towards the end of the decade at Joseph Thompson's sly-grog den in Hunter Street and Phil Jeffs's infamous 400 Club.

Between 1935 and 1952 Dick Reilly appeared in court on 15 different matters, the charges including assault, robbery, demanding money by menaces, stealing and carrying an unlicensed pistol. In 1937 he was charged with the murder, but acquitted, of fellow standover man Clarrie Thomas — Reilly had gunned him down in a central Sydney street.

During the war Reilly moved into the rationing rackets. A vast black market in basic living commodities had developed and Reilly made a small fortune distributing forged clothing ration coupons. But in February 1945 Reilly, six other men and two women, were arrested as part of an organised fraud ring. Reilly, his partner William James Sedgwick and well-known Sydney solicitor Abraham George Brindley were described in court as the key figures in the operation.

In the late 1940s Reilly worked for a period as a doorman at Abe Saffron's glitzy Roosevelt Club in Kings Cross. Then, when the sly-grog rackets were at their height during the early 1950s, he moved on to manage the southern suburb nightspot, Oyster Bill's, which had been renamed the Colony Club. Reilly also worked for Joe Taylor at Thommo's two-up school for a time, escorting the big winners back to hotels or driving them home.

It was during the 1950s that Reilly skilfully developed the key political and police contacts which subsequently allowed him, during the early 1960s, to emerge as one of Sydney's most feared and powerful criminals. He became a partner with the notorious Dr Reginald Stuart-Jones in Sydney's sleazy abortion rackets, and managed the high-profile illegal gambling joint, the Kellett Club, in the heart of Kings Cross.

By 1967 Dick Reilly had become renowned as a tough, ruthless thug who provided the muscle for any problems around Sydney's booming illegal gambling clubs. He drove a $17,000 Maserati, wore $200 suits and owned both a palatial home in exclusive Castle Cove and a unit in the fashionable eastern suburbs.

But it all ended in a blaze of gunfire in June 1967 when he was blasted with both a shotgun and rifle as he descended the front steps from his mistress's flat in Double Bay. The murderer was fellow gunman Johnny Warren.

Hayes recalls those years: "I was at Maitland when Reilly and Abe Brindley were pinched over that rationing coupon fraud. Reilly copped a couple of years and Brindley was finished as a solicitor after that. But up to that point — even though Brindley was never a top criminal lawyer and you wouldn't hire him to fight a case for you — he was always available to appear for you at short notice and arrange a remand and so on. Brindley and Phil Roach and Harold Munro had that business all tied up for years.

"Harold Munro's major 'earner' was to travel around with the coppers, to dark city parks such as Green Park opposite St Vincent's Hospital. The police would arrive and pinch a bloke for something like exposing himself or propositioning someone — they were all trumped-up charges. Then they'd take him back to the police station and lay the charge. It was always an innocent man — they never tried it on criminals, because no-one would believe them. Then they'd tell the bloke there was a good solicitor they could recommend named Harold Munro. And often the victim would accept their advice and hire Munro. Then Munro would put the bite onto the poor sap and inform him that he (Munro) could arrange for the matter to be dropped for £50 or £100. That way the victim would be able to avoid newspaper coverage, with all the resultant embarrassment in front of friends and family and so on. The mug would hand over the cash and Munro and the coppers would split it up. Eventually there was a big inquiry into the racket and Munro was charged."

• • •

In 1967 — the same year as Dick Reilly was murdered — Chow Hayes returned to civilian life after 15 years in custody. He was "on licence", a condition of which was that he was not allowed to drink alcohol or enter a hotel (though he was permitted to attend nightclubs).

Hayes did not have to worry about finding employment, since the Corrective Services Department had arranged that he receive the invalid pension immediately upon release.

He went to live in the unit in Park Street, Campsie, with his wife, Topsy. She had suffered a stroke two years earlier, and was now an invalid. Though bedridden after the stroke, Topsy had continued to write letters to Hayes once a week, every week, throughout his prison term. Her niece, Dolly Simmons, who lived across the road, and her daughter, Little Topsy, had looked after her in Chow's absence. Now, upon his return from prison, Dolly would walk across each day and help Chow wash Topsy; Dolly would also cook their meals and attend to most of the housework. When Topsy eventually died in 1969, Hayes went to live at Dolly's place. "Dolly would always drink two or three cans of beer with me each day until she died a number of years later," Hayes recalls.

"When Topsy died, Joe Taylor paid for a double plot at Rookwood Cemetery. So my grave was already paid for. But I gave it to my son when he died in 1987. I'm going to be cremated and then they can put the ashes on top of Topsy's grave."

• • •

While he had been in Maitland Jail, Hayes had met two well-known thugs: Jackie "Ratty Jack" Clarke, who was serving three years for breaking and entering and stayed at Maitland for five months; and Donny "The Man with the Iron Glove" Smith, who was serving four years for assault and robbery and was at Maitland for about three months.

Hayes recalls: "Before they'd gone to jail, Clarke had given

Chow Hayes on his release from jail in 1967.

Smith a bad kicking. The police knew who had done it, but they didn't have enough evidence to charge Clarke — and Smith would never have dobbed him in...

"After I was released in 1967, I was at Canterbury races one day and Jackie Clarke walked over and asked: 'How are you going, Chow?' I replied: 'Not very well, because I've only just been let out from jail.' Well, he already knew that, because my release had featured on all the television news bulletins. He told me to meet him at the Forest Lodge Hotel at 6 the following evening and he'd give me a few quid to help me find my feet (it was dollars by then, but I still used to refer to them as quid). Anyway, I never made it to the hotel that evening, basically because I had other things to do and it simply slipped my mind.

"But the following week I was down at the markets, in the Covent Garden Hotel, and I noticed this sheila staring at me. She was a big lump of a woman, about 30 years old, and she was accompanied by another woman, aged around 40. They seemed to be looking me up and down. Eventually the chap with whom I was drinking asked: 'Do you know the blonde-headed sheila over there?' I replied: 'No.' Then he commented that she was definitely looking me over and I said I'd noticed it too. I downed a few more drinks with a couple of blokes and then she stood up to leave. At that point I approached her and asked whether I knew her. She replied that she didn't think so, but she thought she'd seen me somewhere before. Well, it had been on the television, but at that moment she couldn't place me."

The woman was named Linda, and at that point she was Donny Smith's girlfriend. Linda operated several brothels in the Woolloomooloo district in opposition to the then king of Sydney prostitution, Joe Borg.

Hayes continues: "We began talking about various criminals we both knew, and soon she asked if I'd ever met Donny Smith. He'd been released from jail about 12 months earlier. I replied 'Yes,' and pretty soon she recalled that she'd seen me on television. Then she realised I must be Chow Hayes and insisted that she'd like to take me to see Donny. We arranged to meet later that afternoon in a hotel opposite the ABC studio in William Street, just down from Kings Cross.

"I duly arrived at 4 pm and she was already there with Donny Smith. He explained that he'd told Linda all about me. Smith took out $200 in cash to help me find my feet. But then Linda declared that wasn't enough and she gave me another $400. Smith had his hand in this black glove — and at the time I didn't understand why. I'd never heard anything about his infamous glove. I asked: 'What's wrong with your hand?' But he just mumbled something about it being a bit sore. However, of course, he had a piece of lead in it, bound up with padding — though I didn't find that out until several days later when I went back to the same pub and bit him for another $200.

"He gave the cash to me without any trouble. Then, over a few drinks, we began reminiscing about some of the blokes with whom we'd been in jail. After a while, I said I'd seen Jackie Clarke. And that's when Smith informed me: 'He gave me a kicking, you know?' Until that point I didn't know. However, Smith explained that was all forgotten now. So then I mentioned that I might bring Clarke out to a party Smith and Linda were arranging the following Saturday evening at Linda's house in Bronte. Smith said that was okay, as long as Clarke didn't start a blue.

"When Clarke and I arrived at the party there were already 40 people inside the house. Eric Williams was there and the four of us (Clarke, Smith, Williams and I) seemed to team up from that point. And Linda put us on the payroll, through Donny Smith, to look after her interests if she had any trouble with Joe Borg. But she never had any major confrontations with Borg — he seemed quite prepared to concentrate upon his own thriving business. At that point Linda had two brothels down at 'The Loo', but later she expanded to four. She was paying Jackie Clarke and me $400 each a week and we were never really called upon to help her, so it ended up being money for nothing."

Within a matter of weeks, Hayes classed Clarke, Smith and Williams as good friends. He was drinking and playing snooker with them daily, as well as "running around" standing over people for money at every opportunity. Hayes was back into the crime business fulltime.

During one particularly roisterous evening at the Bronte house, a man named Walter "Cyril" Hopegood was shot. Hayes explains: "We were drinking in the Tradesman's Arms Hotel (it was a pub I never frequented much) when Smith told Clarke and me that he had to go out to Linda's place at Bronte to meet a fellow at 7.30 pm. He wanted us to accompany him, because there might be some trouble. We walked in about 7.20 pm and, soon after, Wally Hopegood arrived. We were all sitting around on lounge chairs, and Smith and Hopegood began arguing. Hopegood didn't want Linda to employ a particular sheila as a prostitute; he wanted this girl to leave the whole vice scene. But Donny Smith said no, it was up to her — and if she wanted to work, she could. Clarke and I were sitting there listening and drinking beer when Smith suddenly walked into the bedroom and then returned with a little handgun, a .25.

"Smith threatened Hopegood: 'I'll blow your fucking head off, if you come down interfering again.' I immediately thought to myself: 'This is bloody nice! I'm out on licence from a life sentence. If Smith knocks Hopegood, he'd better make a good job of it.'

"Then Smith began stalking around the lounge room, shaking the gun in the air and threatening Hopegood, who remained seated in the armchair. After about 10 minutes Clarke became agitated and declared: 'Well, don't just talk about it. If you're going to shoot him, shoot the bastard!' And with that Smith shot Hopegood in the shoulder.

"Hopegood tumbled out of the chair and Smith ran over, knelt down beside him and put his ear to his chest. Then he declared Hopegood was still breathing. So I butted in: 'You may as well finish the bastard now! Otherwise he's going to identify the lot of us.' But Smith replied no, he didn't want to kill Hopegood. Then Clarke yelled: 'Come on, kill the bastard and we'll bury him in Waverley Cemetery!' However, Smith insisted: 'No! No! No! I'll take him away and have him attended to by a doctor.' Well, I was very dubious about that plan. I was afraid that if the coppers heard about the shooting, they would try to 'load' me with the whole thing and I'd end up back in jail. However, Smith said he knew exactly where to take Hopegood. They went to a private hospital in Waverley, and thereafter Smith and Linda spent weeks taking him daily bunches of flowers and chocolates. And they gave him $1000 to tell the police he'd been shot in the street by an unknown man."

• • •

Linda operated her main brothels in a row of terraces just up from the Tradesman's Arms Hotel in Darlinghurst. Around the corner and barely 50 metres down the hill, Joe Borg ran half a dozen of his major vice dens (these six sites alone featured 30 working girls).

Hayes recalls: "One night Smith and Clarke and I were sitting in the loungeroom at Linda's place. You could see from the way they talked that Linda and Smith were extremely jealous of Joe Borg, especially the fact that he had about 14 brothels in total. During the conversation Linda suddenly declared: 'Chow would be able to bite Borg for $1000!' Now I've given it plenty of thought since, and I don't know if she was trying to set me up that night or not. But anyway she suggested that Donny Smith should arrange a meeting so that I could go and attempt to bite Borg for $1000. Smith asked whether I wanted to give it a go, and

I replied: 'Of course I do. Borg's only a bludger!' So Smith arranged the meeting for a Saturday evening.

"The night before, on the Friday, I was in the Hampton Court Hotel with Jackie Clarke and we ran into Charles 'Chicka' Williams. It was the first time I'd seen SP bookie Charlie since I'd been released from jail. Williams asked how I was going and I said not too well. He explained that he wasn't travelling very well at that time either. But he gave me $300 on the spot, and said that as soon as he was cashed up again he'd give me more. There was no standover involved in it. You didn't have to stand over Charlie. And anyhow I wouldn't have — not that I was afraid of him, or anything like that, but he was a good fellow and a friend of mine.

"So Williams gave me $300. Then over a couple of drinks I asked whether he knew Joe Borg. Charlie replied that he knew Borg well, why did I want to know? So I detailed how I was going to try and bite him for $1000 the following evening. Williams then explained that he had to be honest and warn me that he didn't know if I'd succeed. And he added that I should also understand that, since I'd been away, things had changed considerably. He said Borg had a lot of people on his payroll. He emphasised that it wasn't so much his shitpot gunmen about whom I should worry, but Borg also had a large number of police on his payroll. And it was those police, Williams emphasised, who were the ones about whom I should worry. Williams explained that Borg had them all on his payroll — otherwise he wouldn't have been able to operate.

"So then I asked Williams for his opinion: would Borg pay me quietly or would I have to stand over him? Bourke advised me to go quietly at first and that I might be a rough chance, even if I only received a few hundred. But, he again warned me, if I decided to push the matter, then I ought not go in too heavy first off, because Borg had 'too many on his payroll' — meaning the police."

The following evening Hayes, accompanied by Donny Smith and Jackie Clarke, made his way to the Tradesman's Arms Hotel in Palmer Street at 8.30 pm. Smith pointed out the car, parked directly opposite, in which Joe Borg was sitting. Smith then remained in the hotel drinking with a couple of fellows whom Hayes didn't know.

"At that stage Borg hadn't even met Jackie Clarke," Hayes recalls. "We walked over to this dark-coloured Buick, and alongside Borg sat a sheila named Julie. I didn't know either of them at that point.

"Borg had the driver's window down (though the others were up) and this big mongrel dog was sitting in the back. When I came up to the side of the car it started barking and howling. I began: 'Donny Smith has told you who I am.' But Borg replied: 'No, he hasn't. Who are you?' So I told him Chow Hayes and so on. Then Borg asked: 'Well, what can I do for you?' I replied that I'd just been released from jail and I wanted $1000 from him until I was back on my feet. He replied, but I couldn't hear what he said, and I yelled: 'Stop that mongrel dog barking and howling or I'll bash its fucking head in!' It was a monstrous thing, almost as big as a small pony. So he quietened it down, but he never stepped out of the car. I was still standing in the street and Clarke was beside me — and, of course, Clarke had a gun with him.

"Borg then said: 'Look, I don't know you. I'll give you the thousand, but I don't want you to make a habit of it or you're likely to end up back where you've just come from.' I immediately replied: 'What's that, a fucking threat?' He answered: 'No. No. But I have a lot of overheads and expenses.' And I know that was true, with all the coppers and everything, because he had an 'open go' as far as prostitution was concerned.

"So he handed me the $1000 — he simply peeled the cash from a huge bankroll there and then — and Clarke and I walked back over the road and into the hotel. We didn't return to where Smith was drinking with the other blokes, but I nodded over to him to indicate that I'd received the money okay. Then I handed Clarke $400, and later I gave Smith $200 and I kept $400 myself.

"But about 20 minutes later, Julie walked in and announced Joe wanted to see Clarke and me again. I asked where, and she said he was still sitting in the car. We walked back across the street, and he explained: 'Look, I've been thinking it over and I don't want you coming back asking for thousands. I'll put you both on my payroll at $100 a week. Will that suit you?' I replied that was alright. However, we didn't tell Donny Smith or Linda about this arrangement with Borg, because we were on their payroll as well and they were dirty on each other's operation. But, of course, it only lasted three weeks because then Borg was blown up one morning when he started his car at Bondi."

Joe Borg, 35, the "King of Palmer Street", was listed in police records as a "gunman, thief, shopbreaker and pimp". Maltese migrants of the era had been attracted to the low rents in East Sydney's narrow lanes around the Palmer Street brothel area, which was known as the Doors for the way prostitutes solicited from doorways that fronted on to the footpaths. In the 1960s Borg, who had migrated from Malta in 1952, began buying terraces and converting them into brothels. By renting rooms to prostitutes at $20 per eight-hour shift, Borg had an income which police estimated at between $8000 and $10,000 a week. His operation therefore turned over millions of dollars annually.

Borg always slept with a loaded pistol under his pillow, but he never saw his killers. At 11 o'clock one May morning in 1968 Borg strolled from his house in Brighton Boulevard, North Bondi, jumped into his white Holden utility van and turned the ignition. A bomb under the driver's seat, containing two kilograms of gelignite, exploded — destroying the lower half of his body.

Police said Borg was killed because he refused to share his vice empire, branding the bombing part of a "reign of terror for control of Sydney prostitution". (Two months later they charged two Maltese men, Paul Mifsud, 29, and Paul Attard, 24, with Borg's murder. In addition Keith Keillor, 50, was charged with having incited the two men to murder Borg. Mifsud and Attard were eventually sentenced to life imprisonment, and Keillor to seven years in jail.)

"I was living at Campsie at the time," Hayes remembers. "My wife was still alive, but she was an invalid. I heard the news about Borg's murder over the radio and, soon after, the coppers arrived at my door. They wanted me to accompany them to Darlinghurst to answer some questions, but wouldn't reveal what it was about. I insisted I couldn't leave because my wife was an invalid. But, in the meantime, Dolly Simmons had seen the two police cars arrive and she walked across the street to our unit and agreed to look after Topsy.

"So they drove me in to Darlinghurst police station. And as I walked along an upstairs corridor, I spotted Jackie Clarke in one room and then Julie in the next room. The coppers took me into a separate room and explained that I'd been called in about Joe Borg's murder. They wanted to know where I was when he was murdered because, they said, I'd recently threatened to bash his brains in. Well, I immediately jumped up and insisted that was wrong, that I'd threatened to bash his dog's head in. There was no doubt in my mind either Clarke or Julie had told them that.

"Then they asked why I went and stood over Borg for $1000. I replied that I didn't stand over him — rather, I'd bitten him for a loan of $1000. Of course, they wanted to know what reason I had to bite him for a loan of $1000. And I replied that the explanation was simple: I was just out of jail and had no money. But the police insisted it was a standover payment, adding that I later went back and tried to squeeze even more out of Borg. Then, they said, when I couldn't have any more, I'd blown up his car. Of course, they only suggested that to see what I answered. So I replied it wasn't like that at all. Then I added that I'd seen Julie down the corridor and if they didn't believe me they should go and ask her. They replied that they already had her statement. Then they left the room, but two uniformed cops remained to keep an eye on me.

"Finally, after about three hours, the head copper came back on his own and admitted they knew I hadn't blown up Borg, but they also knew Clarke and I had gone there and stood over Borg for the $1000. Again I insisted I hadn't stood over him for the money and that, in fact, Clarke hadn't even said a word to Borg. I emphasised that I'd only bitten Borg for a loan of the $1000. But the copper said I'd returned to the car afterwards. So I explained Julie would confirm that that was only after Joe had sent her into the hotel to fetch us and put us on the payroll, at $100 a week each, to stay away from him. And, I explained, I was certainly not going to knock that back.

"The copper said they didn't know anything about that. But he said he'd been making a lot of inquiries about me and, if he'd wished, he could have charged me there and then with having been in the company of molls and criminals, which would automatically have revoked my licence. I replied that if he was going to do that, he might as well let me walk down the stairs and blow my fucking head off — because, I said, I could never serve another life sentence. Then he answered: 'No, look, you're just out of jail and it's the only thing that's saving you. I don't know you, and I don't want to know you. But if I see you running around with criminals again — or up here anywhere near the Cross — I'll put you back in jail.' Then he told me to leave immediately, and don't come back. So, to tell the truth, I went and gulped down two or three stiff brandies at the Court House Hotel.

"I saw Clarke that night over at Linda's place at Bronte. The police had also taken Smith and Linda in for questioning during the day. I asked them whether they'd said anything about the threats to Borg, and they all said no. But it could only have come from Clarke or Julie."

Despite his suspicions, Hayes did not pursue the matter. And in any case, each of the unsavoury gents met his maker early. Donny Smith was shot dead in the notorious Venus Room at Kings Cross in 1970 by "Big Jim" Anderson, who succeeded in maintaining the shooting was justified in self-defence. Jackie Clarke had a falling-out with his one-time mate Johnny "Mad Dog" Regan in 1974. A few days later, at 10.25 on a Friday eveing, Clarke was sitting in a Petersham hotel, barely 150 metres from his home, when Regan shot him dead through the window. And Eric Williams, after a three-year prison sentence during which he bumped into Hayes again at Parramatta Jail, was shot dead at his front door in Waverley by an unknown gunman.

24 "Gouged a Man's Eye Out with a Beer Glass"

In mid-1969 Jackie "Ratty" Clarke suggested to Hayes that they visit a small social club in Camperdown, known as the Prince Alfred Club. It was directly opposite Sydney's historic Royal Prince Alfred Hospital, with the club entrance about 50 metres along Brown Street from the corner of busy Missenden Road.

Hayes recalls: "Initially, the club was mainly for doctors and nurses. But eventually the crims took it over. We started drinking there and it became our meeting place — especially for Clarke and me. A lot of police from Newtown drank there too, including many female police. We used to go there nearly every day and stay four or five hours. Half a dozen of us would contribute $20 each into a bowl on the table, for drinks and taking turns at pushing $10 at a time into the poker machines. Anything you won went back into the bowl."

This daily routine continued for about five months — until one Sunday afternoon in December 1969. "I was over at the bar talking to a chap," Hayes recalls, "and I happened to look across and thought I spotted Gerald Hutchinson, a petty criminal, take some money out of the tray and put it in his pocket. I didn't take much notice at the time. About half an hour later I returned to our table and the bowl was three-quarters full of coins. It was Hutchinson's turn to go to the machines. But as he moved to put his hand in and grab a fistful of silver (they were 20-cent pieces) I said: 'You don't need them, Gerry, because you already have some in your pocket.' He immediately replied that he didn't, but I insisted he did because I'd seen him take them out of the tray. With that, Clarke slapped the outside of Hutchinson's pocket — and it was bulging with coins. Clarke called him every name under the sun, but I didn't give it much thought, because I couldn't have cared less about $10 or $12 in coins.

"Just then two women aged about 35 walked into the club and

soon after they joined us at our table. Hutchinson asked if we wanted to come around to his place — about 10 minutes away in Hordern Street, Newtown — for a drink and a good time with these sheilas. We immediately said yes and four of us jumped into a car with the two women.

At Hutchinson's place, we had a couple of drinks and then I asked one of the sheilas: 'Do you want to be in it?' But she replied: 'No, I'm a respectable woman!' Then someone yelled: 'Oh, take your gear off.' But they wouldn't be in it. So we took them back to the club and they sat down at our table.

"After a while Hutchinson said to me: 'You made a nice cunt out of me. That wasn't the money that was in the bowl, that was my own money.' I told him to forget about it, because I'd already put it out of my mind. But he repeated that I'd made a cunt out of him. So then I replied: 'Well, if you want it that way, you are a cunt, because I saw you put the coins into your pocket!' Immediately Hutchinson retorted: 'Righto, we'll go outside and fix it up.' And I said 'Okay.' But one of the owners intervened and told us both to sit down and forget it — and I noticed that Hutchinson was only too happy to sit down again, even though he'd offered to go outside.

"Soon after, I walked out to the toilet. But on the way I snatched a glass from the bar. In the toilet I smashed the rim of the glass and wrapped it in my handkerchief. At that stage I'd decided to give it to Hutchinson; I'd made up my mind that I'd fix this bastard. I walked back to the table with the glass in my pocket and, instead of sitting opposite Hutchinson — where I had been — I sat down beside him. I said: 'When are we going to go outside?' But one of the other blokes chipped in again: 'No. Forget all about that.' But I replied: 'Forget nothing!'

"With that I hit Hutchinson on the head with the glass. Then I quickly jabbed him three or four times in the face. He started to put his hand up, but he didn't sing out and hardly anyone saw it. One of our mates picked Hutchinson up off the chair and said to me: 'Beat it, while I take him over to the hospital.' Prince Alfred Hospital was only across the road. But I said I wasn't going anywhere. Then one of the club officials came over and asked what had happened. I said I thought Hutchinson had fallen on a glass on the table.

"I stayed there with a couple of blokes, but Clarke and the two women left. Soon after, a plain-clothes copper from Regent Street police station arrived. At that stage, they didn't know that I'd done it, because if anyone had told the coppers I did it, they'd have come and pinched me straightaway. But they didn't — only this young fellow from Regent Street arrived. He walked in and talked to a couple of the club officials and a few other hangers-on at the bar. I sat watchig the young copper very closely and he never looked in my direction.

"About 10 minutes later, he finally came over to our table. He asked: 'Where was the man sitting?' One of the club officials told him, and then he spotted the blood, because Hutchinson had been bleeding like a pig when he was taken out. The young copper followed the blood outside and right over to the hospital's main entrance. (Our mate hadn't taken Hutchinson into the casualty ward, he'd taken him into the main office, and then they'd taken him to casualty from there.)

"About 10 minutes after the young copper left, the heavies arrived from Newtown. I knew the copper in charge well, because I'd seen him in the Prince Alfred Club many times. It was now about 7.30 pm. The police walked around asking patrons whether they'd seen anything. But everyone told them they'd seen nothing. Finally they came over to me and asked where I'd been sitting. I said 'Alongside him'. So they asked what happened. I said that I went to the toilet and when I came back he was bleeding. Then the head copper asked: 'Wasn't he assaulted while you were in his company?' To which I replied: 'No, he'd already been assaulted when I returned to the table.' Then they asked one of the blokes who'd been drinking in our group what he had to say about it all, and he replied: 'The same as Chow.' He said he was there, but he didn't see it. Then the copper asked what did he mean that he didn't see it, and he told them: 'I know the fellow who did it, but I'm not going to tell you.' Then the police threatened to take him down to the CIB. But after half an hour they had to let him go, because they had nothing on him and he didn't have enough bookings to be charged with consorting.

"I went to Dolly's place at Campsie. I didn't have any blood on me. My wife had died about four months before and, though I was still living across the road, I went to Dolly's place. When I arrived she asked whether I'd been in any trouble. I replied: 'No. Why?' Dolly explained that the police had been trying to enter my unit. When I asked how she knew that, she said she and half the other residents of Park Street had seen them. Apparently they'd then gone to the real estate agent for the keys, and the agent let them in. Then they'd searched my unit, but didn't take anything."

The next day the *Daily Mirror* reported: "Doctors at RPA Hospital performed emergency surgery on a man who staggered into the casualty section early today with severe cuts to his face and arm. Doctors said the injured man, Gerald John Hutchinson, 37, of Hordern Street, Newtown, was semi-conscious. He had lost a considerable amount of blood. He had a deep wound over one eye and his mouth and face were deeply cut."

The *Sun* noted: "Police are trying to find out how a man, now in a critical condition in RPA Hospital, came by his injuries..."

Hayes continues: "The next day only a few details were reported in the newspapers about a man being assaulted in the Prince Alfred Club. So I rang Jackie Clarke — at that stage I didn't know the extent of Hutchinson's injuries. Hutchinson had actually required 50 stitches in his head, he'd lost his left eye and he'd also needed a lot of stitches in his arms and hands where he'd tried to protect himself.

"So Clarke told me that Hutchinson was in a bad way. Initially the doctors described him as critical and said he looked like dying. But, said Clarke, he'd made a statement and said he didn't know who had done it. I asked Clarke whether he was sure on that last point, and Clarke replied yes, because he'd been over to see Hutchinson. Clarke also told me two of the club officials had been over to visit Hutchinson. Then I telephoned the Prince Alfred Club and spoke to one of them. He confirmed that Hutchinson had made a statement, but hadn't identified anyone.

"So then I returned to my own flat — across the other side of Park Street. But within a matter of hours, Clarke rang and warned me that a policeman from the CIB had taken over the case and persuaded Hutchinson to identify me. Clarke said Hutchinson had now made a new statement, which implicated me. Clarke warned that the police were on their way to pinch me. I left the flat, naturally, and went to Dolly's sister Margaret's place at Villawood for about a week. Everyone in Sydney was telling me that the police were looking for me and that Hutchinson had given me up. So I sent a few messages to him, threatening that if I went to jail over it I'd arrange for someone else to do a fair dinkum job on him. But Hutchinson was like the proverbial meat in the sandwich: he didn't know whether to go along with me or the police. But the police told him that they'd put me away for another life sentence and all this shit, and that I'd have no chance of doing anything more to him.

"Anyway, Clarke arranged a lawyer for me. The lawyer said he'd ring Newtown police station and inform them that I was coming in there with him, and that would stop any verbal. So he rang Newtown — but he was told they didn't want to see me because it was now out of their hands and it was a CIB matter. So he rang the CIB, but the copper in charge of the case wasn't there. Finally he made arrangements for me to go to Newtown police station the next day — which was 16 or 17 days after the incident. The police agreed to my one condition for surrender — that I'd be granted bail. Otherwise, I said, they could find me. But they agreed I'd be given bail. I knew it would be heavy — but I also knew that I could borrow it from Joe Taylor."

Hayes, accompanied by his lawyer, duly walked into Newtown police station to surrender at 4 o'clock on Tuesday afternoon, 2 January 1970. He recalls: "There were half a dozen coppers waiting for me. The bloke in charge said he had a statement from Hutchinson which identified me. I replied that Hutchinson couldn't have identified me because he'd made a statement saying it wasn't me. But the copper said Hutchinson had been half out of his mind at that point, with all the pain, and was only semi-conscious. He explained they were now going to take me to Prince Alfred Hospital. We drove there and, sure enough, Hutchinson pointed me out. In fact he screamed at the top of his voice: 'That's the man!'"

A fortnight later Hayes faced Newtown Court of Petty Sessions, charged with maliciously wounding Hutchinson with intent to do grievous bodily harm.

The *Sun* reported that Hutchinson said he'd gone to the Prince Alfred Club on a Sunday morning, where he joined a number of people, including Hayes, at a table. Later in the day two women had joined the group. Hutchinson claimed Hayes asked the women: "Would you like to go for a drink?" They agreed, and four men and the two women had then decided to go to Hutchinson's home nearby. Hutchinson then told how, in the lounge room, "two or three minutes" after they arrived at the premises, Hayes took all his clothes off bar his socks, and then said to the women "Get your gear off!" Hutchinson said one woman began to complain and said: "I don't want anything to do with this." Hutchinson said he then told the group, "Everybody out!" and they left the building.

Hutchinson told the court he returned to the club later in the afternoon and saw Hayes and several other men sitting drinking: "I went to a table where Hayes was sitting. I took my beer with me and just sat down. I said: 'How are you going?' Chow said: 'You have been making a —— of me all day.' Then he put a glass in my eye. I don't know whether it was in his shirt sleeve or a bit of paper, but it was covered. I felt my eye bust as if it was cut out."

The court heard Hutchinson had, in fact, been repeatedly jabbed in the face with a broken beer glass, resulting in the loss of both his left eye and several teeth, plus a large scar on his lip.

The *Sydney Morning Herald* also noted that police prosecutor Sergeant N. Webber, told the court several witnesses to the attack had been threatened that they would be blinded and "their eyes used to play marbles" if they appeared in court. Webber said police alleged the men who made the threats to the witnesses had been "acting on Hayes's behalf".

Hayes continues: "So I was committed for trial. In the meantime, while I was out at Long Bay, a prisoner bashed another inmate and put 30 or 40 stitches in his head. I said that I was talking to the screw — I wasn't, but I said I was — at the time. They charged the bloke, and I appeared as a witness for him. I said I was in the Wing at the time (10 Wing) and I was talking to the screw, who was in his office so that he couldn't see anything. But the screw denied I was in the Wing, and said he'd seen everything.

"The bloke who was on trial was a barber. When he went before Judge Curlewis, it was the first time I'd ever come in contact with that judge. But as soon as I stepped into the witness box to give evidence for the prisoner, instead of the crown prosecutor examining me, Curlewis took over, from the bench. He referred to my criminal record and said I was a man of violence and that I'd mixed with violence all my life. He emphasised that he was putting it to me that, if I'd seen the prisoner do it, I'd say I didn't see him do it. I replied that I was only speaking the truth and that he didn't do it. Anyway, to cut a long story short, the prisoner was acquitted — it was a miracle and I don't know how it happened.

"Anyway, Curlewis had announced his retirement, but I suspected that he wanted to take my case. Of course, I didn't want him to sit on my case because he'd already told me in the witness box what he thought of me. So the night before my case was set to come on, I put some nose drops in my eyes — you weren't supposed to put them near your eyes — so that I'd receive another remand and miss Curlewis. I 'knocked up' about 9 that night ('knock up' means to bang on your cell to seek assistance) and the screws rushed in. I couldn't open my eyes. I told them that I'd leaned back to put the drops in my nose, but I was thinking of something else and I'd mistakenly put them in my eyes. They said I was mad because I could have blinded myself.

"So they sent a letter to the court the next morning, explaining that I couldn't appear because I was hospitalised. They asked for a month's adjournment. But I was only given a week — if I'd received a month Curlewis would have retired.

"Anyhow, I duly copped Curlewis the next week and I pleaded not guilty. I appeared for myself. I'd heard a lot of whispers about the barristers around the police courts during that era — how they'd win one case in 10 and then let the coppers win nine. So I thought I'd have a better chance on my own."

The assault upon Hutchinson had occurred in December 1969. Eventually, 10 months later, Hayes's trial began at Sydney Quarter Sessions court in October 1970. The *Daily Mirror* noted that Hutchinson told the jury how, after the first jab with the glass, Hayes tried to strike him in the other eye, but he had put his arm across his face. The broken glass then cut his arm to the bone: "Hayes then jabbed me a third time... catching me in the mouth, knocking five teeth out." But, the newspaper noted, Hayes told the jury he had nothing to do with Hutchinson's injuries. He said Hutchinson had left the table, returning soon after with his face covered in blood. Hayes said he believed Hutchinson had fallen on a broken bottle.

"The case went on for two weeks," says Hayes, "and I kept asking Hutchinson about the original statement he'd made to police. He replied that he was under sedation at that time, and didn't know what he was saying. I explained to the jury how the police had come into the club and never asked me any questions. I explained how I'd remained sitting at the same table for the rest of the afternoon and that night. And I emphasised how I didn't leave the club and how I'd freely entered the witness box — it was the first time I'd been in the box on my own behalf in my life. I started off by telling the jury that I wasn't a man of good character — to stop the Crown from cross-examining me on my criminal record. I said I was set up and that I hadn't assaulted Hutchinson. I told the jury I was out on licence on a murder charge and that, no matter what the jury decided, my licence had already been revoked — which it had — because I'd been in the company of criminals such as Clarke.

"Now the charge was 'malicious wounding with intent to do grievous bodily harm' which could mean a penalty up to a life sentence. But the alternate charge was 'malicious wounding', which carries a maximum five years with hard labour. The jury went out and deliberated for about three hours. When they came back they found me not guilty on the first charge, but guilty on the lesser charge of malicious wounding.

"Well, Curlewis nearly fell off his seat. He brought the victim Hutchinson in and paraded him up and down in front of the jury, as though he was a model, and declared that he didn't know how they'd arrived at guilty on the second charge rather than the first. He said he wanted the jury members to look at this victim, and he showed them his head and arms and so on — Hutchinson had a patch where his eye was missing. Then Curlewis asked whether I knew the maximum for the charge? I said five years. And he replied: 'Yes, well that's what you've got — and I only wish that I could give you more.' But all he could do was give me the maximum five years, though he also directed that '$2000 compensation be paid to the complainant out of the property of the accused.' "

The *Daily Mirror* reported: "Addressing Hayes in the dock, Judge Curlewis told him that he couldn't imagine a more vicious, brutal crime. He said: 'In my opinion you are not fit to be released to move about among decent members of our community. I am giving you the maximum penalty for malicious wounding and it is such a serious one that I decline to set a non-parole period.' "

Hayes returned to Long Bay for a fortnight, before being sent to Parramatta, where he quickly took over that jail's large SP bookmaking operation.

25 Winning the Lottery — and the Weekend Detention Caper

As a result of the Hutchinson assault, Hayes received an additional five years on his resurrected life sentence.

At Parramatta Jail he resumed his previous prison status as the leading SP bookmaker "inside", and quickly established a lucrative operation which averaged a profit of around $200 a week. Of that, he would pass on $40 each fortnight to Dolly Simmons, who never missed a visit.

Hayes recalls: "When she came to see me, she'd ask what I wanted for my birthday and Christmas and those type of occasions. And I'd always reply that there wasn't anything I needed, especially with the SP money I was averaging. So I'd instruct her to buy a lottery ticket for me. At one point in 1973, I gave her $20 and told her to buy two Opera House lottery tickets — and a fortnight later we won second prize of $40,000! So I gave Dolly $20,000, my son and daughter $4000 each, and half a dozen others smaller amounts."

Briefly, Chow Hayes was back in the headlines. The *Daily Mirror* reported on 23 September: "Jailed killer John Frederick 'Chow' Hayes learned this week he had won a $20,000 slice of a big lottery win. . . half of the $40,000 second prize in an Opera House lottery. . . 'His sister [*sic*] held the ticket and will hold Hayes' share in trust until he is released,' a Justice Department spokesman said. . . Hayes, now 63, was once one of Sydney's toughest criminals."

Six months later, as part of an interview with Hayes from his jail cell, the *Daily Mirror* reported on 9 June 1974: ". . . during a visit last year Chow and his sister [*sic*] decided to buy an Opera House lottery ticket. 'My sister said she'd get the ticket and send me the number,' said Hayes. 'I forgot all about it and one afternoon I was sitting on my bed looking through an afternoon newspaper — and I saw our names as the winners of the second prize, $40,000. I fell off the bed. They thought I'd taken a turn...I have given most of it away. My sister has bought a home unit...and with what remained I put a bit away and gave the rest to my son and daughter'."

After another interview in February 1977, the *Daily Mirror* trumpeted: "Chow Hayes, convicted murderer and gangland criminal, revealed today how he gave away nearly all the $20,000 he won in an Opera House lottery...'Most people probably think I've held on to the money until today,' he said. 'But money means nothing to me. If I had been free when I won it, I would have blown it all on a horse the next day...I finished with $100 to call my own.'"

• • •

Inmates were never supposed to stop the Prisons Department boss (the Comptroller-General of Prisons had now become the Commissioner for Corrective Services) during one of his inspection visits to a prison. Instead, they were required to file in advance a formal application, to go "on request", if they wanted to speak to him personally.

"Now Wally McGeechan was the Commissioner for Corrective Services," Hayes recalls. "One day he was walking past 3 Yard, and I was there with two other blokes. I'd heard a rumour that they were about to open something called a 'weekend detention centre'. It was the first of its kind, to be established in the old governor's house right opposite the jail.

"Anyway Harris Bush, the superintendent of Parramatta Jail, and Coleman, the chief warder, and another chap were walking with McGeechan. They had to pass through 3 Yard to head across to Bush's office. So at that moment I butted in: 'Excuse me, Mr McGeechan, but I want to have a word with you.' He immediately stopped to listen. But then Bush jumped in and warned: 'You know you shouldn't stop the Commissioner for Corrective Services. If you want a word with him you have to go on request.' However, McGeechan replied: 'Oh no, it doesn't matter. He's already pulled me up now. What is it, Chow?' So then I asked: 'This new weekend detention centre which you're opening outside the jail. What about giving me a go?'

"At that, the others all laughed. And McGeechan declared: 'Oh gee, I couldn't give you a job outside!' But I persisted: 'Why not? I had an outside job while I was at the camp at Kirkconnel.' Then McGeechan inquired: 'How much of your sentence have you served?' I replied: 'About two and a half years.' He thought for a moment, but then responded: 'Oh no, the newspapers will play up about it. And anyhow, who told you about this weekend detention?' I answered cautiously: 'Oh, I hear things.' Then he said: 'Well, you know more than I do. I know nothing about it.' But I retorted: 'Oh, don't tell me that. Of course you do. You're the main man behind it.' Finally he said: 'No, no, I couldn't take the odds to putting you outside.'

"So then McGeechan moved on. Soon after, Coleman, the chief warder, came back and declared that Superintendent Bush wanted to see me. I walked into Bush's office and he gave me a real dressing-down about pulling up the Commissioner for Corrective Services. But I said that if he'd put me down for a 'request' I'd be the last one on, while he (Bush) was in charge of the place. Then he threatened that I could be charged over it, and told me to get out of his office and out of his sight.

"However, about 10 days later McGeechan came to Parramatta again. And he called me into the office. He asked me bluntly: 'Would you give me your word that you wouldn't 'go through' if I put you out there?' I immediately said: 'Yes.' So he explained: 'I'm going to take a punt on you. We're trying to change jails around a bit and let other prisoners know that, if they behave themselves, then they might also be moved to a camp early. But if you shoot through, then you'll set them all back years.'"

The weekened detention centre opened the following Monday. At about 7.30 each morning, Hayes would walk over the road from the main jail to the detention centre, look after it during the day, and go back to the jail about 5 pm. "To tell the truth," says Hayes, "it was a home away from home. It had eight rooms (there were 16 men, two in each room) and I was in charge of everything. There were two screws with me, but they spent most of their time either travelling down to the shops to buy things for the prisoners who were coming in, or over at the jail drinking tea. So I virtually had the run of the place.

"The screws had a locker, a sort of silver thing as big as a wardrobe, and they used to unplug the phone and hide it in there and lock it up whenever they weren't at the centre. But one day I walked into the front room, which they had converted into an office for themselves, and the keys were lying on the table. I ran back to the kitchen and grabbed a piece of soap. Then I took an impression of the locker key, wiped it clean and put it back in its place.

"I had it for about a fortnight. There was a male nurse with whom I was friendly, and I offered to pay him $50 to have a key made from the impression. He asked where it came from, so I told him. He had the same sort of locker in the surgery, so he said he'd have one made. He did that and tried the new key in his locker and it worked perfectly. But when I took it over the road for weekend detention, it fitted into the lock okay but it wouldn't turn. So then he gave me his own key to test and see if it worked. It did, so then he said he'd have another copy made from it, which he did. Hence, from that point we had access to the telephone. Of course, I immediately began ringing everyone in Sydney, telling many of them I was out of jail — and quite a few believed I really was out because, as far as they knew, there was no such thing as this weekend detention centre. I also rang a couple of enemies and threatened that I was coming over to their homes and all that shit to frighten them. I even rang one mate, told him I was free and arranged to meet at 7 pm on such and such a night — but then I rang back later and explained it was a joke, because I didn't want him going there to meet me when I wouldn't turn up...

"On Friday evenings, the men coming to the house for their period of weekend detention would arrive at 4 pm. They'd sweep the hospital grounds and church yards and other similar tasks over the weekend. Sometimes they'd all simply remain at the centre, and not go anywhere. They were allowed to bring their own food. And they'd leave stuff for me in an enormous fridge — in fact, I had so much food there that I used to give it to the other poor bastards working on the road gangs which cleaned up outside the jail.

"When Dolly Simmons came to visit me, I'd arrange for her to arrive at 2 pm and I'd have the visit outside the jail in the house. Then she wouldn't have to enter the jail at all. We'd spend a couple of hours at the detention house. She'd always ask what I wanted her to bring and I replied I wanted nothing because now I had everything.

"But one day I said there was something. I asked her to walk around the corner and buy me half a dozen beers at the local hotel. So she did that and I duly drank them. Then I began to arrange for one fellow, who used to come each weekend for his detention, to drop in at Dolly's place on his way and collect a dozen cans for me each Friday afternoon. He used to hide them under his bed when he was leaving again on Sunday afternoon, and I'd pick them up on the Monday.

"However, one Monday morning I went over to the house, after the weekend detention, and walked straight up to this bloke's room. But there was no beer under his bed. I couldn't understand it, because I'd seen Dolly on the Saturday and she'd told me she'd given the bloke the dozen cans as usual. So I couldn't work out what had happened to the beers, because they definitely weren't under the bed.

"Anyway, there was an announcement that the Minister for Justice, John Maddison, was coming on inspection with McGeechan and two or three other members of parliament. And, of course, whenever either the minister or McGeechan was due, the administrators would all be running around like blue-arse flies at the jail — the screws would insist that everything was cleaned and dusted and so on. So Coleman, the chief warder, came over to the weekend detention house and checked: 'How's everything over here, Chow?' And I replied: 'Alright. What's wrong?' Coleman said that Maddison was visiting that afternoon.

"Now for some reason I didn't go to the refrigerator that morning — yet previously I'd always gone straight to it to see what the weekend detention blokes had left for me. But this day I hadn't looked. Instead I sat down and played the card game patience, at the kitchen table.

"So after they'd inspected the jail, Maddison and McGeechan and the parliamentarians came over with Bush and Coleman to inspect the detention house. Maddison quipped to me: 'Gee, I'm surprised to see you out here, Chow! How do you like it?' I replied it was okay. Then he asked if the detainees left me anything when they returned home? I replied yes, they often left little bits and pieces in the refrigerator. And with that I pulled the door open to show him — and there, sitting at the front, were the dozen cans of beer!

"Well, McGeechan dropped his eyes as though he didn't want to see it, but Maddison exclaimed: 'Yes, I see! How long's this been going on?' He declared that I had more drink there than he had at home. But I jumped in and replied: 'They all belong to one of the blokes who is here on weekends. He leaves them in there. I never touch the stuff.' Then Maddison commented that he thought they were only allowed two cans each weekend. But one of the warders covered up quickly and, going for broke, retorted: 'Oh yes, but they bring in a dozen cans and then have two each week.' Then Maddison smiled: 'I know you wouldn't have a drink of that beer, Chow.' And of course I immediately replied: 'Oh no, no way would I ever have one!' So then they all laughed and left the house.

"But that was only the start of the matter. After Maddison and his group had left the jail, Bush and Coleman and so on instantly marched straight back over to the detention house. They wanted to know where the beer was, because by this time I'd taken it out of the refrigerator and hidden it back up in his bedroom. So I told them it was in the bedroom. Then they wanted to know why I'd left it in the refrigerator? I told them the truth: that I simply didn't know it was there."

Meanwhile, the word spread inside and outside the prison system that Chow Hayes was running the weekend detention centre, that he was now viewed as a model prisoner, and that he was likely to be released shortly. On 2 June 1974, the *Daily Mirror* reported: "Sydney's most notorious criminal, John Frederick 'Chow' Hayes is about to be released from jail...man who received the death sentence for murder 22 years ago...Asked if he has any regrets, Hayes said: 'Of course I have — plenty! A man is a mug to finish up in a place like this. I've spent 45 of my 67 years behind bars and I'll tell you this — if I could wind back the clock, I'd be a squarehead in a second.'"

However, back inside Parramatta Jail the big lottery win momentarily interrupted Hayes' new lifestyle. Hayes recalls: "When I won that $40,000 second prize in the lottery, Superintendent Bush called me into his office and announced that he couldn't let me go over to the weekend detention house that day. Too many 'solid' men had been in to see him and informed him that he'd be taking a risk by leaving me outside with $40,000 in my pocket. And he told me there'd been half a dozen of my supposed mates who'd warned him about that — including two whom I'd class as close mates. But later Bush spoke to McGeechan and they decided to let me return across to the house the next day, because if I was going to shoot through I'd have done it before, and the $40,000 was not going to make any difference."

Hayes had been based in the weekend detention house for seven or eight months when a reporter from the *Daily Mirror* came to Parramatta Jail to see Superintendent Bush. Hayes explains: "He wanted to write a story about Chow Hayes and his work outside the jail and so on. Bush said they could walk over and ask me whether I wanted to cooperate with them. I immediately said: 'No. No way. I don't want my name in the newspapers again.' But the reporter talked me into it by arguing that everyone in Sydney knew I was working outside, so why didn't I give him a break. Finally I felt a bit sorry for him, so I told him the full story about my new role outside the jail walls.

"Of course that made the front page of the *Mirror*. It was all stuff about 'How's a notorious criminal allowed outside the jail?' and that type of rubbish. Two days later I was called in to see Bush. The newspaper story had put the kybosh on the whole thing: I had to return inside Parramatta Jail. But Bush told me not to worry because I wouldn't lose much by it. And he asked me how I would like to go back to Kirkconnel. But I replied 'No way in the world,' because it was too far away. Besides, I was doing very well at Parramatta with the SP bookmaking.

"There was a lot of money involved in SP betting inside the jails. And the prison authorities didn't really try to stop the practice because, as long as everyone was happy and people weren't trying to climb over the walls, then they were content to more or less allow the jail to run itself. I only used to bet on the Wednesday and Saturday meetings. I'd hold about $300 on a Wednesday and anything up to $1000 on a Saturday. And I averaged about $200 a week profit over the 3½ years I ran my book. I was regularly passing on the profits to Dolly Simmons when she came to visit. I maintained a 'bank' of about $3000 at the jail, because you had to have enough cash to pay out. A screw kept it safe for me. I paid him $5 a week and he used to take it home. I think he had it in the bank all the while and was drawing interest on it too. However, I also had several other hiding places for some of my cash inside the jail — I didn't keep it all in the one place...

"So I told Superintendent Bush that I didn't want to return to Kirkconnel, ostensibly because it was too far away. Then he asked: 'What about Emu Plains?' But I replied: 'No, stick that too, because it's only for young fellows!'

"However, the following Saturday Dolly Simmons came to visit and she asked: 'Why have you lost your job at the weekend detention centre?' I simply explained about the bastard from the *Mirror*. Then she became worried that I was doing it a lot tougher again. But I assured her I was okay. As a matter of fact, I explained, I could have gone back to Kirkconnel but I'd knocked the opportunity back. Then I told her about the minimum security institution at Emu Plains, and she asked why I didn't go there. I explained there was no SP bookmaking at Emu Plains.

However, Dolly argued that I should forget about the book-making and give it a go. Initially I refused. But, after another six weeks, jail really started to play upon my nerves again. So I thought about it, and decided that Emu Plains wasn't really very far away. Then I spoke to Bush and asked for the chance to give Emu Plains a trial."

Hayes was duly sent to Emu Plains in late 1975.

26 Fifty-six Pints of Blood

Hayes was at Emu Plains for about 18 months. "But I'd heard a lot about the Malabar Training Centre, where they were planning to introduce a 'day leave' scheme," Hayes adds. "So that seemed extremely attractive. The only drawback was that you had to work there. Of course, I was supposed to be working in the garden at Emu Plains, but I wasn't really doing anything other than lying around the yard most of the time.

"Hence, when 'day leave' was first introduced, I asked for a transfer to Malabar. Day leave was available once a month. On day leave, the person you nominated was supposed to come out to the jail and pick you up at 8 am, and then bring you back at 5 pm. But you weren't allowed to have a drink or go to the races or anything like that. And you weren't allowed to go into hotels or associate with criminals and so on.

"So I moved to Malabar and nominated Dolly Simmons. I used to go to her unit in Lidcombe. I'd talk to her and drink all day, and other people would drop in there to visit me. And I used to walk around a bit. I knew half a dozen crims at the nearby Railway Hotel — including two ex-murderers with whom I used to drink. I would go and see those blokes, but I wouldn't walk inside the hotel itself. I'd go into the milk bar and borrow two milkshake cartons. Then my mates would take them into the hotel and pour a schooner into each. Then we'd sit outside in the sun and I'd pretend that I was drinking milkshakes."

At Malabar, Hayes shrewdly arranged a "job" for himself: making tea and coffee in one of the administration offices. "That saved me from having to work hard, unlike most of the others who went to Malabar," Hayes explains. "Later the parole board came out there a few times, and I fronted them on each occasion. But they always told me to see them again next time. However, on one occasion I fronted them and they told me to come again the next time as usual — which meant in another four or five months. But later I was walking past the office of one parole officer, and he whispered to me to step inside. He informed me not to tell anyone, but I was going to be released the next Monday — 14 February 1977.

"Now this was on the Friday before that, and the parole officer explained that even the prison superintendent didn't know about it yet. However, I didn't see any reason why he'd tell me a lie. So I walked over and told a friend of mine, Jimmy Edds, and a couple of other blokes that I'd just been informed I was leaving on the Monday.

"Then I was called down to the superintendent's office that afternoon. He told me to sit down — and they never tell you to sit down unless they have some very good or very bad news. He announced that he had good news for me, and I replied that I already knew it. He asked how the hell did I already know? He said he'd only found out himself half an hour earlier, when he'd received a telephone call from 'in town'. So I had him on, and declared: 'Oh, our information is much better than that. I knew two days ago.' Well, of course I didn't, I only knew about two hours earlier.

"I rang Dolly Simmons at 6 that evening to inform her that I'd be home the following Monday. She normally came to see me on a Sunday, but that weekened she came out on the Saturday. Then she and her son returned to pick me up on the Monday morning."

Hayes walked to freedom with, officially, $73.83 to his name. However, soon after, he was able to bite his long time buddy Perce Galea for "$2000 cash to help me establish myself again."

On the afternoon of his release the *Daily Mirror* reported: "John Frederick 'Chow' Hayes, convicted murderer and standover man from Sydney's wild post World War II era of crime, walked to freedom today. Hayes was released after serving 22 years in jail..."

He had to report to his parole officer at Parramatta at 4 o'clock that afternoon. "One of the conditions of the parole," Hayes recalls, "was not to go to hotels and the races and so on. But eventually I asked my parole officer if I could go to the races, because I really enjoyed a day at the track. He said he'd find out. And then Dolly suggested the trots. So he arranged permission for me to go to the trots, as long as I took Dolly along with me. From that point I took Dolly along to the trots for about six or seven months... Eventually I saw out my licence, and I haven't been back to jail since."

• • •

Chow Hayes, in his mid-seventies, relaxes at home in Lidcombe in the late 1980s.

During the 1980s Chow Hayes lived in a single-bedroom unit in John Street, Lidcombe.

One of his neighbours was another criminal with a lengthy record, Billy Walsh. Hayes and Walsh were now sick old men, both requiring frequent medical attention for serious health problems. Over the next half-dozen years they spent much of their spare time reminiscing about "the old days".

Bernard William "Billy" Walsh was originally from Brisbane. Hayes met him in the late 1930s after he'd come down to Sydney. "Breaking and entering was Billy's caper," Hayes recalls. "Eventually he was declared an habitual criminal. And when a person was declared an habitual criminal, he was given two parts to his sentence: the first for the crime itself in that particular court proceeding, and the second for being declared an 'habitual' offender. The prisoner served the first part of his sentence wearing a normal khaki prison uniform; then he would change into a special blue uniform (like a policeman's outfit without any stripes or badges) for the remaining portion of the sentence which related specifically to his declarataion as an 'habitual criminal'."

Walsh hit the headlines in late 1953, when he was charged

with breaking, entering and stealing from the Haymarket store of the Mick Simmons group. "Walsh and his mates pinched three truck-loads of cigarettes worth over £100,000," Hayes explains. "Then they disposed of the loot by selling the cigarettes to Joe Taylor and Perce Galea and company for resale through Thommo's and their gambling clubs. But then Walsh and his partners became greedy and attempted to rob Mick Simmons again some months later. This time they were caught and Walsh copped a three-year jail sentence."

Half a dozen years later Walsh and an associate, William Louis Heydon, were sentenced to life imprisonment after being convicted of murdering a labourer named Neil George Johnson in the doorway of his Bondi Junction home in November 1961. Crown prosecutor, Mr J. W. Knight, QC, told the court that when Johnson answered a knock at his front door, Walsh shot him three times. Knight explained the motive was "friction over a woman", and added that Heydon had accompanied Walsh to make sure that no-one unexpected "came on" Walsh.

Chow Hayes recalls: "Walsh had discovered that he'd been two-timed by a sheila, so he went and shot the bloke involved. Billy Heydon had been drinking in the hotel with Walsh, when Walsh announced that he was going off to fix this bloke. So Heydon went along for the ride. Heydon spent time at 'The Bay' and then Parramatta, while Walsh was at Parramatta and then Silverwater."

• • •

Chow Hayes turned 79 on Wednesday, 5 September 1990.

He has, via a lengthy series of transfusions, received 56 pints of blood over the last four years.

He spends his time reading newspapers, drinking daily at local hotels and licensed clubs, and punting modestly on the horses. At weekends he still attends the Sydney metropolitan racetracks as often as possible.

His personal reminiscences, unlike those of most elderly gents of his generation, are not of happy family occasions and smiling grandchildren. Rather, they are almost exclusively of hardened criminals and crooked policemen and long, late, boozy nights around the illegal gambling dens and seedy flop-houses of inner Sydney during the 1930s, 1940s and early 1950s.

In his old age Chow Hayes has few memories of carefree, winter weekend outings or lazy, summer seaside picnics. "I only ever went to the beach occasionally," he recalls. "If I wanted a swim I walked over to the Domain baths on the edge of the harbour. And I never went along on family picnics, though I do remember my wife and kids and Aunt Ninny travelling up to the Blue Mountains once a year by train...

"The racetrack was always my favourite pastime. I didn't really follow a footy team, and only went to the occasional match. However, when I was younger I always attended the cricket Tests at the Sydney Cricket Ground with a group of fellows including Arthur Messenger, Arthur Bedford and Eddie Weyman. I stayed there all day, from the first ball through to the last ball, even if I had to remain behind by myself. The others tended to decide whether to stay or not depending on who was batting..."

The return trip from the historic SCG to Hayes's home turf around Central Railway and Ultimo involves a journey down the narrow streets of Surry Hills. In 1990 there are few remnants of the Surry Hills where Chow Hayes ruled the roost — the overcrowded rows of rented hovels, the numerous rat-infested sly-grog dens and the dimly lit bordellos. Hayes chuckles when he recalls his regular standover collections from many of these sites. "All the fancy restaurants in Surry Hills today — we'd have been demanding money from all of them. Either that or they'd be closed!"

Throughout his life Chow Hayes has been a crook, a thief, a ruthless thug and a cold-blooded murderer. He does not attempt to resile from these blunt descriptions. He admits his largely indefensible — and often abominable — crimes against society.

To the detached observer, however, he represents, most of all, the classic product of a wayward, undisciplined, tragic upbringing: his father left for war when he was three years old and remained overseas for nearly six years; when his dad returned he spent much of his time in hospital and eventually died before young Chow had reached his teens; within 18 months his mother re-married and permanently abandoned her children.

As a result, by the age of 11, young Hayes was selling newspapers outside Central Railway Station, skipping school and living a life centred upon the criminal activities of the Railway Mob. He spent most of his youth unsupervised, running wild around the streets.

Hayes was still only 11 years old when he was initially packed off to Guildford Truant School. From there he progressed to a home for uncontrollable youths at Gosford, the "breeding ground for crims" where he first met "blokes like Guido Calletti and 'Scotchy' McCormack — blokes who were murdered later in life. All the kids up there later became heavy criminals and many ended up being killed in underworld activities. I'd say that, of the boys at Gosford, I finished up seeing 99 per cent of them again at Long Bay Jail. . . All I basically did there was learn more bad habits for later on."

From that point Hayes's destiny seemed as inevitable as the nightly flow of losers out the back door from his beloved Thommo's two-up school.

But the observer, perhaps seeking an explanation for Chow Hayes's brutal, violent, largely wasted life, is left to ponder one nagging, overwhelmingly simple quesiton: did a fatherless young boy — whose shocking crime was to skip a spot of school — really need to be sent away and locked up in a state institution at 11 years of age?

Appendix: Hayes's Criminal Record

NEW SOUTH WALES POLICE DEPARTMENT

CRIMINAL RECORD OF JOHN FREDERICK HAYES, BORN 5 SEPTEMBER, 1911

COURT	DATE	OFFENCE	RESULT
NEW SOUTH WALES			
Redfern P.C.	10·10·28	Break and enter	Discharged.
		Malicious damage	Recognizance self and surety £10 Good Behaviour 12 months, compensation £4.2.3 or a further 21 days. APPEALED.
Central P.C.	10·12·28	Indecent language	£2 or 14 days hard labour.
Sydney Q.S.	11· 2·29	Appealed against conviction of 10·10·28. Appeal allowed, conviction quashed. No order as to costs.	
Central P.C.	18· 2·29	Indecent language	£1 or 7 days hard labour.
Central P.C.	19· 2·29	Riotous behaviour	10/– or 48 hours hard labour.
Central P.C.	8· 4·29	Steal from the person	£3 witness expenses 15/– or 1 month hard labour.
Central P.C.	1· 5·29	Demand money by menaces	Discharged.
		Threatening words	Recognizance self £20 keep peace for 6 months or 14 days.
Central P.C.	18· 6·29	Assault	60/– or 1 month hard labour.
		Evade tram fare	£2 or 14 days hard labour.
Kogarah P.C.	25· 6·29	Suspected person	Withdrawn.
Central P.C.	22· 7·29	Riotous	£1 or 7 days.

COURT	DATE	OFFENCE	RESULT
NEW SOUTH WALES			
Central P.C.	2· 9·29	Riotous	£1 or 7 days.
		Indecent language	£3 or 10 days.
		Not pay for drinks	No evidence to offer. Discharged.
Paddington P.C.	19·10·29	Riotous	Enter recognizance £25 and security £25, Good Behaviour for 12 months or 1 month hard labour.
		Indecent language	£3 or 1 month hard labour.
		Assault Police	£5 or 3 months hard labour.
Paddington P.C.	6·11·29	Stealing (2 charges)	No evidence to offer. Discharged.
Central P.C.	6·11·29	Riotous	£2 or 14 days hard labour.
Central P.C.	15·11·29	Stealing	£10 and £2.12.0 witness expenses or 2 months hard labour.
Central P.C.	19·11·29	Assault	Recognizance self £10, Good Behaviour for 12 months and come up for sentence if called.
		Stealing	14 days hard labour. APPEALED.
Central P.C.	1· 2·30	Malicious damage	£5 pay damages 22/6 witness expenses 10/– or 1 month.
Sydney Q.S.	12· 2·30	Appeal withdrawn, conviction confirmed without costs.	
Central Summons Court	1· 4·30	Called up for sentence on surety of 19·11·29	£10 or 3 months hard labour.
Central P.C.	17· 5·30	Offensive	£1 or 7 days hard labour.
Burwood P.C.	2· 6·30	Suspected person	3 months hard labour and pay 10/– witness expenses or 2 days hard labour accumulated.
Central P.C.	16· 6·30	Assault	39/– or 10 days hard labour.
		Indecent language	£3.2.0 or 21 days hard labour.
Sydney Q.S.	1· 7·30	Appeal withdrawn, conviction confirmed without costs. Sentence to date from 17·6·30.	
Redfern P.C.	3·10·30	Riotous behaviour	£5 or 2 months, and sureties or 1 month accumulative.
Central P.C.	10·10·30	Vagrancy	Discharged.
Central P.C.	15·10·30	Riotous behaviour	£3.4.0 or 7 days hard labour.

COURT	DATE	OFFENCE	RESULT
NEW SOUTH WALES			
Central P.C.	20·10·30	Indecent language	£2 or 14 days hard labour.
Central P.C.	27·10·30	Indecent language	£5 or 1 month hard labour.
Central P.C.	6·11·30	Stealing	6 months hard labour.
		Assault Police	1 month hard labour accumulative.
Sydney Q.S.	19·11·30	Appeal dismissed, conviction confirmed.	
Central P.C.	6· 6·31	Riotous behaviour	Recognizance forfeited.
		Indecent language	Recognizance forfeited.
Central P.C.	9· 6·31	Riotous behaviour	20/– or 2 days hard labour.
		Indecent language	£5 or 10 days hard labour.
Central P.C.	29· 6·31	Indecent language	£3 or 6 days hard labour.
Central P.C.	14· 7·31	Assault and robbery	Discharged.
Central P.C.	20· 7·31	Riotous behaviour	40/– or 4 days hard labour.
Central P.C.	27· 7·31	Common assault	3 months hard labour.
		Malicious damage	£2 or 4 days hard labour. Pay damage £2 or 4 days.
Glebe P.C.	28· 7·31	Riotous behaviour	£5 or 10 days hard labour.
		Malicious damage	No evidence to offer. Discharged.
Sydney Q.S.	8· 9·31	Appeals dismissed, confirmed the convictions and ordered costs £1.11.6 to be paid in each case within 14 days.	
Central P.C.	28·12·31	Indecent language (2 charges)	£4 or 8 days hard labour on each charge.
Central P.C.	6· 1·32	Suspected person	3 months hard labour. APPEALED.
Central P.C.	12· 1·32	Steal from person	Discharged.
Central P.C.	18· 1·32	Indecent language	£5 or 10 days hard labour.
		Assault Police	6 months hard labour.
		Stealing	6 months hard labour.
Central P.C.	1· 2·32	Assault and robbery	Discharged.
Sydney Q.S.	8· 2·32	Appeal withdrawn; conviction confirmed.	
Central P.C.	11· 7·32	Indecent language	£5 or 10 days hard labour.
Central P.C.	18· 7·32	Riotous behaviour	£1 or 7 days hard labour.

COURT	DATE	OFFENCE	RESULT
NEW SOUTH WALES			
Glebe P.C.	26· 7·32	Indecent language	£3 or 6 days hard labour.
Glebe P.C.	6· 8·32	Street betting	Discharged.
		Assault police	£5 costs 10/6 or 12 days hard labour.
Central P.C.	23· 8·32	Assault occasion actual bodily harm	Discharged.
Central P.C.	26· 8·32	Indecent language	£5 or 10 days hard labour, Good Behaviour for 12 months or 3 months hard labour.
Central P.C.	10·10·32	Indecent language	£5 or 10 days hard labour.
		Assault Police	£3 or 6 days hard labour.
		Resist arrest	£1 or 2 days hard labour.
Central P.C.	11·10·32	Suspected person	6 months hard labour. APPEALED.
Sydney Q.S.	11·10·32	Appeal dismissed, conviction confirmed. Costs £3.3.0. (re Central P.C. 10·10·32).	
Central P.C.	13·10·32	Consorting	6 months hard labour. APPEALED.
Sydney Q.S.	2·11·32	Appeal withdrawn. Conviction confirmed. Costs £3.3.0. to be paid within 14 days.	
Sydney Q.S.	8·11·32	Robbery	Acquitted.
Central P.C.	26· 4·33	Stealing	6 months hard labour.
Central P.C.	9· 6·33	Stealing	12 months hard labour.
Sydney Q.S.	12· 6·33	Appeal withdrawn, confirmed conviction, without costs.	
Sydney Q.S.	3· 7·33	Appeal withdrawn, conviction confirmed without costs, the sentence to date from 13·6·33.	
Central P.C.	22· 2·35	Consorting	6 months hard labour. APPEALED.
Glebe P.C.	14· 3·35	Stealing	3 months hard labour. APPEALED.
		Threatening words	Admonished and discharged.
Glebe P.C.	16· 3·35	Drunk	30/– or 3 days hard labour.
Central P.C.	4· 4·35	Evade taxi fare	No prosecutor. Discharged.
Central P.C.	9· 4·35	Stealing from person	4 months hard labour.

COURT	DATE	OFFENCE	RESULT
NEW SOUTH WALES			
		Stealing	3 months hard labour.
		Demand money by menaces	No evidence to offer. Discharged.
		Stealing	No evidence to offer. Discharged. APPEALED.
Sydney Q.S.	15· 4·35	Appeals withdrawn. Convictions confirmed without costs.	
		Appeal withdrawn. Conviction confirmed without costs.	
		Appeal withdrawn. Conviction confirmed without costs.	
QUEENSLAND			
Brisbane P.C.	3· 2·37	Stealing	3 months hard labour.
NEW SOUTH WALES			
Central P.C.	26· 5·37	Demand money by menace	Discharged.
		Maliciously wounding	Discharged.
Central P.C.	2·12·37	Stealing	No evidence to offer. Discharged.
Glebe P.C.	10· 5·38	Indecent language	£2 or 4 days.
Glebe P.C.	11·10·38	Indecent language	£5 or 10 days hard labour.
		Resist arrest	£2 or 4 days hard labour.
		Indecent language	50/– or 5 days hard labour.
Glebe P.C.	3·11·38	Stealing £2 in money. 40/1900 S.501	3 months hard labour. APPEALED.
		Stealing (4 charges)	No evidence to offer. Discharged.
Glebe P.C.	15·12·38	Insulting words	£2 or 4 days hard labour.
		Assault constable in execution of duty	6 months hard labour. APPEALED.
		Assault Police	Merged in above charge.
Central P.C.	19·12·38	Assault constable	3 months hard labour. APPEALED.
		Break enter and steal (2 charges)	No evidence to offer. Discharged.
Glebe P.C.	3· 1·39	Drunkenness	£1 or 2 days hard labour.
		Indecent language	£1 or 2 days hard labour.

COURT	DATE	OFFENCE	RESULT
NEW SOUTH WALES			
		Threatening words	£5 or 10 days and utter recognizance self and surety £10 Good Behaviour 12 months or 1 month.
Glebe P.C.	26· 1·39	Consorting	6 months hard labour. APPEALED.
Central P.C.	1· 3·39	Carry pistol at night	Discharged.
Glebe P.C.	2· 3·39	Drunk	Dismissed.
		Malicious damage	£5 damage, 6/– or 11 days hard labour. APPEALED.
Sydney Q.S.	3· 4·39	Appealed against the conviction imposed at Glebe P.C. on 26·1·39. The appeal having been withdrawn the Judge confirmed the conviction without costs.	
		Appealed against the conviction imposed at Glebe P.C. on 2·3·39. The appeal having been withdrawn the Judge confirmed the conviction without costs.	
		Appealed against the conviction imposed at Central P.C. on 19·12·38. The appeal having been withdrawn the Judge confirmed the conviction without costs.	
		Appealed against the conviction imposed at Glebe P.C. on 3·11·38. The appeal having been withdrawn the Judge confirmed the conviction with costs £5.5.0 to be paid within 14 days.	
		Appealed against the conviction imposed at Glebe P.C. on 15·12·38. The appeal having been withdrawn the Judge confirmed the conviction without costs.	
Sydney Q.S.	12· 4·39	Demand money with menaces	Acquitted.
Sydney Q.S.	24· 4·39	Break enter and steal	Jury discharged without a verdict. Accused remanded for Trial.
Sydney Q.S.	28· 4·39	Break enter and steal (re-trial)	Acquitted.
Redfern P.C.	29· 2·40	Indecent language	£2 or 4 days hard labour.

COURT	DATE	OFFENCE	RESULT
NEW SOUTH WALES			
Glebe P.C.	15· 8·40	Riotous behaviour	£1 or 48 hours.
		Indecent language	£2 or 4 days hard labour accumulative with above charge.
		Resist arrest	£2 or 4 days hard labour.
Glebe P.C.	4· 3·41	Assault whilst armed	No evidence to offer. Discharged.
		Illegally use car	No evidence to offer. Discharged.
Sydney Q.S.	25· 3·41	Robbery being armed	4 years hard labour to date from 20·2·41
		Receiving	18 months hard labour concurrent.
Redfern P.C.	16· 4·41	Unlicensed pistol	Not before court; in gaol under sentence.
Central Criminal Court	14· 3·45	Murder	Acquitted.
Central P.C.	10· 4·45	Found in disorderly house	6 months hard labour. APPEALED.
		Consorting	6 months hard labour, accumulative, and recognizance self and surety £100 Good Behaviour for 3 years or 3 months hard labour. APPEALED.
		Indecent language	£3 or 6 days hard labour.
		Assault Police	£5 or 10 days hard labour.
		Assault Police	£2 or 4 days hard labour.
Redfern P.C.	13· 4·45	Indecent language	£5 in default 10 days hard labour.
		Assault Police	£7 default 14 days hard labour.
Central P.C.	26· 4·45	Assault	Not before court. Recognizance forfeited.
		Offensive behaviour Resist arrest Indecent language	Not before court. Recognizance forfeited.

COURT	DATE	OFFENCE	RESULT
NEW SOUTH WALES			
Sydney Q.S.	21· 5·45	Assault occasioning actual bodily harm	3½ years penal servitude.
Paddington P.C.	30· 5·45	Insulting words Assault Resist arrest	Not before court; in gaol.
Sydney Q.S.	30· 5·45	Appealed against the convictions recorded at Central P.C. on 10·4·45. Appeals dismissed withdrawn and convictions and sentences confirmed without costs.	
Central P.C.	4· 6·45	Indecent language	Not before court; in gaol.
Central P.S.	27· 8·48	Assault and rob	No evidence to offer. Discharged.
Central P.S.	10· 9·48	Stealing from dwelling clothes jewellery and radio 40/1900/148	Committed for trial Sydney Quarter Sessions 5·10·48.
Sydney Q.S.	2·11·48	Stealing in a dwelling house	5 years hard labour to date from 5·11·48.
		Common assault	2 years hard labour concurrent.
Court of Criminal Appeal	17·12·48	Appealed against conviction at Sydney Quarter Sessions of 2·11·48 for stealing in a dwelling. The Appeal was allowed, set aside the conviction and entered a verdict of acquittal.	
Redfern P.S.	6·11·50	Offensive behaviour	£5 or 10 days hard labour.
Newtown P.S.	4·12·50	Indecent language	£3 or 6 days hard labour.
Central P.S.	19· 1·51	Offensive behaviour	£3 or 6 days hard labour.
Paddington P.S.	22· 1·51	Indecent language	£5 or 10 days hard labour.
		Resist arrest	£2 or 4 days hard labour.
		Take liquor into Public Hall	£2 or 4 days hard labour. APPEALED (3).
Sydney Q.S.	1· 3·51	Appealed against convictions of 22·1·51. Appeal dismissed, convictions confirmed.	
City Coroners Court	10·10·51	Murder	Trial Central Criminal Court 19·11·51.
Central Criminal Court	26·11·51	Murder	Jury failed to agree.
Central Criminal Court	10· 3·52	Murder	Jury failed to agree.
Central Criminal Court	26· 5·52	Murder	Sentenced to death.

COURT	DATE	OFFENCE	RESULT
NEW SOUTH WALES			
Central P.S.	5· 6·52	Unlicensed pistol	Not before court; in gaol.
		Consorting	Not before court; in gaol.
Minute from Under Secretary of Justice	17·10·52	His Excellency the Governor, with the advice of the Executive Council, has approved of the sentence of death in this case being commuted to penal servitude for life.	
Newtown P.S.	1· 5·70	Malicious wounding	Committed for trial Sydney Quarter Sessions 4·5·70.
Sydney Q.S.	4·11·70	Malicious wound with intent to do grievous bodily harm	5 years hard labour. His Honour directed that $2000 compensation be paid to the complainant out of the property of the accused.

INDEX